Trapped by History

Indigenous Nations and Collaborative Futures

Series Editor:

Larissa Behrendt, Simone Bignall, Daryle Rigney and Linda Tuhiwai Smith

'Indigenous Nations and Collaborative Futures' showcases new thinking about Indigenous nation building and decolonisation in the regional contexts of Australia, Aotearoa-New Zealand and other countries of the Southern Pacific Rim. Attending critically to legacies of settler-colonialism in this region, the series supplements and enriches scholarship emerging from Indigenous perspectives and experiences in the United States, Canada and other Occupied Territories. The Indigenous-led and Indigenous-centred research appearing in this series explores the diverse ways in which Indigenous authorities are designing and utilising modern political institutions that match their cultural values and assert a continuing right and responsibility to care for traditional lands and waters. Conceived through the optic of the political, 'Indigenous Nations and Collaborative Futures' publishes innovative and important research that studies the transformative potential of cross-cultural interaction, collaboration and agreement-making to successfully mediate culturally diverse political interests and values in settler-colonial jurisdictions. The series contributes new thinking about the reparation of historical injustice and the terms and future conditions of positive coexistence after colonisation.

Titles in the Series

The Children's Country: Creation of a Goolarabooloo Future in North-West Australia, by Stephen Muecke and Paddy Roe

Developing Governance and Governing Development: International Case Studies of Indigenous Futures, edited by Diane Smith; Alice Wighton; Stephen Cornell and Adam Vai Delaney (forthcoming)

Trapped by History: The Indigenous-State Relationship in Australia, by Darryl Cronin

Trapped by History

The Indigenous-State Relationship in Australia

Darryl Cronin

ROWMAN & LITTLEFIELD
Lanham • Boulder • New York • London

Published by Rowman & Littlefield
An imprint of The Rowman & Littlefield Publishing Group, Inc.
4501 Forbes Boulevard, Suite 200, Lanham, Maryland 20706
www.rowman.com

British Library Cataloguing in Publication Information Available

Library of Congress Cataloging-in-Publication Data
Names: Cronin, Darryl, 1957- author.
Title: Trapped by history : the indigenous-state relationship in Australia / Darryl Cronin.
Description: Lanham : Rowman & Littlefield, 2021. | Series: Indigenous nations and collaborative
    futures | Includes bibliographical references and index. | Summary: "The Australian nation has
    reached an impasse in Indigenous policy and practice and fresh strategies and perspectives are
    required. Trapped by History will highlight a fundamental issue that the Australian nation must
    confront to develop a genuine relationship with Indigenous Australians. The existing relationship
    between Indigenous people and the Australian state was constructed on the myth of an empty
    land - terra nullius. Therefore, interactions with Indigenous people have been constrained by
    eighteenth-century assumptions and beliefs that Indigenous people did not have organised soci-
    eties, had neither land ownership nor a recognisable form of sovereignty, and that they were
    'savage' but could be 'civilized' through the erasure of their culture. These incorrect assumptions
    and beliefs are the foundation of the legal, constitutional and political treatment of Indigenous
    Australians over the course of the country's history. They remain ingrained in governmental
    institutions, Indigenous policy making, judicial decision making and contemporary public atti-
    tudes about Indigenous people. Trapped by History shines new light upon several historical and
    contemporary examples where Indigenous people have attempted to engage and dialogue with
    state and federal governments. These governments have responded by trying to suppress and
    discredit Indigenous rights, culture and identities and impose assimilationist policies. In doing so
    they have rejected or ignored Indigenous attempts at dialogue and partnership. Other settler
    countries such as New Zealand, Canada and the United States of America have all negotiated
    treaties with Indigenous people and have developed constitutional ways of engaging cross cultu-
    rally. In Australia, the limited recognition that Indigenous people have achieved to date shows
    that the state is unable to resolve long standing issues with Indigenous people. Movement
    beyond the current colonial relationship with Indigenous Australians requires a genuine dialogue
    to not only examine the legal and intellectual framework that constrain Indigenous recognition
    but to create new foundations for a renewed relationship based on intercultural negotiation,
    mutual respect, sharing and mutual responsibility. This must involve building a shared under-
    standing around addressing past injustices and creating a shared vision for how Indigenous
    people and other Australians would associate politically in the future"-- Provided by publisher.
Identifiers: LCCN 2020054897 (print) | LCCN 2020054898 (ebook) | ISBN 9781786611451 (cloth) |
    ISBN 9781538152614 (pbk) | ISBN 9781786611468 (epub)
Subjects: LCSH: Indigenous peoples--Australia--Government relations. | Multiculturalism--Austra-
    lia. | Australia--Race relations
Classification: LCC DU124.G68 C76 2021(print)|LCC DU124.G68(ebook)|DDC 323.199/159--dc23
LC record available at https://lccn.loc.gov/2020054897
LC ebook record available at https://lccn.loc.gov/2020054898

Contents

Acknowledgements   vii
Introduction   ix

 1   No Just Relationship   1
 2   The Intellectual and Legal Origins of Terra Nullius   39
 3   Promise, Hope and Disappointment: 1970–1990   69
 4   Recognition and the Limits of Tolerance   109
 5   Dialogue and Indigenous Recognition   157
 6   The Pathway Ahead   197

Epilogue   227
Bibliography   231
Index   251
About the Author   259

Acknowledgements

This book is the result of my frustrations with the slow pace of change in regard to Aboriginal and Torres Strait Islander recognition in Australia. I am also displeased with the continuing lack of respect that Indigenous people endure within Australian society. As an Aboriginal Australian I witnessed the enormous social and political strides of Indigenous people from the 1970s to the early 1990s. I was optimistic that progress would be made on some of the tougher issues of Indigenous recognition. However, as the Australian nation approached the new millennium, Indigenous policy and practice moved backwards. At the onset of the new millennium in Australian society, disrespect for the human rights of Indigenous people became public. It was obvious that Australian society had learnt little about Indigenous people. Clearly, there was a need to educate new generations of Australians about Indigenous issues, particularly the impact of colonialism on their culture. Therefore, I decided to contribute to the education of Australians on Indigenous people with this book.

In writing this book I am indebted to the older generations and ancestors who had the strength and resilience to withstand the forces of colonialism. They experienced brutal and oppressive governmental policies and practices, and under difficult circumstances they continued to assert their cultural and human rights. In doing so they have educated and imparted knowledge to Australians. Educating Australians is an ongoing process. It is tiring, frustrating work but each and every Indigenous person must do it throughout their life, never stopping. I am also indebted to the current and future generations of Indigenous people who continue the legacy of their ancestors.

I am grateful to Patrick Dodson, a formidable Aboriginal leader, who is now a senator in the Australian Parliament. This book takes its title from an opinion piece he wrote for the *Sydney Morning Herald* on 20 August 2009, where he refers to the Australian nation as being trapped by its history and paralysed by the failure to imagine any relationship with Indigenous peoples other than assimilation. In August 2007, after the Commonwealth government's intervention into Northern Territory Aboriginal communities, Dodson felt the Australian nation had reached a low point in its relationship with them. In a speech at La Trobe University in Melbourne in October 2007, he said there was need for a formal dialogue between the government and Indigenous peoples for the unfinished business of reconciliation. He has also argued the need to question the philosophical underpinnings of the relationship between Indigenous peoples and the Australian nation and for a need to create a new national framework to transform the nation. These words and insights of Dodson inspired me to question the philosophical underpinnings of how governments relate to Indigenous people and to write about how social and political transformation can happen in Australia in regards to Indigenous cultural and political rights.

I am immensely grateful to Phil Glendenning, the Director of the Edmund Rice Centre for Justice and Community Education in Sydney, Australia. As an employee, I was allowed use of resources plus given time and space to bring this book to completion. Indeed, this book complements the research, education and advocacy focus of the Edmund Rice Centre regarding Aboriginal and Torres Strait Islander peoples. Those at the Edmund Rice Centre believe that Aboriginal and Torres Strait Islander peoples should be treated justly and with dignity as self-determining peoples in Australia. In educating and advocating about rights and justice, those at Edmund Rice Centre also focus on the rights of refugees and people seeking asylum and the rights of the peoples of the Pacific, especially those struggling for climate justice.

Lily Murphy at the Edmund Rice Centre volunteered to read the entire manuscript in her free time, making important editing suggestions. Professor Paul Patton at the University of New South Wales, Sydney, initially guided, encouraged and assisted me with submitting a book proposal to the publisher and read earlier versions of my chapters. As book series editor, Dr Simone Bignall, now at the University of Technology, Sydney, also guided and assisted with the book proposal and encouraged me during the writing process. She made valuable comments and suggested helpful editorial changes. I thank all for their support, which I deeply appreciate.

Finally, I am grateful to my wife, Julie Darnell, and my children—Jas, Daly, Mali and Tully—who were living at home when I was writing. I thank them for their support and encouragement. I also acknowledge my eldest adult children, Katon and Coby, and my grandchildren, Aiden and Kiara.

Introduction

As an Aboriginal person who has been involved in the struggle for the rights of Aboriginal and Torres Strait Islander peoples in Australia, I despair about the parlous state of Indigenous policy in this country and the way in which Australia receives and perceives Indigenous claims for recognition. These claims have encompassed demands for land and recognition of cultural and political distinctiveness, as well as demands for equality and civil rights. But Indigenous Australians have encountered significant societal, political and legal opposition to their claims throughout history. My experience with the political process and the impact of government policies on Indigenous people has led me to question why Indigenous policy continues to be such a top-down, government dominated approach. This in turn has led me to ask why governments and the Australian population largely respond in negative ways to Indigenous claims for recognition of rights. Today, there is a historical basis for why Indigenous people are treated as such in Australia. It is reflected in the assumptions and beliefs that Australians hold about Indigenous people and in the inability of Australian governments to adequately address Indigenous claims for recognition. Understanding how colonial assumptions of Aboriginal inferiority have historically underpinned and continue to inform Indigenous policy, lays a foundation for answering these questions.

In 1992, I started work at the Kimberley Land Council (KLC) in Derby, Western Australia. It was an important time in Australian nation-building as the federal government had just established the formal reconciliation process and the High Court was on the eve of handing down its *Mabo (No. 2)* judgment.[1] *Mabo (No. 2)* concerned a claim for native title by the Meriam people of Murray Island in the Torres Strait region of Australia (see chapter 2). I had previously worked for the Northern Land Council (NLC) in Darwin and had witnessed the Northern Territory government's aggressive and negative response to Aboriginal land claims under the Aboriginal Land Rights (Northern Territory) Act 1976. I had also witnessed the historic occasion of the Northern and Central Land Councils presenting the Barunga Statement to Prime Minister Bob Hawke at Barunga in the Northern Territory in June 1988, and subsequently I observed, with others, the Hawke government's failed commitment to a treaty with Indigenous people.[2]

My time with the KLC and NLC was significant because I experienced first hand how Australian governments respond to Indigenous claims for recognition. In 1992–1993, after the *Mabo (No. 2)* judgment, I participated in several significant events relating to native title. To me, these events emphasised the hopes and frustrations of Indigenous people in dealing with governments. The subordination of Indigenous people by state and federal governments is evident in the way governments both colonial and contemporary have dealt with Indigenous people in Australia. Having no constitutional status, Indigenous people are at the mercy of governments, parliaments, government agencies and industry that have the authority and power to limit Indigenous rights and to discriminate against Indigenous people. The way the Western Australian government responded to the High Court's recognition of native title is a key example.

On 26–27 June 1992, I was at Wamalu (Cadjebut Springs) on Leopold Downs station, the traditional country of the Bunaba people and a Bunaba-owned pastoral property. About 150 Aboriginal people from throughout the Kimberley gathered to discuss the changes that the then Labor government in Western Australia intended to make to the Aboriginal Heritage Act 1972, and to hear about the High Court's *Mabo* judgment. The KLC had called the meeting. Patrick Dodson in his new role as chairman of the Aboriginal Reconciliation Council was also in attendance. After two days of discussion, the amendments were rejected as discriminatory and a threat to the newly recognised 'Aboriginal title'. The key resolution from the meeting considered the *Mabo* decision as a turning point and therefore insisted the Western Australian government had to give effect to it by commencing formal negotiations with Aboriginal people in the Kimberley region.

The Western Australian Labor government's proposed amendments to the heritage legislation merely reflected the way governments had always treated Aboriginal people in that state.[3] The High Court of Australia had just recognised the existence of native title at common law, but the Western Australian government was changing its Aboriginal Heritage legislation to potentially impact upon native title. The irony was not lost on the KLC. In a media release on 3 July 1992, the KLC said the Western Australian government was hypocritical and deserved no respect from Aboriginal people because it was intent on acting contrary to the High Court's decision and the common law. On 20 July 1992, the KLC wrote to the Hon. Carmen Lawrence, MLA, labour premier of Western Australia, stating that the lack of response by her government to the High Court decision had not given them any confidence that her government would consider Aboriginal interests. The KLC called for governmental negotiations to ensure the recognition of native title in Western Australia.

The first public response of the Western Australian Labor government to the *Mabo* decision was through the Aboriginal affairs minister at the time, Judyth Watson, who said it was unlikely the decision would have an immediate impact on Western Australia because it related to the Murray Island people.[4] This attitude would change, however, after the government realised that there was a substantial portion of Crown land in Western Australia that could be subject to native title. When the government in Western Australia changed in February 1993, the new Liberal-National Party premier, Richard Court, set his government on a course of extinguishing native title in Western Australia. Soon after he was elected, the KLC wrote to the new premier on 3 March 1993, suggesting he give serious consideration to establishing a process to enable negotiations to take place on issues relating to the *Mabo* decision. In the letter the KLC set out several issues and expressed their concern that no formal discussions had taken place and also requested a meeting with the premier.

Court made it clear that he was going to protect mining and business interests as well as their land titles against the *Mabo* decision. He said he wanted to talk with Aboriginal groups but was not prepared to deal with representatives of Aboriginal organisations or Aboriginal legal advisers. Court said legislation would be required to protect land and mining titles issued before the *Mabo* decision. To this end his government was developing a proposal to protect land titles from native title claims.[5] At a KLC meeting I attended in late July 1993 at 'Blue Hole' in Purnululu National Park, Premier Court confirmed his government would validate existing land titles and extinguish native title.[6]

Not one government at either federal or state level responded positively to the *Mabo* judgment. The Commonwealth government focussed on identifying and restricting the impact of native title while at the same time validating non-Indigenous land titles by extinguishing native title. However, of all the state governments, the Court government expressed the greatest opposition to native title and the proposed Commonwealth legislation. The Court government's response was to eliminate native title through the Land (Titles and Traditional Usage) Act 1993. The act extinguished all native title remaining in Western Australia with no compensation payable for extinguishment. Native title was replaced with 'rights of traditional usage' that would be subordinate to all other grants or interests and could not be enforced against those interests. Traditional usage rights could be extinguished or suspended with payment of compensation, although payment would be inferior, and a court could not challenge any advice or recommendation of a minister. Only the relevant minister could grant title to or interests in land for advancing the interest of Aboriginal people.[7] Therefore, the Aboriginal relationship to land was subordinate to all other property rights and interests protected by the Crown. Further, after having extinguished native title, the Court government's legislation also empowered the relevant minister to grant titles and interests in land to Aboriginal people for their 'advancement'. According to the historian Henry Reynolds, the assumption underpinning the Court government's legislation was 'that Aboriginal society was so backward, so primitive that it was never able to establish rights of possession', not even in thousands of years of occupation of the continent.[8]

Within a day of the Land (Titles and Traditional Usage) Act 1993 coming into operation, the Wororra and Yawuru people from the Kimberley region challenged the constitutional validity of the Western Australian Act in the High Court on the basis that it was inconsistent with the Commonwealth Native Title Act 1993 pursuant to Section 109 of the Australian Constitution.[9] The Martu people of the eastern Pilbara region also issued a legal challenge. Meanwhile, the Western Australian government challenged the Commonwealth Native Title Act in the High Court on the basis that it had no application to Western Australia because native title had been extinguished on settlement of the colony; that the Native Title Act was a law about land management therefore a state responsibility; that it impaired the capacity of the state to govern and hence discriminated against Western Australia; and that it also offended the Racial Discrimination Act by discriminating against non-Indigenous Western Australians.[10]

The Western Australian government had prepared for a 'glorious victory', having briefed journalists on six possible outcomes of any High Court decision, only one addressing possible loss.[11] But the High Court, on 16 March 1995, unanimously declared the Western Australian legislation invalid because it breached the Racial Discrimination Act 1975 and upheld the Native Title Act 1993.[12] The Aboriginal groups who had challenged the Western Australian legislation were pleased that the High Court had thrown out the Western Australian Government's 'racist' legislation.[13] On 17 March 1995, the front-page headlines on the *West Australian* screamed, 'Court's $4m Mabo Folly'.[14] The paper devoted nine pages to what it described as Premier Richard Court's 'foolhardy pursuit of an ideological fantasy', which 'has left WA morally isolated, derided, out of pocket and beset by increased confusion and uncertainty about the effects of Aboriginal claims to their traditional lands'.[15] Premier Court was defiant, saying the government accepted the High Court ruling but does 'not accept the Federal Government's native title legislation and we will use whatever means we can to politically fight that'. He believed 'the state was the loser and it was his responsibility to protect WA's interests'.[16] Peter Yu of the Kimberley Land Council said, 'the Premier and his government should hang their heads in shame' because the government had adopted 'a highly dishonest and reckless and arrogant position in the way it has treated Aboriginal rights' in Western Australia. Taking note of the behaviour of the mining industry he said, 'the mining industry has also been quite gutless', as some mining representatives had obviously been intimidated by the State government.[17]

I have always been intrigued by the extraordinary lengths the Western Australian government went to extinguish native title rights. Why was Premier Richard Court and his government so resistant to the recognition of native title? Their response in attempting to extinguish native title has led me to think deeply about why the Australian nation is so challenged by the recognition and acceptance of Indigenous people and their rights. Why are governments and the Australian population so resistant to recognising the humanity of Indigenous people and recognising Indigenous rights? Colonial ideologies and practices in respect to Indigenous people play a significant role in the way the Australian state responds to Indigenous claims or develops Indigenous policy. These ideologies have been influential in constructing the relationship between the Australian state and Indigenous peoples, and they continue to define that relationship. This relationship is based on key erroneous assumptions: that Indigenous people did not have organised societies, did not own the land and had no recognisable form of sovereignty.[18] Throughout history these false assumptions have formed the background discourse for governments to exterminate Indigenous culture and difference.

This book tackles a fundamental issue that the Australian nation must confront if it is to develop a genuine relationship with Aboriginal and Torres Strait Islander peoples. The existing relationship is constructed on the myth of an empty land—terra nullius. Therefore, interactions with Aboriginal and Torres Strait Islander peoples have been influenced and constrained by erroneous eighteenth-century assumptions and beliefs, which regard Aboriginal people as 'savages' who had to be 'civilised' through the erasure of their culture. These false assumptions and beliefs are the foundations of the legal, political and societal discourses about Aboriginal and Torres Strait Islander peoples over the course of the country's history. They remain ingrained in governmental institutions, Indigenous policymaking, judicial decision-making and contemporary public attitudes, and they influence how government and society treat and respond to Indigenous people.

The colonial mindset that traps the Australian state and the Australian population has created barriers for Indigenous people in their claims for recognition and justice. The historical and contemporary episodes in this book show how Indigenous people have attempted to challenge colonialism and engage in dialogue and negotiation with colonial, state and federal governments. However, terra nullius discourse and thinking has constrained or prevented these governments from having a genuine political and policy engagement with Indigenous peoples. In that regard, governments have responded by trying to suppress and discredit Indigenous rights, culture and identities and impose assimilationist policies. In doing so they have rejected or ignored Indigenous attempts at dialogue and engagement. Other settler countries, such as New Zealand, Canada and the United States, have all negotiated treaties with Indigenous people and have developed constitutional ways of engaging cross-culturally. In Australia, the limited recognition that Indigenous people have achieved to date shows that the state is unable to resolve long-standing issues with Indigenous people. Movement beyond the current colonial relationship requires a new dialogic approach to engaging with Aboriginal and Torres Strait Islander peoples.

Dialogue is the ability for people to talk to each other, to listen, to think, to explore and reflect and to develop mutual understandings in order to co-create meaning. In dialogic conversation people set aside their assumptions; they do not attack the ideas or integrity of others and do not make judgement about others. In conversation they also step back to self-reflect on their own thoughts and feelings in order to become more open to the views and opinions of others and in doing so change their thinking. The process of self-reflection enables people to explore their underlying tacit thought, which is the knowledge that is used to think, and which governs how views are formulated, how differences are dealt with and so on. People see and understand the world through various frameworks of thought and interpretations of life which are perceived to be valid or literally true. Therefore, when these underlying thoughts or interpretations of life are challenged, threatened or questioned, they are, generally, fiercely defended. This is the fundamental obstruction to Indigenous recognition in Australia because settler Australians understand the history of the nation and perceive Indigenous people through historical discourses that have erroneous and racist origins.

The views of Lieutenant James Cook and the botanist Joseph Banks, who sailed up the east coast of Australia in 1770, became influential in framing the discourse about Indigenous people. Their views were taken for granted as fact and became embedded in the language and attitudes of non-Indigenous people towards Indigenous people, and they continue to frame the discourses on Indigenous issues.[19] The basis of the tacit knowledge that formulates how Australians engage with Indigenous people or perceive Indigenous rights is the discourse of terra nullius. Terra nullius discourse has been the underlying thinking in how governments make Indigenous policy or respond to Indigenous claims for recognition. Terra nullius discourse encompasses the various discussions that developed in international law, domestic law and in the belief systems that informed Australian attitudes and policy. Engaging differently with Indigenous peoples and resolving long-standing issues requires a genuine intercultural dialogue to discuss and repudiate the terra nullius discourse.

A genuine intercultural dialogue requires truth telling to examine the history and continuing impact of colonisation on Indigenous peoples to deconstruct the colonial relationship and create a framework for a fair and just relationship. Therefore, a genuine dialogue is required to not only examine and understand the thinking or discourse that underlies the resistance to Indigenous recognition but to also create new foundations for a renewed relationship based on intercultural negotiation, mutual respect, sharing and mutual responsibility. A genuine intercultural dialogue would entail a process of reflection on how these erroneous attitudes and assumptions about Indigenous people, which have their genesis in terra nullius discourse and thinking, continue to be influential in government policy making, judicial decision-making and societal behaviours and attitudes. The outcome should be a repudiation of terra nullius discourse, thinking and practice by governments and a focus on creating a renewed relationship where Indigenous Australians are recognised, respected and politically empowered within society and government. It should also involve building a shared understanding around addressing past injustices and creating a shared vision for how Indigenous people and other Australians would associate politically in the future.

This book informs and challenges thinking about the relationship between Indigenous people and the Australian state to understand why there is an impasse in Indigenous policy and practice; to understand Australian history from an Indigenous counternarrative perspective; and to use the lessons of the past to identify fresh strategies and perspectives for Indigenous recognition in the Australian political and constitutional structure. I argue for a transformation of the current colonially-based relationship between Indigenous people and the state. This is done by analysing and interpreting the colonial and contemporary relationship of Indigenous people and the Australian state; identifying and understanding how colonial assumptions about Indigenous people have determined the relationship; contextualising how Indigenous people have challenged these assumptions through dialogue and various forms of protest; and examining the applicability of intercultural dialogue in Australia as the means to change thinking in order to transform the relationship between Indigenous and non-Indigenous societies.

This work proceeds by examining historical and contemporary episodes where Indigenous people in their struggles have challenged government authority to assert claims for recognition and in doing so have attempted to engage in dialogue and negotiation with government. In discussing these episodes, I show how erroneous colonial views and assumptions about Indigenous Australians are the basis of rejecting, constraining, misconstruing or ignoring Indigenous attempts at dialogue and negotiation. Clearly, as evidenced by the historical and contemporary episodes, what has occurred in Australia between governments and Indigenous peoples can hardly be considered 'dialogue'. The episodes discussed in this book provide evidence of the way government policies in Australia work to eliminate the specificity of Indigenous existence, including a distinctive connection to land and political difference. While Australia is often referred to as a postcolonial state, it is hardly so because there has never been a transformative moment in which the nation has restructured its relationship with Indigenous people to recognise Indigenous political difference. Governmental policy in Australia continues to frame Indigenous people as a 'political problem' that needs to be eliminated because Indigenous political difference challenges colonial sovereignty.[20]

Indigenous attempts to reclaim land, language, knowledge and sovereignty have usually contested the colonisers' account of the past.[21] In that regard I have privileged Indigenous voices to bring their perspectives to the surface: not only to critique government policies and practices but also to highlight the intractable nature of the relationship between Indigenous people and governments, as well as present a counternarrative in regard to the struggles of Indigenous peoples. An Indigenous perspective is critical to understanding Indigenous political agency because Indigenous people have been mobilising in various ways to fight for their rights. But an Indigenous perspective also counters the discourse about Indigenous people as having cultural deficiencies or as being problematic within society and against the structure of the Australian government. I draw on history to examine whether the current relationship between Indigenous peoples and governments can be reconceptualised through an intercultural dialogue. There is potential for genuine dialogue in Australia, providing the settler Australian population is prepared to listen to Indigenous people and reflect on colonial attitudes and assumptions with a view to being more open and accepting of Indigenous difference. Dialogic conversation may be a possibility if the federal government is willing to address the Indigenous claims for recognition that came out of the process to recognise Aboriginal and Torres Strait Islander people in the Australian Constitution, and which are outlined in the Uluru Statement from the Heart.

Chapter 1 provides historical context to explain why the Australian nation is trapped by history and why there is no just relationship with Indigenous people. Three historical stories about how Aboriginal people have consistently attempted to dialogue with government to claim recognition or to protect their rights, only to be rebuffed, are presented. The struggle of Aboriginal people in Coranderrk from 1863 in the colonial state of Victoria against paternalistic and authoritarian protection policies; the claim for citisenship and land rights by Aboriginal activists in New South Wales and Victoria during the 1930s; and the assertion of land ownership by the Yolngu people in Arnhem Land in the Northern Territory in the 1960s demonstrate that colonial assumptions and discourses about Aboriginal people influence how governments dominate and disempower Aboriginal people in Australia. As examples of settler colonial governance these stories show a familiar pattern of domination and disempowerment of Indigenous peoples. Colonialism not only happened in the distant past but also is implicit in contemporary forms and recent events such as the closure and threatened closure of Aboriginal communities in Western Australia, and the federal government's response to the stolen generations and the formal reconciliation process. Australian governments have not been able to accommodate Indigenous aspirations. Instead, they have worked to undermine, suppress, extinguish or discredit Indigenous claims. Consequently, there is no just relationship between Indigenous people and Australian governments.

Chapter 2 traces the intellectual origins of the doctrine of terra nullius and its reformulation and application in Australia. Terra nullius is a product of European imperial expansion around the world and was formulated as a legal principle at the time of colonisation of the Australian continent. The discourse surrounding terra nullius and its application to Australia emanates from the journals of Lieutenant James Cook and his colleague Joseph Banks. Despite having limited contact and understanding, they judged Indigenous Australians to be incapable of having a system of law or government, instead portraying Indigenous people as inferior or having 'deficits' in respect to European society. This discourse has been deeply influential in Australian judicial and political decision-making in regard to Indigenous claims for recognition. Such discourse is reflected in the poor relationship between Indigenous people and the Australian state. The application of terra nullius discourse in Australian judicial decision-making became unquestioned law for more than one hundred years. It is still influential in how politicians make decisions about Indigenous people and how the judiciary regards Indigenous claims for sovereignty.

Chapter 3 discusses the promise, hope and ultimate disappointment of a period of significant political and judicial recognition for Indigenous people from the early 1970s to the early 1990s. In 1972, Gough Whitlam's Labor government discarded the assimilation policy in favour of a policy of self-determination. This recognition opened the political space for a national Indigenous political voice through the National Aboriginal Conference (NAC) as well as enabled claims for land rights and a treaty—or Makarrata—to be placed on the government's policy agenda. However, the NAC was disbanded until the Aboriginal and Torres Strait Islander Commission replaced it in 1987, and issues of treaty and land rights were likewise abandoned. Indigenous aspirations for a treaty, or Makarrata, were stymied by the Federal Liberal government and eventually rejected by the Indigenous leadership in 1981. In 1986, in the face of the mining industry's strong opposition to the land rights campaign, the federal Labor government abandoned national land rights.

Chapter 4 outlines the limits of political and societal tolerance in regard to Indigenous land ownership. In 1993, the High Court of Australia recognised that Indigenous Australians had a form of land ownership, called native title, which preceded British colonisation. The recognition of native title and its subsequent legislative recognition was a high point for Indigenous claims for land rights and their involvement in government law making processes. It shows how strong political leadership in Australia can support Indigenous rights; however, it was also a low point, as the recognition of native title brought out a negative backlash at the same time, grounded in assumptions and perceptions about Indigenous people that have their genesis in terra nullius discourses. These negative attitudes took hold in politics and societal thinking after a change of federal government in 1996. These attitudes led to what can only be described as a racist political agenda against Indigenous rights. This is an example of how an unsympathetic political leader can dismantle Indigenous political gains and suppress Indigenous rights.

Chapter 5 examines the limitations of politics for Indigenous recognition in Australia and the lack of an adequate political framework for relationship-building between governments and Indigenous peoples. It discusses the need for new foundations, which can only be created through a process of intercultural dialogue to build a renewed relationship with Indigenous people. The theory and practice of dialogue is examined in consideration of its applicability to transforming the Indigenous-state relationship in Australia. This chapter looks at the Canadian Royal Commission on Aboriginal Peoples and the Canadian Truth and Reconciliation Commission as examples of public dialogue which attempted to create a transformative vision for a new relationship enabling political change.

Chapter 6 subsequently argues that the fundamental issue facing Australia, if the nation is to move forward to a renewed relationship with Indigenous people, is to change the master narrative evidenced in the earlier chapters of this book. This chapter examines the limits of reconciliation in Australia and how truth-telling is an essential step for reconciliation. Truth-telling involves the establishment of an intercultural dialogue to examine the colonial foundations of the nation and the treatment of Indigenous people. A truth-telling process is integral to changing attitudes and creating the foundations for a renewed and just relationship between governments and Indigenous peoples.

This book is not a study of Indigenous policy but rather an examination of how Indigenous policy and practice has been shaped by erroneous colonial assumptions and beliefs about Indigenous people. The political and legal episodes discussed provide the evidentiary basis to argue for a renewed political and policy approach that moves beyond the current legal and intellectual framework of Indigenous policy in Australia. Intercultural dialogue is the means for the Australian nation to progress to a renewed relationship with Indigenous people. Accordingly, this book closes with a conceptual account of the principles required for genuine intercultural dialogue. The intention of this book is not to moralise the unjust treatment of Indigenous people or to highlight the guilt of settler Australians, but rather to promote an understanding of how false colonial attitudes and assumptions stop the Australian nation from moving towards a just relationship with Indigenous peoples.

Throughout the book I use the terms 'Indigenous' and 'Aboriginal' interchangeably. Both these terms share similar meanings. Generally, I use the term 'Aboriginal' when referring to mainland Australian Aboriginal groups and 'Indigenous' to include all Indigenous Australians, including Torres Strait Islanders.

NOTES

1. Mabo and Others v The State of Queensland [No. 2] [1992], 175 CLR 1; 107 ALR 1; 66 ALJR 408.

2. The Barunga Statement presented to Prime Minister Hawke on 12 June 1988, calls for recognition of Indigenous self-determination; national land rights; compensation for loss of lands; protection of sacred sites, objects and knowledge; respect for Indigenous identity and culture; a national organisation for Indigenous affairs; support for an international declaration of principles for Indigenous rights and negotiation of a treaty.

3. P. L. Dodson, *Regional report of inquiry into underlying issues in Western Australia*, Royal Commission into Aboriginal Deaths in Custody, Canberra, Australian Government Publishing Service, 1991. Volumes 1 and 2 examine in detail the social, cultural, legal and economic matters as they directly and indirectly affected Aboriginal people in Western Australia.

4. W. Pryer and S. Manchee, 'Historic win in fight for land rights', *The Western Australian*, 4 June 1992, 3.

5. 'Court: Act on Mabo', *Northern Territory News,* 13 May 1993; G. Meertens, 'State acts over Mabo', *The West Australian*, 17 May 1993, 5.

6. Kimberley Land Council, Transcript of Richard Court's meeting with the Kimberley Land Council Executive and Representatives of the Council of Kimberley Aboriginal Organisations at Purnululu National Park, Friday, 30 July 1993.

7. R. H. Bartlett, 'The Land (Titles and Traditional Usage) Act Western Australia, A Racist and Invalid Enactment', in *Mabo: The Native Title Legislation*, ed. M. A. Stephenson (St Lucia, Queensland: University of Queensland Press, 1995).

8. H. Reynolds, 'Western Australian justice won't come from within', *The Sydney Morning Herald*, 22 November 1993.

9. The Land (Titles and Traditional Usage) Act 1993 came into operation on 2 December 1993.

10. G. Nettheim, 'Western Australia v The Commonwealth: The Wororra Peoples and Anor v Western Australia; Teddy Biljabu and Ors v Western Australia', *Aboriginal Law Bulletin* 3, iss. 73 (1995), 4–7; Aboriginal & Torres Strait Islander Social Justice Commissioner, *Native Title Report* (Canberra, ACT: Human Rights and Equal Opportunity Commission, January–June 1994), 201.

11. K. Brown and M. Duffield, 'Lawyers kept hopes high', *The West Australian*, Friday, 17 March 1995, 6.

12. Nettheim, 'Western Australia v The Commonwealth', 4–7; Aboriginal & Torres Strait Islander Social Justice Commissioner, *Native Title Report* 1994, 201–10.

13. 'Victorious Day in the High Court', *Kimberley Land Council News*, June 1995, Number 1, 5; K. Stoney, 'Victory comes with mixed emotions', *The West Australian*, Friday, 17 March 1995, 9.

14. 'Courts $4m Mabo Folly', *The West Australian*, Friday, 17 March 1995, 1.

15. 'Court ruling ends foolish adventure', Editorial, *The West Australian*, Friday, 17 March 1995, 14.

16. M. Quekett, 'Court vows to fight decision', *The West Australian*, Friday, 17 March 1995, 7.

17. Stoney, 'Victory comes with mixed emotions', 9.

18. B. Buchan and M. Heath, 'Savagery and civilization: From terra nullius to the "tide of history",' *Ethnicities* 6, no. 1 (2006), 5–26.

19. L. Tuhiwai Smith, *Decolonizing Methodologies: Research and Indigenous Peoples*, second edition (London, UK: Zed Books, 2012), 82.

20. E. Strakosch and A. Macoun. 'The Vanishing Endpoint of Settler Colonialism', in *Stolen Lands, Broken Cultures: The Settler-Colonial Present*, John Hinkson, Paul James, Lorenzo Veracini, eds. (North Carlton, Vic: Arena Publications, 2012), 44–45.

21. Smith, *Decolonizing Methodologies*, 35.

ONE

No Just Relationship

Indigenous peoples have occupied the Australian continent for at least forty thousand to forty-five thousand years,[1] and there is increasing evidence that occupation extends for at least sixty thousand years.[2] Yet when the British came to Australia in 1788, they regarded the continent as uninhabited by established societies. They considered the Indigenous inhabitants as 'savages': almost nonhuman and without civil rights, rights to land or sovereignty. These erroneous assumptions provided a justification for the British to treat the Australian continent as terra nullius. Indigenous Australian lands were regarded as either wholly unoccupied, or occupied by people who were considered too 'barbarous' to have legal, social and political systems worthy of recognition by international law.[3] Justice Brennan in the *Mabo (No. 2)* case refers to this as the 'barbarian theory', which underpinned the reception of English common law in Australia.[4] Australia was established as a penal colony by the British imperial government and, based on the reports of Lieutenant James Cook and Joseph Banks, formulated a policy to take the land and use military force to defend it from Indigenous people.[5]

British, and subsequent Australian, policies and practices had a catastrophic impact on Indigenous people. Not only were Indigenous people forcefully dispossessed of their land, waters and sovereignty by invasion and extermination, they were also dispossessed of their identity and dignity by policies and practices of protection and assimilation. The application of the terra nullius doctrine in Australia and its associated demeaning discourse about Indigenous people continue to underlie the way they are treated. There is no relationship of mutual respect or recognition. In Australia Indigenous people are treated as a disadvantaged minority social group rather than as peoples with political rights and responsibilities. Therefore, Indigenous people are treated as having no legitimate status

1

or independent political authority in Australian society and no stake in policy and law-making processes. Despite more than two hundred years of occupation by the British-Australian colonisers, there has been limited efforts on the part of governments to address the injustice of the terra nullius doctrine and its associated discourse. Justice for Indigenous Australians is largely limited to addressing inequality and socioeconomic disadvantage through distributive measures, often called 'social justice'. The broader issues of 'political justice' addressing historical wrongs of colonisation through restorative, reparative or relational measures to restructure the relationship with Indigenous people, are rejected by the federal government. Unlike other countries colonised by the British, there were no treaties with Indigenous Australians nor is there any constitutional recognition of their rights.

Between 2016 and 2019, the state of Victoria, South Australia and the Northern Territory each committed to negotiating treaties with Indigenous people, but a change of government in South Australia saw a retreat from the treaty process. A treaty is a political mechanism that transforms the relationship between Indigenous peoples and the state and serves to reconcile pre-existing Aboriginal sovereignty with Crown sovereignty, thus distributing constitutional authority.[6] However, we are yet to see whether these proposed treaty commitments will amount to a 'fair and just relationship' with Indigenous people.[7] The stumbling block to securing justice for Indigenous Australians is an intellectual and legal framework that has its genesis in colonial thinking and which has been shaped by erroneous assumptions about them. These assumptions and attitudes originated from European theories about property ownership, civil society and sovereignty and were introduced into the British-Australian colonies through social, political and judicial discourses and practices. These assumptions and attitudes are embedded in the institutions of Australian constitutional government and in the attitudes and opinions of ordinary Australians. This colonial thinking has created a political and public mindset that has thwarted Indigenous claims for recognition and whose defining attitudes have become barriers to dialogue and political change. History shows that most government approaches to Indigenous people have been based on the extinguishment or suppression of their rights and identities or have involved the use of assimilationist policies to resolve issues and claims.[8] The colonial relationship is characterised by the assumption that Indigenous people are subordinate and subject to the imposed system of government.[9] Therefore the Indigenous-state relationship in Australia is underpinned by enduring colonial beliefs that have been central to the subordination of Indigenous people. Indigenous people have consistently attempted to engage in dialogue and negotiation with governments to change this colonial relationship, but they have largely been rebuffed.

A new approach is necessary. However, to create one it is necessary to understand the historical context of the Indigenous-state relationship, to explain why there is no mutually respectful and just relationship between Indigenous people and the Australian state. This chapter presents three historical episodes that show how the Australian state has historically related to Indigenous people. In these episodes we will see how Indigenous people struggled against colonialism and attempted to dialogue with governments, but their claims were rebuffed on the basis of false assumptions and discourses. These historical episodes are significant because they indicate the standing approach of governments in developing Indigenous policy or responding to Indigenous claims. Today, this is reflected, for example, in Western Australia's attempt to extinguish native title, in the continuing removal of Indigenous children though policies of assimilation, in the dismissal and dismantling of the formal reconciliation process, and in the Western Australian government's attempt to 'close' remote Aboriginal communities. There is a crucial need for new perspectives and strategies to transform the existing Indigenous-state relationship through pathways of political dialogue.

PROTECTION AND MANAGEMENT

In 1863, in the colonial state of Victoria, Aboriginal people were regarded as having no sovereignty, rights and interests in land. Government policy was formulated on the basis that Aboriginal people would eventually disappear by dying out or through biological absorption and assimilation into the broader population. The 'doomed race' theory, which gained a foothold in the colonial imagination of the 1830s, formed the impetus for policies of protection. Dovetailing with Charles Darwin's theory of the 'survival of the fittest', when the principle of 'natural selection' was applied to human races, it was considered inevitable for the so-called low races to become extinct when they encountered so-called civilised races. [10] However, Aboriginal people at Coranderrk asserted their claim to land, highlighting their grievances and challenging the policies of protection by showing that they were equal to any person in the colony of Victoria. The key demand for land was not only to secure their traditional country but also as a resource to farm like Europeans and to be self-sufficient. Central to their demand for land and improved living conditions was the demand for self-determination.

During the 1830s and 1840s, reformist groups in England were influential in the British colonial administration of colonised Aboriginal people. Their humanitarian views were influential in the 1837 *Report from the House of Commons Select Committee on Aborigines (British Settlements)*. The report looked at measures to secure justice and protect the rights of 'native inhabitants' in British colonies and to promote the spread of civilisation and Christianity. Regarding the Australian colonies, the committee noted the dispossession of Aboriginal people, stating they were entitled to the protection of the Queen and considered subject to British law. Further, the committee said the government of New South Wales should maintain missionaries to instruct tribes and protectors to defend them.[11] Five protectors were appointed by the British Government in 1838 to 'civilise and protect' Aboriginal people in New South Wales. The Office of the Protector of Aborigines was to alleviate 'acts of cruelty, oppression or injustice' against Aboriginal people and to 'civilise and Christianise' as well as conciliate Aboriginal people to colonial authority.[12] In 1838, a protectorate was established in Port Phillip under Chief Protector George Augustus Robinson to safeguard Aboriginal people from injustices of white settlement, but it was considered a failure because of continuing Aboriginal and settler violence and a belief that the system was undermined by the protectors' lack of 'sound judgment and zealous activity'.[13]

In 1858, the colonial government in Victoria enacted a comprehensive scheme to govern the administration of Aboriginal affairs. It included reserving land for agricultural purposes where Aboriginal people could be 'civilised and Christianised' by missionary managers and establishing a Central Board for Aborigines to supervise Aboriginal welfare and control the reserve and rationing system. In 1869, parliament passed legislation—An Act to Provide for the Protection and Management of the Aboriginal Natives of Victoria. It gave legislative recognition to the 'Board for Protection of Aborigines', power to the governor to prescribe where Aboriginal people could live, and to distribute money granted by Parliament. An amending act in 1886 known as the Half-Caste Act aimed to assimilate, or merge, so-called half-castes into the white community as low waged or unpaid members of the labour force, making them 'useful' members of society and relieving the state of the cost of their maintenance. Both the 1886 act, and later the Aborigines Act of 1890, had devastating impacts on Aboriginal people. The acts limited their freedom, forced them from their homes on reserves, broke up families by removing children from their parents and closed reserves over a forty-year period.[14]

The Coranderrk Struggle

Coranderrk reserve was established by John Green, a Presbyterian lay preacher and inspector general of the Protection Board, and Kulin leaders Simon Wonga and William Barak, after they were forced off their original reserve by a powerful squatter and pastoralist. The Kulin built huts, cleared the land, fenced, planted wheat, oats, potatoes, and other vegetables, and raised cattle for milk and meat. Between 1864 and 1866 most survivors of Kulin clans had moved to Coranderrk. Aboriginal people from other areas of Victoria were also sent there including 'neglected' and 'abandoned' orphaned children or children who might be surrendered under the Aborigines Protection Act of 1869.[15] Coranderrk residents created their own reserve court in April 1865, which laid down rules of conduct and punishment for law offenders.[16] The farm was self-managed with the Kulin men organising into four companies to oversee farm tasks. The community was almost self-supporting, producing its own food and cultivating hops as a successful cash crop. However, settler farmers in the district began to pressure for alienation of Coranderrk's agricultural land and in 1869 the surveyor general recommended the resumption and sale of the reserve.[17]

From 1863 until Coranderrk's closure in February 1924, Kulin and other Aboriginal leaders fought for better living conditions, to retain their land and for self-determination. However, they had to contend with the Aborigines Protection Board as well as the various protection and management acts of 1869, 1886 and 1890. These acts comprised a paternalistic and authoritarian regime underlain with assumptions that Aboriginal people were subordinate and inferior. The 'doomed race' theory predicted that the so-called primitive Aboriginal race would eventually become extinct: so-called full bloods would die out and so-called half-castes would be uplifted and merged into white society, losing their Aboriginal identity. While enlightened humanitarian reform policies concerned with the protection of Aboriginal people enabled the Kulin and other Aboriginal groups to obtain land for community preservation and for self-sufficiency, the system of 'protection' instituted by colonial governments was more oppressive than protective. The reservation of land did not recognise Aboriginal traditional ownership; reserves were simply precincts that controlled Aboriginal people and regulated their movements. As Aboriginal people were considered incapable of self-management, they were subjected to authoritarian policies and paternalistic practices by the Aborigines Protection Board who did not consider it necessary to engage with Aboriginal people as fully human agents of self-determination.

During the 1870s, the composition of the Aborigines Protection Board became more hard-line and authoritarian as founding members were replaced by conservatives with a pastoral background. The Aborigines Protection Board advocated for the closure of Coranderrk and over a period of fifty years it pursued various strategies to move people off the reserve. Efforts to close Coranderrk persisted despite recommendation by an 1877 Royal Commission for the retention and funding of reserves to encourage self-sufficiency. Coranderrk eventually succumbed because of the policies of removal and banishment adopted in 1884. Policies of removal were implemented to encourage so-called half-castes to make their way in white society, with the eventual goal of absorption into the general community. Those aged between thirteen and thirty-five were removed from the reserves for apprenticeships as servants, and orphans were transferred to public institutions. The various protection and manage-

ment acts were intended to dispossess Aboriginal people from their reserved land and destroy their traditional society.[18] The forced removals
and assimilatory policies of the 1886 'merging of the half-castes' act is
considered legal genocide by some commentators who believe that it was
aimed at eliminating the existence of Aboriginal people as a distinct
group.[19]

Coranderrk leaders challenged the oppressive polices of protection
through protest and resistance, deputations and lobbying of politicians,
as well as by petitions, letter writing and providing evidence to an 1881
parliamentary board of inquiry that investigated conditions and management at Coranderrk. Despite their lack of political status and even though
they were not always successful, Coranderrk protest leaders developed
informal political relationships through which they could engage in
cross-cultural conversations. In 1876, William Barak and his deputation
took their grievances to Chief Secretary John MacPherson. They turned
his attention to establishing a Royal Commission that would inquire into
the conditions of Aboriginal people in Victoria. In 1878, when the Protection Board continued to advocate for the closure of Coranderrk after the
Royal Commission, William Barak and his deputation gained access to
Premier Graham Berry to protest the closure. Coranderrk leaders secured
an investigation into its management and, because of their relationship
with Berry, they secured a rescindment of a banishment order against
Tommy Bamfield and the gazettal of Coranderrk as a permanent reserve.

Despite their subordinate position within colonial society, Coranderrk
leaders thus engaged in dialogic and respectful relationships with significant individuals. The most significant, respectful relationship was with
John and Mary Green, Scottish emigrant lay preachers. As Inspector-
General for the Board of Protection and manager of Coranderrk, John
Green empowered Aboriginal people and enabled a level of self-determination.[20] While he held colonial notions of 'civilisation' and 'progress', he
did not subscribe to racial superiority and instead treated the Kulin as
free and independent people.[21] However, Green's support and advocacy
for Coranderrk threatened the Aborigines Protection Board, prompting
his removal. Likewise, Anne Fraser Bon, a wealthy pastoralist, had strong
interest in the welfare of Aboriginal people, whom she regularly employed.[22] She supported their struggle to undermine or subvert the power of the Protection Board and was thus accorded special treatment and
vitriol by colonial officials who accused her of betraying her race and
behaving in ways unbecoming of a woman of her class.[23] The dialogic
relationships established with two politicians who were ministers and
chief secretaries of the Aborigines Protection Board are also significant:
John MacPherson consequently promised and instituted a Royal Commission and Graham Berry listened, sympathised and respected the Coranderrk delegations who met with him. He acted on some matters, ga-

zetting Coranderrk as a permanent reserve, but he was also restricted in what he could do by the minority status of his government.

Ultimately, power rested with the Aborigines Protection Board who considered Coranderrk people inferior and their aspirations to become self-determining a threat, and so continually undermined their struggle. The Protection Board had its own agenda and was run by several seemingly vindictive and authoritarian individuals who attempted to coerce people at Coranderrk into leaving. The Protection Board had enormous power over the lives of Aboriginal people and used it in destructive ways. Coranderrk station managers appointed by the Protection Board had similar disrespectful and authoritarian relationships with the Coranderrk people. Coranderrk's demise came in July 1948 when the Coranderrk Land Bill was passed. It revoked the reserve's permanent status so the land could be handed over for soldier settlement. The Kulin and other Aboriginal people in Coranderrk attempted to subvert the prevailing norms of settler colonialism that treated them as inferior and subordinate. They challenged the authority of the Protection Board and the injustice of the laws and societal attitudes that denied them the right to be self-determining, self-sufficient and to make their own way in the colony as free and independent people with their own identity. They formed respectful dialogic relationships with various individuals in colonial society and government. In the process these individuals were able to transcend underlying assumptions about Aboriginal people to recognise the claims and grievances of the Coranderrk people. But the Coranderrk struggle for recognition ultimately challenged the limits of tolerance of government and colonial society. Although the Coranderrk Aboriginal community maintained their struggle for a long period of time, they were ultimately unable to significantly transform the attitudes and opinions of government and the Aborigines Protection Board.

CIVIL RIGHTS AND CITIZENSHIP

In the 1930s and 1940s, Aboriginal people in New South Wales were not entitled to citizenship rights and had no recognised rights to land. They were considered 'backward' and inferior, not 'civilised' enough to be Australian citizens and were destined to die out or be biologically absorbed and assimilated into white society. In the context of the protection and assimilation regimes, a group of Aboriginal activists including William Cooper, William Ferguson and Jack Patten organised politically to agitate for land ownership, economic self-sufficiency, citizenship rights and the elimination of the Aborigines Protection Board. Assumptions regarding Aboriginal inferiority were significant in the Aborigines Protection Board's removal of Aboriginal children from their families to be indentured as domestics and labourers for white society as well as the dispersal of Aboriginal people off the reserves into towns and their sub-sequent imprisonment on reserves for civilisation training. The purpose of dispersal was to force Aboriginal people to assimilate into white soci-ety, but the racist rejection of them by whites forced many Indigenous individuals back to the reserves. At the same time assumptions about Aboriginal people as being unproductive and not needing much reserve land resulted in white Australians pressuring the government to repur-pose Aboriginal reserves and to turn the land over to white farmers.

Assumptions about Aboriginal inferiority also sustained the denial of Australian citizenship to Aboriginal people. They were excluded from the substantive rights and benefits of citizenship such as the right to vote, the right to speak and move freely, the right to a minimum wage, to be equally protected by the law, to enjoy basic health care, a minimum level of social security and a basic level of education.[24] Assumptions about their inferiority were also implicit in the exclusion of Aboriginal people from political processes and the lack of engagement by government with Aboriginal people regarding Aboriginal policy. However, Aboriginal ac-tivists in New South Wales and Victoria were able to develop forms of cross-cultural dialogue, directly appealing to the broader population for citizenship and land rights. Activists such as Bill Ferguson, Jack Patten and others used the white Australian celebration of the 150th anniversary of the landing of the First Fleet on 26 January1938, to stage a Day of Mourning, appealing to the conscience of white Australians and high-lighting Aboriginal grievances against the policies of protection. They also developed national policies for the recognition of Aboriginal rights. But their efforts at dialogue and their demands were largely ignored by the New South Wales government. Prime Minister Joe Lyon and the Commonwealth Minister for the interior, John McEwan, met the activists and were sympathetic to their cause, however the activists' efforts were thwarted by the Australian system of federalism that granted the states regional control of Aboriginal affairs. The Commonwealth government had no power to legislate for Aboriginal people and did not gain such power until after the 1967 referendum.

Various forms of Commonwealth legislation introduced from 1901 granted rights and entitlements of citizenship but deliberately and uni-formly excluded 'Aboriginal natives'.[25] The term 'Aboriginal native' not only referred to Indigenous Australians but also to people from Asia, Africa and the Pacific Islands. The lack of definition of Australian citizen-ship also meant that both Commonwealth and states through their parlia-ments, governments and bureaucracies systematically excluded Aborigi-nal people from citizenship rights and entitlements.[26] An Australian citi-zen was considered white and European. The exclusion of 'Aboriginal natives' of Asia, India, Africa and the Pacific Islands was dropped in 1920 under a new Nationality Act, however Aboriginal Australians including Torres Strait Islanders, Papuans as well as other 'Aboriginal natives' were still excluded from voting and benefits. The Commonwealth also refined its definition of an 'Aboriginal native' making Aboriginality a question of blood rather than identity, so any person with a preponderance of 'Aboriginal blood' was excluded from citizenship rights. When the Commonwealth government passed new legislation relating to pensions and social security benefits in the 1940s, it continued to use 'Aboriginal native' as an exclusionary category, however, the category was narrowed to 'Aboriginal natives of Australia', thereby excluding the Australian Aboriginal population from welfare benefits. Most Aboriginal Australians were excluded from receiving invalid and old-age pensions, widow's pensions, maternity allowances, child endowment and unemployment and sickness benefits.[27] It was not until 1948 that the Commonwealth government gained power over citizenship when it created the Australian citizen as a legal entity under the Nationality and Citizenship Act. However, the act only provided an 'empty category' of citizenship for Aboriginal people because they were still excluded from citizenship rights and entitlements including welfare benefits by other Commonwealth and state legislation.[28]

In New South Wales the cultural assertiveness of a growing 'mixed blood' Aboriginal population who identified as Aboriginal and who were living on reserves was perceived as a racial and cultural threat to the nation. Along with the increasing financial liability of funding rations and maintaining Aboriginal reserves, the Aborigines Protection Board sought stronger powers to disperse the Aboriginal population off reserves, gain control over Aboriginal children to indenture them as domestics and labourers and to reduce the birth rate of the Aboriginal population by taking adolescent girls away from their communities.[29] There was also pressure to revoke Aboriginal reserves and for the land to be turned over to white Australians. The soldier settlement scheme of 1917, whereby returned soldiers could select a block of agricultural land, created further demand for Aboriginal land although returned Aboriginal soldiers did not benefit from this scheme. The Aborigines Protection Board initially resisted the pressure to turn Aboriginal land over but would eventually do so to raise funds for its activities.

By 1901, each state except Tasmania had regimes of Protection Boards or protectors.[30] These policies and practices of protection were eventually formalised by legislation after Victoria was the first to pass legislation in 1869.[31] A key assumption of protection policies was that Aboriginal people of full-descent would die out and mixed-descent Aboriginal people would be biologically absorbed into the white population through interracial relationships.[32] Western Australia and Northern Territory established processes to speed up biological absorption through interracial marriage. Administrators in Victoria, New South Wales and South Australia were more focussed on the cost of Aboriginal people to the state, but they did have similar policies of absorption which divided the Abo-

riginal people into mixed-descent and full-descent groups, removing financial support from the mixed-descent groups. The mixed-descent
groups were also removed from the reserves and children were removed
from their families to destroy Aboriginal identity. In Queensland interracial marriage was conditional on written permission from a protector but
was not viewed as a preferred method to absorb Aboriginal people into
the white population.[33] By 1911, the Protection Board in New South
Wales had sought more power from the government to take away children. To generate revenue to fund its programme of child removal, it
began leasing Aboriginal reserve land to white settlers for residential and
farming expansion.[34]

During the 1920s, Aboriginal people moved to live in town camps on
the outskirts of white townships, but a rising tide of protest from white
town people demanded their exclusion from schools, shops, streets and
town boundaries. It was during this time that the Australian Aboriginal
Progressive Association (AAPA) emerged. Led by Fred Maynard who,
with the support of friends and family, including the support of Elizabeth
McKenzie-Hatton, the secretary of the AAPA, agitated for land based on
prior ownership as an economic base and for the cessation of removal of
Aboriginal children from families under the apprenticeship system and
for the protection of Aboriginal girls. AAPA also demanded the dissolu-
tion of the Aborigines Protection Board and full privileges of citizenship
for Aboriginal people. The Protection Board was threatened by AAPA
and sought to discredit the organisation and its leaders. However, as the
economic recession deepened, AAPA broke up in 1927. In the 1930s,
unemployment forced many Aboriginal people back to the reserves to
obtain rations because they were denied unemployment and work relief.
But the Protection Board could not support those who were previously
employed in the mainstream economy and in 1932 it urged the incoming
conservative government to remove widespread discrimination being
practiced in New South Wales. Having suffered funding cuts, the Protection Board took control of family endowment payments to Aboriginal
people on reserves to meet its rations and maintenance costs. But the
government was eager to cut costs and ruled that unemployed Aboriginal people were only entitled to income security benefits if they could
prove they had done 'white man's work' in the previous years of employment. Aboriginal people from all over the state protested the injustice.[35]
By the mid-1930s, the Protection Board initiated a policy of concentrating
Aboriginal people on reserves. The intention was to remove and confine
any person with 'Aboriginal blood' on reserves where they would be
provided with 'disciplinary supervision' and not be allowed to leave
until they could be effectively assimilated into society.[36]

Aboriginal activists and white Australian support groups had been
calling for Commonwealth control of Aboriginal Affairs, however, in
1936, state premiers said this was impractical; instead, they instituted

regular conferences of chief protectors and protection boards. The initial conference of chief protectors, Commissioner of Native Affairs, and representatives of Aborigines' protection boards in Canberra in April 1937 resolved that the administration of Aboriginal Affairs should remain with the individual states, but that legislation should be uniform as much as possible, and the Commonwealth should provide financial assistance towards the states for the 'care, protection and education of natives'.[37] In their first resolution they decided that 'the destiny of the natives of aboriginal origin, but not of the full blood, lies in their ultimate absorption by the people of the Commonwealth' and that 'all efforts be directed to that end'.[38] They considered the increase in the population of 'mixed-blood' Aboriginal people a threat to the nation; the solution being their ultimate absorption into the white population.[39]

William Cooper, William Ferguson and Jack Patten led different regional groups of activists who came together to stage the Day of Mourning conference. This Aboriginal movement had begun to emerge in October 1937 with a campaign of public speeches, support meetings and press interviews attacking the discriminatory unemployment relief system, the increase in Protection Board powers and the appalling conditions of Protection Board stations and reserves. Their protests attracted the attention of the NSW premier who established a Parliamentary Select Committee to inquire into the policies and administration of the Aborigines Protection Board. But the Select Committee lapsed without reporting, and eventually the Public Service Board took up this task.[40]

The Day of Mourning

On Wednesday, 26 January 1938, Sydney was celebrating the 150th anniversary of the 1788 landing of the First Fleet, which involved a re-enactment of Governor Phillip's landing in Sydney Cove and a parade of floats through the streets commemorating the unfolding story of 'Australia's March to Nationhood'.[41] Aboriginal men from Menindee and Brewarrina participated in the re-enactment at a specially prepared beach at Farm Cove in Sydney Harbour. Dressed in cloth and gum leaves, and armed with boomerangs, they rushed forwards as a boatload of actors representing the British seamen and marines rowed towards the shore from a replica of the HMS *Supply*. In the presence of marines with fixed bayonets, the Aboriginal men retreated but not too far, as an English actor playing Governor Phillip approached and placed a red cloth around the neck of Hero Black, the leader of the group. An actor playing Judge Advocate David Collins read an abbreviated version of Phillip's commission, although in 1788 this was not read until twelve days after the initial landing. In a short speech, the actor portraying Phillip expressed the hope that this country would become the most valuable acquisition the

British had ever made. There was a toast to the king, three cheers and a *feu de joie*.[42]

In stark contrast, on 26 January 1938, Aboriginal people, led by Cooper, Ferguson and Patten, held a protest objecting to their living conditions and plight. More than one hundred Aboriginal people, plus two white policemen and two white journalists, attended the Aboriginal Day of Mourning conference. Protest delegates arrived from around New South Wales and Melbourne in Victoria. Among those in attendance were William Cooper, William Ferguson, Jack Patten, Douglas Nicholls, Margaret Tucker, Pearl Gibbs, Jack Kinchela, Helen Grosvenor and Tom Foster. The Day of Mourning protest was planned to coincide with Australia's 150th anniversary celebration after a dismal and dismissive response from the prime minister's office to William Cooper's petition to King George VI in 1937. In the petition Cooper stated that white Australians had a moral duty to care for Aboriginal people because they had been dispossessed of land and denied status. Cooper called on the king to intervene to prevent the extinction of Aboriginal people, to provide better living conditions and for the representation of Aboriginal people in Federal Parliament.[43]

At the conference Jack Patten and William Ferguson spoke of the deplorable living conditions of Aboriginal people in New South Wales, arguing strongly for full citizenship rights and benefits, and for the abolition of the Aborigines Protection Board. Jack Patten stated that the lack of opportunity and citizenship rights was related to white Australian attitudes about Aboriginal people being inferior and incapable of bettering themselves. According to Patten the malnourishment and poor education of Aboriginal people was a disgrace and a major handicap to equality. Both Patten and Ferguson argued that the apprenticing of young Aboriginal women for domestic labour without payment amounted to slavery.[44] Ferguson spoke of the 'dreadful suffering' of people on the reserves and argued for access to health care, education, training and other opportunities including land ownership. Ferguson said that the absence and denial of opportunity prevented Aboriginal progress. He had scathing criticism towards the system of Aboriginal protection, believing that Aboriginal people did not need government protection.[45] Doug Nicholls believed that Aboriginal people needed to fight hard for equality because after 150 years they were still being influenced and oppressed by white people even though they were capable of self-determination if given the chance. William Cooper urged continuation of the struggle. He focussed on the lack of protection provided by the Aborigines' Protection Board, stating that 'protect' should mean 'protect from injury', and asserted the board did 'not act in accordance with British justice'.[46] The one and only resolution that came from the Day of Mourning protested the treatment of Aboriginal people and called for a new policy to enable full citizenship and equality for Aboriginal people.

Jack Patten and Bill Ferguson launched the Aborigines' Progressive Association's manifesto titled *Aborigines Claim Citizen Rights*.[47] The manifesto sought repeal of the official policy of protection because it was based on the belief that Aboriginal people were backward, inferior and required supervision by the government. The manifesto explained that 26 January 1938, was a day of mourning for Aboriginal people because white invasion had imposed misery and degradation upon the original inhabitants when they had taken the land by force and almost succeeded in exterminating the original Australians. It sought the abolishment of the boards for the protection of Aborigines because their unlimited power of control deprived Aboriginal people of their citizenship rights and reduced the Aboriginal 'standards of living below life-preservation point.' The manifesto also pointed out that labour parties and trade unions were indifferent to the use of Aboriginal people as cheap labour and had given no real support to them in achieving civil rights. Finally, the manifesto said the attitudes of racial prejudice and misunderstanding towards Aboriginal people had to change. It asked white Australians whether their conscience was clear regarding the treatment of Aboriginal people; it asserted that white Australians could hardly claim to be 'civilised, progressive, kindly and humane' given the cruel and callous treatment of Aboriginal people. The manifesto also highlighted the hypocrisy of the policy of 'protection'; rather than protect it had degraded, humiliated and exterminated Aboriginal people. The manifesto stated that Aboriginal people were not asking for 'protection', 'charity' or 'sentimental sympathy' but were asking for 'equal education, equal opportunity, equal wages, equal rights to possess property, or to be our own masters'; in other words 'equal citizenship'.[48]

Newspapers in Sydney and Melbourne were generally dismissive of the Day of Mourning, although their response indicates that the message from the protest had reached its target. An editorial in Melbourne's *The Argus*, 17 January 1939, said fair-minded Australians would welcome the opinions expressed in the manifesto however the Aboriginal people 'cannot be treated as a modern civilised race' as 'they are properly regarded as a dying relic of a dead past'. The paper's reasoning was that Aboriginal culture had not advanced beyond the stage of nomadic hunters. Aboriginal people, according to *The Argus*, belonged to an early stage of human development.[49] The *Sydney Morning Herald* stated that any attempt to mar the 150th anniversary celebrations by staging a Day of Mourning protest must be deplored. It said the Day of Mourning movement was political and largely emotional, sponsored by sympathetic white people and 'half-castes'.[50] However, in another editorial from 22 January 1938, *The Sydney Morning Herald* said the Day of Mourning 'offers deserved criticism of the nation, reminding us that the inevitable clash of white and black cultures has produced a sad disintegration of aboriginal life which we have failed to remedy'.[51]

Following the Day of Mourning protest, on 31 January 1938, a deputation of twenty people, including Jack Patten, William Ferguson, Helen Grosvenor, Pearl Gibbs and Tom Foster, met with Prime Minister Joe Lyons and his wife as well as John McEwen, minister for the interior in Sydney. Jack Patten provided a copy of the 'Policy for Aborigines' expressed in a ten-point statement to the prime minister. The prime minister received the delegation and policy statement sympathetically, however he indicated that there would need to be an alteration to the Constitution or an agreement by all states before the Commonwealth could take control of Aboriginal affairs.[52] The national Aboriginal policy statement given to the prime minister had two aims: full citizenship for all Aboriginal people and land settlement. The policy statements sought a national Aboriginal policy and Commonwealth control of Aboriginal affairs; a minister of Aboriginal affairs to be a member of the cabinet; a departmental head to oversee a department of Aboriginal affairs, which should be advised by an advisory board of six people, three of whom should be Aboriginal and nominated by the Aborigines' Progressive Association. The aim of the department would be to raise all Aboriginal people to full citizen status and ensure they receive certain entitlements relating to education, work and wages, pensions and benefits, and owning land and property. This also included equality in marriage and freedom to marry; the same privileges in respect to housing; and that free maternity and hospital treatment be provided to Aboriginal women. Regarding land, the policy called for a special land settlement scheme to assist Aboriginal people to settle on the land and to provide them with advice and financial support. However, the policy also sought the retention of reserves for 'aged and incompetent Aborigines' who are unable to take their place in white society. Other aspects of the policy related to training Aboriginal men and women as patrol officers and having nurses and teachers working with 'uncivilised and semi-civilised' Aboriginal people.[53]

Justice, Decency and Fair Play

Nothing came of the meeting with Prime Minister Joe Lyons because the Commonwealth was reluctant to pursue an alteration to the Australian Constitution or to seek agreement from the states in that regard. In any case, in 1937 Aboriginal affairs administrators from the states and Northern Territory had concluded that the administration should remain with the individual states. There was no change in Aboriginal policy in New South Wales and in the administration of the Aborigines Protection Board. This is evidenced by the behaviour and response of the government and Protection Board to the claims of Aboriginal people in Cumeroogunga reserve on the Murray River and their walk-off in 1939. The Cumeroogunga protest was defeated when the Protection Board and New South Wales government refused to listen to the complaints of Aboriginal people about their living conditions and the reserve's management.[54]

Nonetheless in June 1940, after an inquiry by the Public Service Board into the Aborigines Protection Board, the Aborigines Protection Act was amended. The inquiry recommended reconstitution of the Protection Board into a Welfare Board, the appointment of a superintendent and a policy for the gradual assimilation of Aboriginal people 'into the general and social life of the general community'. It also recommended developing Aboriginal stations to produce crops and foodstuffs, providing training to Aboriginal people and improving housing and other necessary buildings on reserves. New appointments were made to the Welfare Board, including anthropologist A. P. Elkin.[55] In 1944, the Commonwealth government attempted to hold a referendum and secure Aboriginal law-making power, but it was defeated. However, activism and public campaigning in the late 1950s and early 1960s forced the government to hold a referendum in 1967 to amend discriminatory sections of the Australian Constitution and to enable the Commonwealth government to have legislative power over Aboriginal people.[56]

The Day of Mourning Aboriginal activists employed the language of equal rights to influence and seek the support of white activists, white political organisations and the general population to pressure the government to change Aboriginal policy. William Cooper emphasised the importance of the Aboriginal voice and perspective in advocating for rights and interests because white Australians could not 'think black'. According to Cooper the Aboriginal perspective was different to that of whites and he argued for an Aboriginal point of view in government policy.[57] Similarly, Jack Patten and Bill Ferguson supported Aboriginal people speaking in their own voice and enabling public airing of an Aboriginal perspective. They wanted white Australians to face the truth—that the so-called policy of protection was in fact exterminating Aboriginal people. They wanted white Australians to hear the Aboriginal point of view and to view the problems and issues from an Aboriginal perspective. They argued that Aboriginal people were not asking for charity or to be studied as 'scientific freaks' and were also not asking for 'protection' but wanted 'justice, decency and fair play'.[58]

While largely suspicious of white people and their intentions, Aboriginal activists formed relationships with unions, feminist groups, Christian groups, the Australian Labor Party and the Communist Party as well as with white individuals such as P. R. Stephensen, a publisher and leader of the right-wing Australia First movement. Although in a paternalistic manner, these organisations and individuals campaigned on behalf of Aboriginal people. These political connections provided the resources to support Aboriginal agency and the political platform to enable Aboriginal activists to pursue their rights agenda.

In the 1930s, the entry of anthropologists to the public debate over Aboriginal policy changed the language and issues of the discussion. Their closeness to government and their desire for roles in Aboriginal administration were met with suspicion and derision from Patten and Ferguson. Anthropologist A. P. Elkin believed that anthropological expertise could interpret the current conditions and future needs of Aboriginal people. However, Patten and Ferguson believed that anthropologists such as Elkin would use their power and expertise to continue white control of and interference in Aboriginal communities.[59] The advice anthropologists provided government denied Aboriginal people a voice and agency in shaping their own future. Anthropologists had limited political connections to Aboriginal activists and they did not work directly with them on the frontline of their struggle. Elkin's interest lay with traditional Aboriginal communities in the north of Australia. However, he did have significant influence over Aboriginal policy in New South Wales and nationally, which undermined the Aboriginal political platform for social and political change.

The intercultural relations forged by Jack Patten, William Ferguson, William Cooper and other Aboriginal activists enabled them to play a constructive and historical role in agitating for citizenship, land rights and economic self-sufficiency. Due to their efforts, white Australian humanitarian organisations and individuals began to take up their concerns, arguing for equality for Aboriginal people and for Commonwealth control of Aboriginal affairs. As an Aboriginal-only forum, the Day of Mourning protest enabled Aboriginal people to develop and assert their own political agenda. It operated in stark contrast to the white Australian celebrations taking place on 26 January 1938. There was significant divergence between Aboriginal and white Australians regarding the meaning of the day, and this divide could not be bridged because of the assumptions, beliefs and practices of government and the public towards Aboriginal people. Every January 26 this continues to be played out although Indigenous people and their supporters now celebrate Indigenous survival, while mainstream Australia celebrates the birth of the settler nation.

ASSIMILATION AND PATERNALISM

By the late 1930s, the policy of protection was widely considered to have failed. The Commonwealth government initiated a policy of assimilation in the Northern Territory and in the early 1950s state governments followed by instituting assimilation as a policy. Assimilation assumed that all Aboriginal people would eventually transition from their 'tribal' or 'detribalised' lives and live as white Australians in a homogenous Australian community. However, underlying the assimilation policy was the assumption of Aboriginal cultural inferiority and the belief that Aboriginal people had no 'civilised' society or rights of land ownership. The assimilation policy was paternalistic, deeming Aboriginal people to be wards of the state and only entitled to full citizenship if they assimilated into non-Indigenous society. For assimilation to be successful, white Australians would have to abandon their discriminatory attitudes and practices and accept Aboriginal people as their equals; and Aboriginal people — particularly those no longer living a traditional life — would have to readily accept assimilation as an inevitable passage, forgoing their identity and culture.

In the 1960s, government authorities assumed that Aboriginal culture and society had nothing to offer and therefore a process of assimilation would transition Aboriginal people into a superior 'civilisation'. Adolphus P. Elkin, an Anglican minister, anthropologist, and lobbyist for the rights of Aboriginal people, believed protection was authoritarian and failed to protect Aboriginal people from injustice and violence, and did not envisage a future for Aboriginal people.[60] Elkin advocated a policy for protecting and advancing the welfare of Aboriginal people so they could become worthy citizens and not 'hangers-on to station and townships'. A key aspect of this policy was that Aboriginal people would not only be protected from injustice but also assured of a livelihood.[61] The essential features of the policy included health services, education and improved conditions of employment. As of 1934, the humanitarian Aboriginal rights campaigners were increasingly influenced by Elkin's ideas. In 1933, the National Missionary Council of Australia endorsed a national policy calling for several changes in Aboriginal policy, especially Commonwealth oversight and control of Aboriginal people, a separate Department of Aboriginal Affairs and uplifting Aboriginal people to become 'capable, industrious and self-reliant'.[62]

The move away from the protection policy to a new one of assimilation began with Elkin's involvement in developing a new federal government policy for Aboriginal people in the Northern Territory. It was referred to as the 'new deal' for Aborigines.[63] It aimed at taking care of the immediate physical needs of Aboriginal people including their health, education and training for 'useful community service', with a long-term objective, taking place over many generations, of assimilation into the Australian community in order to secure the rights of citizenship.[64] Western religion would provide a philosophy and moral code for Aboriginal people and would involve religious training through church missions. This training was aimed to elevate the 'native' from the 'tribal state' who was seen to be a 'hanger-on' with 'no objective in life'.[65] Under the policy a Native Affairs Branch was created in the Northern Territory supported by district and patrol officers.

In accordance with the 'new deal' policy so-called fully detribalised natives would be provided housing, education and health care in Aboriginal compounds in Darwin and Alice Springs. There they would be able to engage in gardening, fishing and animal husbandry and to have entertainment that would keep them away from town. So-called half-castes born in wedlock to half-caste parents would be cared for by their parents, and those born of an Aboriginal mother and non-Aboriginal father would be cared for in government institutions, given elementary education and later put in separate institutions according to gender. Girls would be trained to be domestic servants and boys trained for pastoral station work as a source of labour for whites. The near-white children would be trained apart from the half-caste children. So-called myalls still living in a tribal state and 'semi-detribalised' Aboriginal people would be left alone and protected from white intrusion, and exploitation of resources on reserves would be prevented. District Officer Stations were to be established on the boundaries of reserves 'as buffers between tribal natives and outer civilisation' and as centres for gradual contact with 'civilisation'. The stations would become training and employment centres for 'natives', preparing them to gradually develop in their own way rather than drift into towns only to become 'hangers-on'.[66]

The assimilation of Aboriginal people was integral to an Australian vision of a uniform nation. Aboriginal people would be inculcated with white Australia's values and aspirations and conform to its established way of life to become members of the nation. The assimilation policy was associated with greater Commonwealth government involvement in Aboriginal affairs. In many respects this was because the government was concerned with its international reputation in relation to the treatment of Aboriginal people, as MP Paul Hasluck argued in Parliament in June 1950.[67] In September 1951, the Commonwealth and states agreed that assimilation was the objective for 'native welfare' but that executive responsibility for 'native affairs' would remain with respective governments. While the Commonwealth and states acknowledged that many Aboriginal people were capable of accepting citizenship responsibilities, they believed a number of them in northern Australia needed special legislation to assist their advancement into 'civilisation'. The governments did not think they were treating persons defined as 'native' and 'Aboriginal' as a different class of citizen but viewed them as wards of the state in need of guardianship. They would cease to be wards once they obtained full citizenship, achieved only by living and working as accepted members of the community.[68] Thus, the benefits of full citizenship for Aboriginal people were linked to their successful assimilation into white society.

Hasluck did not view this as 'suppression of Aboriginal culture' but considered that Aboriginal people would eventually lose their 'tribal life' and grow into white society. He asserted that more than two-thirds of Aboriginal people were 'detribalised' and that assimilation provided an alternative to the loss of 'tribal customs'. Nonetheless, he said that there would be some Aboriginal people at a 'lower level of civilisation' who would remain segregated for a temporary duration.[69] In fact, Aboriginal people were already Australian citizens by reason of birth and by virtue of the Nationality and Citizenship Act of 1948 but were not entitled to full citizenship rights and responsibilities. To justify limited citizenship entitlements, the Commonwealth government said Aboriginal people were of equivalent status to minors under twenty-one years of age: that is, they could not do everything others were able to do and needed to be protected and assisted in ways in which adults were not. The government argued that being placed under the provisions of native welfare legislation did not take away Australian citizenship. While it may limit the exercise of some rights enjoyed by other non-Aboriginal Australians, it also afforded assistance which was not given to other citizens. This included building more houses, providing transitional housing, ensuring supervision and guidance from welfare workers, creating employment interest in a new way of life and educating Aboriginal children.[70]

The assimilation and citizenship process was controlled by the exemption provisions of Aboriginal legislation whereby Aboriginal people—including so-called half-castes—gained citizenship rights only by being exempt from the provisions of special Aboriginal legislation. However, such exemptions did not always imply full citizenship. In New South Wales (NSW), Queensland (Qld), South Australia (SA), Western Australia (WA) and the Northern Territory (NT) a certificate of exemption could exempt Aboriginal people from the provisions of the Aborigines Acts. The exemption was based on the opinion of the board in NSW and SA, the director in QLD and NT and the minister in WA. In SA the legislation specifically stated that an Aboriginal person had to have a certain standard of character and level of intelligence and development to be granted exemption; and in WA there were conditions related to having a certain standard of health and freedom from disease.[71]

A Native Welfare Conference on 26 January 1961, advanced a detailed definition of assimilation outlining the methods for advancing the policy of assimilation. Paul Hasluck outlined this policy in Parliament stating that assimilation 'means that all aborigines and part aborigines are expected eventually to attain the same manner of living as other Australians and to live as members of a single Australian community enjoying the same rights and privileges, accepting the same responsibilities, observing the same customs and influenced by the same beliefs, hopes and loyalties as other Australians'.[72] This attitude was reflected in government approaches to Aboriginal peoples and typically was met with strong resistance by Aboriginal communities intent on preserving their cultures, values and connections to traditional territories.

Exclusion and Assimilation

Accordingly, in 1963, when the Commonwealth government excised a large area of the reserve on the Gove Peninsula in the Northern Territory for bauxite mining, they did not consider this land to be the traditional country of the Yolngu people living in Yirrkala, a Methodist mission founded in 1934 in the Arnhem Land Reserve. In their view it was merely land on which mining could take place and incidentally offering a means to advance Yolngu assimilation. Yolngu were regarded as having no title or rights to land or to the resources of the land, and were therefore not consulted regarding the development of a mine. The Methodist Mission Board and the Welfare Department believed they understood the needs and concerns of the Yolngu and that mining would be beneficial to the Yolngu to assist their transition into mainstream society. They assumed that gainful employment through home industries linked to the mainstream economy would be a stepping-stone for advancement and that industrial development would complement the home industries and enhance Yolngu transition towards assimilation into non-Indigenous society.

The Yolngu asserted their ownership of the land by protesting the mining on their lands and by petitioning the Commonwealth Parliament, also calling to account the actions of the welfare authorities and the federal minister. They had to overcome assumptions that they were inferior and unintelligent and therefore incapable of protesting and articulating their concerns or making decisions about their well-being and future. They managed to secure a parliamentary Select Committee inquiry, vindicating Yolngu grievances about the lack of explanation and consultation from the government regarding the mining project. This also enabled the Yolngu to highlight the deficiencies of the guardian/ward relationship—which treated them as though they were children—and of the assimilation policy through which their lives were managed. However, the Select Committee could only recommend certain protections and benefits for the Yolngu. The Yolngu were ultimately unsuccessful in securing a fair exchange regarding the mining project and in gaining recognition of their native title rights in a court action.[73] The court action also exposed the deficiencies in the Australian judicial system, which at the time persisted in applying Australian legal authorities based on a 'barbarian theory' in respect of Aboriginal people. It was difficult for the Yolngu to overcome the entrenched assumptions and attitudes about Aboriginal people in the political and legal institutions of Australian government.

In March 1963, a series of events took place when the minister for territories, Paul Hasluck, signed a forty-two-year lease to enable the Gove Bauxite Corporation, in association with the French aluminium company Péchiney, to establish an alumina plant and mine bauxite on land near Yirrkala, a Methodist mission with more than five hundred Yolngu inhabitants. The Yolngu had no say in the decision because they were considered wards of the state. However, the Yolngu considered themselves owners of the country, as affirmed by anthropologist Ronald Berndt.[74] Discussions over the possibility of bauxite mining at Yirrkala had been underway since early 1958. The agreement, in principle, about the mine was reached between Reverend Cecil Gribble, general secretary of the Board of Methodist Overseas Missions, Reverend G. S. Symons, chairman of the North Australia District of the Methodist Church, and Roger Nott, representing the Commonwealth government. According to the Yirrkala mission superintendent, Edgar Wells, the decision 'had been kept quiet as possible'. No Aboriginal people were present at the meeting of the mission's board, which ratified the agreement in the presence of the technical director of the Gove Bauxite Corporation. The board made no request for either the direct representation of Aboriginal people or for a report to be submitted on their behalf.[75] In negotiating the mining lease, Hasluck said the federal government wanted to ensure that there were no harmful effects on Aboriginal people and that the Yirrkala mission work would continue, thereby ensuring that the older generation would maintain access to their 'totemic sites' and the younger generation would obtain benefits from employment and training. The Yolngu were not consulted because the government deemed their interests to be represented by the director of welfare in the Northern Territory and officials of the Methodist Board of Missions. The general secretary of the Methodist Board of Missions was satisfied that the federal government and the mining company had 'taken all possible care to safeguard the interest' of the Aboriginal people. [76]

The mission superintendent, Edgar Wells, felt that the exclusion of the Yolngu and the expected impact of mining warranted a protest. He understood the nature of the Yolngu's relationship to their land and was angry that the mission board did not consider Yolngu consent for the transfer of reserve land for mining, nor their views on it. He sent dramatically worded telegrams to church officials in Sydney, Perth and Adelaide as well as the *Courier Mail*, the *Sydney Morning Herald*, Stan Davey, secretary of the Federal Council for Aboriginal Advancement, and the leader of the Federal Opposition, Arthur Calwell, advising that the people at Yirrkala were being squeezed into half of a square mile from the original holding of two hundred square miles as a result of the bauxite land grab, making it impossible to house the population of the mission and cultivate and graze the land. He also sent telegrams to the director of welfare in the Northern Territory, H. C. Giese, Reverend Professor Trigge, president of the Methodist Church of Australasia and Reverend Cecil Gribble, recommending that no document of transfer of facilities be signed and that there be no negotiations with the mining company or government over transfer of land tenure or living space of Aboriginal people for thirty days.[77] Stan Davey condemned the Commonwealth government and the mission board for 'defrauding' the Aboriginal people of their tribal land. He called for suspension of mining development until certain conditions were met and for negotiations with the Yolngu. He also demanded that the Australian government enact legislation to grant title to tribal lands to people living on reserves and to assure Aboriginal people they had inalienable rights that could only be set aside by negotiation and just compensation.[78]

The uncertainty of what the mining company was doing, a lack of explanation concerning company activities and absence of negotiation in relation to the land caused anxiety among the Yolngu and mission staff. The Yolngu were concerned that strangers could walk about the country boring holes, marking off areas, erecting buildings and delaying mission shipments on the wharf without any real attempt at explaining their future intentions.[79] The Yolngu leaders said the mining company could use the country, but they wanted to hunt freely and did not want mining to encroach on the mission. Giese responded by stating that the mining would be beneficial to the Yolngu, assuring them they would not be pushed out of Yirrkala and that he would send the chief welfare officer, Ted Evans, to explain what the mining company can do and how people would benefit. In May 1963, the Yolngu leaders wrote to both Harry Giese and Paul Hasluck requesting compensation because the government would benefit financially from the mining. In exchange for mining on their land they wanted brick houses, including housing for single people, a shop, bakery, tables and chairs and two toilet blocks, as well as a truck and four-wheel drive vehicles for hunting.[80]

The dispute over mining at Yirrkala focussed public attention on the policy of assimilation. Paul Hasluck said the government was trying to foster home industries such as gardening, fishing, beef cattle, forestry and production of artifacts for sale on all missions in Arnhem Land to transition Aboriginal people into gainful occupations. These home industries would complement the industrial development in east Arnhem Land, which according to Hasluck should not be a source of harm but a valuable opportunity for advancing Aboriginal people.[81] Cecil Gribble believed that assimilation was inevitable for Aboriginal people in Arnhem Land and that the church's role was to comfort them during this transition. Gribble's position endorsed assimilatory beliefs that Aboriginal people would progress if merged into the white community. However, in June 1963, the National Missionary Council of Australia questioned its policy on assimilation and supported the desire of Aboriginal people to retain their distinctive culture, identity and their right to contribute to decision-making and policies that affect their lives.[82]

To the government, however, assimilation was incompatible with rights to land or maintaining Aboriginal language and culture. Hasluck pointed out that reserves were created to protect 'tribal nomads' from other Australians by isolating them on inviolable reserves and did not create any legal title to the land or its resources for Aboriginal people. Under the assimilation policy the issue was how to best transition Aboriginal people from a 'sheltered life on the mission' to a full life in the community. This involved providing 'gainful occupation' and ensuring development on reserves promoted their welfare.[83] Peter Howson, who would later have ministerial responsibility for Aboriginal affairs, believed that assimilation meant individual ownership of land and housing—not sharing on a communal basis—as well as taking up non-Indigenous forms of employment. Howson also believed that Aborigines should be treated similarly to other Australians and have the same opportunities.

The Federal Labor Opposition believed that there should be a 'revolutionary approach' to the position of Aboriginal people on reserves. Labor politician Kim Beazley Sr. believed the time had come for the Commonwealth Parliament to create an Aboriginal title to reserve land in the Northern Territory as it was within the constitutional power of the government to do so. He asserted that the proclamation of reserves by the Commonwealth would mean nothing if areas where minerals had been found were excised from reserves leaving Aboriginal people less desirable country. Beazley was also critical of the government for not consulting with the Aboriginal people and for accepting the mission as the representative of Aboriginal people. He said Aboriginal rights should be safeguarded by discussions with Aboriginal leaders of the Gove Peninsula. [84] Labor member Gordon Bryant argued that Aboriginal people had a right to their traditional lands and should be consulted regarding its use. He believed the rights of Aboriginal people in Yirrkala had not received proper consideration and noted that tribal elders were concerned about what had happened. He also argued that if this part of Arnhem Land was to be developed then it must be for the benefit of Aboriginal people. Bryant recognised that the Australian conscience could not be clear because Aboriginal people were not being treated equally and that governments had given little consideration to the fundamental human dignity of Aboriginal people.[85] In response to the Labor Party's call for an Aboriginal title in land, Howson believed that to create Aboriginal title and hand over land would be treating Aboriginal people differently to other Australians.[86]

Yolngu traditional values relating to their relationship to the land was the source of their strength and power. Edgar Wells understood that reaffirming Yolngu traditional association with their land and their spirituality would reinforce survival values, increase intellectual power and ensure a full and free discussion among the Yolngu. The Yolngu were also artists and emphasis on art at Yirrkala brought the clan leaders together where they exchanged views on other issues including the mining of their land.[87] It was the Yolngu paintings in the Yirrkala church that provided the inspiration for a bark petition to the Federal Parliament.

The paintings impressed Labor Party politicians Gordon Bryant and Kim Beazley Sr. when they both visited Yirrkala in July 1963. They saw a working mission cultivating peanuts, vegetables, sorghum and bananas, and they noted the improved pasture. But the area of the mission had been reduced to about one square mile because of the mining lease.[88]

The two large paintings in the new church building in Yirrkala represented the essence of Yolngu existence by depicting theie relationship with the land. They also linked Christianity and Yolngu spirituality as a meeting of cultures. Over a discussion about the cultural meaning of the paintings, Beazley suggested the Yolngu make a bark petition surrounded by an Aboriginal painting to convey their concerns. He provided the wording to the petition in English while the paintings and the matching Yolngu Matha petition was done by the Yolngu.[89] The bark petition was presented to the Federal Parliament by John (Jock) Nelson, member for the Northern Territory, on 14 August 1963. The petition asked that: (1) the House of Representatives appoint a committee with competent interpreters to hear the views of the people of Yirrkala before permitting the excision of any land from the Aboriginal reserve in Arnhem Land; and (2) no arrangement be entered into with any company that will destroy the livelihood and independence of the Yirrkala people.[90]

The Yolngu Bark Petition

The Yolngu bark petition was considered the first of its kind in the Australian Parliament. *The Age,* in its 15 August 1963, edition said, 'House Hears Plea in Strange Tongue', stating that the House of Representatives had received the 'strangest petition' written in 'Aboriginal language on a length of stringy bark'.[91] *The Canberra Times* headline read, 'Novel Plea By Tribal Group', stating that a petition written in English and an Aboriginal language, and mounted on stringy bark decorated with ochre pictures of turtles, fish, goannas and bandicoots, was presented by members of a Yirrkala group of tribes to the House of Representatives. *The Canberra Times* went on to say that the 'bark petition' caused 'a ripple of surprise and interest'.[92] The Yolngu petition was a political statement that highlighted the deficient approach of government in excising the land from the reserve without consultation and recognition of the rights of the Yolngu. The Yolngu felt that their needs and interests had been completely ignored and they feared their fate would be much the same as the Larrakeyah people in Darwin.[93] The petition had considerable impact not only because it was different but also because Yolngu culture was recognisable to settler Australians due to the work of anthropologists such as Donald Thomson and Ronald and Catherine Berndt. Yolngu art had also won Australian and international audiences.[94]

Representatives of the federal government and the Methodist Overseas Mission tried to identify a missionary organiser in Yirrkala responsible for the petition, implying that Europeans were pressuring the Yolngu. Gribble said that Aboriginal leaders in Yirrkala had assured him that they did not object to the development. He claimed that the Methodist mission was instrumental in safeguarding the rights and welfare of the people and their sacred places.[95] In Parliament, Paul Hasluck rejected the petition because only about six of the thirteen tribal groups in Yirrkala were represented by the signatories and none of the twelve signatories were more than thirty years old, therefore they could not be regarded as having the authority to speak on behalf of the people of Yirrkala.[96] In response, the Yolngu prepared a second bark petition as proof of their support for the petition. Wandjuk Marika organised the taking of names and thumbprints that were witnessed by a missionary. Most of the community sent their witnessed thumbprints to Canberra.[97] Gordon Bryant said it was disappointing that Hasluck and Gribble, who were responsible for protecting the people of Yirrkala, should attempt to silence the Yolngu voice.[98]

Representatives of the Welfare Department in the Northern Territory, such as Harry Giese, believed the Yolngu were happy about what was happening to their land. Giese said the petition surprised him because he believed that people at Yirrkala were happy about the arrangements to safeguard their interests and those of the mission. Ted Evans, chief welfare officer, said he had no knowledge of the petition and that people at Yirrkala had not raised their fears with him. Giese was of the view that there was a movement by one or two mission staff to instigate the petition.[99] He said it was 'factually incorrect' that the lease excision had been kept secret from the Yolngu because full facts of the matter were made known to mission authorities. He indicated that certain people at the mission had misrepresented the truth or made statements that caused misunderstandings among the Yolngu and had endeavoured to influence them. Evans said there was no specific request made to him to convey anything to government and that it was 'grossly untrue' to say that Yolngu had been ignored in the past.[100]

Parliament agreed to appoint a Select Committee to inquire into the grievances of the Yolngu people. The approach of the Coalition government and the opposition were in direct contrast. Kim Beazley Sr. spoke about Australia's obligations for justice and restitution toward Aboriginal Australians for dispossession and the need to enable an Indigenous voice in Parliament. He argued that if Indigenous communities can be dispossessed without consent, consultation, compensation, or offer of alternatives then they were being treated as conquered people. He recommended the ratification of the International Labour Organisation Convention 107, which recognises the rights of Aboriginal peoples.[101] Paul Hasluck believed the Select Committee inquiry would remove any doubts and misunderstandings. He also hoped the Select Committee would educate the Yirrkala people so that any grievances that may exist in their minds would be assuaged by having a true understanding of their situation. Hasluck said the government's policy in relation to Aboriginal reserves was not about providing reserves for Aboriginal people to 'retreat and live in a tribal state' but to meet the future needs of Aboriginal people as they 'advanced further towards civilisation'. [102]

As decisions had already been made in regard to mining on Yolngu land, the Select Committee could only recommend certain protections and benefits for the Yolngu such as ensuring access to the land for hunting; protection of sacred sites; restricting unauthorised access to the mission; providing compensation for loss of traditional occupancy; building of homes; making provision for land within the town; and ensuring consultation on the location of the proposed town. [103] The only consolation for the Yolngu was the vindication of their grievance about the lack of explanation and consultation. While the committee was impressed with the quality of the Aboriginal evidence presented, it found that no discussion had taken place between the government representatives and the Yirrkala people prior to the land excision. The committee noted that the chief welfare officer was on leave during the 'vital period' when consultations could have taken place and there was a 'failure in clear communication' when welfare officers met with the people in May 1963 to explain the mining proposal. The committee was also of the opinion that the welfare officers and government officials had not conveyed the views and feelings of the Yirrkala people to the government. [104]

The Yolngu [105] who gave evidence were clearly of the view that the Gove peninsula was their country, that they had first rights of ownership and that wealth made from their country should be shared. [106] The Yolngu explained to the Select Committee that the lack of communication from the government caused them to worry about their country and what the mining company was doing. They said that they wanted to stay on their country and for their children to be able to enjoy it as well. They were concerned about sacred sites and wanted to be able to hunt and hold ceremonies. They were also concerned about the use of water and the impact of large numbers of white people coming onto their country. They agreed that the company could use the country provided they received something in exchange as compensation. The Yolngu felt that there should be an equal partnership arrangement between them, the mining company and the government. [107]

The government had undertaken limited consultations with the Yolngu. Ted Evans visited Yirrkala on 16 May and did not return until 30 August 1963. He said on neither occasion was he 'spontaneously approached' by elders regarding the proposed mining activity. He saw the purpose of his visit was to explain the government's reasons, communicate what the government thought people could derive from the mining activity and to clear up any possible misunderstandings. Harry Giese visited Yirrkala on 17 May 1963, to explain what the government was proposing to do and the arrangements for the leases. Giese left the meeting with a 'fairly clear impression' that the people were satisfied with the general arrangements regarding the leases and the financial assistance from the government, including the safeguarding of their interests and those of the mission. In their evidence to the Select Committee, some of the Yolngu said that Giese's visit to Yirrkala was short. He arrived and flew out the same afternoon. They said they did not really understand him in the meeting. There was no opportunity to ask him questions and Giese did not make clear that a decision had already been made about mining. Money was apparently mentioned but the Yolngu did not think it was sufficient compensation. Giese spoke about the township but did not speak about water or sacred sites.[108]

The Yolngu anchored their struggle in their traditional values — especially their spiritual and physical connection to country. They wanted to show that they owned the land through their desire to protect sacred sites, to access country for hunting, to undertake ceremonies on country and to ensure the country was not damaged or exploited. They were worried about their future and about maintaining connection to country, as well as fearing that mining and the influx of white people would force them off their country into small living areas. Reciprocity was an important value to Yolngu, and they expected that white people — particularly the Mission Board, the government and the mining company who had made decisions about using their country — would share this respect and respond accordingly: that is, by entering into an arrangement with the Yolngu to provide a share of the wealth from bauxite mining.

While the Yolngu used the political processes of the Australian government to present their concerns and grievances, the petition was grounded in an alternative discourse that expressed the Aboriginal relationship and title to land. The petition was presented as a bark painting; however, it was not just a novel petition written in a 'strange tongue'. It constituted a political statement and a claim to land, and although its significance and sophistication was lost on the media and most parliamentarians, it forced the government to listen. It was no ordinary petition because the painting showed the clan designs of all the areas threatened by mining and represented a claim to land or title to land.[109] The artwork was an expression of the relationship between the Yolngu and the identified land, and symbols used in the painting depicted the sacred significance of that relationship.[110]

The complex meaning of the bark petition was not fully grasped, however it raised the profile of the Yolngu grievances. The Yolngu were able to subvert the power of the church and the government by demanding the right to speak for themselves, to speak with their own authority and to speak in their own language.[111] They challenged the government's authority in Arnhem Land, and the petition's authoritative nature indicated that the Yolngu connection to land could not be relegated to the periphery of the white agenda.[112] The subsequent establishment of the Select Committee highlighted the deficiency of the guardian/ward relationship and the shortcomings of the policy of assimilation, which was incompatible with Aboriginal difference and Aboriginal rights. The evidence provided to the Select Committee also highlighted the lack of concern for and engagement with the Yolngu by the Welfare Department. The Select Committee inquiry was, however, unable to change the relationship between the government, the Methodist Overseas Mission and the Yolngu. In chapter 2, we will see how the Yolngu clans lodged an unsuccessful claim for native title in the case of *Milirrupum v Nabalco* (1970), arguing they had rights to land under their laws and customs that should be respected by government and that could not be terminated by the government without their consent. The failure of this claim by the Yolngu and the subsequent Aboriginal Tent Embassy protest in Canberra in 1972 would lead Gough Whitlam, leader of the opposition, to commit his government to recognising land rights in the Northern Territory.

Although they were considered inarticulate and primitive, the Yolngu—with the support of some white Australians—engaged in a sophisticated dialogue with the Commonwealth government and with the wider Australian community at the time. Despite significant opposition from the church and the government, they established agency and were able to speak in their own voice that was anchored in their cultural values, particularly in that of reciprocity. The bark petition had a significant impact in challenging the authority of the government. However, the government was not respectful of the Yolngu and, in that regard, was not open to the Yolngu perspectives; nor was it open to recognising Yolngu claims for recognition of their rights to land. Ultimately, the government was not able to transcend assumptions that the Yolngu were culturally inferior and had to live and be the same as white people to be recognised and gain full citizenship rights.

The Yolngu ultimately were unsuccessful in their protest and challenge, but their struggle resonated with a new generation of Aboriginal activists who emerged in the late 1960s and early 1970s in Sydney and elsewhere on the east coast of Australia. This new generation challenged the paternalistic and assimilationist policies of the Commonwealth government by challenging parliamentary authority with an ingenious form of protest and resistance to bring attention to the lack of recognition of Aboriginal rights to land. At the time, the Commonwealth government believed that Aboriginal people had no legal or moral right to land and that any recognition of land ownership based on tradition amounted to separatism.

A MODE OF DOMINATION

In trying to understand why Australian governments have dominated, suppressed, excluded and assimilated Indigenous Australians, it is necessary to engage with the ideologies and practices that define settler colonialism. Australia is regarded as a settler colonial society because its politics and governance are substantially based on settler colonial institutions, ideas and norms that have been institutionalised and normalised.[113] In the nineteenth century, settler colonialism encompassed settler invasion, progressive occupation of Indigenous lands, frontier violence including state-sanctioned retributive violence, Indigenous resistance and rebellion, policies and practices of protection, and control and assimilation of Indigenous peoples.[114] The elimination of the Indigenous population was often the consequence of the desire for territory by settler colonists.[115] By the twentieth century, settler colonialism persisted with policies and practices of protection, control and containment of Indigenous people that excluded Indigenous people from the benefits of civil rights and from the national identity. This was followed by policies and practices of assimilation to absorb Indigenous people into settler society. Indigenous people resisted and struggled against settler domination by making claims for civil rights, land rights and self-determination.[116]

Settler colonialism involves the permanent settlement of people in a new territory where they bring their own external source of sovereignty with them and establish a new political order. Settler sovereignty dominates, suppresses and displaces Indigenous political sovereignty and identity through strategies of extermination, expulsion, incarceration, containment and assimilation to remove, transfer or erase the Indigenous population. The removal of Aboriginal children from their families, referred to as the 'stolen generations' in Australia, was an attempt by the government to eliminate a rapidly growing population of 'mixed-blood' Aboriginal people, so-called half-castes. Therefore, the term 'stolen generations' refers to the separation of thousands of Aboriginal children of mixed descent from their mothers and communities. They were forcibly removed by agents of the state or relinquished by Aboriginal mothers who were pressured into doing so by those who thought they knew best. The 1997 *Bringing Them Home* report of the Human Rights and Equal Opportunity Commission (Wilson-Dodson Inquiry) states that in Australia during the period 1910 to 1970 between one in three and one in ten Aboriginal children had been separated by either force, duress or undue pressure from their mothers, families, and communities. The report recommended various forms of restitution for the separated children, including monetary compensation and apologies from the church and government. The inquiry also concluded that the policies and practices of removal to absorb and assimilate the children into non-Indigenous society amounted to the crime of genocide.[117]

In his quarterly essay on the stolen generations, Robert Manne distinguishes pre– and post–World War II policies and practices of Australian governments according to whether the thinking behind these policies and practices was genocidal. He argues that the programme of eugenics advocated by chief protectors in Western Australia and the Northern Territory in the 1930s, which removed children from their families in order to biologically absorb them into white society, demonstrates genocidal intention. The programme of eugenics encompassed: (1) the prohibition of mating between 'full-bloods' and 'half-castes'; (2) the systematic removal of 'half-caste' children from their families; and (3) the encouragement of marriage between 'half-caste' females and white males. However, according to Manne the removal of children under the policy of assimilation instituted in the 1950s, although 'racist and paternalistic', was not driven by genocidal intentions.[118] The destruction of Indigenous culture through coercive assimilation policies is not considered genocide under the 1948 United Nations Convention on the Prevention and Punishment of the Crime of Genocide. However, for Indigenous people it is equivalent to genocide because it is a direct attack on their cultural continuity. Cultural genocide is the destruction of language, traditions, identity, livelihood, cultural practices, resource management systems, knowledge, norms and institutions of a group.[119] The full impact of the cultural genocide implemented through these policies was felt by Indigenous Australians both then and today.

The Howard Coalition government refused to officially apologise to the stolen generations on the basis that present generations of Australians are not legally or morally responsible for actions of earlier generations, particularly when those actions were sanctioned by laws and were considered to be in the best interest of the children. Instead, the Howard government only expressed a 'deep and sincere regret' about past mistreatment of Aboriginal people.[120] The ensuing debate about genocide and dispossession of Indigenous people, known as the Australian History Wars, saw a concerted intellectual and political campaign against the *Bringing Them Home* report by right-wing think tanks and magazines, conservative journalists writing for popular daily newspapers and former Aboriginal affairs administrators and patrol officers.[121] The campaign was largely conducted to not only prevent Australians from accepting the truths of the stolen generations but to also dissuade any discussion about historical injustice.[122] Former Prime Minister John Howard argued that any blemishes in Australian history could not alter the overall story of great Australian achievement. The question of whether these policies and practices amounted to genocide was controversial with the Howard Coalition government and subsequent Australian governments that have rejected the view.

However, the damaging effects of government policies tell a different story. Through such policies eventually the settler population becomes the majority, imposing European political, legal, economic, social and cultural structures over the territory.[123] Settler colonial regimes disavow the very existence of Indigenous people and their claims on the basis that the land is empty or sparsely populated and perceive 'settlement' as peaceful, thus denying any founding violence against Indigenous people. Ultimately, Indigenous people become transformed into intruders.[124]

The narrative of settler colonialism is premised on an understanding of 'progress' as being the displacement or erasure of Indigenous people, thereby generating a discourse of national identity that legitimises the political and economic structures and justifies policies and forms of privilege.[125] Settler ideology informs and determines perceptions of Indigenous people, justifying the denial of Indigenous humanity.[126] Indigenous identity is viewed as synonymous with failure, inferiority and primitiveness in biological, cultural, social, economic and political terms. The power to define 'the Indigenous' has the effect of silencing the Indigenous population, leaving little space for them to make claims against the state because settler nationalism is presented as the only legitimate state formation or conception of the national identity. The ideology of settler nationalism thus informs not only the operation of the settler state but also the thinking of settler citizens. This results in the creation of a colonial state that is engaged in a process of continual and self-perpetuating colonisation.[127]

Settler colonisation in Australia is persistent and ongoing, encompassing myriad forms of domination and disempowerment that go beyond the historical and continuing dispossession of land and resources.[128] It is evident in how Aboriginal people are governed and how governments and the Australian society responds to Aboriginal claims in contemporary debates.[129] Contemporary forms of domination and disempowerment by Australian governments are apparent in the way governments have sought to undermine Indigenous culture and ways of life and to eliminate Indigenous difference. The removal of Indigenous children though policies of assimilation, the intervention into Indigenous communities in the Northern Territory and the dismissal and dismantling of the formal reconciliation process are contemporary examples.

TRAPPED BY HISTORY

Patrick Dodson, former chairman of the Reconciliation Council and now senator in the Australian Parliament, has spoken of the Australian nation as being trapped by its history and paralysed by the failure to imagine any relationship with Aboriginal peoples other than assimilation.[130] The ongoing failure of government to resolve questions of justice for Indigenous peoples highlights that the nation is trapped by history, colonial thinking and outdated practices. The ongoing influence of erroneous and negative colonial assumptions about Indigenous people in Australia has widespread effects. The current relationship between government and Indigenous people has been constructed on these colonial assumptions, which have become ideological and legal barriers. These barriers explain why governments, through policies of dispossession and assimilation, have prevented Indigenous people from maintaining their cultural distinctiveness and have not been able to negotiate a postcolonial settlement with Indigenous polities. It also explains why government and industry have opposed Indigenous land rights and native title and why there has been political and intellectual attacks on the repeated calls for recognition of Indigenous sovereignty and criticism directed towards the scholarship investigating colonial genocide and Indigenous dispossession.

These negative and erroneous assumptions have denied Indigenous people their right to speak, to be heard and to negotiate a different relationship throughout the course of history. They have also constrained the ability of settler Australians to genuinely engage in dialogue with Indigenous people, thus diminishing prospects for change. In that regard, these entrenched colonial attitudes have become barriers to reconciliation and dismantling the colonial relationship. For this reason, Patrick Dodson argues that we need to question the philosophical underpinnings of the relationship between Aboriginal peoples and the Australian nation and create a new national framework for dialogue to transform the nation.[131] An alternate pathway is required to transform the relationship between Indigenous people and other Australians. Patrick Dodson has called for a national dialogue about the relationship between the British and succeeding settler generations and the Indigenous peoples; a national dialogue about the 'unfinished business' of reconciliation.[132]

An intercultural dialogue is necessary to construct a decolonised relationship with the settler state. It can contribute to political discussion and deliberation because it opens up new potential to transform the way people relate to each other and is relevant to resolving intercultural conflict. Australians prefer not to dwell on the history of Indigenous dispossession and mistreatment. Many Australians would prefer to 'avert their gaze from the history of what happened' and 'to think of their country as largely innocent of wrongdoing'.[133] To open new possibilities for the future of the nation, a genuine dialogue is necessary to confront truths and falsehoods about the colonisation of Australia in order to move settler Australians out of their comfort zone and thus change attitudes.[134] Therefore, the type and level of dialogue in Australia must be suited to truthfully critiquing colonialism and fully recognising and respecting Indigenous cultural and political difference.

NOTES

1. J. F. O'Connell and J. Allen, 'Dating the colonization of Sahul (Pleistocene Australia–New Guinea): A review of recent research', *The Journal of Archaeological Science* 31 (2004), 835–53.

2. S. Cane, *First footprints: The epic story of the First Australians* (Crows Nest, NSW: Allen & Unwin, 2013).

3. S. N. O'Neill and R. Douglas, *Retreat from Injustice: Human Rights in Australia*, second edition, (Leichhardt, NSW: The Federation Press, 2004), 564.

4. Mabo and Others v The State of Queensland [No. 2] [1992] 175 CLR 1; 107 ALR 1; 66 ALJR: 39.

5. S. Banner, 'Why terra nullius? Anthropology and property law in early Australia', *Law and History Review* 23, no. 1 (2005), 110–11.

6. S., Grammond, 'Treaties as Constitutional Agreements', in *The Oxford Handbook of the Canadian Constitution*, Peter Oliver, Patrick Macklem, and Nathalie Des Rosiers, eds. (New York: Oxford University Press, 2017).

7. J. Tully, 'A Fair and Just Relationship. The Vision of the Canadian Royal Commission on Aboriginal Peoples', *Meanjin* 57, no. 1 (1998), 146–66.

8. D. Short, 'Australia: a continuing genocide?' *Journal of Genocide Research* 12, nos. 1–2 (2010), 61.

9. J. Tully, *Public Philosophy in a New Key, Volume 1: Democracy and Civic Freedom* (Cambridge, UK: Cambridge University Press, 2008), 223–27.

10. R. McGregor, *Imagined Destinies, Aboriginal Australians and the Doomed Race Theory, 1880-1939* (Carlton South, Vic: Melbourne University Press, 1997), 13–16, 48–59.

11. *Report from the Select Committee on Aborigines (British Settlements)*, Great Britain Parliament, House of Commons, Select Committee on Aboriginal Tribes, London (1837), 82–83.

12. A. Nettelbeck, 'A Halo of Protection': Colonial Protector and the Principle of Aboriginal Protection through Punishment', *Australian Historical Studies* 43, no. 3 (2012), 397–98.

13. Nettelbeck, 'A Halo of Protection', 399–400.

14. R. Broome, *Aboriginal Victorians, A History Since 1800* (Crows Nest, NSW: Allen & Unwin, 2005), 188–93.

15. Broome, *Aboriginal Victorians,* 134–36; A. Massola, *Coranderrk. A History of the Aboriginal Station* (Kilmore, Vic: Lowden Publishing Co.,1975), 17–18.

16. Broome, *Aboriginal Victorians*, 167–68; D. Barwick. *Rebellion at Coranderrk* (Canberra, ACT: National Capital Printing, 1998), 68.

17. Barwick, *Rebellion at Coranderrk*, 82–84.

18. A. Dirk Moses, 'An antipodean genocide? The origins of the genocidal moment in the colonization of Australia', *Journal of Genocide Research* 2, no. 1 (2000), 90.

19. T. Barta, 'Sorry, and not sorry, in Australia: how the apology to the stolen generation buried a history of genocide', *Journal of Genocide Research* 10, no. 2 (2008), 202; M. F. Christie, *Aborigines in Colonial Victoria 1835–1886*, (Sydney, NSW: Sydney University Press, 1979), 205.

20. Broome, *Aboriginal Victorians*, 166–67.

21. G. Nanni and A. James, *Coranderrk. We Will Show the Country* (Canberra, ACT Aboriginal Studies Press, 2013), 162–63.

22. Nanni and James, *Coranderrk*, 26.

23. L. Reed, 'Mrs Bon's Verandah Full of Aboriginals,' Race, Class, Gender and Friendship', *History Australia* 2, no. 2 (2005), 1–15.

24. J. Chesterman and B. Galligan, *Citizens Without Rights, Aborigines and Australian Citizenship*, (Cambridge, UK: Cambridge University Press, 1997), 2–5; J. Chesterman and B. Galligan, *Indigenous people and Citizenship. Individual, Community, Nation: the 50th Anniversary of Australian Citizenship Conference*, University of Melbourne, 1999, web.archive.org/web/20100706073856/http://www.law.unimelb.edu.au/events/citizen/chesterman.pdf [Accessed 28 August 2013].

25. See Chesterman and Galligan, *Citizens Without Rights*, 85-86 for a list of these legislative regime.

26. Chesterman and Galligan, *Citizens Without Rights*, 58–62, 82, 84–86.

27. Chesterman and Galligan, *Citizens Without Rights*, 109–14, 115–17, 117–18.

28. Chesterman and Galligan, *Citizens Without Rights*, 3.

29. H. Goodall, *Invasion to Embassy: Land in Aboriginal Politics in New South Wales 1770–1972*, (St. Leonards, NSW Allen & Unwin with Black Books, 1996), 118–20.

30. The Northern Territory was part of South Australia until 1911.

31. See chapters 1 and 2 of Chesterman and Galligan, *Citizens Without Rights*, where they examine the policies in Victoria and Queensland prior to and after 1901.

32. K. Ellinghaus, 'Absorbing the 'Aboriginal problem': Controlling interracial marriage in Australia in the late 19th and early 20th centuries', *Aboriginal History* 27 (2003), 183, 185–86.

33. Ellinghaus, 'Absorbing the "Aboriginal problem"', 190–91, 193–96, 197–200.

34. Goodall, *Invasion to Embassy*, 115–16, 120–24.

35. Goodall, *Invasion to Embassy*, 149–56, 162–66, 173–74, 179–82.

36. Goodall, *Invasion to Embassy*, 193–99; Chesterman and Galligan, *Citizens Without Rights*, 137.

37. Northern Territory (C. E. Cook); Queensland (J. W. Bleakley); and South Australia (M. T. McLean); Western Australia (A. O. Neville); New South Wales (D. E. Morris, B. S. Harkness, and A. C. Pettit); and Victoria (H. S. Bailey and L. L. Chapman).

38. Commonwealth of Australia, *Aboriginal Welfare: Initial Conference of Commonwealth and State Aboriginal Authorities* (Canberra, ACT: Commonwealth Government Printers, 1937), 21, 33–34.

39. Commonwealth of Australia, *Aboriginal Welfare*, 10.

40. Goodall, *Invasion to Embassy*, 230–31.

41. 'Rehearsal at Farm Cove, Preparation for Pageant', *The Sydney Morning Herald*, Saturday, 15 January 1938, 11.

42. G. Souter, 'Skeleton at the Feast', in *Australians 1938*, Bill Gammage and Peter Spearritt, eds. (Sydney, NSW: Fairfax, Syme & Weldon Associates, 1987), 13–18.

43. B. Attwood, *Rights for Aborigines* (Crows Nest, NSW: Allen & Unwin, 2003), 59, 70.

44. J. T. Patten, 'Our Historic Day of Mourning and Protest, Aborigines Conference, Held at Australian Hall, Sydney, 26 January 1938, Report of Proceedings', *The Australian Abo Call*, April 1938, 2, http://www.aiatsis.gov.au/_files/archives/r000006632049n1p2.pdf [Accessed 19 September 2013].

45. Patten, 'Our Historic Day of Mourning and Protest, Aborigines Conference'.

46. Patten, 'Our Historic Day of Mourning and Protest, Aborigines Conference'.

47. R. Egan, *Neither Amity nor Kindness: Government policy towards Aboriginal people of NSW 1788 to 1969* (Paddington, NSW: Richard Egan, 2012), 151–52; J. Horner and M. Langton, 'The Day of Mourning', in *Australians 1938*, Bill Gammage and Peter Spearritt, eds. (Sydney, NSW Fairfax: Syme & Weldon Associates, 1987).

48. J. T. Patten and W. Ferguson, *Aborigines Claim Citizen Rights. A Statement of the Case for the Aborigines Progressive Association* (Sydney, NSW: The Publicist, 1938).

49. 'Aborigines' Protest', *The Argus*, Melbourne, Monday, 17 January 1938, 10.

50. 'Aborigines' Day of Mourning. Emotional Protest Criticised, David Unaipon's Statement', *The Sydney Morning Herald*, Thursday, 13 January 1938, 8; '150 Years After', *The Sydney Morning Herald*, Tuesday, 18 January 1938, 10.

51. 'Aboriginal Art', *The Sydney Morning Herald*, Saturday, 2 January 1938, 10.

52. J. Horner, *Bill Ferguson, Fighter for Aboriginal Freedom* (Canberra, ACT: Published by Jack Horner, 1994), 68–70.

53. Horner, *Bill Ferguson*, 69–70; J. T. Patten, 'Our Ten Points', *The Australian Abo Call*, April 1938. http://www.aiatsis.gov.au/_files/archive/r000006632049n1p1.pdf [Accessed 11 October 2013].

54. Attwood, *Rights for Aborigines*, 31–53.

55. Aborigines Welfare Board, *Report for the Year Ending 30th June 1940* (Parliament of New South Wales, Sydney: Government Printer, 1941).

56. B. Attwood and A. Markus, *The 1967 Referendum. Race Power and the Australian Constitution* (Canberra, ACT: Australian Institute of Aboriginal and Torres Strait Islander Studies, 2007).

57. Attwood, *Rights for Aborigines*, 62–63; B. Attwood and A. Markus, *Thinking Black. William Cooper and the Australian Aborigines' League* (Canberra, ACT: Aboriginal Studies Press, Australian Institute of Aboriginal and Torres Strait Islander Studies, 2004).

58. Patten and Ferguson, *Aborigines Claim Citizen Rights*, 3–4.

59. Goodall, *Invasion to Embassy*, 234–36.

60. A. P. Elkin, *Understanding the Australian Aborigine* (The Morpeth Booklets, No. 2, 1933), 3–5. http://handle.slv.vic.gov.au/10381/121093 [Accessed 24 October 2013].

61. A. P. Elkin, *Citizenship for Aborigines. A National Aboriginal Policy*, (Sydney, NSW: Australasian Publishing Co. Pty Ltd, 1944), 12; A. P. Elkin, 'Anthropology and the Future of the Australian Aborigines', *Oceania* 5, no. 1 (1934), 1–18.

62. A. P. Elkin, *The Australian Aborigines. How to Understand Them* (Sydney, NSW: Angus & Robertson, 1964), 367; Elkin, *Citizenship for Aborigines*, 15–16.

63. 'New Deal' Policy, Education of Aborigines',' *The Argus*, Wednesday, December 14, 1938, 13.

64. J. McEwen, *The Northern Territory of Australia: Commonwealth Government's Policy with respect to Aboriginals* (Canberra, ACT: Department of the Interior, February 1939), 1–2. National Library of Australia, http://nla.gov.au/nla.aus-vn4690481 [Accessed 30 October 2013].

65. McEwen, *The Northern Territory of Australia*, 11.

66. McEwen, *The Northern Territory of Australia*, 4–10.

67. Commonwealth of Australia, Parliamentary Debates, House of Representatives, Thursday, 8 June 1950, No. 23, 3979-80 (Paul Hasluck).

68. Commonwealth of Australia, *Native Welfare, Meeting of Commonwealth and State Ministers held at Canberra, 3rd and 4th September 1951* (Canberra, ACT: Commonwealth Government Printer, 1951).

69. Commonwealth of Australia, Parliamentary Debates, House of Representatives, Thursday, 18 October 1951, No. 42, 875–76 (Paul Hasluck).

70. Commonwealth of Australia, Parliamentary Debates, House of Representatives, Thursday, 20 April 1961, No. 16, 1052–53 (Paul Hasluck).

71. Commonwealth of Australia, *Native Welfare, Meeting of Commonwealth and State Ministers 3rd and 4th September 1951*.

72. Commonwealth of Australia, Parliamentary Debates, House of Representatives, Thursday, 20 April 1961, No. 16, 1051–52 (Paul Hasluck).

73. Milirrupum and Others v Nabalco (1970) 17 FLR 141.

74. R. M. Berndt, 'The Gove dispute: The question of Australian Aboriginal land and the preservation of sacred sites'. *Anthropological Forum: A Journal of Social Anthropology and Comparative Sociology* 1, no. 2 (1964), 263.

75. J. Clark, *Aborigines & Activism. Race, Aborigines & the Coming of the Sixties to Australia* (Crawley, WA: University of Western Australia Press, 2008), 94–95; E. Wells, *Reward and Punishment in Arnhem Land 1962–1963* (Canberra, ACT: Australian Institute of Aboriginal Studies, 1982), 41–42.

76. Commonwealth of Australia, Parliamentary Debates, House of Representatives, Tuesday, 9 April 1963, No. 15, 482 (Paul Hasluck).

77. Attwood, *Rights for Aborigines*, 215–18; Clark, *Aborigines & Activism*, 95–96; Wells, *Reward and Punishment*, 41–44, 51–54.

78. Attwood, *Rights for Aborigines*, 219–21.

79. Wells, *Reward and Punishment*, 14–16, 19.

80. Wells, *Reward and Punishment*, 71–72.

81. Commonwealth of Australia, Parliamentary Debates, House of Representatives, Tuesday, 9 April 1963, No. 15, 482 (Paul Hasluck).

82. Clark, *Aborigines & Activism*, 99–100, 102–03.

83. Commonwealth of Australia, Parliamentary Debates, House of Representatives, Tuesday, 9 April 1963, No. 15, 482 (Paul Hasluck).

84. Commonwealth of Australia, Parliamentary Debates, House of Representatives, Thursday, 23 May 1963, No. 21, 1795–97 (Kim Beasley).

85. Commonwealth of Australia, Parliamentary Debates, House of Representatives, Thursday, 23 May 1963, No. 21, 1800–03 (Gordon Bryant).

86. Commonwealth of Australia, Parliamentary Debates, House of Representatives, Thursday, 23 May 1963, No. 21, 1798–1800 (Peter Howson).

87. Wells, *Reward and Punishment*, 17–18, 70.

88. G. M. Bryant, *Report on Yirrkala, Northern Territory, and Bauxite Deposit Leases*, (The Federal Council for Aboriginal Advancement, 1963). National Museum of Australia. http://indigenousrights.net.au/document.asp?iID=684.

89. Clark, *Aborigines & Activism*, 108–09; Wells, *Reward and Punishment*, 58–62, 79–80.

90. Commonwealth of Australia, Parliamentary Debates, House of Representatives, Wednesday, 14 August 1963, No. 33, 81 (Jock Nelson).

91. 'House Hears Plea in Strange Tongue', *The Age*, Thursday, 15 August 1963.

92. 'Aboriginal Petition on Bark. Novel Plea by Tribal Group', *The Canberra Times*, Thursday, 15 August 1963, 3.

93. Commonwealth of Australia, *Report from the Select Committee on Grievances of Yirrkala Aborigines, Arnhem Land Reserve. Part 1—Report and Minutes of Proceedings, House of Representatives* (Canberra, ACT: Commonwealth Government Printer, 1963).

94. Attwood, *Rights for Aborigines*, 231–32.

95. Wells, *Reward and Punishment*, 81–82.

96. Commonwealth of Australia, Parliamentary Debates, House of Representatives, Tuesday, 20 August 1963, No. 34, 276–77 (Paul Hasluck).

97. Attwood, *Rights for Aborigines*, 232; Clark, *Aborigines & Activism*, 117; Wells, *Reward and Punishment*, 85.

98. Wells, *Reward and Punishment*, 84.

99. Commonwealth of Australia, *Report from the Select Committee on Grievances of Yirrkala Aborigines*, 9–10, 12, 59–60.

100. Commonwealth of Australia, *Report from the Select Committee on Grievances of Yirrkala Aborigines*, 18, 20, 59, 63.

101. Commonwealth of Australia, Parliamentary Debates, House of Representatives, Thursday, 12 September 1963, No. 37, 927–30 (Kim Beasley).

102. Commonwealth of Australia, Parliamentary Debates, House of Representatives, Thursday, 12 September 1963, No. 37, 930–33 (Paul Hasluck).

103. Clark, *Aborigines & Activism*, 113; Commonwealth of Australia, *Report from the Select Committee on Grievances of Yirrkala Aborigines*, 12.

104. Commonwealth of Australia, *Report from the Select Committee on Grievances of Yirrkala Aborigines*, 10.

105. Milirrpum, Dadayna and Djalalinba were senior Yolngu men who gave evidence to the House of Representative Select Committee Inquiry on Yolngu grievances. Milirrpum represented Yolngu in the case of *Milirrpum and Others v Nabalco Pty Ltd and the Commonwealth of Australia* (1971). Others who gave evidence were Wandjuk, Djalalinba, Dadayna, Narritjin, Mungurrawuy, Mawalan and Garramali. Two Yolngu women also gave evidence—Yinitjuwa and Nyubililnu.

106. Commonwealth of Australia, *Report from the Select Committee on Grievances of Yirrkala Aborigines*, 29–30, 31, 50, 51.

107. Commonwealth of Australia, *Report from the Select Committee on Grievances of Yirrkala Aborigines*, 31, 49, 50, 51–53, 54–55, 73.

108. Commonwealth of Australia, *Report from the Select Committee on Grievances of Yirrkala Aborigines*, 12, 16, 49, 50–51, 52–53, 56.

109. J. Schwarz, 'Beyond Familiar Territory: Decentering the Centre (An analysis of visual strategies in the art of Robert Smithson, Alfredo Jaar and the Bark Petitions of

Yirrkala)', (PhD dissertation, The Australian National University, 1999), 54, 57; H. Morphy, 'Title to their land', *Quadrant* 22, no. 9 (1978), 38.

110. Clark, *Aborigines & Activism*, 109.

111. Clark, *Aborigines & Activism*, 110–11.

112. Schwarz, 'Beyond Familiar Territory', 82.

113. M. Lovell, 'Settler Colonialism, Multiculturalism and the Politics of Postcolonial Identity', Australasian Political Studies Association Conference, 23–26 September 2007, Melbourne, 1–2. https://digitalcollections.anu.edu.au/bitstream/1885/9387/3/Lovell_Settler2007.pdf [Accessed 1 May 2013].

114. P. Edmonds and J. Carey, 'Australian Settler Colonialism over the long Nineteenth Century', in *The Routledge Handbook of the History of Settler Colonialism*, Edward Cavanagh and Lorenzo Veracini, eds. (Abingdon, Oxon, UK: Routledge, 2017), 371–89.

115. P. Wolfe, 'Settler Colonialism and the elimination of the native'. *Journal of Genocide Research* 8, no. 4 (2006), 388–89.

116. S. Maddison, 'Settler Australia in the Twentieth Century', in *The Routledge Handbook of the History of Settler Colonialism*, Edward Cavanagh and Lorenzo Veracini, eds. (Abingdon, Oxon, UK: Routledge, 2017), 425–38.

117. R. Manne, 'In Denial: The Stolen Generations and the Right', *Quarterly Essay*, no. 1 (2001), 2, 5, 35.

118. Manne, 'In Denial', 39, 27–40.

119. D. Short, 'Australia: a continuing genocide?', *Journal of Genocide Research* 12, no. 1–2 (2010), 46–53, 55, 62.

120. Manne, 'In Denial', 75–76; T. Barta, 'Sorry, and not sorry, in Australia: how the apology to the stolen generation buried a history of genocide', *Journal of Genocide Research* 10, no. 2 (2008), 203.

121. R. Manne, 'Comment, The History Wars', *The Monthly* (November 2009), 15–17.

122. A. Gunstone, *Reconciliation, Nationalism and the History Wars*. Refereed paper presented to the Australasian Political Studies Association Conference, University of Adelaide, 29 September–1 October 2004, 5. http://pandora.nla.gov.au/pan/39515/200607190000/www.adelaide.edu.au/apsa/docs_papers/Aust%20Pol/Gunstone.pdf [Accessed 12 February 2016].

123. L. Veracini, *Settler Colonialism, A Theoretical Overview* (Basingstoke, UK: Palgrave Macmillan, 2010), 3–5, 16–17, 33, 53; J. Greene, 'Colonial History and National History: Reflections on a Continuing Problem', *William and Mary Quarterly* 6, no. 2 (2007), 237–38; L. Veracini, 'Settler Colonialism and Decolonisation', Borderlands e-journal [online] (2007), 6. http://www.borderlands.net.au/vol6no2_2007/veracini_settler.htm [Accessed 1 May 2013].

124. Veracini, *Settler Colonialism, A Theoretical Overview*, 77, 82–83, 86.

125. Veracini, *Settler Colonialism, A Theoretical Overview*, 99, 101; Lovell, *Settler Colonialism, Multiculturalism*, 2.

126. S. Wright, *International Human Rights, Decolonisation and Globalisation* (London & New York: Routledge, 2001), 57; C. Lane West-Newman, 'Anger in Legacies of Empire, Indigenous Peoples and Settler States', *European Journal of Social Theory* 7, no. 2 (2004), 192.

127. Lovell, 'Settler Colonialism, Multiculturalism', 4–5.

128. A. Maguire, 'Law Protecting Rights: Restoring the law of self-determination in the neo-colonial world', *Law Text, Culture* 12 (2008), 23.

129. M. Dodson and L. Strelein, 'Australia's Nation-Building: Renegotiating the Relationship between Indigenous Peoples and the State', *University of New South Wales Law Journal* 24, no. 3 (2001), 838.

130. P. Dodson, 'Intervention turned our backs on reconciliation', Opinion Piece. *The Sydney Morning Herald*, 20 August 2009, 17.

131. P. Dodson, *Dialogue and Nation Building in Contemporary Australia*, So What? Lecture, 20 August 2009, University of New South Wales, Sydney.

132. P. Dodson, *Reconciliation: Two Centuries On, Is Dialogue Enough?* La Trobe University Centre for Dialogue Working Paper (2008), 11–12. www.latrobe.edu.au/dialogue/publications/workingppaper-series/past-issues [Accessed 19 January 2012].

133. Manne, 'Comment, The History Wars', 17.

134. A. Leigh, 'Leadership and Aboriginal Reconciliation', *The Australian Journal of Social Issues*, 37, no. 2 (2002), 140–42.

TWO

The Intellectual and Legal Origins of Terra Nullius

The contention that the Australian nation is trapped by colonial thinking and outdated political and policy practices when it comes to Indigenous people may well elicit a defensive or dismissive response. However, for Indigenous people who are on the receiving end of political decision-making or public disrespect, the contention is legitimate. Indigenous Australians are not respected or taken seriously by governments. Therefore, Indigenous attempts to engage equally with governments invariably fail because the relationship between Indigenous people and the Australian state is one of subordination and dominance, underpinned by ideologies of racial superiority where colonial perceptions and portrayals of Indigenous people as savage and inferior justifies the denial of their rights. This established a 'fundamental disrespect' for Indigenous people that not only occurs in the relationship between the state and Indigenous peoples but also engenders a personal disrespect towards them daily.[1]

Australian governments and public institutions have largely failed to accommodate Indigenous rights and difference. Such indifference, exclusion and nonrecognition has been referred to as 'psychological terra nullius'; a term that refers to the dismissal of the legitimate rights of Indigenous people and ignores the history of their dispossession in order to maintain the myth of terra nullius and the romanticised view of Australia's colonisation.[2] These ideological, legal and also political barriers have become ingrained in the structure, traditions, practices, norms and conventions of governmental institutions and in contemporary public attitudes about Indigenous people.

The relationship between Indigenous people and the Australian state is thus underpinned by a multifaceted discourse of terra nullius. This discourse portrays Indigenous people as inferior or as having 'deficits' in respect to European society. Over the course of history, this discourse and thinking has been framed to resist the recognition of Indigenous rights and has also spawned an array of negative and demeaning views and opinions about Indigenous people. It influences how Australian society perceives and understands Indigenous people and its impact is seen in how Indigenous claims for recognition are treated by governments. It has become an intellectual or psychological barrier that has significant influence in government Indigenous policymaking. Terra nullius discourse influences those who have the power to interpret and make decisions about Indigenous claims for recognition.

The term 'terra nullius discourse' used throughout this book refers to the complex discourse that has developed in different ways and at different rates in international law, domestic law, and in the belief systems that informed Australian attitudes and policy. Terra nullius discourse encompasses the following: (1) the erroneous beliefs and observations of Lieutenant James Cook and his colleague Joseph Banks; (2) the emergence of the doctrine in international law, from Emmerich de Vattel in the eighteenth century to its consolidation as a formal doctrine in the 1870s; (3) the English common law version as prescribed by William Blackstone that was applied to the colonisation of Australia in the form of the 'desert and uncultivated' doctrine; (4) the 'Barbarian theory', as described by Justice Brennan in the *Mabo (No. 2)* case; and (5) the 'psychological' obliteration of Indigenous people, their law and customs that persists in law and public policy. The High Court decision of *Mabo (No. 2)* has partially dismantled the legality of this discourse in relation to Indigenous ownership of property, although a psychological terra nullius discourse remains. *Mabo (No. 2)* is a claim for native title by the Meriam people in the Torres Strait region of Australia and is discussed later in this chapter.

This chapter examines the terra nullius discourse in Australia and its influence in judicial decision-making. It explains how the intellectual underpinnings of terra nullius as reproduced in the Indigenous and British-Australian relationship contributed to a lack of respect and recognition for Indigenous people.

INTELLECTUAL BEGINNINGS OF TERRA NULLIUS

As of the sixteenth century, the basis of terra nullius thinking gained traction in Europe. A particularly striking example of thinking about non-European peoples this way was displayed by Lieutenant James Cook and Joseph Banks in 1770. Cook's encounters with Indigenous peoples display the kind of Eurocentric racial viewpoint that led them to assume that Indigenous people were without property or law. Cook and Banks provided erroneous information that allowed colonial office officials to believe that the country was only thinly populated by people who had no attachments to particular places and therefore no land ownership. Despite having limited contact with the local Aboriginal peoples and no understanding of them, Cook and Banks judged Aboriginal people to be incapable of having a system of law, organised society or government. These early erroneous assumptions provided the justification for concluding that the entire continent was terra nullius. Terra nullius was a convenient conclusion used to legally justify British occupation of an inhabited territory without consent and to deny Indigenous rights in Australia.[3] The Australian continent was treated as unclaimed territory, therefore, according to British law, Indigenous Australians lost all rights, titles and interests in land in 1788. This view was consistently articulated in various legal cases from 1863 to 1992 when the *Mabo (No. 2)* decision was handed down.

In 1768, Lieutenant James Cook received instructions from the Lords of the Admiralty to observe the transit of the planet Venus on Tahiti. He was also instructed to search for what was thought to be a great southern continent. In doing so he was required to survey and chart the coast, observe the nature of the continent and its wildlife, take plant specimens as well as 'observe the genius, temper, disposition and number of natives' and cultivate friendships and alliances through gift giving and trade. Cook was instructed to take possession of territory with consent; or if the country was uninhabited, to take possession by making the appropriate marks and inscriptions as first discoverer and possessor.[4] He sailed the east coast of Australia in 1770 stopping over in what is now known as Botany Bay in April of that year. However, he did not gain the consent of the people in Botany Bay in accordance with his original instructions.

At the entrance of Botany Bay, a group of Aboriginal people were watching the ship. Some of the men were 'threatening and menacing' with their spears.[5] After anchoring in the bay, Cook and his party rowed to the south point of the bay (Kurnell)—the country of the Gweagal people—seeking to speak with them. However, his party was challenged by two men armed with spears and throwing sticks. They were calling out 'very loud in a harsh sounding language' and shaking their spears in a menacing way to stop the landing. Cook's interpreter, Tupia from Tahiti, could not understand the language so they attempted to signal that they wanted water and meant no harm and threw strings of beads and nails to the Aboriginal men. When the Aboriginal men continued their opposition to the landing, Cook's men shot musket fire over their heads. A small shot was fired at the elder, striking him in the leg with little effect so Cook's men shot at him again. He ran to the hut and returned with a shield. Both men threw spears at the party that landed, although no one was hurt. Two more shots were fired. The elder man threw another spear and then both men slowly backed off.[6] Clearly, Cook and his party were not welcomed at Botany Bay as armed groups of Gweagal men attempted to intimidate them when they were on shore.[7] Gweagal people also chose to avoid, ignore or intimidate Cook and his party. Despite leaving strings of beads, cloth, looking glasses, combs, nails and so on, Cook was unable to make contact as the Gweagal refused to even acknowledge him. Cook tried—to a limited degree—to cultivate contact with Aboriginal people in Botany Bay but he failed.

In June and July 1770, while repairing one of his ships, Lieutenant Cook had a friendlier encounter with the Guugu Yimithirr people near present-day Cooktown in North Queensland, at the mouth of the Endeavour River. Although he had the opportunity, he still failed to gain consent. The Guugu Yimithirr at first avoided Cook's party, but a few weeks into their stay four men fishing in a canoe came alongside the *Endeavour* and were given 'trifles', as described by Cook. As the men returned to shore, Tupia asked them to lay down their arms and sat with them. Later, Cook and his crew joined them and invited them to dinner, which they declined.[8] In a later encounter, ten or so Guugu Yimithirr men were prevented from taking two of the twelve turtles the Englishmen had caught as a food source. Instead, Cook offered the men bread, which they 'rejected with scorn'. The men began throwing ship items overboard and went ashore setting fire to the dry grass in an attempt to burn out Cook's camp. A musket with small shot was fired at one of the leaders, wounding him and sending the men into the bush. Cook, Banks and some of his men followed but were met by the Aboriginal men with spears. In return, Cook and his men grabbed spears causing the Aboriginal men to retreat. Cook and his men then followed, calling after the Aboriginal men who eventually laid down their spears and came back, as Cook describes, 'in a very friendly manner'.[9]

This incident underlines how Cook was blinded by his assumptions of Aboriginal people. He failed to understand that Aboriginal people had property rights to the land, seas and their resources. Neither Cook nor Banks understood the significance of what had happened that day. Cook would not share two turtles with his hosts. The Guugu Yimithirr people were generous enough not to take the incident any further and instead agreed to conciliate when an elderly Aboriginal man spoke to the men to lay down their spears and to join with Cook and his men.[10] Cook and Banks failed to see this incident as an opportunity to develop a more formal relationship based on mutual recognition and consent.

Cook wrote that Aboriginal people fled on his approach, kept their distance or threw spears at them. Cook admits that he knew little of Aboriginal customs because he was 'not able to form any connections with them', and the Aboriginal people had not touched the beads, ribbons and trinkets he had left in their huts.[11] Banks on the other hand wrote that the Aboriginal people in Botany Bay 'have turned out such rank cowards' because they walked or ran away from the Englishmen when encountering them on shore. But he also wrote that Aboriginal people ignored the presence of the Englishmen, especially when canoe fishing, or on occasions they watched, followed or shadowed the Englishmen and even challenged them by shouting or menacing behaviour and even throwing spears at them.[12] In reality, the people at Botany Bay were more cautious than cowardly because Cook had shot at two men on first landing and because there was no reason to engage with Cook as he had nothing of value to offer in a trade except beads, ribbons and trinkets.

Cook chose not to recognise Aboriginal people or their property rights. Taking possession of the eastern coast of Australia seems preposterous not only because it was an act of extraordinary territorial acquisition but also because Cook carried out the ceremony for possession on an island that he named 'Possession Island', which was detached from the mainland. At Possession Island Cook hoisted the English flag, fired a volley of shots and duly took possession of the eastern coast for the British Crown.[13] If claiming an entire continent while situated on an outer-lying island were not ironic enough, Cook also knew the island itself was inhabited by Aboriginal people – the Kaurareg.[14]

Cook's failed engagements with Aboriginal people and his manner of claiming the east coast of Australia in August 1770 without their consent set the scene for how the British would relate to Aboriginal Australians. While Cook believed Aboriginal people lived in a state of nature with no magnificent houses, household items, or clothing and having all necessities of life provided by the land and sea,[15] he in fact considered the people, their lifestyle and their society to be inferior. According to Cook, the people in Botany Bay were not numerous and did not live in large groups, but rather were dispersed in small parties around the bay.[16] Cook concluded that the 'natives' of New South Wales were not a 'warlike people' but a 'timorous and inoffensive race, no way inclined to cruelty' and 'neither are they numerous'. He wrote that they lived by the sea and along the banks of lakes, rivers and creeks having no fixed habitation, but move about from place to place 'like wild beasts in search of food'. Cook said he did not see 'one inch of cultivated land in the whole country'.[17]

Banks wrote that the land is 'thinly inhabited' and speculated that the country inland may be totally uninhabited. He said they 'never but once saw so many as thirty Indians together' and that people at Botany Bay could muster no more than fifteen fighting men and in other places they generally ran away. He believed that the sea was the chief source of supply for the 'Indians' because the wild produce alone would scarcely support them and they were ignorant of cultivation.[18] Banks also said that Aboriginal people do not have permanent homes because they wander 'like Arabs from place to place' and set up a house when they come upon a sufficient supply of food; when the food is exhausted, they move, leaving the house behind.[19]

Cook's and Banks' observations of Aboriginal people did not fit with British perceptions of civilisation, government and sovereignty. Therefore, they dismissed any notion of Indigenous polity, forming the opinion that Aboriginal people were too uncivilised to have any form of society, property or sovereignty. According to Europeans, one indicator of civility was a willingness to engage in trade, and this also indicated that Indigenous people had a level of moral, social and political development. Trade was a device by which the British interpreted and made judgments about Indigenous development.[20] The refusal to trade with Cook was interpreted as a lack of 'civilisation' on the part of the Aboriginal people, even though Cook offered nothing of value in return. Cook wrote that Aboriginal people did not value anything given to them, nor did they part with anything of their own in exchange for European articles.[21] Joseph Banks said Aboriginal people had no idea of trade nor could they teach them because Aboriginal people did not value what they had, and so they could not be induced to part with their items.[22]

While Cook had nothing of value to trade with Aboriginal people, he helped himself to water, shot animals for food, took turtles, fish and shellfish, cut grass and timber, took spears belonging to Aboriginal people, and did not ask for permission for any of these items. Cook's and Banks' observations and perceptions of Aboriginal people are significant because their accounts have contributed to a dominant colonial discourse of a sparsely populated continent with a culturally inferior people. This terra nullius discourse dispossessed Aboriginal people of their land, rights and dignity.

Savages, Civilisation and Property Rights

European beliefs in their own progress and superiority were very much part of the cultural baggage that was transported to Australia. They viewed non-Europeans as at a lower stage of political, social and economic development.[23] These attitudes were part of a belief formulated by European intellectuals in their attempts to understand their existence and the world around them, especially through the perspectives of European colonialism, capitalism and Christianity. Given this assumption of superiority, Europeans believed it was 'not necessary either to comprehend others in their own terms or to attempt to deal with them as equals'.[24]

While the first Europeans in Australia were ethnocentric and believed they were culturally superior to Aboriginal people, most early colonial officials believed that Aboriginal people had the ability to be as capable as Europeans if provided with European education and culture.[25] The more enlightened European settlers believed that Aboriginal people displayed acumen and sharp intellect; hence they saw a possibility of 'civilizing' them. Other Europeans believed Aboriginal people were 'disgusting', 'barbarous' and 'stupid'.[26] From the second half of the nineteenth century, racist ideas came to dominate the thinking of English colonists who considered Aboriginal people as racially inferior. The shift to hardline racism stemmed from many different factors including cultural and physical differences between European and Aboriginal people, racial ideology, beliefs about Aboriginal 'savagery' and, above all, the need for Europeans to rationalise the dispossession of Aboriginal people and the accompanying exploitation and violence.[27]

By 1780, social and political theorists in Europe subscribed to a 'stages theory' of evolution in which mankind passed through several stages transitioning from savagery to civility. It was accepted that Europeans and other 'advanced' societies had passed through four stages of development. The first stage was hunting, followed by pastoralism, agriculture and the development of commerce-based economies. Each stage was distinguished by different modes of subsistence, institutions of law, property and government, and different sets of customs, manners and morals. Civilisation was considered at the high end of a process of historical development, to the extent that colonisation was not seen as dispossession but as carrying out the essential task of bringing civilisation to the uncivilised. Indigenous peoples were considered to be in the first stage of development. Terms such as 'wild men', 'savages' and 'barbarians' were used to set apart the 'civilised' from the 'uncivilised' and to establish the superiority of European culture and political organisation.[28] Both savages and barbarians were considered less than human, incapable of exercising sovereignty and represented an external threat to 'civilisation'. [29] In large part this was because they did not practice European culture, submit to European social norms and were not Christian.

The term 'savages' became part of the negative discourse employed to categorise Aboriginal peoples as culturally and racially inferior because of their cultural and physical differences to Europeans. The belief system behind the use of the terms 'savages' and 'barbarians' was linked to European colonial expansion, the rise of capitalism in Europe with its focus on land ownership and private property, and belief in Christianity. Colonialism constructed other people as 'savages' and 'barbarians' to situate them within the language and discourse of civilisation. Indigenous people in Australia were commonly referred to as 'savages'. The so-called savage could be noble or ignoble, both of whom lived outside of civil society and were considered as an example of the first stage of human development. The 'noble savage' was an example of a simple state of existence where 'uncivilised' man lived in a state of nature, whereas the ignoble savage was considered to have a brutal and barbaric state of existence.[30] In nineteenth-century Australia, Aboriginal people were regarded as both brute savages and noble savages; 'brute savages' lived a 'poor, solitary, nasty, brutish, short life', while 'noble savages' were uncorrupted by the vices of civilisation. In Australia, the 'noble savage' construction declined as frontier racial attitudes hardened.[31]

Scientific racism further hardened the idea that Aboriginal people were 'savages'. Inferiority, for scientific racists, was defined by physiology. Phrenology was one of the most influential of racist scientific theories about differences between races and was widely accepted in Australia from the 1820s onwards. Phrenology claimed that the size and bumps of a person's skull represented the size and shape of the brain within, as well as the different skills and personality traits of the person. According to phrenologists the Aboriginal skull was large and thick. Its shape indicated that Aboriginal people had moral and intellectual deficiencies as well as a propensity to roam and an aversion to a fixed place of residence.[32]

Beginning in the second half of the nineteenth century, negative views of Aboriginal people were also supported by social Darwinism, which depicted Aboriginal people as less evolved and suggested they would eventually die out. Charles Darwin's theory[33] on the evolution of species by way of 'natural selection' and 'survival of the fittest' was used to explain and support European views of racial superiority and the inevitable demise of Aboriginal people. Social Darwinism was widely accepted in Australia and provided a justification for the decline of the Aboriginal population.[34]

The 'stages theory' of human development played an important role in the construction of colonial property rights. It assumed that the laws and institutions of society were dependent upon the mode of subsistence. Therefore, those societies deemed to be at the higher stages of development had property rights whereas Indigenous people were considered to be at a 'lower' stage of development that did not incorporate property rights, and so their dispossession was justified.[35] English philosopher John Locke made several assumptions about Aboriginal systems of property and political organisations in North America that influenced European theories of property and were used to dispossess Aboriginal people of their land and territory. These assumptions deemed Aboriginal Americans as being in a pre-political 'state of nature', having no established system of property or government and having no rights in their territories except in what they hunted or gathered. It was assumed that the hunting and gathering economy was economically inferior to the European commercial system of private property in land. In this assumption, Aboriginal people had no fixed and recognisable system of property in land, and did not have an institutionalised system of law, therefore were not 'political societies' or states.[36]

These theories not only undermined Indigenous rights in property; they established links between property rights, civil society and sovereignty[37] that were deemed not to exist in Indigenous societies. Civil society was defined by the idea of agrarian labour, which gave men a right to property. Property was the rightful possession of land and, according to John Locke, was derived from investing labour in the land, especially by means of English agricultural practices.[38] Therefore, it was incorrectly assumed that people living in a state of nature did not have property rights. Property rights included ownership of land as well as rights of sovereignty against others. Civil society was considered a prerequisite for sovereignty because it enabled 'civilised' man to collectively transfer power to a sovereign. On that basis only, 'civilised man' was regarded as having property rights and civil society. Indigenous people who were considered non-farmers, were not regarded as having property rights or civil society and therefore it was assumed that they were unable to collectively authorise a sovereign to act on their behalf and to order the relations between individuals.[39]

The belief that Indigenous people lack sovereignty stems from the fact that Indigenous authority was considered inferior or non-existent. In the European constitutional tradition, authority is derived from a centralised and uniform system of legal and political authority that is formed by people exercising popular sovereignty. Free and equal individuals deliberate and reach agreement on how they should form political associations, how they should recognise European institutions and traditions, and how their society should be constituted. The idea is that people free themselves from customary ways and practices and become more self-determining. This was contrasted with Indigenous forms of governance, which are considered to be constituted by customary ways and therefore Indigenous constitutions are closely tied to the customs of their societies. Indigenous constitutions are accordingly considered an 'earlier' or 'lower' stage of historical development.[40] They were devalued by virtue of not having a sovereign or a uniform system of government. European constitutional government is considered to represent the historical progression of society and is regarded as the only legitimate legal authority.[41] This combination of ideas about European civil society, property and sovereignty were used to justify dispossession of Indigenous people.

Discovery, Occupation and Indigenous People

The ideas about civil society, property and sovereignty are reflected in the rules developed by Europeans regarding the acquisition of foreign territory and in particular the lands of Indigenous peoples. According to these rules, Lieutenant James Cook's claim to the east coast of Australia on behalf of the British Crown only provided an inchoate title that had to be perfected by effective occupation of the new territory. British occupation of eastern Australia followed in January 1788 when Governor Phillip conducted ceremonies to assert British authority over New South Wales and establish governmental administration.[42] The British claim and subsequent occupation was underpinned by the assumption that the Australian continent was unclaimed territory: that Aboriginal people had no sovereignty; or if they did, then they had lost it when Britain occupied the continent in 1788. But according to Henry Reynolds, Aboriginal tribes had land ownership and sovereignty, which was recognisable by the law of the time, if only the law had been applied with more impartiality.[43]

It took many years after 1788 to assert authority and establish governmental control in the colony of New South Wales. Indeed, the assertion of governmental authority over Aboriginal people continues today.[44] The Crown was not able to maintain effective occupation over the continent because white administrative control was so feeble that it could not have extinguished Aboriginal sovereignty.[45] Aboriginal sovereignty continued to coexist with British sovereignty. In that regard British colonial officers in the outposts of empire sought accommodation with local Aboriginal people to avoid violence.[46]

By 1788, there had been significant developments in international law and the British common law. However, at the beginning of the colonial era, towards the end of the fifteenth century, there was no accepted set of international rules for acquiring territory that was not under the control of any recognised sovereign. A sovereign who succeeded in exercising a sufficient degree of exclusive control was generally regarded as having acquired sovereignty.[47] Over time the practice of states and the opinions of political thinkers and jurists produced recognised modes for acquiring new territory, which also regulated the respective claims of the European nations.

From the fifteenth to the nineteenth century, the Doctrine of Discovery justified claims to territory outside of Europe. Discovery gave the first European country to 'discover' unknown lands, the right to pre-empt or preclude other European nations from gaining an interest in the new lands. Discovery was designed to control exploration and manage conflict between European nations who were making claims of ownership and sovereignty over the territory of Indigenous peoples.[48] Discovery and conquest was originally authorised by the issuing of papal bulls, a form of authority from the Pope that authorised Catholic colonial powers such as Spain and Portugal to explore, invade, take property and slaves, assert sovereignty, and convert non-Christians to Christianity and civilisation.[49] But England, France and Holland refused to recognise papal claims and a new rule of discovery was developed. To prevent extravagant claims over vast tracts of territory, discovery was extended to include actual occupation of the discovered lands to perfect the discovery title. Hence, discovery only provided an inchoate title that had to be followed by actual possession.[50]

Actual possession involved occupation or settlement, the founding of a colony, and the establishment of governmental administration for control and administration of the territory.[51] Some Europeans argued that they could occupy territory inhabited by non-Christians because non-

Christians had no sovereign rights and war could be waged against them. But there has been a 'persistent preponderance' of juristic opinion in favour of the view that so-called politically organised 'backward' peoples have sovereignty over their land. Francesco de Vitoria, a Spanish theologian and jurist in the sixteenth century, argued that Indian people—although 'sinners and infidels'—possessed complete sovereignty over their territory and were the owners of their lands. However, the Spanish could still wage war and take possession of Indigenous peoples' lands under certain circumstances.[52]

By the eighteenth century, acquisition by settlement usually referred to territories that were totally uninhabited—that is, no one lived in the territory. This is evidenced in writings of philosophers and jurists such as Emmerich de Vattel (*The Law of Nations*) and William Blackstone (*Commentaries on the laws of England*) in the eighteenth century. Vattel argued that European nations were justified in taking possession of and colonising territories that had 'no prior owner' or were 'desert' or 'uninhabited without an owner' after they had made their intentions sufficiently known. However, this assertion of title had to be followed by taking real possession.[53] Similarly, Blackstone said that 'desert and uncultivated' territories could be colonised by occupancy and the colonist would take such English law as applicable to the situation and conditions of the infant colony. On the other hand, he said that 'cultivated' colonies could only be gained by conquest or ceded by treaty. In such cases the 'ancient laws of the country'—unless they are against the law of God—would remain until altered by the king.[54]

But Vattel went further. He said countries that were uncultivated but inhabited by politically 'unorganised' and 'thinly populated' people who did not occupy the whole of their territory, could be lawfully claimed and occupied, at least in part. According to Vattel, European nations could lawfully possess and colonise those countries where so-called savages had no need for or made no use of land because they could not claim more land than they needed for cultivation or habitation.[55] It was the European nation that made the determination about whether the territory was uncultivated, unorganised or thinly populated. Vattel's extension of his 'desert' and 'uninhabited' doctrine was directed at the acquisition and colonisation of territories populated by Indigenous or tribal peoples, particularly in North America. By this reasoning a country that is inhabited, although uncultivated, could be possessed and occupied if the Indigenous society did not use or occupy all their territory or if it was thinly populated and politically unorganised. Vattel's view is evident in James Cook and Joseph Banks' assumptions about Aboriginal Australians. Vattel's view was taken up by other jurists who held the view that the territory of 'backward' people is open to occupation so long as the Indigenous people did not resist encroachment of the occupying state by force.[56]

As legal perceptions were reformulated and reinterpreted it became common in nineteenth-century legal thinking to deny sovereignty to Indigenous or so-called backward or savage people on the grounds that they had not progressed in 'civilisation' and had no statehood or sovereignty.[57] Territory regarded as cunclaimed', 'uninhabited' or inhabited by people considered to be 'less advanced' without political society could be acquired by occupation or settlement.[58] Settlement, either when it was authorised by the Crown or through an unauthorised private venture, involved acquisition of territory where there was 'no civilised government and legal system'.[59] If, however, the inhabitants of a territory had a collective political society, although crude and rudimentary, acquisition could only be made by way of cession, conquest or prescription.[60]

If there was no treaty with the colonising power to transfer title of an inhabited territory then possession of a territory could be taken by force (conquest) from either a sovereign state or an Indigenous political society, and title to the territory passed to the victorious sovereign.[61] The colonising power assumed sovereignty upon the establishment of a civil government and extended jurisdiction over the territory.[62] If a colonising power had no title or insufficient title to a territory but had effective, continuous and undisturbed sovereignty for a long period then title was acquired by prescription.[63]

The change in denying sovereignty to Indigenous people, so-called backward or savage people, produced the modern doctrine of 'terra nullius'. As to its application in Australia, some writers argue that the term 'terra nullius' was not originally used to justify dispossession at the time of the establishment of New South Wales[64] nor was there British policy or a legal doctrine that enabled possession of inhabited lands as though they were uninhabited or ownerless.[65] The established theory and practice of international law at the time, in regards to acquiring new territories, was by conquest, cession or purchase.[66] However, terra nullius-thinking became entrenched in British land policy from the 1780s onwards as a result of James Cook's and Joseph Banks' description of an enormous continent sparsely populated by 'primitive' hunter-gatherers.[67] This is the point at which the different layers of terra nullius discourse intersect and became fundamental to the way colonial authorities treated Indigenous Australians.

Terra nullius may not have been a legal doctrine in 1788 but it was embedded in the assumptions and practices of the British at the time. It was a product of the legal tradition and New South Wales played a significant role in the development of the legal theory that lands inhabited by hunters and gatherers were ownerless.[68] By 1873, international jurists were not only classifying Indigenous occupation as res nullius but also as territorium nullius and terra nullius. Territorium nullius was applied to African colonies that might have lacked territorial sovereignty but not people and which were not necessarily void of property rights or even sovereignty; hence treaties were required to subsume the territory. Terra nullius on the other hand was used to describe land that had literally no one inhabiting it or a country where the people were regarded as having no rights in land and no sovereignty.[69] Terra nullius would eventually acquire the same level of authority as that attributed to territorium nullius. Its English common law counterpart is the 'desert and uncultivated' doctrine;[70] both classified inhabited land as uninhabited although the doctrine of terra nullius legitimised the acquisition of sovereignty at international law and the 'desert and uncultivated' doctrine determined the law which governed a territory on colonisation at common law.[71]

TERRA NULLIUS DISCOURSE AND AUSTRALIAN LAW

While the British occupation of the Australian continent in 1788 followed the practice laid down by international law, the acquisition of New South Wales was also determined by the English common law. The common law determines the classification of the territory and this in turn determines the law in force in the territory and the powers of the Crown to make law.[72] The general rule in regard to the introduction of English law was that in conquered and ceded territories, local laws and customs remained in force until altered by the Crown insofar as they were not incompatible with the change in sovereignty, whereas in settled territories English law was introduced to the extent that it was applicable and adaptable to local circumstances.[73]

But many of Britain's territorial acquisitions did not readily fit into the settled, conquered or ceded classification, and this was the case regarding New South Wales.[74] To determine whether a territory is classified as conquered, ceded or settled, it is necessary to look at the intention and conduct of the Crown based on its perceptions of the nature of the Indigenous society. Although the Crown had prerogative to acquire sovereignty of new territory or make treaties and proceed as it liked, it lacked the legal authority to determine the constitutional status of its acquisition; only courts could determine this.[75] In the colony of New South Wales, this uncertainty played out in sporadic debates about the status of the colony.

The British Crown treated the colony of New South Wales as terra nullius. This was largely based on the observations and assumptions of Cook and Banks that New South Wales was practically unoccupied.[76] Banks' evidence to the Committee of Transportation in 1779 and 1785 reiterated his observations and assumptions that the continent was sparsely populated, that Aboriginal people lacked defensive capacity and did not have the capacity to sell land because they did not understand trade.[77] These erroneous views and assumptions about New South Wales and its inhabitants were largely accepted as fact.

The perceptions and assumptions of James Cook and Joseph Banks neatly fit the classification that an inhabited territory could be claimed on the basis that Indigenous people had no land ownership because they supposedly roamed over the land like wild animals. This persuaded the British Crown that there was no need to buy land from Aboriginal people.[78] Governor Phillips' second commission provides evidence that New South Wales was assumed to be unclaimed territory because all land in the colony was vested in the Crown to be disposed of by the governor.[79] No provision was made for Aboriginal people and their lands.

Some writers suggest a purported or implied recognition of Aboriginal rights and jurisdiction. Both Justices Deane and Gaudron in the *Mabo (No. 2)* case speculated that the land needs of the penal establishment could have been satisfied without impairing the existing interests of Aboriginal people or that matters could have been resolved on the spot with the assent or acquiescence of Aboriginal people.[80] Merete Borch suggests that the British government believed there would be room for everyone without making further arrangements with Aboriginal people and that the policy would be reviewed in the light of better knowledge of actual conditions. However, Governor Phillip failed to suggest that a settlement ought to be made in regard to land for the colony.[81] Lisa Ford agrees, arguing that early colonial governments did not assume that they had jurisdiction over Indigenous people, though this changed, as Indigenous jurisdiction became a growing threat to the territorial aspirations of the colony.[82] These authors point to signs of persistent confusion about the reception of law in the colony and the legal status of Aboriginal people in regard to the Crown.

But the question remains why the British did not negotiate with Aboriginal people once they encroached further into Aboriginal territory and when Aboriginal people resisted this encroachment. The convergence of discourses and theories of European racial superiority present at the time of colonisation and the development of the terra nullius doctrine in international law suggest possible explanations. In 1819, the British attorney general and solicitor general confirmed that the power to impose taxes was based on New South Wales being acquired as 'desert and uninhabited'. Similarly, advice from the Colonial Office in 1822 regarding the law-making powers in the colony was also confirmed on that basis.[83] The case of *Cooper v Stuart* revisited the status of the colony in 1889 reaffirming the principle that New South Wales was 'desert and uninhabited'.

The application of terra nullius discourse in Australian law is evident in two significant cases that became unquestioned law for more than one hundred years. Both cases show how the judiciary transported erroneous colonial assumptions and discourse about Australia being 'peacefully settled'—because it was 'practically unoccupied' and was considered without settled inhabitants, settled law or a recognised system of land tenure—into the common law, thereby enshrining them into Australian constitutional government.

The case of *R v. Jack Congo Murrell* before the Supreme Court of NSW in 1836 concerned the rights of Aboriginal people, the application of tribal laws of punishment, and the application of British law.[84] In deciding whether the Court had jurisdiction to try Jack Congo Murrell and George Bummaree who were charged with murder of two of their countrymen, Justice Burton held that the Court did have jurisdiction to try Murrell because Aboriginal people had no sovereignty and the British government had exercised rights of domain over the country for a long period. Murrell's lawyer argued that the Court had no jurisdiction to try Murrell because he was not a subject of Great Britain and so not bound by its law but bound by tribal laws and customs and liable for tribal punishment. He also argued that New South Wales was not originally desert because it was populated by a people who had their own manners and customs and were not bound by British law because they were not protected by it.[85]

Justice Burton said that while Aboriginal people might be entitled to be recognised as free and independent, on the taking of possession of the colony 'they were not in a position with regard to strength as to be considered free and independent tribes'. He further held that the offence had been committed within the boundary of the colony of New South Wales where the law of England applied and there was no distinction in liability for punishment whether the offense had been committed on a white person or one of his own tribe.[86] The *Murrell* decision asserted Crown sovereignty over the colony of New South Wales.

The 1889 New South Wales Supreme Court case of *Cooper v. Stuart* revolved around Crown grants of land, public purpose reservations and the introduction of English law into the colony of New South Wales.[87] In deciding the extent to which English law was introduced into the colony of New South Wales, Lord Watson of the Privy Council held that New South Wales was a settled colony and therefore the Crown, through the Imperial Parliament or the colonial legislature, may by statute declare what parts of English common law and statute law apply to the colony.

In deciding the case, Lord Watson looked at the extent to which English law was introduced into the colony of New South Wales and decided that it consisted of a tract of 'territory practically unoccupied, without settled inhabitants or settled law, at the time when it was peacefully annexed' by the British. In the case of a settled colony, the law of England becomes the law of the colony. Lord Watson also said that because there was no land law or tenure existing in the colony at the time of annexation and it was inevitable that when colonial land became the subject of settlement and commerce, all land transactions were governed by English law, in so far as that law could be justly and conveniently applied to the colony.[88]

Both cases assumed Aboriginal people had no sovereignty or land ownership at the time of British colonisation of New South Wales, with the judge in *R v. Jack Congo Murrell* saying that Aboriginal people were too small in numbers and so did not have the strength to be considered a sovereign independent nation and that the British had asserted dominion over New South Wales for a long period of time. The rule of prescription is relied on in the assertion of British dominion; however, according to Henry Reynolds, the strength (in numbers) or weakness of a nation was not relevant in considering whether a nation was sovereign.[89] *Cooper v. Stuart* assumed there was no existing land law or tenure in the colony at the time of its annexation because according to the Privy Council, New South Wales was without settled inhabitants or settled law.

From 1836 to 1992, courts in Australia largely accepted the erroneous views and assumptions that New South Wales was 'peacefully settled' on the basis that so-called wandering tribes were not considered settled inhabitants with settled law. The courts reached their decisions without any evidence in respect to the nature of Aboriginal society,[90] and merely applied the uninformed perceptions and erroneous assumptions of Cook and Banks that were accepted without question or inquiry by the British Crown.[91]

The Barbarian Theory and Australian Law

Until *Mabo and Others v. The State of Queensland (No. 2)*, Australian law accepted, without question, that the Australian continent was without settled inhabitants or settled law and that Indigenous people in Australia had no sovereignty or ownership in land.[92] In effect, according to British law, Indigenous people had rights to nothing because the acquisition of sovereignty of a so-called terra nullius territory by occupation or settlement was also equated with absolute Crown ownership of the land. Justice Brennan in *Mabo (No. 2)* refers to this as the 'barbarian theory' where Indigenous people were regarded as 'barbarous' or unsettled without law or sovereignty and were considered 'primitive' in their social organisation. In a settled colony the Indigenous inhabitants were regarded as low on the scale of social organisation, so their occupancy of land was ignored in considering title to land in the colony. The colony of New South Wales was treated as 'uninhabited' on the basis that there was no proprietor of the land.[93] This is clearly wrong. Regarding the barbarian theory, Justice Brennan said,

> The facts as we know them today do not fit the 'absence of law' or 'barbarian' theory underpinning the colonial reception of the common law of England. That being so, there is no warrant for applying in these times rules of the English common law which were the product of this theory. It would be a curious doctrine to propound today that, when the benefit of the common law was first extended to her Majesty's

indigenous subjects in the Antipodes, its first fruits were to strip them of their right to occupy their ancestral lands. Yet the supposedly barbarian nature of indigenous people provided the common law of England with the justification for denying them their traditional rights and interests in land.[94]

The 'barbarian theory' was applied by the courts in *R v. Jack Congo Murrell* and *Cooper v. Stuart* and continued to be applied, or at least followed, by Australian courts in their decision making up to 1979; although the common law continued in that form up until 1992 when the Australian High Court discredited and rejected the 'barbarian theory' as the underlying basis for Australian law.

The 1979 case of *Milirrpum v. Nabalco* concerned Yolngu clans (Rirratjingu, Gumatj and Djapu) who took action to assert their rights under 'native law and custom' against the Nabalco mining company and the Commonwealth government in relation to the grant of mining and ancillary leases in 1968, enabling Nabalco to mine bauxite and establish a township on the Gove peninsula in Arnhem Land.[95] The Yolngu accepted that political sovereignty over the land and ultimate radical title vested in the Crown; however, they argued that they had occupied the land from time immemorial and that their rights to the land were proprietary. They also argued that these rights of ownership still existed and should be respected by the Crown and that the activities of Nabalco were unlawful and an invasion of their proprietary rights.

In deciding whether a doctrine of communal native title existed at common law and was recognised by the common law, Justice Blackburn cited *Cooper v. Stuart* as binding authority that New South Wales was a settled or peaceably occupied colony and so English law applied to the whole of the colony. The Yolngu clans argued that *Cooper v. Stuart* was historically inaccurate considering anthropological knowledge and the land was not without settled inhabitants or settled law. Justice Blackburn said this was not a question of fact but a question of law, which he was not about to overturn.

Blackburn relied on the authority of Australian common law decisions, none of which expressly or implicitly referred to communal native title. According to Justice Blackburn they all affirmed that the Crown is the source of title, therefore all title, rights and interests in land, which existed after the foundation of New South Wales and South Australia, were the direct consequence of a grant from the Crown. The Crown acquired title to land when it acquired sovereignty over Australia and so the land became the property of the Crown in demesne. According to Justice Blackburn the Yolngu clans were unable to point to a grant from the Crown as the basis of their title, and therefore their case failed.

Justice Blackburn also said the Yolngu clans failed to show that in 1788 their predecessors had the same links to the same areas of land as those which the Yolngu now claimed. He further said that the Yolngu relationship to the land was not proprietary in nature. Although the evidence showed that the Yolngu clans had 'a subtle and elaborate system highly adapted to the country', which 'provided a stable order of society' and which was recognised by Justice Blackburn as a system of law, he concluded that the system 'did not provide for any proprietary interest in the plaintiffs in any part of the subject land'. He said that the Yolngu rights and obligations regarding their land did not resemble the characteristics of Australian (English) property law, which is the right to use and enjoy, the right to exclude others and the right to alienate land.[96]

Applying principles of English property law to deny that Aboriginal people had ownership of land and to suggest that the Yolngu could not prove the same links to the land in 1970 as in 1788 is clearly unjust. Justice Blackburn merely accepted the colonial discourse of terra nullius and incorrectly assumed that in 1788 Aboriginal people throughout Australia lost all their rights, entitlements, and interests in land. Although he recognised that the Yolngu have an elaborate system of governance and a stable order of society, he regarded *Cooper v. Stuart* as binding authority that could not be overturned.

Cooper v. Stuart was also the authority for the 1976 case of *R v. Wedge* where an Aboriginal man, James Leslie Wedge, argued the Court had no jurisdiction to try him for murder because Aboriginal people were and still are sovereign people and as such not subject to English law.[97] Wedge also argued that even if Aboriginal people are not sovereign people, the English colonists brought with them only so much of the English law as was applicable to their circumstances and these laws only affected British settlers. Further, he argued that the acquisition of New South Wales in the presence of Aboriginal people did not conform to any recognised method of acquisition in English law, namely conquest, cession, and settlement; and that Aboriginal people were neither regarded nor recognised as British subjects or citizens.

Justice Rath held that the Court had jurisdiction on the basis that Aboriginal people were not sovereign and were subject to the laws of New South Wales. He said that Wedge's propositions were untenable because, based on *Cooper v. Stuart* and according to William Blackstone's commentaries, New South Wales was acquired by settlement as uninhabited territory without settled inhabitants or settled law. Justice Rath said that it is not the presence of an Indigenous population that is significant for classification of a colony but the absence of 'settled inhabitants', 'settled law' and cultivation. Therefore, in a colony founded by settlement, the law of England becomes from the outset the law of the colony. On that basis, there was only one sovereign, the king of England; and only one law, the English law, which provided for the protection of Aboriginal people as subjects. Justice Rath said he was bound by *R v. Murrell*, stating the Court 'would not lightly reverse a historic decision that has stood for nearly one and a half centuries'.[98]

Clearly, challenging British and Australian sovereignty in a criminal case such as *Murrell* and *Wedge* will always fail, first and foremost because they are criminal cases but also because the legal community accepts that the law of England is the applicable law in Australia, even though this is based on erroneous assumptions that Aboriginal people had no form of sovereignty or land ownership. Further, the courts have now asserted that the British acquisition of Australia cannot be challenged in an Australian court. Australia is regarded by the Australian judiciary as a 'settled' colony and not a 'conquered' colony. But during the 1970s, Australian courts continued to apply *Cooper v. Stuart*. While the case was regarded as badly pleaded, causing some antagonism from the judges, the case of *Coe v. the Commonwealth* also relied on *Stuart v. Cooper* as authority.[99] In the High Court, Paul Coe asserted Aboriginal sovereignty on behalf of the Aboriginal community and nations of Australia against the Commonwealth of Australia and the government of the United Kingdom. He argued that the claims by Lieutenant Cook were wrongful and contrary to the exclusive sovereignty of Aboriginal people and nations, that the continent was not terra nullius because it was occupied by the sovereign Aboriginal nation, and that Aboriginal people were unlawfully dispossessed after January 26, 1788, thereby destroying their culture, customs, and way of life.

Paul Coe sought to amend his statement of claim, accepting that the British had claimed Australia but that Aboriginal people retained a limited form of sovereignty; however, his application was dismissed. In an appeal to the Full Court of the High Court in the case of *Coe v. Commonwealth of Australia and Another* (1979),[100] Coe accepted the legality of British occupation in 1770 but sought to argue that Aboriginal people were domestic dependent nations as expressed in the case of *Cherokee Nation v. State of Georgia*.[101] The basis of Coe's argument was that while radical title vested in the Crown it was subject to the possessory and proprietary right of the Aboriginal people and the Aboriginal nation. Aboriginal people were domestic dependent nations in that they still retained rights and interests in respect to their land until or unless these rights were taken away by bilateral treaty, compensation or international intervention. Because of unlawful dispossession by governments of the United Kingdom and the Commonwealth of Australia, Coe asserted that Aboriginal people had lost the benefit of their common law rights in the land and suffered harm to their culture, religion, customs, language and way of life.

The appeal was dismissed by the High Court based on the finding in *Cooper v. Stuart* that Australia was acquired by settlement. Justice Gibbs stated that the annexation of the east coast of Australia by Lieutenant James Cook in 1770 and subsequent acts from which Crown dominion extended over the continent were acts of state that could not be validly

challenged. Regarding whether there is an Aboriginal nation with sovereignty as a domestic dependent nation, Justice Gibbs said the Cherokee
nation case provided no assistance in determining the position in Australia. He said it is not possible to say that Aboriginal people of Australia
were organised as a distinct political society separate from others or that
they had been uniformly treated as a state. Justice Gibbs concluded,

> The aboriginal people are subject to the laws of the Commonwealth
> and of the States or Territories in which they respectively reside. They
> have no legislative, executive or judicial organs by which sovereignty
> might be exercised. If such organs existed, they would have no powers,
> except such as the law of the Commonwealth, or of a State of Territory,
> might confer upon them. The contention that there is in Australia an
> aboriginal nation exercising sovereignty, even of a limited kind, is quite
> impossible in law to maintain. [102]

Justice Gibbs cited the decision of *Cooper v. Stuart* as authority that the
Australian colonies have always been regarded as a territory acquired by
settlement, not conquest, and this was fundamental to the Australian
legal system. Justice Gibbs also said that the claim of Aboriginal people to
rights and interests in land that were recognised by the common law (and
which continue to subsist) was too general, as the case identified no
particular land. Moreover, he said it was erroneous to posit that the hold-
er of proprietary or possessory rights could not be dispossessed without
treaty, compensation or international intervention. [103]

Although a minority judgment, it was Justice Murphy who addressed
the issue of whether Aboriginal people had social and political organisations and whether *Cooper v. Stuart* was good law. Justice Murphy said
Coe was entitled to prove that the concept of terra nullius had no application in Australia, that the lands were acquired by conquest and that the
acquisition of sovereignty acquired by the British Crown did not extinguish ownership rights of Aboriginal people in land. [104] Justice Murphy
said the view of *Cooper v. Stuart* was not binding on the Court and that a
cardinal condition of 'occupation' was that the territory should be terra
nullius; that is, belonging to no one at the time of occupation. He said that
there was a wealth of information to support the claim that Aboriginal
people had occupied Australia for many thousands of years, and although nomadic, they were attached to defined areas of land, they had a
complex social and political organisation, and their laws were settled and
of great antiquity. [105] In regard to the authority of *Cooper v. Stuart* and its
reference to peaceful annexation, Justice Murphy said,

> the aborigines did not give up their land peacefully; they were killed or
> removed forcibly from the lands by United Kingdom forces or the Eu-
> ropean colonists in what amounted to attempted (and in Tasmania
> almost complete) genocide. The statement by the Privy Council may be

regarded either as having been made in ignorance or as a convenient falsehood to justify the taking of aborigines' land. [106]

The decision of *Cooper v. Stuart* achieved almost gospel status in Australian law as it was applied without question for more than one hundred years. However, by the late 1970s it was becoming untenable because of the political calls for Aboriginal land rights. Even though in 1979 Justice Murphy had raised doubts about the underlying assumptions upon which *Cooper v. Stuart* was based, it was not until the case of *Mabo and Others v. The State of Queensland (No. 2)* [107] in 1992 that the court decided that it was unjust to continue to uphold the erroneous assumptions underlying Australian law—but this decision was made only regarding the rights of Indigenous people to land.

The *Mabo* case began in 1982 when Eddie Mabo, David Passi and James Rice, members of the Meriam people who occupied Murray Island in the Torres Strait, asserted a claim for traditional native title against the State of Queensland and the Commonwealth of Australia in the High Court. They claimed that their traditional native title survived acquisition by the British Crown, that it was a possessory title recognised by the common law and that they could still establish local legal customary rights. The case did not question whether Australia was conquered or settled. It accepted that the British Crown had acquired sovereignty over Australia by settlement but argued that traditional native title rights survived acquisition and were still in existence. The case had a long and difficult track through the Court as the Queensland government unsuccessfully attempted to retrospectively extinguish native title to put an end to the native title claim. [108] However, on 3 June 1992, the High Court declared the Meriam people were entitled, as against the whole world, to the possession, occupation, use and enjoyment of the Murray Islands. All the judges except Justice Dawson agreed that the common law of Australia recognises a form of native title that comes from the laws and customs of Indigenous people in relation to the occupation and use of land, but that native title could be extinguished by a clear and plain intention as evidenced by government action or by legislation, so long as this did not breach the Racial Discrimination Act 1975 (Cth).

The High Court examined the issues of the acquisition of sovereignty and the introduction of common law in Australia in deciding whether the Crown had acquired beneficial ownership of the land in the Murray islands. The majority held that Australia was not terra nullius at the time of European settlement. While the Crown gained sovereignty and radical title upon settlement, it did not prevent the protection of the pre-existing rights and interests of Indigenous people. Justice Brennan, who wrote the majority judgment, said that the proposition that the Crown became the universal and absolute beneficial owner of all land in Australia upon the acquisition of sovereignty, extinguishing the interests of the Indigenous inhabitants, was by 'any civilised standards' unjust because Indigenous people had neither ceded the lands nor was the land taken in conquest. Further, based on case law, the common law was also unjust because it took away the right of Indigenous people to occupy their traditional land, depriving them of the sustenance that the land provided, making them 'intruders in their own home and mendicants for a place to live'.[109]

Justice Brennan looked at the enlarged concept of terra nullius in international law as it was applied in New South Wales. It justified the acquisition of inhabited territory by settlement and facilitated the reception of common law into the colony. As a 'settled' colony, New South Wales was assumed to have no local law in existence because Aboriginal people were regarded as 'barbarous or unsettled and without settled law', therefore English law became the law of the colony. Brennan said the 'absence of law' or 'barbarian' theory that underpinned the reception of the common law does not fit the facts as they are known today and in that regard the barbarian theory was false, unacceptable in today's society and could not be accepted in contemporary law.[110] Therefore, the common law was no longer in step with international law, particularly in respect to the Advisory Opinion on Western Sahara, which condemned the concept of terra nullius.[111] Justice Brennan rejected the assumption of terra nullius as part of the common law of Australia because the barbarian theory depended on a discriminatory denigration of Indigenous inhabitants, their social organisation and their customs. According to Brennan to continue to embrace the enlarged notion of terra nullius would perpetuate injustice. On that basis the notion that the Crown acquired absolute beneficial ownership of the land when it acquired sovereignty over parts of Australia was also rejected.

The Crown only acquired radical title to land, which enabled the Crown to grant interests in land or to acquire land for the Crown but did not prevent recognition of Indigenous interests in that land. In this regard, Aboriginal people were not dispossessed in 1788 but were dispossessed by subsequent grants of land to colonists and by the exclusion of Aboriginal people from their traditional territory. However, this recognition of the rights and interests of the Indigenous people could not overturn the doctrine of tenure, a 'skeletal principle' of the Australian legal system in respect to land ownership.[112] In rejecting terra nullius regarding Aboriginal land ownership, the High Court did not reclassify Australia as 'conquered'[113] because the court was not prepared to hold that European occupation of Australia was unlawful. In this regard, terra nullius was the 'scapegoat' to explain why the common law had not recognised Aboriginal rights to land; however, the *Mabo* decision reiterated Australian sovereignty and 're-legitimated the political economy and moral foundation of Australian society and nationhood', at the same time reaffirming the structure of power relations in Australia.[114] Accordingly, the *Mabo* judgment was not necessarily rejecting terra nullius but reviving it to critique the justice of colonisation; hence the *Mabo* judgment was defending Indigenous rights while at the same time rescuing liberal democracy from the threat posed by the dispossession of colonised peoples.[115]

ONGOING INTELLECTUAL BARRIERS

While the courts are prepared to entertain Indigenous claims for rights to land within the framework of British and Australian common law, they are not prepared to entertain any claims that question the classification of Australia as a colony acquired by settlement. The claims that have been presented to Australian courts are denied on the basis that the acquisition of New South Wales was an act of state, which cannot be challenged, and that there is no basis in law for these types of claims. In the case of *Coe v. Commonwealth* (1993), Isabel Coe asserted against the Commonwealth and the State of New South Wales (NSW) that the Wiradjuri are a sovereign nation of people and as a domestic dependent nation they are entitled to self-government and full rights over their traditional lands.[116] Coe also claimed the Commonwealth had wrongfully and unlawfully acquired Wiradjuri land and that the State of NSW had committed crimes against humanity as a result of its wrongful and unlawful seizure. Further, Coe claimed that the Commonwealth and State of NSW had a fiduciary trust relationship with the Wiradjuri nation and had breached that obligation by dispossessing the Wiradjuri from their land and alienating Wiradjuri land.

Chief Justice Mason said that Coe's sovereignty claim was an abuse of process because she was using the proceedings for improper political purposes. He followed the judgment set down in *Coe v. The Commonwealth* (1979) to reject the claim of Aboriginal sovereignty, thereby affirming the decision that the annexation of the east coast of Australia and the subsequent acts of the Crown were acts of state whose validity could not be challenged. Therefore, it was settled law that the Australian colonies were acquired by British settlement not conquest. He also said that based on *Mabo (No. 2)* the Crown's acquisition of sovereignty over Australia could not be challenged in a municipal case and further stated that *Mabo (No. 2)* does not support the notion of Aboriginal sovereignty nor does it support the notion that Aboriginal people are a domestic dependent nation and a free and independent people. He said this claim has no basis in domestic law and no independent legal significance. [117]

The High Court has also rejected the assertion that customary laws of Aboriginal people survived colonisation, including claims that state or Commonwealth statute law cannot apply to Aboriginal people until adopted by them. *Walker v The State of New South Wales* (1974) concerned the question of whether Aboriginal criminal law could be recognized by the common law and whether such laws continued in a similar way as Aboriginal land tenure laws were held to continue after colonization as recognised in the case of *Mabo v Queensland (No. 2)*.[118] Charged with a criminal offense in New South Wales, Denis Walker argued that the common law is only valid in its application to Aboriginal people to the extent to which they have accepted it. His argument was that statute law of the states and Commonwealth cannot apply to Aboriginal people without their consent and has no effect until Aboriginal people adopt it. It was argued that the criminal law imported into New South Wales upon colonisation only affected the colonists and was, therefore, only applicable to them.

Chief Justice Mason stated that Walker's pleadings were untenable because the New South Wales legislature had power to make laws for the peace, welfare and good government of New South Wales. Citing *Coe v. The Commonwealth* (1979), he rejected the claim that Aboriginal people were sovereign. He also said *Mabo v. Queensland (No. 2)* (1992) does not support the notion that the Commonwealth and NSW Parliaments lacked legislative competence to regulate or affect the rights of Aboriginal people or that Commonwealth or state laws are subject to the acceptance, adoption, request or consent of Aboriginal people. Such a notion, he said, amounts to a contention that a new source of sovereignty resides in Aboriginal people. As to the question of whether customary Aboriginal criminal law survived colonisation and hence the criminal law of NSW did not apply to Aboriginal people, Mason rejected the proposition because English and Australian criminal law do not accommodate an alternate body of law operating alongside the sovereign law of the state. He went on to say that even if customary criminal law survived British settlement, it was extinguished by the passage of criminal statutes of general application. He said there was no analogy with the situation in *Mabo (No. 2)* where native title survived colonisation.

Except for *Mabo (No. 2)*, all Indigenous claims for recognition presented and adjudicated within the common law failed. In this context, on the face of it, *Mabo (No. 2)* seems an aberration. However, *Mabo (No. 2)* did not recognise Indigenous laws and customs as giving rise to a political right such as self-determination. These vital institutions of Indigenous culture are not 'accorded the equal recognition and status of settler institutions', hence 'white law would continue to trump Indigenous law'.[119] *Mabo (No. 2)* reinforced the legitimacy of Australian sovereignty on the basis that Crown acquisition of the Australian territory, and consequently its sovereignty, was an act of state that could not be challenged in an Australian court.

The courts in *Coe v. Commonwealth* (1993) and *Walker v. NSW* (1994) also followed this reasoning; the assumption behind these decisions is that Indigenous people either had no sovereignty prior to 1788 or British sovereignty extinguished Indigenous sovereignty in 1788. Elements of the colonial discourse of terra nullius were perpetuated in these two cases because the courts used *Coe v. The Commonwealth* (1979) as the authority to reject the claim of Aboriginal sovereignty, yet the authority used by *Coe v. The Commonwealth* (1979) to reject Aboriginal sovereignty was *Cooper v. Stuart,* in which it was erroneously stated that the colony of NSW was practically unoccupied and peacefully annexed by the British. Hence, the courts are applying law based on erroneous assumptions about Indigenous Australians to consistently and emphatically reject any notion that Indigenous people in Australia retain any form of sovereignty. In the courts' view there is no other source of sovereignty other than that exercised by the Commonwealth and state governments.

The High Court asserts the exclusivity and legitimacy of British-Australian sovereignty as the means to extinguish any suggestion or contention that Indigenous people have a form of residual sovereignty existing in Australia. Land or native title rights not attached to any notion of Indigenous sovereignty are much more acceptable to the common law. Assertions of Indigenous sovereignty with respect to criminal matters have been equally unsuccessful. Although the two *Coe* cases were not presented correctly in accordance with the language and conventions of the common law, claims to domestic dependent nationhood were rejected by the courts based on the principle in *Cooper v. Stuart*. Indigenous people sought recognition of continuity of their culture, their rights and authorities, and recognition of plurality, but the common law sees these claims as a threat or challenge to Australian sovereignty and constitutionalism.

When the High Court rejected terra nullius in *Mabo (No. 2)*, it did not follow through and consider whether Australia had been conquered by the British or ceded by treaty. For it follows that if there was no terra nullius and no treaties then the only available method of acquisition of Australia was conquest.[120] Alternatively, if the Australian continent was 'settled' then Indigenous sovereignty continues today because it was not lost by cession or conquest; therefore, Indigenous sovereignty was never ceded or conquered. The High Court also refused to recognise that native title originates from the collective authorities and powers of Indigenous people over their territory and that these powers have continuity. These powers did not cease in 1788 and while governments and courts have tried over the course of history to eliminate this authority and power by various means, they have not been able to eliminate Indigenous people within whom the power resides.

Australian courts have played a significant role in perpetuating uninformed and erroneous colonial assumptions and terra nullius discourses that construe Indigenous people as having deficits in regard to European 'civilisation'. They have assumed that the Australian continent was in fact terra nullius. However, this 'barbarian theory' is still part of the common law to the extent that the High Court in *Mabo (No. 2)* accepted that Australia was established as a settled British colony. According to the assumptions currently embedded in the common law, Indigenous people were not and are still not 'civilised' enough to be a sovereign people. The High Court also said the acquisition of sovereignty of the Australian continent was within the prerogative power of the Imperial Crown and as such it is an act of state that could not be challenged in an Australian court. Therefore, the international law and British common law still view Australia as legally uninhabited for the purpose of acquisition of sovereignty.

According to Aboriginal scholar Irene Watson, the legal theory of terra nullius remains intact because the High Court in *Mabo (No. 2)* merely replaced the term 'terra nullius' with the 'act of state' doctrine allowing the High Court to sanction 'colonialism, dispossession and disempowerment' of Indigenous people as a 'legitimate act of state'.[121] Henry Reynolds argues that it is not enough for the Crown to assert that at the moment of annexation Indigenous sovereignty disappeared over vast areas of land and among people; this fiction cannot continue to underpin Australian national life or Australian jurisprudence.[122] However, *Mabo (No. 2)* has effectively confirmed that the acquisition of sovereignty of the Australian continent is an act of state that cannot be challenged in an Australian court.

Australian governments and courts now hide behind the 'act of state' doctrine to sanction colonialism and deny Indigenous sovereignty. Therefore, challenging colonialism through the judicial system is almost impossible. This is evidenced by the application of the 'barbarian theory' and the 'act of state doctrine' by the courts in Australia. Judicial challenge is now beyond the reach of Indigenous people. However, there is a history of Indigenous anticolonial resistance and political struggle in Australia. The Indigenous struggle in Australia has encompassed various approaches in seeking justice. It has involved asserting Indigenous rights as they relate to culture, land and sovereignty, but also rights to equality such as citisenship, economic self-sufficiency and human rights, such as the right to self-determination as well as making claims for justice in the form of legal and political recognition. It is the political arena where Indigenous people have been able to make the most significant gains. A change in Indigenous policy in 1972 opened the political space for Indigenous Australians to assert their right to self-determination, which in turn ushered in a period of significant political, social and economic progress for Indigenous people.

NOTES

1. M. Dodson and L. Strelein, 'Australia's Nation-Building: Renegotiating the Relationship Between Indigenous Peoples and the State', *UNSW Law Journal* 24, no. 3 (2001), 826.

2. L. Behrendt, *Achieving Social Justice: Indigenous rights and Australia's future* (Leichhardt, NSW: Federation Press, 2003), 3.

3. M. Borch, 'Rethinking the Origins of Terra Nullius', *Australian Historical Studies* 32, no. 117 (2001), 239.

4. A. G. Price, *The Explorations of Captain James Cook in the Pacific as told by selections of his own Journals 1768–1779* (New York: Dover Publications Inc., 1971), 17–20.

5. P. Brunton, *The Endeavour Journal of Joseph Banks* (Angus and Robertson & the State Library of New South Wales, 1998), 22.

6. J. C. Beaglehole, *The Journals of Captain James Cook on his Voyages of Discovery. The Voyage of the Endeavour 1768–1771*, Part Two (Millwood, NY: Hakluyt Society, 1988), 305; A. W. Reed, *Captain Cook in Australia: Extracts from the journals of Captain James Cook* (Wellington: New Zealand, A H & A W Reed, 1969), 39–41; Brunton, *The Endeavour Journal*, 23.

7. Beaglehole, *The Journals of Captain James Cook*, 306, 308; Reed, *Captain Cook in Australia*, 42; Brunton, *The Endeavour Journal*, 25.

8. Beaglehole, *The Journals of Captain James Cook*, 357–58; Price, *The Explorations of Captain James Cook*, 63–85; Reed, *Captain Cook in Australia*, 94.

9. Beaglehole, *The Journals of Captain James Cook*, 361ö62; Reed, *Captain Cook in Australia*, 97–99.

10. Brunton, *The Endeavour Journal*, 66–67.

11. Reed, *Captain Cook in Australia*, 50.

12. Brunton, *The Endeavour Journal*, 25.

13. Price, *The Explorations of Captain James Cook*, 80; Reed, *Captain Cook in Australia*, 50, 122–24.

14. Beaglehole, *The Journals of Captain James Cook*, 387–88; Reed, *Captain Cook in Australia*, 123.

15. Beaglehole, *The Journals of Captain James Cook*, 399; Reed, *Captain Cook in Australia*, 136.

16. Reed, *Captain Cook in Australia*, 49.

17. Beaglehole, *The Journals of Captain James Cook*, 396; Reed, *Captain Cook in Australia*, 133–34.

18. Brunton, *The Endeavour Journal*, 96–97.

19. Brunton, *The Endeavour Journal*, 103.

20. B. Buchan, 'Traffick of Empire: Trade, Treaty and Terra Nullius in Australia and North America, 1750–1800', *History Compass* 5, no. (2007), 386–405.

21. Beaglehole, *The Journals of Captain James Cook*, 399.

22. Brunton, *The Endeavour Journal*, 99.

23. P. Keal, *European Conquest and the Rights of Indigenous Peoples* (Cambridge, UK: Cambridge University Press, 2003), 56.

24. Keal, *European Conquest*, 83.

25. R. Broome, *Aboriginal Australians: Black Response to White Dominance 1788–1980* (North Sydney: Allen & Unwin, 1982), 88.

26. H. Reynolds, *Dispossession: Black Australians and White Invaders* (St Leonards: Allen & Unwin, 1989), 101–07.

27. Broome, *Aboriginal Australians*, 88–91.

28. Keal, *European Conquest*, 73, 74.

29. Keal, *European Conquest*, 67–69.

30. Keal, *European Conquest*, 72, 74–76.

31. Reynolds, *Dispossession*, 97.

32. Broome, *Aboriginal Australians*, 89; Reynolds, *Dispossession*, 107–09.

33. C. Darwin, *On the Origins of Species by Means of Natural Selection or the Preservation of Favoured Races in the Struggle for Life* (London: John Murray, 1859).

34. Broome, *Aboriginal Australians*, 92–93; Reynolds, *Dispossession*, 111–18.

35. Keal, *European Conquest*, 75.

36. J. Tully, 'Aboriginal property and Western theory: Recovering a middle ground', *Social Philosophy and Policy Foundation* 11, no. 2 (1994), 159–62.

37. Keal, *European Conquest*, 76–77.

38. J. Locke, *Two Treatise of Government* (New York: Hafner Publishing, 1947), 133–46.

39. Keal, *European Conquest*, 76–78, 78–80.

40. J. Tully, *Strange Multiplicity, Constitutionalism in an age of diversity* (Cambridge: Cambridge University Press, 1995), 59–64.

41. Tully, *Strange Multiplicity*, 66–67.

42. A. Castles, *An Australian Legal History* (Sydney: The Law Book Company, 1982), 20–21, 23–25.

43. H. Reynolds, *Aboriginal Sovereignty, Reflections on race, state and nation* (St Leonards: Allen & Unwin, 1996), 41–46, 54–55.

44. H. Douglas and M. Finnane, *Indigenous Crime and Settler Law. White Sovereignty after Empire* (United Kingdom: Palgrave MacMillan, 2012), 8.

45. H. Reynolds, 'Reviving Indigenous Sovereignty', *Macquarie Law Journal*, 6 (2006), 11.

46. Douglas and Finnane, *Indigenous Crime and Settler Law*, 34.

47. K. McNeil, *Common Law Aboriginal Title* (Oxford: Clarendon Press, 1989), 110.

48. R. J. Miller, J. Ruru, L. Behrendt and T. Lindberg, *Discovering Indigenous Lands, The Doctrine of Discovery in the English Colonies* (Oxford: Oxford University Press, 2010), 2–6.

49. Miller et al., *Discovering Indigenous Lands*, 9–15.

50. M. F. Lindley, *The Acquisition of Government of backward Territory in International Law* (London: Longmans, Green and Co., 1926), 124–28, 129–38; Miller et al., *Discovering Indigenous Lands*, 18–19.

51. Lindley, *The Acquisition of Government*, 139–41.

52. Lindley, *The Acquisition of Government*, 10–11, 12–17, 20.

53. E. de Vattel, 'The Law of Nations; or, Principles of the Law of Nature, applied to the Conduct and Affairs of Nations and Sovereigns', in *The Law of Nations*, J. Chitty ed., (Philadelphia: T & J W Johnson & Co., 1863), 98.

54. W. Blackstone and T. M. Cooley, *Commentaries on the Laws of England* (Chicago: Callaghan and Cockcroft,1871), 105.

55. de Vattel, 'The Law of Nations', 97–100.

56. Lindley, *The Acquisition of Government*, 17.

57. Lindley, *The Acquisition of Government*, 18–20; Borch, 'Rethinking the Origins of Terra Nullius', 238–39.

58. Lindley, *The Acquisition of Government*, 45.

59. K. Roberts-Wray, *Commonwealth and Colonial Law* (London: Stevens & Sons Ltd, 1966), 99–100.

60. Lindley, *The Acquisition of Government*, 45.

61. Lindley, *The Acquisition of Government*, 160.

62. Roberts-Wray, *Commonwealth and Colonial Law*, 105–7.

63. Lindley, *The Acquisition of Government*, 178–79.

64. A. Fitzmaurice, 'The Genealogy of Terra Nullius', *Australian Historical Studies* 38, no. 129 (2007), 2.

65. Borch, 'Rethinking the Origins of Terra Nullius', 230.

66. Borch, 'Rethinking the Origins of Terra Nullius', 225–27.

67. S. Banner, *Possessing the Pacific. Land, Settlers, and Indigenous People from Australia to Alaska* (Cambridge, MA: Harvard University Press, 2007), 13–17.

68. Borch, 'Rethinking the Origins of Terra Nullius', 224, 238.

69. A. Fitzmaurice, 'Discovery, Conquest, and Occupation of Territory', in *The History of International Law*, Bardo Fassbender and Anne Peters, eds. (Oxford, UK: Oxford University Press, 2012), 855–59; Fitzmaurice, 'The Genealogy of Terra Nullius', 9–13.

70. U. Secher, 'The High Court and Recognition of Native Title: Distinguishing between the Doctrine of Terra Nullius and "Desert and Uncultivated," *University Western Sydney Law Review* 11, (2007), 12; D. Ritter, 'The "Rejection of Terra Nullius" in Mabo: A Critical Analysis', *Sydney Law Review* 5 (1996), 8.

71. Secher, 'The High Court and Recognition of Native Title', 2–3.

72. McNeil, *Common Law Aboriginal Title*, 111, 113.

73. McNeil, *Common Law Aboriginal Title*, 113–16; B. H. McPherson, *The Reception of English Law Abroad* (Brisbane: The Supreme Court of Queensland Library, 2007).

74. McNeil, *Common Law Aboriginal Title*, 117–18.

75. McNeil, *Common Law Aboriginal Title*, 130–32.

76. A, Frost, 'New South Wales as terra nullius: The British denial of Aboriginal land rights', *Historical Studies* 19, no. 77 (1981), 518–21.

77. R. Standfield, '"These unoffending people": myth, history and the idea of Aboriginal resistance in David Collins Account of the English Colony in New South Wales' in *Myth, Memory and Indigenous Australia,* Francis Peters-Little, Ann Curthoys, and John Docker, eds. (Canberra: ANU E Press, 2010), 126.

78. Banner, *Possessing the Pacific*, 13–20.

79. Castles, *An Australian Legal History*, 23.

80. Mabo and Others v The State of Queensland [No. 2] [1992] 175 CLR, 98.

81. Borch, 'Rethinking the Origins of Terra Nullius', 235–36.

82. L. Ford, *Settler Sovereignty. Jurisdiction and Indigenous People in America and Australia 1788–1836* (Cambridge, MA: Harvard University Press, 2010), 27–30.

83. 83 Banner, *Possessing the Pacific*, 26–28.

84. R. v Jack Congo Murrell [1836] 1 Legge 72.

85. *R v Murrell and Bummaree* [1836] NSWSupC 35 (5 February 1836).

86. R v Jack Congo Murrell [1836], 73.

87. Cooper v Stuart [1889] 14 App. Cas, 286.

88. Cooper v Stuart [1889] 14 App. Cas, 291–92.

89. H. Reynolds, *Aboriginal Sovereignty, Reflections on race, state and nation* (St Leonards: Allen & Unwin, 1996), 42–43.

90. McNeil, *Common Law Aboriginal Title*, 123.

91. B. Buchan, 'The empire of political thought: civilization, savagery and perceptions of Indigenous government', *History of Human Sciences* 18, no. 2 (2005), 3, 12.

92. Mabo and Others v The State of Queensland [1992] 175 CLR 1; 107 ALR 1; 66 ALJR 408.

93. Mabo and Others v The State of Queensland [No. 2] [1992] 175 CLR, 39.

94. Mabo and Others v The State of Queensland [No. 2] [1992] 175 CLR, 39.

95. Milirrpum and Others v Nabalco Pty Ltd and The Commonwealth of Australia [1970] 17 FLR, 141.

96. Milirrpum and Others v Nabalco Pty Ltd and The Commonwealth of Australia [1970] 17 FLR, 262–74.

97. R v Wedge [1976] 1 NSWLR 581.

98. R v Wedge [1976] 1 NSWLR 586.

99. Coe v the Commonwealth [1978] 18 ALR 592.

100. Coe v Commonwealth of Australia and Another [1979] 24 ALR 118.

101. Cherokee Nation v State of Georgia [1831] 5 Pet 1.

102. Coe v Commonwealth of Australia and Another [1979] 24 ALR 129.

103. Coe v Commonwealth of Australia and Another [1979] 24 ALR, 129–30.

104. Coe v Commonwealth of Australia and Another [1979] 24 ALR, 131, 136, 138.

105. Coe v Commonwealth of Australia and Another [1979] 24 ALR, 137–38.

106. Coe v Commonwealth of Australia and Another [1979] 24 ALR, 138.

107. Mabo and Others v The State of Queensland [No. 2] [1992] 175 CLR 1.

108. D. Cronin, 'Trapped by history: democracy, human rights and justice for Indigenous people in Australia', *Australian Journal of Human Rights* 23, no. 2 (2017), 229.

109. Mabo and Others v The State of Queensland [No. 2] [1992] 175 CLR, 29.

110. Mabo and Others v The State of Queensland [No. 2] [1992] 175 CLR, 31–40.

111. Western Sahara Advisory Opinion [1975] ICJ Reports, 12.

112. Mabo and Others v The State of Queensland [No. 2] [1992] 40–58.

113. D. Ritter, 'The "Rejection of Terra Nullius" in Mabo: A Critical Analysis', *Sydney Law Review* 5 (1996), 26.

114. Ritter, 'The Rejection of Terra Nullius in Mabo', 7–9, 32.

115. A. Fitzmaurice, 'The genealogy of Terra Nullius', *Australian Historical Studies* 38, no. 129 (2007), 14–15.

116. Coe v Commonwealth [1993] 118 ALR 193.

117. Coe v Commonwealth [1993] 200–205.

118. Walker v The State of New South Wales [1994] 182 CLR 45.

119. D. Short, 'Australia: a continuing genocide?' *Journal of Genocide Research* 12, nos. 1–2 (2010), 54.

120. G. Simpson, 'Mabo, International Law, Terra Nullius and the Stories of Settlement: An Unresolved Jurisprudence', *Melbourne University Law Review* 19 (1993–1994), 195–210.

121. I. Watson, 'Indigenous Peoples' Law-Ways: Survival Against the Colonial State', *The Australian Feminist Law Journal* 8 (1997), 47–48.

122. H. Reynolds, 'Reviving Indigenous Sovereignty', *Macquarie Law Journal* 6 (2006), 6, 11.

THREE

Promise, Hope and Disappointment: 1970–1990

The 1970s and 1980s were a period of significant growth and development for Indigenous Australians after the Whitlam government abandoned the policy of assimilation in 1972 in favour of a policy of self-determination. However, the lead up to the change in Indigenous policy witnessed a reinforcement of the assimilation policy and a strenuous denial of Indigenous rights to land by the Commonwealth government. This chapter examines the political and policy environment in regard to assimilation and the Indigenous experience of challenging the authority of the Commonwealth government. It also examines the experience of Indigenous people after the change in policy by the Whitlam Labor government. The initiatives of the Whitlam and Hawke labour governments opened a new era in Indigenous policymaking. Both the Whitlam and Hawke labour governments attempted to engage Indigenous people in policy and decision-making processes. However, despite well-meaning intentions, Indigenous hopes were dashed as governments backtracked on significant policy initiatives such as national political representation, land rights and treaties. The failure of these policy initiatives is a clear example of how colonial assumptions and discourses about Indigenous people were still influential in the way government engaged and dealt with Indigenous issues.

Assimilation was directed at creating a homogenous Australian society wherein Aboriginal people would be absorbed into white society, having the same culture, lifestyle and rights as white Australians. The foundations of assimilation were laid down in the late 1930s by state and territory governments. The Commonwealth government had initiated an assimilation policy in the Northern Territory at this time; however, it was not until the early 1950s that state governments in Australia endorsed assimilation. Based on historical assumptions that Aboriginal culture and society was inferior, governments in Australia believed that assimilation into white society was the method by which so-called Aboriginal disabilities would be overcome. The provision of services in housing, health care, welfare, education, employment and enterprise development, including mining on Aboriginal land, was presented as a means to transition Indigenous people into mainstream Australian society.

The Commonwealth government considered Aboriginal people to have neither legal nor moral rights to land and that any recognition of land ownership based on tradition amounted to the creation of a separate and different land system in Australia that would threaten or dispossess white Australians of their rights and benefits. Under the assimilation policy, Indigenous people could only own land through purchase or by government grant under Australian law. The change in policy came about in January 1972 after the Aboriginal Tent Embassy protest on the lawns of what is now the former Parliament House in Canberra. The protest challenged the paternalistic and assimilationist policies of the Commonwealth government, demanding self-determination, ownership of land, rights to minerals, protection of sacred sites and compensation for land taken. The activists spoke in the language of international black revolution.[1] They advocated autonomy and empowerment as the means to strengthen Aboriginal culture and identity and to advance Aboriginal interests and aspirations.[2] Rights to land based on indigeneity, Aboriginal self-determination, cultural integrity and black pride anchored the political thoughts of the activists and formed the basis of their struggle.

The Aboriginal activists had to overcome prejudices within the government that they were not truly 'Aboriginal' but rather a group of 'unrepresentative militants'. The government believed that Aboriginal representatives could only be appointed and endorsed within the structure of the Australian government. Therefore, in the view of the government it was not necessary to engage with the Aboriginal Embassy representatives. The Commonwealth government was contemptuous and passed legislation to remove the Embassy. But the activists succeeded in starting a dialogue with the Australian population and the international community. They challenged the settler colonial assumptions that Aboriginal people had no form of land title or sovereignty.

The Aboriginal Tent Embassy protest ushered in an era of positive change to Aboriginal policy during the 1970s and 1980s, extending into the early 1990s. Assumptions regarding Aboriginal rights to land began to change after the Whitlam government came to power in December 1972. Whitlam instituted a policy of self-determination and recognised Aboriginal ownership of land in the Northern Territory based on tradition. The policy of self-determination enabled Aboriginal people to gain a national political voice within government. As of the 1970s, Indigenous political voices were forceful and became even more so as Indigenous people gained national political representation through the National Aboriginal Consultative Committee (NACC) and thereafter the National Aboriginal Conference (NAC). The NACC was a representative advisory body established by the Whitlam Labor government in 1973 and the NAC replaced the NACC when the Fraser Liberal Party came to power in 1976. The rise of Aboriginal community organisations, particularly statutory land councils, also began to assert their authority and influence on the Indigenous political agenda. Sympathetic voices in government acknowledged the fact and injustice of Aboriginal dispossession and the need for redress, allowing for discussions about a new direction in Indigenous affairs. Issues such as treaties and national land rights emerged to influence the Indigenous policy agenda.

At the same time, however, these issues were only open for discussion within a nationalist framework providing they did not challenge Australian sovereignty. There was a firm belief that Indigenous people lacked sovereignty or any form of political authority, which placed limits on Indigenous aspirations for self-determination. Further, continuing attitudes of paternalism within government and the bureaucracy relegated the status of Indigenous voices in the policy discussions, effectively treating them as rubber stamps for the government agenda. Indigenous aspirations for a treaty and national land rights would ultimately be dashed. Historical assumptions and attitudes about Indigenous people were, without question, the dominant contributing factors to the failure of national land rights and treaties.

THE POLICY BACKGROUND

The 1967 referendum gave the Commonwealth government power to make laws for Aboriginal people, but the government was reluctant to assume responsibility for Aboriginal administration that had previously been a state responsibility.[3] Prime Minister Harold Holt did not want to intrude unnecessarily into an area of state responsibility. He believed that the needs of Aboriginal people were predominantly a social problem.[4] Holt established a Council for Aboriginal Affairs in November 1967 to advise the government on national Aboriginal policy and to consult with Commonwealth departments as well as ensure official cooperation between the Commonwealth and state authorities. Herbert 'Nugget' Coombs, retiring Reserve Bank governor, was appointed as chairman of the council. Other appointees were Professor W. E. H. Stanner and Barrie Dexter, who was also the director of the Office of Aboriginal Affairs.

After Harold Holt's death in January 1968, Prime Minister John Gorton pursued assimilation stating he wanted to avoid measures that would set Aboriginal citizens apart from other Australians through separate development or different standards. The government's objective, according to Gorton, was the assimilation of Aboriginal people into a 'single Australian society'.[5] Gorton saw no justification or need for new policies to assist Aboriginal people and it was 'wholly unacceptable' to him that Aboriginal people had valid rights to land based on traditional title.[6] When William McMahon became prime minister in March 1971, Aboriginal policy began to change its emphasis with the advice and guidance of Coombs and the Council for Aboriginal Affairs.[7] While the policy focussed on equality of opportunity for Aboriginal people in mainstream society, it accepted that Aboriginal people could maintain their culture and tradition.[8] However, there were those within the government who believed assimilation required enforcing cultural and political uniformity on Aboriginal people.

McMahon proposed the establishment of a special ministerial committee, presided over by the minister for Aboriginal Affairs and advised by the Council and Office of Aboriginal Affairs. Its role was to consult with state and Commonwealth departments for a programme to increase the economic strength and independence of Aboriginal people through employment opportunities and individual or community enterprises. Consideration would be given to ensuring Aboriginal groups had access to land for recreational and ceremonial purposes as well as for the development of enterprises. Legislation would also be examined to remove any discrimination against Aboriginal people. Finally, McMahon said Aboriginal people must be helped to manage their own affairs through representative and consultative bodies at state, regional and local levels.[9]

But the McMahon government policy did not recognise Aboriginal rights to land based on traditional ownership or prior occupation. In the Northern Territory, where the Commonwealth had jurisdictional responsibility, Aboriginal people could only secure a lease over reserve land. The Council for Aboriginal Affairs had recommended that the government examine Aboriginal claims to land based on traditional association and examine the Gurindji demands for land in that regard, but Northern Territory pastoralists opposed such claims.[10] The Gurindji people worked on Wave Hill station (their traditional land) in the Northern Territory on property owned by Lord Vestey of England. In 1966, under the leadership of Vincent Lingiari, they walked off the station to protest low wages, poor working conditions and bad treatment. They refused to return to work and campaigned for the return and ownership of their traditional land. In 1975, Prime Minister Gough Whitlam handed the Gurindji a lease over part of their traditional land.

There was opposition within the government to the policy direction on land rights and to the influence of Coombs and the Council for Aboriginal Affairs. When Peter Howson became minister for the Environment, Aborigines and the Arts, in late May 1971, he set about reining in and isolating Coombs and the Council for Aboriginal Affairs. Howson chaired the newly created Ministerial Committee on Aboriginal Affairs and established an interdepartmental committee to examine the details of Aboriginal policy.[11] It was within this committee that the Department of the Interior and the Northern Territory administration strongly resisted proposals made by Coombs and the Council for Aboriginal Affairs. The Commonwealth government's attitude towards Aboriginal rights to land did not match its stated policy of allowing Aboriginal people to preserve their culture and tradition. The government saw no moral or legal obligation to recognise Aboriginal land ownership because, in their view, Aboriginal people should secure land through the same system as all Australians. This was summed up by Peter Nixon, the minister for the Interior, responding to the Gurindji demands for their traditional land. He said it would be wrong to encourage Aboriginal people to think that because their ancestors had long association with land that they could demand ownership of it. Aboriginal people, he said, should secure land ownership under the same system as applied to all Australians.[12]

While the government clearly understood the basis of Aboriginal demands for their traditional lands, erroneous historical assumptions that Aboriginal people had no sovereignty, laws, society or rights, continued to form the basis of government policy. As we saw in chapter 2, the Yolngu people in the 1971 *Milirrpum* case challenged this assumption but the court denied their traditional claim to the land.[13] In light of the *Milirrpum* decision and growing public support for legislative recognition of Aboriginal land rights, the Council for Aboriginal Affairs recommended to the Ministerial Committee on Aboriginal Affairs that Aboriginal reserves should be protected by an act of Parliament and that an Aboriginal land fund be established to purchase properties for Aboriginal communities. It also recommended that Aboriginal claims for land should be investigated and land identified by 'traditional claim or long occupancy' should be vested in communities through ninety-nine-year leases. But such land claims should fit within the existing Australian legal system and should not question the Crown title of 1788. For Aboriginal communities not on reserves, the government should set aside small areas for residential, recreational and ceremonial purposes.[14]

The Department of the Interior opposed this approach, suggesting that to set apart Aboriginal people from other Australians with new forms of assistance could encourage 'part Aboriginal' people to 'identify themselves as Aborigines' and lead 'resentment and bitterness' from white Australians. The department also rejected the establishment of an Aboriginal land fund because in their view it was 'discriminatory and separatist in character'.[15] The ministerial committee supported several measures but would not accept 'traditional association' as a criterion in granting a lease to an Aboriginal community.[16]

Nonetheless, Coombs' influence with Prime Minister McMahon forced Howson to propose 'long association' as one of the grounds on which the Northern Territory Land Board could lease land to Aboriginal people. However, the Council for Aboriginal Affairs argued that leases based on tradition should include social purposes and should be for larger areas of land.[17] This was supported by the ministerial committee which decided, in December 1971, that Aboriginal communities, groups or individuals on reserves in the Northern Territory could apply to the Lands Board for multipurpose leases of land, and such leases would be granted if Aboriginal people could demonstrate the 'intention and ability to make reasonable use of the area for economic and social purposes'.[18]

While the proposals by the Council for Aboriginal Affairs recognised Aboriginal people in the Northern Territory had rights to land, this recognition of Aboriginal land rights only amounted to leasing of Aboriginal reserve land. There was resistance within government to Aboriginal land ownership based on tradition. The Department of the Interior and Minister Peter Howson believed that land ownership or leases for Aboriginal communities based on maintenance of tradition and culture would create a separate and different land tenure system in Australia. Further, there was an erroneous belief that Aboriginal rights to land would threaten or dispossess white Australians of their rights and benefits and would lock away land from potential development.

Against the advice of the Council for Aboriginal Affairs, Prime Minister McMahon released his government's Aboriginal policy to coincide with Australia Day, 26 January 1972[19]—known as the Day of Mourning, or Invasion Day by Aboriginal people. The government's policy focussed on: (1) providing assistance to Aboriginal people to become part of Australian society but allowing them to preserve and develop their own culture, language and traditions; (2) recognising that Aboriginal people could choose the degree and pace at which they identified with Australian society; (3) ensuring that programmes evolve in accordance with the effects of action taken so far, the needs of the times and the expressed wishes of Aboriginal people; (4) collaboration with the states to deal with problems faced by Aboriginal people and encouraging and strengthening Aboriginal capacity to manage their affairs, increase economic independence, reduce existing social and other handicaps, and promote enjoyment of normal civil liberties; and (5) recognising that special 'temporary and transitional' measures will be necessary to overcome the disabilities experienced by Aboriginal people.[20]

However, the government's statement on Aboriginal rights to land was most controversial. The government would create general purpose leases for a period of fifty years, which Aboriginal individuals, groups and communities could apply for, providing they could demonstrate 'reasonable and economic and social use of the land'. Such leases were only available on Aboriginal reserves in the Northern Territory and provided for economic and social purposes that included Aboriginal educational, recreational, cultural and religious activities. For Aboriginal people in the Northern Territory not living on reserves, the government would purchase land for their economic and social development. McMahon said the government decided not to translate the Aboriginal affinity with land into a legal right under the Australian system because it would have unforeseen implications and could lead to uncertainty and challenges to land titles elsewhere in Australia.[21]

The government's Aboriginal policy also included funding for the establishment of enterprises by Aboriginal communities, such as market gardening, fishing, poultry, brick making, forestry, service stations, and tourist accommodation. Additional measures included: a flexible form of incorporation for Aboriginal communities; protection of reserves from being revoked without a review by Parliament; access for Aboriginal people to hunt and forage on land reserved for their benefit and on pastoral leases; and protection of land both on and off reserves for Aboriginal religious and ceremonial use. As mining was in the national interest, mineral exploration and development would continue on Aboriginal reserves in the Northern Territory, however double royalties would be paid to the Crown, which would then be paid into the Aboriginal Benefits Trust Fund.[22]

Coombs said that the prime minister had done his best to use his authority to acknowledge Aboriginal traditional rights in land and to provide a means by which they could obtain a limited title to land.[23] But the choice of January 26 by the government to deliver its Aboriginal policy was in poor taste and offensive to Aboriginal people, as was pointed out in an editorial in *The Australian*.[24] Clearly, the Australia Day policy statement of the McMahon government reflected the limits of the political influence of the Council for Aboriginal Affairs.[25]

THE ABORIGINAL EMBASSY

Aboriginal people had hoped conditions would improve after the 1967 referendum; that land rights would be a possibility and that Coombs' advice would help the prime minister see the righteousness of Aboriginal claims.[26] The government's policy statement on Australia Day stirred Aboriginal activists in Sydney and around Australia to strongly reject it, despatching a small group of activists (Michael Anderson, Billy Craigie, Tony Coorey and Bert Williams) to Canberra to establish a presence, erecting a beach umbrella and a sign that read 'Aboriginal Embassy' on the lawns of Federal Parliament.[27] On 28 January 1972, the *Canberra Times* reported that three Aboriginal men had set up their own embassy and would remain there until the government withdrew its statement about Aboriginal land rights, reconsidered the issue of land rights and consulted Aboriginal people before forming policy.[28] Peter Howson, minister for the Environment, Aborigines and the Arts, said there was a 'disturbing undertone' in the use of the 'Aboriginal Embassy' sign as it 'implied another sovereign state or separate development' of the Aboriginal race and was 'kindred to apartheid'.[29] The police did not move on the Aboriginal Embassy protestors as there was no law against camping on the lawns of Parliament; however a twenty-four-hour police surveillance was established.[30]

By early February 1972, the Aboriginal Embassy was preparing to fly its own flag and it issued a comprehensive statement of demand as an assertion of sovereignty. Early versions of symbolic flags were replaced in July 1972 by the black, red and yellow Aboriginal flag.[31] On February 5, John Newfong, an Indigenous journalist, released a comprehensive statement of demand on behalf of the Aboriginal embassy. The statement of demand contained a five-point plan calling for: (1) statehood for the Northern Territory with a predominantly Aboriginal Parliament; (2) Aboriginal ownership of existing reserves and a settlement throughout Australia, including rights to minerals; (3) the preservation of all sacred sites in Australia; (4) Aboriginal ownership of areas of land in and around all capital cities, including mineral rights; and (5) compensation for all lands taken with a down payment of $6 billion and an annual percentage of the gross national income.[32] The demand for compensation recognised the original dispossession of Aboriginal people and was a central component of the idea of economic empowerment through self-determination rather than reliance on 'paternalistic' government funding.[33] Aboriginal activists regarded legal ownership of land as the basis for development and economic self-sufficiency for impoverished Aboriginal communities to enable economic, social and political reconstruction.[34]

In early February Gough Whitlam, the Opposition Labor Party leader, visited the Aboriginal Embassy with Kep Enderby, Labor member for the Australian Capital Territory. Whitlam promised that a Labor Party government would grant full freehold title to 'Aboriginal tribes and clans' and would not hesitate to use the power of the Federal Parliament to overrule any state laws that discriminated against Aboriginal people. He noted there was precedent in Canada and the United States for communal land ownership and this was supported by the International Labour Organisation Convention (No. 107) on Indigenous peoples' rights.[35] However, the Labor Party's policy only related to those peoples who had ongoing traditional connections to land, thus excluding dispossessed and dislocated Aboriginal people based in the eastern states, and not benefitting urban-based Aboriginal people.[36]

Gough Whitlam thought the government's policies were 'patronising proposals' because Aboriginal people were being treated differently from any other identifiable group in Australia. He said the Commonwealth had the power to recognise communal ownership of land but had done little for Aboriginal people since the 1967 referendum. In Parliament, Whitlam explained that exclusive land rights vested in a trust would be granted to Aboriginal communities who retained a strong tribal structure or could demonstrate potential for corporate action regarding land presently reserved for Aboriginal people, or where traditional occupancy could be established by anthropological or other evidence. Land rights would also carry the full rights to minerals in the lands, and no Aboriginal land would be alienated unless approved by the Trust and Parliament. Sacred sites would be mapped and protected.[37]

Peter Howson tabled the prime minister's Australia Day policy statement in Parliament and outlined the government's aim of 'one Australian society' in which all Australians, including Aboriginal people, would have equal rights, responsibilities and opportunities and would be encouraged to preserve and develop their own culture, language, traditions and arts. Howson stated 'separate development' was completely alien to the government's objectives. Ralph Hunt, the minister for the Interior, reiterated this policy, explaining that the government was opposed to recognising any form of Aboriginal land ownership. Hunt implied that left-wing movements were behind the protest, using Aboriginal people as a launching pad for their own motives. He said that neither emotional speeches nor land rights would overcome the 'disabilities' of Aboriginal people; and further, he said that welfare policies based on race rather than need would create a white backlash. He asserted that there should not be one land law for Aboriginal people and another for Australians.[38]

Embarrassed by the protest, the Department of the Interior began drafting an ordinance, making it an offense for persons to camp on unleased Commonwealth land and empowering authorities to move their possessions.[39] To assist the removal of the Tent Embassy, Ralph Hunt suggested that an Aboriginal place could be developed to incorporate a lobby at the federal level for Aboriginal people, but Embassy activists firmly opposed the idea.[40] Peter Howson also rejected the idea, stating that the government should not have to bow to the demands of the Aboriginal Embassy, which he considered not representative of all Aboriginal people.[41] The Council for Aboriginal Affairs also opposed the removal of the Tent Embassy and the idea of an Aboriginal place because they saw it was an attempt to bribe the Embassy.[42] In early May the Federal Cabinet endorsed the removal of the Embassy, to be achieved with reasonable notice and carried out tactfully, with the least disturbance.[43]

Within days of the Black Moratorium protest marches on 14 July 1972, the federal police moved on the Embassy. The Black Moratorium was a series of coordinated rallies across the country focussed on ownership and rights to land and minerals, compensation for loss of land since 1770, the right of communities to control their lives and land and support for struggles regarding health care, employment, housing and education.[44] Thousands of Aboriginal people and white supporters marched on the streets of the major capital cities, except the northern city of Darwin where the march was banned by the city council. The images of mass support for Aboriginal land demands alarmed Ralph Hunt, who has-

tened passage of the ordinance to remove the Embassy from the lawns of
Parliament House.[45]

On 17 July, Federal Police Inspector Johnson handed a copy of the
proposed ordinance and explanatory notes to Ambrose Golden-Brown at
the embassy, advising that camping would become prohibited and that
the police would enforce the law.[46] On 20 July, one hundred and fifty
police officers marched in paramilitary fashion from behind Parliament
House and were met by Embassy representatives who informed Inspector Osborne they would vigorously defend the Office Tent. The police
ejected people from several tents, pulling them down without resistance.
However, the protestors linked arms around the Office Tent and chanted
while Inspector Osborne called on the protestors to move or be arrested
for obstructing police. The police then advanced and with extraordinary
brutality attacked the protestors, ripping down the tent.[47]

On ABC television, Ralph Hunt said he regretted the violence, and
blamed the demonstrators, saying they had tried to prevent the police
from executing their duty and so police had no alternative but to do what
they did.[48] Peter Howson felt that 'this is only the first round of the
battle', with more 'worry and trouble' expected.[49] A *Canberra Times* editorial argued that Australian apathy towards Aboriginal people had resulted in only small economic, social and political gains, and this had led
directly to the establishment of the Embassy.[50] Opposition Leader,
Gough Whitlam, criticised the government's actions and stated that as
result of the Embassy efforts, the public were now aware that the aspirations of the Aboriginal population could only be satisfied by recognising
their rights to land.[51]

An application by Tent Embassy activists for a High Court injunction
to prevent any further removal of the tents was denied on 21 July.[52]
Continuing the protest was therefore a priority. On the morning of 22
July, a protest march was held in Canberra Civic. The following day,
activists marched and assembled on the road and lawns in front of Parliament House. A crowd surrounded a tent set up to symbolise the erection
of the embassy. There were speeches by Shirley Smith, Bob Maza and
Paul Coe. Inspector Osborne approached the rally and called on them to
disband, but they refused, jeering loudly. The protestors formed themselves into a circle. Some three hundred and sixty police, including rein-
forcements from the New South Wales department emerged in paramilitary style. The violent encounter that ensued was described as more brutal than the previous confrontation, with people being smashed in the
face, knocked to the ground and kicked. Having superior numbers, the
police dismantled the tent. Anger, shock and disbelief characterised the
feelings of the protestors in the aftermath of the violent clash. Opinions
varied regarding further protests, including retaliation, however no decisions were made other than to rebuild the embassy.[53] Some of the Aboriginal protestors were seeking a compromise and wanted to talk with

someone from the government, but Ralph Hunt and the prime minister were not in Canberra and no other minister emerged. The government wanted the Embassy removed with a show of force and so a reluctant Inspector Osborne had to order his men forward.[54]

The idea of an Aboriginal place in Canberra was raised again as a conciliatory measure. A broad cross-section of Aboriginal protestors at the Embassy had signed a letter to Peter Howson seeking a meeting to discuss an 'Aboriginal peoples' place' in Canberra with status equivalent to an embassy. The Council for Aboriginal Affairs also endorsed long-term Aboriginal representation in Canberra.[55] But Howson said he would only 'negotiate with a fully representative Aboriginal body and not with a group of unrepresentative militants'. He had called a national consultation conference scheduled for 10 and 11 August 1972, and in his view, this was the opportunity for Aboriginal people to present their demands. Howson worked on strengthening his hand against the idea of an Aboriginal place and in support of his hard-line approach to the Aboriginal Embassy. Howson was also concerned that the prime minister was weakening. He said the government would be 'showing great signs of weakness' if it handed over an Aboriginal place. Howson obtained Hunt's agreement to a joint statement, inviting protest organisers to meet with them, to hear the government's position and to discuss how best to ensure the peaceful Aboriginal contribution to the government's policy. Howson also obtained confirmation and support from all state ministers that the national conference and his hard-line approach was appropriate.[56]

Coombs and the Council for Aboriginal Affairs prepared a report for a meeting of cabinet ministers in Canberra on 29 July to defuse the situation and avoid confrontation by negotiating an interim arrangement.[57] Coombs also met a group of about fifteen Aboriginal protestors in Canberra to obtain specific proposals, making a summary of the issues and providing the brief to the cabinet office. Coombs said the original issues of land rights, greater expenditure on education and health, and so on had become overwhelmed by concern about police action, the right to meet ministers and a desire for a continuing Aboriginal presence in Canberra.[58] Howson was 'extremely annoyed' that Coombs and the council had advocated the proposal he had already rejected and was annoyed at Coombs for meeting with the protest leaders to discuss matters with them before discussing it with him.[59] Coombs felt the Council for Aboriginal Affairs had 'an overriding obligation to ensure that significant Aboriginal voices were heard'. But Howson felt that talking with the Embassy protestors made a mockery of the national consultation he had authorised for August. In the cabinet meeting, Coombs recommended a partial list of the Embassy's demands to the ministers, including temporary representation housed in an Aboriginal place in Canberra, the dropping of all charges from the previous two demonstrations and permission to re-erect the tent and subsequently move it to a new temporary location. The ministers were then offered Howson's option of a national conference in August with the advice that Aboriginal people could lobby through those channels. Nonetheless, the Council for Aboriginal Affairs' efforts were partly successful as cabinet ministers agreed for Howson, Ralph Hunt and Malcolm Fraser to meet the Aboriginal protestors and police were instructed to avoid a show of force in dealing with the next demonstration. [60]

In a meeting with Embassy protestors on 29 July, Howson's contempt was blatant. In his diary he records the meeting with a 'deputation from the militant Aborigines' was mainly a 'public relations exercise' and, they got rid of the Aboriginal deputation after about two hours, then reported to the cabinet which unanimously agreed to move the Tent Embassy. [61] Coombs said the Aboriginal deputation spoke of their grievances, frustrations and fears, but the ministers were of the attitude that the protestors did not have the mandate to represent Aboriginal opinion and had to submit proposals for consideration through state and territory advisory groups. [62] In a later press release, Peter Howson and Ralph Hunt said a national meeting of Aboriginal advisory councillors from six states and the Northern Territory would convene to obtain a 'truly representative expression of Aboriginal views'. The Aboriginal protestors were invited to submit proposals for a national Aboriginal hub, which would be discussed at the national conference. [63]

On the morning of Sunday, 30 July, Aboriginal supporters came from Sydney, Melbourne, Brisbane and Adelaide, converging in Canberra. With support from many white Australians, the crowd was a tenfold increase on the numbers of previous demonstrations. Led by Paul Coe, Michael Anderson, Sol Bellear, Alana Doolan, Bobbi Sykes and Isobel Coe, the demonstrators arrived on the lawns of Parliament House mid-morning. A police presence of some three hundred, supported by two NSW police vehicles, faced the protestors from across the road. With an additional one thousand or more tourists and spectators, there were an estimated three thousand people at the event. [64] But no action was taken by police that day, other than to issue a further deadline for dispersal.

Over the preceding week the activists concluded the Embassy had achieved more than they had dreamed possible and they announced they would end the protest in an honourable way. They would declare the Embassy project a success and claim the moral high ground by allowing the police to remove the canvas from over the heads of a group of activists. [65] Hal Wootten, then president of the Redfern Legal Service, was requested to contact the police commissioner advising that Aboriginal leaders did not want violence and with restraint by police it would be possible for the day to pass peacefully. The police were suspicious but accepted assurances that the crowd would disperse peacefully. Seven police officers, led by Inspector Osborne, walked through the crowd and removed the tent, and although some booed the police, there was no resistance. In a final symbolic act, the protestors moved to the side holding a piece of canvas over their heads. When the police came running across to tear it down, they found a number of people smiling at them making the V-sign of peace and raising the original Aboriginal Embassy placard.[66]

Speeches on the day of the protest march reflected fear and anger, as well as confidence in the Aboriginal protestors. The Embassy protests not only stood for Aboriginal land rights but also Aboriginal equality, and the demonstration proved that the Aboriginal claims for land rights had moral ascendancy. Criticism was directed at the government's 'racist actions' in destroying the Embassy and at the lack of support from trade unions. White Australians were called upon to support Aboriginal rights because it was recognised that Aboriginal people would not succeed without their support. Police also came under criticism although they were not considered the primary problem for Aboriginal people. The main barrier for Aboriginal people was the racism and apathy of the Australian people. Other issues raised included the lack of political processes to create change and the lack of discussion, negotiation or relationship with government.[67]

Peter Howson had dismissed the Aboriginal Embassy protest, placing his hopes on the national conference of Aboriginal and Torres Strait Island advisory councillors held in August 1972 in Canberra. He promoted the conference as a representative gathering of Aboriginal delegates who had the authority to speak for their people, arguing that the conference would be a truly representative expression of Aboriginal views. Approximately seventy delegates from all states and the Northern Territory attended.[68] In opening the conference Howson said he had been trying to find the best means of establishing a dialogue between Aborigines and the Commonwealth government,[69] but the conference was not the sort of 'dialogue' he envisioned as it was gate-crashed by Aboriginal activists.[70] In full glare of the television media, embassy activists lead by Paul Coe, Chicka Dixon and Bobby McLeod, wearing white mouth gags as a symbol of the government's attempt to silence them, marched into the conference during Minister Howson's opening speech. The protesters were granted full speaking and voting rights by the conference delegates.[71]

Conference delegates discussed big issues such as land rights, Commonwealth control of Aboriginal affairs, Aboriginal political representation and the proposed Aboriginal hub. They passed resolutions on a range of other issues including women's rights, education, housing, employment and training, and social services. The conference resolved that reserve land be returned to Aboriginal ownership and be vested in incorporated Aboriginal groups and exempt from mining. A land fund was to be established to acquire other lands for individuals and Aboriginal communities, and an Aboriginal claims commission would be established to determine claims to land and compensation for land taken from Aboriginal people since colonisation. The delegates resolved that the issue of an Aboriginal place would not be discussed until the Embassy was re-established on the lawns of Parliament House. The conference delegates called for the Commonwealth government to take full financial and administrative control of Aboriginal affairs and for state departments to be abolished. Conference delegates resolved that there should be a national Aboriginal council and conference system for uniform, nationwide policy whereby Aboriginal people would elect Aboriginal councillors without government interference. Conference delegates also resolved that there should be guaranteed Aboriginal representation in each state, in the Federal Parliament and in the Northern Territory Legislative Council.[72]

However, there was evidence of a degree of dissent. Northern Territory delegates were not in favour of an Aboriginal embassy in Canberra or the Northern Territory because they believed they could communicate directly with government themselves. They also felt they were not ready to have Aboriginal representation in the Northern Territory Legislative Council, stating they would gain representation through the normal processes of government 'as our people become more educated'. Northern Territory delegates also expressed dissatisfaction with aspects of the conference, complaining that a small group of people placed most of the motions and there was not adequate time to understand the motions. They also criticised how they were not given a chance to communicate their point of view or the opportunity to discuss issues with their people before the conference.[73]

A TURNING POINT

The Aboriginal Embassy is considered the 'greatest act of defacement' because it ruptured the colonial order and also mocked Parliament and Commonwealth Aboriginal policy by mimicking the state with an embassy and national flag while at the same time symbolising fringe camps and the material deprivation of Aboriginal living conditions.[74] The Aboriginal Embassy asserted sovereignty to challenge government authority and the legitimacy of the Australian state and to assert Aboriginality as the basis of citizenship. This was unsettling for the government because the Aboriginal activists asserted that recognition of an Aboriginal political and legal order is fundamental to any effort to legitimise the Australian state.[75]

The Embassy symbolised the highly political and contested interface between Aboriginal people and settler Australia, challenging underlying colonial assumptions and creating public discussion about Aboriginal land rights and self-determination. The protests engendered popular respect and growing support for Aboriginal people. The Aboriginal activists who emerged in the late 1960s drew their inspiration from the Black Power movement in the United States, which emphasised militancy, black solidarity and struggle. The ideas of Marcus Garvey, Malcolm X and the Black Panther Party influenced Aboriginal activists in Australia. Black Power demanded the right of Aboriginal people to speak for themselves, to organise themselves and work together to effect change; it signified the Aboriginal struggle and resistance against colonisation, but it was also invoked to spread fear amongst white people. Aboriginal activists in Sydney, Melbourne and Brisbane rejected violence in favour of nonviolent, direct action but embraced the language, ideology and practice of black consciousness as a means with which to respond to the political hegemony of the state and police terror tactics against Aboriginal people in inner-city Aboriginal communities.[76] These activists developed a range of self-help organisations for inner-city Aboriginal people to obtain free legal advice, as well as medical and housing assistance. They also developed ideas around land rights, economic independence, cultural integrity and self-determination.[77]

The Tent Embassy protest was sustained for six months and has become a national symbol of Aboriginal protest. Representing the defiant Aboriginal demands for self-determination, the Aboriginal Embassy was the beginning of a new era of Aboriginal resistance and struggle for justice.[78] It is also an example of white Australians taking up the challenge to support Aboriginal aspirations and their claims for recognition.[79] Today, this challenge still remains for white Australians who are again called upon to respond to and cooperate with Aboriginal people in their attempts to decolonise the Australian constitutional order.[80]

The courage of the Aboriginal Embassy protestors, their white supporters and the forceful physical response of the police changed Australian public opinion and led to a turning point in Aboriginal policy. The Whitlam Labor government, elected in December 1972, shifted away from the policy of assimilation, assumed full responsibility for Aboriginal affairs and was committed to addressing the historical disadvantage of Aboriginal people through self-determination and to including Aboriginal people in the process of government.[81] According to Whitlam, the object of his government policy was 'to restore to the Aboriginal people of Australia their lost power of self-determination in economic, social and political affairs'.[82]

The Whitlam government instituted several reforms including the establishment of a Department of Aboriginal Affairs and the taking over of remaining state Aboriginal welfare authorities, except for Queensland's. The Whitlam government also encouraged the development of incorporated community-based Aboriginal organisations to conduct community affairs and deliver government-funded services. It established a Royal Commission to examine how land rights could be recognised, especially in the Northern Territory where the Commonwealth had jurisdictional

control. It also established the National Aboriginal Consultative Committee (NACC), a national elected body of forty-one Indigenous people, to
advise on Indigenous affairs.[83] The government also outlined its intention to ratify International Labour Organisation Convention (No. 107)
dealing with Indigenous and tribal populations and indicated it would
ratify the International Convention for the elimination of all forms of
racial discrimination by introducing general legislation to outlaw acts of
racial discrimination.[84]

Consultation with Aboriginal people, Aboriginal representation in
policymaking, and recognition of land rights were major planks of the
government's self-determination policy. The policy of self-determination
was focussed on self-management and self-reliance in tackling social dis-
advantages in the areas of health care, housing, education and vocational
training, enabling Aboriginal groups and communities to determine their
own decision-making processes and decide their own future.[85] However,
for Coombs and the Council for Aboriginal Affairs, 'self-determination'
was more about empowering local Aboriginal communities to act in a
wide range of issues of community concern so that they may adapt their
customary laws and traditions to the needs of the present. This did not
include a department of Aboriginal affairs, but rather reformed Indigenous programmes carried out by an array of functional departments
dealing with local incorporated Aboriginal organisations that would implement programmes focussing on community welfare, recreation, culture and art, the education of preschool children, and the provision of
legal and medical services. A national representative body would evolve
through initiatives of local Aboriginal organisations, councils and corporations.[86]

For the federal labour government, Aboriginal representation in poli-
cy-making involved the election of an Aboriginal consultative council at
the national level and the recruitment of Aboriginal people into the Australian Public Service to encourage the Aboriginalisation of the public
service. But there was little consideration of whether a national body
could speak authoritatively on behalf of diverse Aboriginal people
around the nation, and the government gave little thought to the potential conflict between the advocacy role of Aboriginal people appointed to
the public service and the traditional expectations of public servants.[87]

The government abolished the Department of Interior in December
1972, however, to the dismay of many Aboriginal leaders, personnel from
the Department and the Northern Territory Welfare Branch were relocat-
ed to the new Department of Aboriginal Affairs. It was a turbulent time
in Aboriginal affairs. Charles Perkins, the assistant secretary in charge of
the consultative and liaison branch, frequently criticised the department
as well as government policy and attitudes. He wanted a much greater
Aboriginal representation with the department and to establish the National Aboriginal Consultative Committee as an independent voice out-

side of the department.[88] Charles Perkins is a significant Indigenous leader and activist who was born in Alice Springs. While studying at Sydney University he led a group of students on a 'Freedom Ride', a bus tour through rural New South Wales, exposing poor living conditions and discrimination against Aboriginal people in country towns. He later joined the Commonwealth Public Service in Canberra and in 1984 became secretary of the Department of Aboriginal Affairs.

While the change from assimilation to self-determination was a turning point, the real transformation was the growing assertiveness of Indigenous people to take control of their affairs and determine their own future. This assertiveness, along with the influence of the Council for Aboriginal Affairs, was effective in changing Indigenous policy. As a result, there were significant advances in the 1970s and 1980s. The policy of self-determination and self-management provided the space for Indigenous people to input government policymaking and enabled key Indigenous aspirations to be discussed as public policy. But residual paternalism within government and societal resistance to recognising Indigenous rights would ensure the ultimate failure of these initiatives.

THE LIMITS TO ABORIGINAL SELF-DETERMINATION

The NACC was not prepared to be a docile consultative body and pushed for greater impact in Aboriginal affairs decision-making. The NACC began as an interim body to advise the minister, Gordon Bryant, on how best to form a national representative body. However, from the start the committee was keen to impose its agenda. They asked for Aboriginal reserve land and settlements to be handed over to Aboriginal ownership, for recognition of prior Aboriginal ownership of Australia including compensation for dispossession and for all monies allocated to federal and state departments for Aboriginal programmes to be placed under the control of the NACC.[89] At its inaugural meeting in December 1973, the NACC specifically pressed for reserved Aboriginal seats in state and federal parliaments as well as the Northern Territory Legislative Council and for Aboriginal representation on several commissions and boards. The NACC also proposed a public relations programme to educate white Australians about the prior occupation rights of Aboriginal people. It further called for a commission on land rights to be established, for compensation for loss of land and for a royal commission into police brutality towards Aboriginal people throughout Australia, especially in Western Australia.[90]

In February 1974, the NACC resolved to become an independent body known as the 'National Aboriginal Congress' with the aim to achieve direct responsibility of government funding for Aboriginal affairs. The NACC also declared its intention to make the Department of Aboriginal

Affairs their secretariat and to assume the role of that department.[91] The NACC sought to incorporate an association to receive funds for a secretariat and for administration of the NACC's affairs, however the NACC was still regarded as an advisory body[92] with no change in role or control over its own expenditure ever eventuating. There was some resistance within the government and the Department of Aboriginal Affairs (DAA). Aboriginal Liberal senator, Neville Bonner, argued that the NACC would be a 'separate Aboriginal Parliament' that would divide Aboriginal people among themselves and from the rest of the Australian community.[93] The DAA was wary of the NACC trying to establish a wider role and felt the NACC did not provide useful advice to the minister, the government or the department. In reality, the DAA rarely sought the advice of the NACC and when it did the advice it sought was limited to seeking nominations of Aboriginal people to various committees.[94] The DAA was unsympathetic to the NACC, believing the NACC's formation was hasty and ill-conceived and that Aboriginal people did not want a national organisation. They felt the NACC was an alien structure to 'tribal Aboriginals', that could not serve their interests, and they found the NACC's assertiveness unacceptable.[95]

But there was more to the DAA's lack of sympathy. Within the department and among government officials, there was a problem of attitude towards Aboriginal people. Public servants in the DAA were unable to throw off colonial attitudes about Aboriginal people and accept the new direction in Aboriginal affairs.[96] According to Charles Perkins, public servants were not happy about being accountable to Aboriginal people. Perkins said he could not tolerate the 'blind ignorance, racism and lack of humanity' from senior officers in government.[97] The persistence of assimilationist and protectionist attitudes as well as 'profound and widespread ignorance' compounded the lack of experience within public service when it came to dealing with Aboriginal people.[98] The consistent view within government at the time was that 'part-descent' or 'mixed-blood' Aboriginal people were not 'real' Aboriginal people and that they shouted down 'traditional' people.[99] Further, DAA officials did not think an Aboriginal officer was any better at mediating between the department and 'traditional' Aboriginal people. They felt that the push for Aboriginalisation of the department came from a group of 'urbanised intellectuals'.[100]

Perkins also considered the Council for Aboriginal Affairs a paternalistic body with too much control over Aboriginal policy.[101] Coombs and his colleagues were concerned about Perkins' outspokenness and its impact on the DAA and about the NACC's aspirations to be the body in charge of Aboriginal affairs policy. It was feared that it would become a channel for the political energies of dissident and ambitious Aboriginal people, reflecting the political ideas and ambitions of urban Aboriginal people rather than traditionally based communities.[102] The Council of

Aboriginal Affairs believed that local organisations were the preferable instruments of Aboriginal decisions and for spending public money. While Perkins and the NACC showed strength and resistance by highlighting the dissatisfaction of Aboriginal people, they had established 'how far the Whites were prepared to go' in allowing Aboriginal people control of their own affairs. When the momentum of demand for change had passed from mainly white people to predominantly black people, Aboriginal people were met with hostility.[103]

The dismissal of the Whitlam Labor Party government in November 1975 and the election of the Fraser Liberal Coalition government saw changes to the NACC and Aboriginal affairs, including terminating the role of the Council of Aboriginal Affairs. The Fraser government's Aboriginal affairs policy focussed on promoting 'self-management and self-sufficiency'.[104] The new minister considered that having a national body sitting between the government and Aboriginal people, able to control and use public funds, was incompatible with the parliamentary system of government. The Fraser government undertook a review of the DAA and established an inquiry into the NACC. The Hiatt Inquiry concluded that the NACC had not functioned as a consultative committee, had not been effective in providing advice to government on Aboriginal policies and programmes and that most Aboriginal people did not know of the activities of the NACC. However, the inquiry found widespread support for a national Aboriginal body, although Aboriginal people in Arnhem Land expressed disgust about the NACC's militancy.[105]

The Hiatt Report recommended the NACC become a National Congress that would have formal meetings at State Branch, National Executive and National Congress level. It also recommended the creation of a statutory commission for Aboriginal development, with both appointed members and National Aboriginal Conference (NAC) delegates to function as an advisory body to the minister for Aboriginal Affairs.[106] The NACC was replaced with the NAC, comprising thirty-five members who would meet annually at the national level, with members in each state or territory meeting twice a year. Ian Viner, the minister for Aboriginal Affairs, also announced the formation of the Council for Aboriginal Development, a formal advisory body to the minister for Aboriginal Affairs.[107] The creation of the Council for Aboriginal Development effectively sidelined the NAC, relegating it to a 'debating society'.[108] Ultimately, the government only wanted an advisory body, not a form of Indigenous government.

The NAC was formalised in October 1978 as an Aboriginal corporation, enabling it to establish a limited secretariat and administer its own budget outside the direct control of the DAA. However, while NAC members aspired to real power and influence over Aboriginal policy, they lacked experience and knowledge of government, had limited resources and were poorly supported in policy research. The Commonwealth government had no intention of bestowing any real power or status on the NAC. Rob Riley and Peter Yu—two Western Australians elected to the NAC in 1981—attempted to bring an organised political approach lifting the profile of the NAC. However, the NAC was undermined by the lack of recognition from state and Commonwealth governments. The NAC became largely irrelevant as the newly emerging statutory land councils in the Northern Territory began to change the dynamics of Aboriginal politics.[109] The NAC was terminated in 1985, but not before it was involved in some significant public policy issues such as a treaty and national land rights.

NO TREATY OR MAKARRATA

Jack Davis, president of the Western Australian Aboriginal Association, raised the need for a treaty with Aboriginal people in 1969.[110] In March 1972, the Gwalwa Daraniki Larrakia group in Darwin sent a petition to the prime minister demanding the government appoint a treaty commission and provide legal assistance to each tribe. But Prime Minister McMahon considered it inappropriate to negotiate with British subjects as though they were foreign powers. In September 1974, Aboriginal Senator Neville Bonner (Liberal Queensland) introduced a motion into the Senate calling for recognition of prior ownership and compensation to Aboriginal and Torres Strait Islander people for their dispossession. The motion was passed unanimously on 20 February 1975, but thereafter lay dormant.[111] Bonner argued that money allocated for Indigenous people was government charity and implied a 'handout mentality'. He wanted a 'true and due entitlement for dispossession'. Bonner asked for an amount of money to be set aside from the annual national budget as compensation for loss of land and 'enforced disintegration', which would be channelled through a statutory Aboriginal and Torres Strait Islander body.[112]

In September 1976, Stewart Harris wrote in the *Canberra Times* that a 'Treaty of Commitment' with Aboriginal people would provide resources for Aboriginal development through the allocation of an agreed fixed proportion of annual royalties on minerals and forestry, fishing and hunting products on all the land of Australia. The treaty would also promise a fixed proportion of the total budget every year for the Department of Aboriginal Affairs. Finally, the exploitation of minerals and forestry, fishing and hunting on Aboriginal reserve land would be a matter of negotiation between the Aboriginal owners, the government and the interested company, giving Aboriginal people a say in exploitation of these resources.[113]

In April 1979, Coombs convened the Aboriginal Treaty Committee with six people, aiming to influence and mobilise Australian opinion for a treaty. He said a treaty was necessary to establish a constitutional relationship between Aboriginal people and Australian society and to bring an end to hostilities between black and white Australians.[114] Coombs felt that white Australians had a serious problem with reconciling invasion, dispossession and violence with their own moral code and that the grievances of Indigenous people would not go away unless white Australians removed the causes.[115] The Aboriginal Treaty Committee took out a full-page advertisement in the *National Times* in August 1979 explaining that a treaty freely negotiated with the Commonwealth government was required to make a just settlement with Aboriginal and Torres Strait Islanders and to recognise their status and rights.[116] The advertisement suggested a method of dialogue, whereby the Commonwealth government should enable the NAC to convene a meeting of Aboriginal representatives to choose negotiators, propose the basis of negotiations and settlement, organise negotiations and submit a treaty to Parliament for ratification.

The NAC took up the idea of a 'Makarrata' treaty in April 1979, forming a sub-committee to consult Aboriginal people in relation to the proposal. Fred Chaney, minister for Aboriginal Affairs, welcomed the NAC initiatives and affirmed the government's willingness to join discussions as the proposal moved forward.[117] But the government's readiness in accepting the NAC proposal raised suspicions among a group of Aboriginal protestors who had set up a tent protest on Capitol Hill in Canberra, calling themselves the National Aboriginal Government of Australia. They called for a federal Aboriginal bill of rights and a treaty of commitment from the federal government. The protestors feared the NAC would come under pressure to conclude an agreement without proper consultation. The Aboriginal Treaty Committee was also suspicious of the government's readiness to consider NAC demands.[118]

The NAC consulted with Aboriginal communities in all States and the Northern Territory over several weeks in 1980 and found that many people were not familiar with the idea of a treaty, wanting more time to consider it. People were also divided on the use of the words 'treaty' and 'Makarrata'.[119] Reporting on its consultations, the NAC stated the Makarrata would recognise prior ownership of Aboriginal people and would involve compensation for loss of culture and land through a percentage of gross national product. It would also pursue recognition for a range of other matters, including teaching of Aboriginal culture in schools; the reservation of seats in Commonwealth, state and local governments; the recognition of National Aborigines Day as a public holiday; the honouring of Aboriginal heroes and the identification of Aboriginal places of struggle; a fixed proportion of Aboriginal people employed in government; and return of Aboriginal human remains and artifacts from museums.[120]

Coombs advised the NAC of the need for an effective communication process with Aboriginal groups and organisations, more time for discussion, and further resources for the NAC to undertake consultations and fund research. Coombs proposed a six-step process in which the NAC would commission options papers to be circulated to Aboriginal communities and organisations. The NAC would then call Aboriginal representatives to a convention to discuss the option papers, after which the representatives would discuss the issues with their communities. Convention representatives would then be recalled to consider a first draft of an agreement for submission to government and the convention would remain in existence to consider issues during negotiations and to approve or reject the provisional agreement.[121] The notion of a treaty was not acceptable to the attorney general, Peter Durack, because in his view Aboriginal people did not constitute a domestic dependent nation and any agreement that was accorded the status of treaty would risk Aboriginal claims to self-determination. The attorney general said Parliament could enact legislation to formalise obligations to Aboriginal Australians and provide compensation for past treatment, but the term 'compensation' could not be used in a legal sense. The attorney general also advised against use of the word 'dispossession'.[122]

In early 1981, the minister for Aboriginal Affairs, Senator Peter Baume, said the government was prepared to acknowledge prior Aboriginal occupation of Australia but could not legitimately negotiate a 'treaty' as this implied an internationally recognised agreement between two nations. The government was not prepared to act unilaterally in areas where states had an interest, and therefore return of tribal lands, including sacred sites and freehold title, should be taken up by NAC with the states. He said the government could not agree to a fixed percentage of gross national product as compensation nor any fixed financial commitment into the future. Further, the government would not agree to reserved seats for Aboriginal people in the Commonwealth Parliament, seeing special representation in state parliaments and local government bodies was a matter for the states. As for employment, the government did not believe in a fixed formula for Aboriginal employment in government bodies and would continue to promote existing employment schemes.[123] Despite having expressed early support for the concept of a treaty, the Fraser government effectively stymied the NAC's aspirations for treaty. The Commonwealth government was not prepared to play a role in leading Makarrata discussions with the states, creating further difficulties, as the NAC would have to negotiate with each State as well as the Commonwealth government. The NAC demonstrated a strong stance on the treaty, arguing that Aboriginal people should at least be recognised as a 'domestic dependent nation'. The NAC also argued it should have corporate standing and statutory functions to enable it to facilitate the Aboriginal discussion to determine the content of the treaty and negotiate the Makarrata on behalf of Aboriginal people.[124]

However, concerns existed regarding whether the NAC, as a government body, had the mandate to represent Aboriginal people. Specifically, there was unease that the NAC was being pressured by the government into a short time frame and was pursuing a treaty without proper consultations. The NAC suggested a two-phase negotiation process for a Makarrata involving: (1) the negotiation of a short nationwide agreement in principle to be possibly entrenched in the Constitution; and (2) the negotiation of a more detailed agreement for various regions. [125] Criticism of the NAC came to the fore during the Third Assembly of the World Council of Indigenous Peoples (WCIP), which was developing an international covenant on the rights of Indigenous people. The NAC hosted the WCIP in Canberra in April through May 1981 and were the only accredited representatives for Australian Indigenous people. The WCIP organising committee was asked to accredit Aboriginal speakers outside the NAC because it was a government created organisation. A separate Aboriginal forum was organised, whereby the NAC was criticised for its monopoly over political representation and it was asked to disassociate itself from any negotiations for a Makarrata. [126]

The NAC called a public meeting in Canberra in August 1981 where more than sixty representatives of Aboriginal communities in southern and western New South Wales called on the NAC to prepare a draft Makarrata proposal and submit it to government. [127] The NAC were determined to pursue the Makarrata, sending a further list of items to the government to be added to the Makarrata proposal. [128] However, scepticism about the role of the NAC in the Makarrata process continued to grow. Concerns were raised that the NAC had buckled to the government's demand to have a draft document prepared in time for the Commonwealth Heads of Government Meeting. [129] The National Federation of Land Councils condemned the Makarrata as a 'confidence trick' by the federal government and rejected the treaty on the basis of insufficient consultation with Aboriginal people and because it would legalise occupation and use of Aboriginal lands by the Australian settler state. The National Federation emphasised that Aboriginal people had never ceded sovereignty and declared that Aboriginal people were being pressured into signing an agreement before the bicentennial year. [130]

There was concern that the government could not be trusted to honour the treaty and that white Australians may see it as a denial of what they regarded as rightfully theirs. There were also concerns about whether a treaty could guarantee every day basic human needs in addition to recognising continuing Aboriginal sovereignty. In September 1981, the Standing Committee on Constitutional and Legal Affairs in the Australian Senate established an inquiry into the feasibility of a 'Makarrata' between the Commonwealth government and Aboriginal people. In its report it concluded that Aboriginal people did not have sovereignty and so could not negotiate with the Commonwealth as a sovereign entity. The

Standing Committee admitted that Aboriginal people had sovereignty at the time of 'settlement', but as a 'legal proposition' no longer held sovereignty except sharing in the common sovereignty of all people in the Commonwealth of Australia. It recommended that the Commonwealth should consider an amendment by referendum to the Constitution by inserting a provision (like Section 105A) that would give the Commonwealth power to enter a compact with the NAC as the representatives of Aboriginal people. The compact should work contemporaneously with resolutions of specific issues such as adequate standard of housing, health care, and welfare facilities as well as recognition of Aboriginal culture and law. Such a compact would go beyond being a 'shopping list' of demands for compensation for injury done to Aboriginal people but would be a 'formal symbol, denoting the achievement of a sound footing in the relationship between Aboriginal and non-Aboriginal Australians'.[131]

According to the Standing Committee, the compact would establish a new framework through which to conduct the relationship. The compact would recognise that Aboriginal people would have legitimate rights to claims, not as a disadvantaged group, but as recognised prior owners of Australia. The Standing Committee also said it would be necessary for the Commonwealth to sponsor programmes to raise community consciousness for an informed discussion, which was necessary in the Aboriginal community to build an understanding of the idea of a compact.[132]

NATIONAL LAND RIGHTS AND THE NEW RIGHT

The election of the Hawke Labor government in March 1983 promised a new approach, including restoring the policy of self-determination and legislating for uniform land rights. According to Clyde Holding, minister for Aboriginal Affairs, the government's approach was based on 'consultation and self-determination', where Aboriginal people would be completely involved in the process. More resources would be provided to the NAC and it would have regular access to the Department of Aboriginal Affairs and the minister. A major government policy issue was land rights based on five principles of inalienable freehold title, protection of sacred sites, control in relation to mining, mining royalty equivalents and compensation for lost land. The Hawke government aimed to establish principles for reconciliation by the bicentennial year of 1988, through which the nation could come to terms with its history and make amends with Aboriginal people. Clive Holding said this would involve the restoration of land rights and recognition of prior ownership and occupation, albeit without undermining Australia's sovereignty. Holding insisted that Australians could no longer live with the 'naive and arrogant concept' that Australia was terra nullius, and that Aboriginal people were not people at all.[133]

The Hawke government came to power promising national land rights, but their good intentions were significantly thwarted by a shift in Liberal Party ideology. The Liberal Coalition Party, which originally supported and passed land rights legislation for the Northern Territory in 1976, began to shift to an increasingly negative position on Aboriginal land rights after the defeat of the Fraser Liberal Coalition government in 1983. This began with attacks by 'radical liberals' on the Fraser government for not implementing free market policies and the rise of a 'counterestablishment' network after the 1980s that advocated for free market polices such as small government, lower taxation, lower protection, low inflation, industry and financial deregulation, decentralisation of wage fixation, needs-based welfare, genuine competition, attack on trade unions and allowing markets to set prices. This was supported by an intellectual movement to promote radical free market philosophy and shape the public debate, as evidenced by the formation or revival of influential right wing think tanks. [134]

The rise of radical free market economic policy referred to as the New Right or Neoliberalism was concerned with wealth creation and the rule of market forces, and so was philosophically opposed to addressing social and economic disadvantage in society through publicly funded programmes. The New Right also set about changing social values and political culture by attacking welfare and affirmative action policies, and by attacking intellectuals and others who supported such policies. Within this context, attacks were launched on Aboriginal culture, so-called revisionist historians and so-called welfare industries. This conservative mobilisation gained traction between 1983 and 1985 through the public advocacy of Hugh Morgan, executive director of Western Mining Corporation, and Professor Geoffrey Blainey of the University of Melbourne. As the New Right aligned itself with the traditions of Australian raced-based nationalism, racial politics began to re-emerge in Australia. Hugh Morgan attacked Aboriginal society and Aboriginal rights. Geoffrey Blainey, although supportive of minimal Aboriginal land rights, was instrumental in attacking Asian immigration. Both men were influential in giving form to public debates as they attacked policies of land rights, immigration, multiculturalism, affirmative action and so-called revisionist history. They attacked policies that they believed catered to minorities, and they attacked and opposed what they believed were interest groups who were trying to overthrow the 'Australian way of life', warning that such policies would lead to national destruction. [135]

Aboriginal land rights were attacked as separatist and a threat to the nation, and government Aboriginal programmes and expenditure were depicted as wasteful. The Opposition Liberal Coalition utilised this negative discourse about Aboriginal policy and expenditure to attack the Labor government's stance on national land rights. The Opposition rejected land rights legislation including the handing back of Uluru and the Kata Tjuta in the Northern Territory, on the basis that the natural rock monoliths were 'national monuments' belonging to all Australians and part of the nationhood of Australia.[136] In their view, handing back the ownership of these rock formations to the Mutitjulu community reduced the rights of other Australians.[137] This nationalistic argument implied that the government was favouring the Aboriginal community by giving away land that belonged to the Australian people.

The liberals argued that national land rights should be abandoned because it was harming the relations between Aboriginal and non-Aboriginal Australians and dividing the nation. They argued that land rights had stalled advancement in areas of real need such as health care, education, housing and employment.[138] However, the liberals also argued that an enormous amount of money was being spent on no more than three hundred thousand Aboriginal people and that funding such programmes ran the risk of creating 'administrative apartheid' where a bureaucratic system was being created for the needs of a specific section of the Australian community. This in turn has resulted in a significant degree of Aboriginal dependence on the Australian population.[139] The subtle use of terms such as the 'divisiveness' of land rights and 'administrative apartheid' was designed to create outrage in the Australian community by presenting a perception that land rights and the funding of Aboriginal programmes was a threat to Australian nationalism.

Australian federalism also proved a stumbling block to the Hawke government. While the 1967 referendum ensured Commonwealth power to legislate for Aboriginal people, the states also retained powers relating to land ownership, land use, health care, education, social welfare and housing, which are not easily overridden by the Commonwealth. In that regard the Commonwealth government could only set standards for national land rights, which it hoped the states would follow.[140] Clyde Holding's strategy was to encourage the state and territory governments to legislate for Aboriginal land rights commensurate with Commonwealth standards; if they didn't oblige then the federal government would adopt overriding legislation.

Clyde Holding established an Aboriginal Land Rights Steering Committee to make political policy for the land rights legislation after consultations with Aboriginal people.[141] He also established a panel of lawyers to draft the legislation.[142] But he tended to disregard the advice of the Steering Committee and imposed rigid deadlines on the committee to endorse policy decisions he and others had made, on occasion even informing the committee after he had made a policy decision. A discussion paper prepared by the Department of Aboriginal Affairs was presented to the Steering Committee in August 1984 outlining the parameters of federal legislation. Neither the Steering Committee nor the panel of lawyers had seen the document before the meeting. Holding argued that setting out the parameters of the legislation was necessary to defuse growing anti-land rights pressure, to ensure it was acceptable to the federal government and to form a basis for consultation with the states, miners, rural and other concerned interests. The Steering Committee rejected proposals regarding the categories of land available for claim, the establishment of state tribunals to hear land claims and the control of Aboriginal land regarding mining. The Steering Committee said they would prepare position papers on areas of disagreement with the discussion paper, but political events would eventually overtake them.[143]

In August 1985, the federal cabinet endorsed the preferred national land rights model put forward by Clyde Holding, which enabled states to implement consistent land rights legislation rather than have overriding Commonwealth legislation. The national model would provide inalienable freehold title to Aboriginal groups pursuant to a claims process, with former Aboriginal reserves and missions, vacant Crown land and Commonwealth national parks available for claim. Land could be granted based on traditional entitlement, historical association, long-term occupation or for specific purposes. There was no right of veto for Aboriginal people over exploration and mining on their land, but only a right to negotiate an agreement.[144]

In response to the Commonwealth preferred model, the states and the Northern Territory said land rights and land use were a state responsibility and that Commonwealth legislation should only apply to those states with no legislation. The mining and pastoral industries similarly argued that the particular land title should not be too restrictive for commercial development and that Aboriginal land should be capable of resumption. The mining industry felt that Aboriginal consent for exploration and mining was a 'de facto' veto. Both the mining and pastoral industries said the Land Rights Act in the Northern Territory should be amended based on the preferred model. By contrast Aboriginal organisations felt the model did not meet the five principles and that there should be further consultations with Aboriginal people.[145] They argued the category of land available for claim was too restrictive and that Aboriginal land should not be appropriated other than by an act of Parliament. Further, Aboriginal people should have the power to veto and control mining and exploration. Church groups expressed similar views.[146]

The Commonwealth government's approach to national land rights changed when Western Australian labour premier Brian Burke met with the federal cabinet in September 1984. Burke opposed major elements of the Seaman Report on recognising Aboriginal land rights in Western Australia and he advised that land rights were politically explosive electorally.[147] The mining industry argued that future growth of the industry would also be affected if mining provisions like the Northern Territory Land Rights Act were adopted nationally. The federal cabinet believed it

necessary to balance Aboriginal land rights with the rights of major economic interests, namely the mining industry. Pressure from Brian Burke
forced Prime Minister Bob Hawke to unilaterally remove Aboriginal
negotiation powers regarding exploration and mining, undermining
Clyde Holding on land rights legislation. This decision was made without consultation with the federal cabinet, ALP caucus or prior discussions with the minister for Aboriginal Affairs. The NAC felt that the
Commonwealth government had caved in on their principles of land
rights and that the Western Australian legislation would become the
model for national land rights. As it was clear the federal government
would not override states in land rights the NAC recommended that all
Aboriginal organisations reject the Western Australian legislation, as well
as all state legislation.[148]

In February 1985, the NAC and the Federation of Land Councils boy-
cotted the proposed Steering Committee meeting and the meeting with
the ALP caucus subcommittee on Aboriginal affairs, marking the end of
their Steering Committee participation. Instead, they resolved to advance
and protect Aboriginal land rights through a public campaign against the
federal government's action. They were angry that the government had
rejected the NAC requests for access to cabinet proposals and for federal
ministers to attend a Steering Committee meeting. In a joint statement,
the NAC and Federation of Land Councils called on the federal government to intervene in Western Australia in regards to its proposed land
rights legislation; to make no changes to the Northern Territory Aboriginal Land Rights Act without the consent of the land councils; not to
proceed with national land rights legislation; to convene a national summit on land rights; and to take immediate action to ensure Indigenous
peoples can develop acceptable national principles for a proper relationship between Indigenous peoples and all governments. The Aboriginal
organisations' public campaign included a national Aboriginal summit in
May 1985 and a delegation to the United Nations in July 1985 to protest
the Hawke government action. But there was little impact on government
land rights policy. In July 1985, the government terminated the NAC. The
land councils in the Northern Territory went on to fight a successful
campaign to stop the federal government from amending the Northern
Territory Land Rights Act of 1976 and removing the mining veto from
that act.[149]

The Western Australian Chambers of Mines supported by the Australian Mining Industry Council (AMIC) successfully campaigned against
the Seaman Inquiry recommendations on Aboriginal land rights in Western Australia and against national land rights. The campaign exerted
public pressure on the Burke government and Hawke government to
influence the political outcome of the land rights issue. It involved an
aggressive 'belt level' newspaper and television advertising campaign to
harness underlying social prejudice against Aboriginal people, reinforc-

ing public opposition to land rights. The campaign forced the Burke Labor government to reach an agreement with the Chamber of Mines on
acceptable principles for state land rights legislation. It also forced the
Burke government into a strategy of co-opting the mining industry to
support the land rights bill, to defuse the issue of land rights in Western
Australia. Industry groups, miners, pastoralists and farmers were included on the committee, which drafted the Aboriginal land rights bill.
When the bill was subsequently defeated in the upper house of State
Parliament, Brian Burke went on to wage a successful political battle
against the federal government's national land rights legislation.[150]

To isolate the Liberal Party in its campaign against land rights in
Western Australia, the Burke government won the support of major industry for the state land rights legislation and sought assurances from the
federal government not to impose overriding national land rights legislation in Western Australia. Brian Burke persuaded the prime minister to
issue a public statement in October 1984 and January 1986 that the federal
government would not override any land rights legislation in Western
Australia. The prime minister and the right wing of the Labor Party were
prepared to compromise the Clyde Holding principles on land rights in
the interest of the political survival of the Burke government. However,
left and central-left factions of the Federal Labor Party opposed this position. Brian Burke's Labor government easily won the Western Australian
election in February 1986 on a platform opposed to any land rights legislation. Burke warned the federal government that if it tried to pursue
national land rights it would encounter the same kind of political opposition it had encountered in Western Australia. A compromise deal was
worked out between the Federal Labor Party government and the Western Australian government shortly after the elections. The elements of the
agreement included no overriding federal land rights legislation and
progress of land rights on a state-by-state basis, although there would be
a funding package for Western Australia, retention of the mining veto in
the Northern Territory Land Rights Act and no change in the national
Labor Party Aboriginal land rights policy.[151]

By March 1986, the federal government had abandoned its promise of
national land rights legislation. In his address to Parliament, Clyde Holding tried to positively spin the government's retreat. The Opposition Coalition Party called Holding's speech an admission of failure of the
government's land rights policy and cynically welcomed the government
in accepting Coalition policy: that land rights for Aboriginal people could
only be achieved through state legislation and with community support.[152] *The Canberra Times* claimed it was the 'obdurate opposition' of the
Western Australian Labor Party to land rights, which precipitated the
government's shameful back down on land rights. The editorial stated
that the government lacked courage, dishonoured undertakings to Aboriginal representatives, and in the middle of the process disbanded the

Aboriginal national voice and had done nothing about replacing it. The editorial further stated that the government did nothing to counter the campaign of fear and misinformation of the mining industry and its negative impact was used by the government to justify its back down.[153]

RECONCILIATION WITHOUT RECOGNITION

The desire for reconciliation with Indigenous people began in December 1983 when Clyde Holding, minister of Aboriginal Affairs in the Hawke Labor government, spoke of a need for reconciliation when presenting a motion to Parliament outlining the major Aboriginal policy initiatives of the government. The impetus for reconciliation from the government's perspective was the approaching bicentennial year celebrations of 1988, providing an opportunity to not only contemplate the nation's achievements but to come to terms with its history and to make amends with the Aboriginal people.[154] Clyde Holding considered the government's policy programme to be the beginning of a process of reconciliation where the nation would come to terms with its own history, make amends and provide some redress to Indigenous people. In its move towards reconciliation as a framework for justice, the Hawke government announced a Royal Commission into Aboriginal Deaths in Custody in August 1987 after a political campaign and lobbying by the National Committee to Defend Black Rights. In July 1987, Hawke announced the creation of the Aboriginal and Torres Strait Islander Commission (ATSIC), established as an instrument of Aboriginal self-determination where Indigenous people would be involved in the decision-making process of government.[155] John Howard, leader of the opposition, said the ATSIC legislation 'strikes at the heart' of Australian unity and that the creation of ATSIC would 'create more resentment and more division'.[156]

When Australia celebrated its bicentenary on 26 January 1988, after two hundred years of European colonisation, it ignored Indigenous aspirations and demands. In opposition to the dominant view of the meaning of Australia Day and to highlight past and ongoing injustices, Indigenous people staged a large protest march for 'peace, hope and justice' from Redfern Oval to Hyde Park in Sydney. There was also a second protest march from Redfern to Lady Macquarie's Chair where activists had established a tent embassy.[157] According to Robert Tickner, who became Aboriginal Affairs minister in April 1990, little attention was paid to Indigenous aspirations as a precondition to celebrating the bicentenary.[158] Avoidance and denial of the historical past were prominent in the public discourse. *The Canberra Times* editorial said it was a shame the original Australians are the most neglected, arguing that the 'problems of Aborigines' would not be solved by 'regurgitating the sins of the past' and that it was 'time for a new cooperative approach that will look to the future'.[159]

Former prime minister Malcolm Fraser said Australians 'should not feel guilty about the sins of 200 years ago because if we are, there isn't a single nation or race on Earth that won't go around feeling guilt-ridden'.[160] A *Canberra Times* opinion piece took the matter further, arguing the current generations of Australians are not responsible for any historical harm and should not have to pay any compensation to today's Aboriginal people.[161]

This rhetoric is unsurprising in the context of the emergence of the New Right and racial politics of the 1980s, which saw the disparaging of Aboriginal rights and culture by conservative intellectuals to reassert colonial values, defend Australian history and sovereignty, and defend the legitimacy of Australian 'settlement'. Hugh Morgan was of the view there was no need for Australians to feel guilty for crimes they did not commit. Geoffrey Blainey believed that Australians were being deceived into doubting their legitimacy and their rights. Morgan and Blainey advocated the extraordinary idea that ideologically-driven anthropologists and historians who were part of a 'guilt industry' were rewriting Australian history to present false and romanticised views of Aboriginal culture and history to create feelings of guilt as a basis for Aboriginal compensation claims.[162]

Indigenous aspirations for a treaty were again placed on the public policy agenda at the Barunga Festival in June 1988, when the Central and Northern Land Councils presented Prime Minister Hawke with a statement of rights and aspirations comprising a series of demands framed by a bark painting, now known as the Barunga Statement. Among the demands was a call for the Commonwealth Parliament to negotiate a treaty or compact 'recognising prior ownership, continued occupation and sovereignty and affirming our human rights'.[163] Hawke promised that a treaty would be negotiated between Aboriginal people and the government by the middle of 1990 and that the government would fund a consultation process that would begin with Aboriginal people deciding what they would like included in the treaty.[164] Opposition leader John Howard said the creation of a treaty between a nation and its own citizens was 'absurd', arguing that it would be divisive, create hostility towards Aboriginal people and 'spawn a form of apartheid'. The Opposition feared that a treaty could open the way for large land claims and a separate sovereign Aboriginal state. Further, the Opposition believed that 'symbolic gestures' would do nothing to 'heal the rift' between Aboriginal people and the rest of Australia and that instead, genuine reconciliation would only be addressed by directing government financial resources towards basic needs.[165]

The idea of a treaty galvanised conservative political opposition, causing Hawke to retreat and instead propose a more politically agreeable concept of reconciliation. Former minister Robert Tickner said the political strategy to achieve change and elevate Indigenous aspirations lay in a reconciliation process to educate Australians about Indigenous issues and build a political movement to address Indigenous aspirations, human rights and social justice.[166] In June 1991, the Australian Parliament unanimously passed legislation instituting a formal ten-year process of reconciliation, conducted through the Council for Aboriginal Reconciliation comprising Indigenous and non-Indigenous members. The aim was to promote reconciliation through education and awareness, address Indigenous disadvantage and aspirations and to consult the Australian community on whether to advance reconciliation by a formal document.[167] However, the formal reconciliation process was destined to fail because at its conclusion the wider community had not become better educated about Indigenous issues, there was no significant improvement in the Indigenous socioeconomic conditions and there was no document of reconciliation.[168]

At the commencement of the formal reconciliation process, the Royal Commission into Aboriginal Deaths in Custody (RCIADIC) delivered its final report. The RCIADIC investigated the overrepresentation of Indigenous deaths in custody, making 339 recommendations. It also looked in detail at issues of Indigenous poverty, inequality and disadvantage in health care, housing, education, employment and income, and made recommendations about reducing and eliminating disadvantage. In his overview report, Commissioner Elliott Johnston contended that understanding the dispossession and deliberate policies and practices of disempowerment of Aboriginal people based on the assumption of superiority and racist attitudes was important in understanding Indigenous disadvantage.[169] Commissioner Johnston saw the 'extraordinary domination' of Indigenous people by non-Indigenous people as the underlying cause of disadvantage, and argued that empowering Indigenous people to control their lives and their communities could eliminate disadvantage, thus affirming the principle of self-determination.

The RCIADIC also recommended that political leaders use their 'best endeavours' to ensure bipartisan public support for a process of reconciliation. Commissioner Johnston said steps needed to be taken to improve relations between Aboriginal and non-Aboriginal people because their relationship was characterised by 'distrust, enmity and disputation'. He said the process of reconciliation must ensure and recognise diversity of Aboriginal opinion and that all Australians needed to understand the country's past and the treatment of Indigenous people. Johnston insisted that only negotiation based on 'mutual respect and equality' would advance reconciliation.[170]

POLITICAL IMBALANCE

Even though the NACC and the NAC were advisory bodies to the Commonwealth government, there were many barriers that excluded Indigenous people from decision-making and constitutional power. Colonial attitudes and ignorance within the DAA denied respect and recognition to Indigenous people and denied the voice of urban Indigenous people. Tensions with Indigenous people from traditional communities caused by the assertiveness of the NACC leadership were reinforced by the DAA, who accused urban or so-called 'mixed blood' Indigenous people of being too assertive. Further, when the NACC was reformed it had no real power or status because the government inserted another advisory body (the Council for Aboriginal Development) between the NAC and the government, thus reinforcing the relationship of subordination. There was a lack of respect and recognition of the NAC from state and Commonwealth governments, which undermined the legitimacy of the NAC.

We have also seen how the Makarrata treaty process was not a joint dialogical process between the federal government, NAC and state governments based on recognition, respect, sharing and responsibility. The Commonwealth and state governments lacked respect for the NAC and Indigenous viewpoints; and their position regarding Indigenous sovereignty was based on 'terra nullius'. Despite the recommendation by the Senate Standing Committee on Constitutional and Legal Affairs for a 'compact', the Commonwealth government considered it could not negotiate a treaty with Indigenous people. There was a distinct lack of commitment from the government, judging by its response to many of the issues raised by the NAC's report on Makarrata and its subsequent reluctance to play a leadership role regarding matters where the states had responsibilities. Criticism and distrust by Indigenous people of the NAC, because of its perceived lack of authority to represent Aboriginal people in negotiations with the government, made it more difficult despite the NAC's strong stance in pursuing the Makarrata.

The Hawke Labor government provided a political platform for Indigenous leaders; however, its approach to national land rights is an example of how government policy approaches can undermine or dismiss Indigenous legitimacy. The government determined the process. Its approach was to draft the legislation and then provide it to the NAC to accept or reject it. Ignoring the advice of the Aboriginal Steering Committee and terminating the NAC at a critical stage of the national land rights process is reflective of ongoing colonial relationships of power between the government and Indigenous people. Although it made progress with several initiatives and achieved 'modest gains' in Indigenous affairs during a period of conservative political resurgence, the Hawke Labor government was not able to deliver its promises in Indigenous affairs.[171]

The Hawke government was balancing the rights and interests of Indigenous people with the interests of state and territory governments as well as the mining and pastoral industries. But government and industry groups have greater political and economic power and privilege and there was no mitigation of any imbalance to give Indigenous people an equal footing in the process. This became obvious when the Western Australian government, under pressure from industry groups, not only opposed the recommendations of its own land rights inquiry but also opposed the Commonwealth's national land rights proposal. In response, the Commonwealth compromised its own principles on national land rights and subsequently abandoned its promise of national land rights using the negative campaign and misinformation of industry to justify its back down. In the conflict between Indigenous policy and Commonwealth-state relations, the Commonwealth favoured the rights and interests of the Western Australian Labor government over the rights and interests of Indigenous people.

The Commonwealth government debacle with the NAC, the treaty and national land rights is a clear illustration of how Australian government is unable to engage equally and respectfully with Indigenous claims for recognition. It is also a reminder of the unequal status and lack of constitutional and political power that Indigenous people have in Australian government. Indigenous claims for recognition are subject to the political whims of Australian federalism and the powerful interests of industry groups. The Hawke Labor government moved to institute a process of reconciliation and created a representative Indigenous body, but by then the social and political environment in Australia had been tainted, especially by the negativity and hostility of the national land rights and treaty debate. Indigenous people had also lost any trust they might have had in the Australian government. Furthermore, judging by the celebration of Australia's bicentenary, the government appeared to lack commitment to cultural pluralism in Australia.

The hostility and negativity regarding national land rights and the treaty was still fresh on the Australian conscience when the Mabo judgment was handed down by the High Court in 1992. Many of the political and social elements affecting the national land rights process can be seen in the way the Commonwealth government dealt with the Mabo judgment in 1992. A major difference by 1992 however, was that a policy of reconciliation with Indigenous people was in place, having been instituted by the Hawke Labor government in the late 1980s. But the power and privilege of state governments and industry and the continuing opposition to Indigenous rights by the New Right would gain further momentum.

NOTES

1. J. Clark, *Aborigines and Activism. Race, Aborigines and the Coming of the Sixties to Australia* (Crawley, WA: University of Western Australia Press, 2008), 203.

2. R. McGregor, 'Another Nation: Aboriginal Activism in the late 1960s and Early 1970', *Australian Historical Studies* 40, no. 3 (2009), 352.

3. The 1967 referendum amended the Australian Constitution to enable Aboriginal people to be counted in the national census and to enable the Commonwealth government to enact special laws for Aboriginal people.

4. Commonwealth of Australia, *Parliamentary Debates*, House of Representatives, Thursday, 7 September 1967, No. 36, 973–75.

5. J. Gorton, *Address by the Prime Minister, Rt. Hon. John Gorton at the Conference of Commonwealth and State Ministers responsible for Aboriginal Affairs at Parliament House*, Melbourne, 12 July 1968.

6. H. C. Coombs, *Trail Balance* (South Melbourne: The MacMillan Company, 1981), 272.

7. Coombs, *Trail Balance*, 279–80; T. Rowse, *Obliged to be Difficult. Nugget Coombs' Legacy in Indigenous Affairs* (Cambridge: Cambridge University Press, 2000), 53, 57.

8. W. McMahon, *Statement by the Prime Minister the Rt. Hon. William McMahon to the Conference of Commonwealth and State Ministers Responsible for Aboriginal Affairs at Cairns*, 23 April 1971.

9. McMahon, *Statement by the Prime Minister at Cairns*, 23 April 1971.

10. Coombs, *Trail Balance*, 281.

11. P. Howson, *The Howson Diaries. The Life of Politics* (Ringwood, Victoria: Penguin Books, 1984), 735, 755–56.

12. Commonwealth of Australia, Parliamentary Debates, House of Representatives, Thursday, 3 September 1970, No. 36, 968 (Peter Nixon).

13. Milirrpum and Others v Nabalco Pty Ltd and The Commonwealth of Australia (1971) 17 FLR 141.

14. Commonwealth of Australia, *Cabinet Minute, Committee on Aboriginal Affairs*, Sydney, 3 August 1971, Decision No. 341 (AA) with attached submission No. 245.

15. Commonwealth of Australia, *Cabinet Minute, Committee on Aboriginal Affairs*, 3 August 1971, Decision No. 341 (AA) with attached Submission No. 285.

16. Commonwealth of Australia, *Cabinet Minute, Committee on Aboriginal Affairs*, Canberra, 13 and 14 October 1971, Decision No. 480 (AA) & 486 (AA).

17. T. Rowse, *Obliged to be Difficult*, 66.

18. Commonwealth of Australia, *Cabinet Minute, Committee on Aboriginal Affairs*, Sydney, 6 December 1971, Decision No. 613 (AA), Submission No. 457.

19. Rowse, *Obliged to be Difficult*, 67.

20. W. McMahon, *Australian Aborigines, Commonwealth Policy and Achievements, Statement by the Prime Minister, the Rt. Hon. William McMahon*, 26 January 1972.

21. McMahon, *Statement by the Prime Minister*, 26 January 1972.

22. McMahon, *Statement by the Prime Minister*, 26 January 1972.

23. Coombs, *Trail Balance*, 290.

24. 'A price on our guilt', *The Australian*, Wednesday, 26 January 1972, 8.

25. Rowse, *Obliged to be Difficult*, 68.

26. K. Gilbert, *Because A White Man'll Never Do It* (Sydney: Angus & Robertson, 1973), 26; G. Briscoe, 'The origins of Aboriginal political consciousness and the Aboriginal Embassy 1907–1972' in *The Aboriginal Embassy: Sovereignty, Black Power, Land Rights and the State*, Gary Foley, Andrew Schaap and Edwina Howell, eds. (Abingdon, Oxon: Routledge Taylor & Francis, 2014), 51.

27. G. Foley, 'An Autobiographical Narrative of the Black Power Movement and the 1972 Aboriginal Embassy' (PhD Dissertation: University of Melbourne, 2012), 95–198; S. Robinson, 'The Aboriginal Embassy: An Account of the protests of 1972', *Aboriginal History* 118, no. 1 (1994), 50–51.

28. 'Aboriginal women gather for conference', *The Canberra Times*, Friday, 28 January 1972, 3.

29. 'Howson hits black power sign', *The Sydney Morning Herald*, 29 January 1972.

30. Foley, 'An Autobiographical Narrative', 199, 201–02; S. Robinson, 'The Aboriginal Embassy', (Master of Arts: Australian National University, 1993), 102–03.

31. 'Aborigines to fly flag', *The Canberra Times*, Wednesday, 2 February 1972, 3; Foley, 'An Autobiographical Narrative',180–84, 200.

32. J. Newfong, 'The Aboriginal Embassy: Its purpose and aims', *Aboriginal & Islander Identity* 1, no. 5, 4–6 July 1972 (Aboriginal Publications Foundation: Perth), 4; Robinson, 'The Aboriginal Embassy', 103.

33. Robinson, 'The Aboriginal Embassy', 104, 135–36.

34. Foley, 'An Autobiographical Narrative', 205.

35. 'Labor promises Aborigines land', *The Canberra Times*, Wednesday, 9 February 1972, 3.

36. P. Eatock, 'Black Demo', in *The Aboriginal Tent Embassy. Sovereignty, Black Power, Land Rights and the State*, Gary Foley, Andrew Schaap and Edwina Howell, eds. (Abingdon, Oxon: Routledge Taylor & Francis, 2014), 143–44; 'Paul Coe & Bobbi Sykes. Monday Conference Interview, ABC Television, 20 March 1972', in *The Aboriginal Tent Embassy. Sovereignty, Black Power, Land Rights and the State*, Gary Foley, Andrew Schaap and Edwina Howell, eds. (Abingdon, Oxon: Routledge Taylor & Francis, 2014), 154–55.

37. Commonwealth of Australia, Parliamentary Debates, House of Representatives, Wednesday, 23 February 1972, No. 8, 125–29 (Gough Whitlam).

38. Commonwealth of Australia, Parliamentary Debates, House of Representatives, Wednesday, 23 February 1972, No. 8, 122–24, 130 (Peter Howson, Ralph Hunt).

39. Commonwealth of Australia, Parliamentary Debates, House of Representatives, Thursday, 11 May 1972, No. 19, 2407.

40. Foley, 'An Autobiographical Narrative' , 225; Robinson, 'The Aboriginal Embassy', 129.

41. Rowse, *Obliged to be Difficult*, 98; Howson, *The Howson Diaries*, 870.

42. Robinson, 'The Aboriginal Embassy', 129.

43. Robinson, 'The Aboriginal Embassy', 124–26; Foley, 'An Autobiographical Narrative', 217–22, 224.

44. H. Goodall, *Invasion to Embassy: Land in Aboriginal Politics in New South Wales 1770-1972* (St Leonards, NSW: Allen & Unwin, 1996), 349.

45. Foley, 'An Autobiographical Narrative', 232–33; Robinson, 'The Aboriginal Embassy', 138–39; Goodall, *Invasion to Embassy*, 350.

46. Police 'to move Aboriginal embassy,' *The Canberra Times*, Tuesday, 18 July 1972, 1.

47. Foley, 'An Autobiographical Narrative', 234–35; Robinson, 'The Aboriginal Embassy 1972', 142–45.

48. 'Criticism follows "embassy" action', *The Canberra Times*, Friday, 21 July 1972, 3.

49. Howson, *The Howson Diaries*, 888.

50. A Turning Point, *The Canberra Times*, Friday, 21 July 1972, 2.

51. G. Whitlam, *The closure of the Aboriginal Embassy*, Statement by the Leader of the Opposition, 20 July 1972 (Canberra, ACT, 1972).

52. Robinson, 'The Aboriginal Embassy', 148, 157.

53. Foley, 'An Autobiographical Narrative', 242–43, Robinson, 'The Aboriginal Embassy', 151–56.

54. S. Harris, *This Our Land* (Canberra, ACT, Australian National University Press, 1972), 28–29.

55. Robinson, 'The Aboriginal Embassy', 159–60.

56. Howson, *The Howson Diaries*, 888–91; Rowse, *Obliged to be Difficult*, 102.

57. Coombs, *Trail Balance*, 291.

58. H. C. Coombs, *Kulinma: Listening to Aboriginal Australians* (Canberra, ACT: Australian National University Press, 1978), 17.

59. Howson, *The Howson Diaries*, 892.

60. Coombs, *Kulinma*, 18–19; Robinson, 'The Aboriginal Embassy', 163; Rowse, *Obliged to be Difficult*, 101–2.

61. Howson, *The Howson Diaries*, 892.

62. Coombs, *Kulinma*, 18.

63. P. Howson and R. Hunt, *Press Statement issued by the Minister for the Interior, Hon. Ralph Hunt, and the Minister for the Environment, Aborigines and Arts, Hon. Peter Howson*, 29 July 1972 (Canberra, ACT, 1972).

64. Foley, 'An Autobiographical Narrative', 250–51; Robinson, 'The Aboriginal Embassy', 166–68.

65. Foley, 'An Autobiographical Narrative', 252–53.

66. Robinson, 'The Aboriginal Embassy', 166, 170–71.

67. 'Speeches at the Aboriginal Embassy 30 July 1972', recorded by Derek Freeman in *The Aboriginal Tent Embassy. Sovereignty, Black Power, land Rights and the State*, Gary Foley, Andrew Schaap and Edwina Howell, eds. (Abingdon, Oxon: Routledge, Taylor & Francis, 2013), 177–80, 182, 186, 188, 189.

68. Harris, *This Our Land*, 99; Robinson, 'The Aboriginal Embassy', 173–74; Rowse, *Obliged to be Difficult*, 109.

69. 'Aboriginal Conference. Demand on land ownership', *The Canberra Times*, Friday, 11 August 1972, 1.

70. Rowse, *Obliged to be Difficult*, 109.

71. 'Aboriginal Conference. Demand on land ownership', *The Canberra Times*, 1; Foley, 'An Autobiographical Narrative', 253–54.

72. *Resolutions by National Conference of Aboriginal Councillors* (Canberra, ACT. 10–11 August 1972).

73. Rowse, *Obliged to be Difficult*, 109–10.

74. E. Howell, 'Black Power—by any means necessary', in *The Aboriginal Tent Embassy. Sovereignty, Black Power, land Rights and the State*, Gary Foley, Andrew Schaap and Edwina Howell, eds. (Abingdon, Oxon: Routledge, Taylor & Francis, 2013), 76, 80.

75. P. Muldoon and A. Schaap, 'The constitutional politics of the Aboriginal Embassy', in *The Aboriginal Tent Embassy. Sovereignty, Black Power, land Rights and the State*, Gary Foley, Andrew Schaap and Edwina Howell, eds. (Abingdon, Oxon: Routledge, Taylor & Francis, 2013), 223, 232.

76. Howell, 'Black Power', 68, 72–74.

77. G. Foley and T. Anderson, 'Land Rights and Aboriginal Voices', *Australian Journal of Human Rights* 12, no. 1 (2006), 89.

78. Howell, 'Black Power', 78; Foley, 'An Autobiographical Narrative', 264–65.

79. Harris, *This Our Land*, 213.

80. Muldoon and Schaap, 'The constitutional politics', 229.

81. B. Attwood and A. Markus, *The Struggle for Aboriginal Rights. A Documentary History* (Sydney, NSW: Allen & Unwin, 1999), 276.

82. G. Whitlam, *Aboriginal and Society*, Statement by the Prime Minister, the Hon. E. G. Whitlam, Conference of Commonwealth and State Ministers concerned with Aboriginal Affairs (Adelaide: Department of Prime Minister and Cabinet, Friday, 6 April 1973).

83. W. Sanders, *Towardss an Indigenous order of Australian Government: Rethinking self-determination as Indigenous affairs policy* (Canberra, ACT: Centre for Aboriginal Economic Policy Research, The Australian National University, 2002), 3.

84. G. M. Bryant, 'Government Policy Towardss Aborigines', *Australian Government Digest* 1, no. 3 (1973).

85. Whitlam, *Aboriginal and Society*; Bryant, 'Government Policy Towardss Aborigines', 899; G. M. Bryant, 'Press Statement 6 April 1973', *Australian Government Digest* 1, no. 2 (1973), 502.

86. Rowse, *Obliged to be Difficult*, 107–8, 110.

87. E. J. Robbins, 'Self-Determination or Welfare Colonialism: Aborigines and Federal Policy Making' (PhD Dissertation: The Flinders University, South Australia, 1994), 130–35.

88. P. Read, *Charles Perkins. A Biography* (Ringwood, Victoria: Penguin Books Australia, 1990), 171–76; Robbins, 'Self-Determination or Welfare Colonialism', 125–26, 133, 138–39; Rowse, *Obliged to be Difficult*, 119.

89. L. R. Hiatt, L. O'Donoghue and J. H. Stanley, *Inquiry into the role of the National Aboriginal Consultative Committee*, Report of the Committee of Inquiry (Canberra, ACT: Commonwealth of Australia, 1976), 13; Robbins, 'Self-Determination or Welfare Colonialism', 136; S. M. Weaver, 'Australian Aboriginal Policy: Aboriginal Pressure Groups or Government Advisory Bodies?' *Oceania* 54, no. 1 (1983), 6.

90. Hiatt et al., *Inquiry into the role*, 16–22.

91. T. O'Leary, 'Advisory capacity to continue', *The Canberra Times*, Wednesday, 13 February 1974, 1, 3; Robbins, 'Self-Determination or Welfare Colonialism', 157–59.

92. Hiatt et al., *Inquiry into the role*, 22–27.

93. Commonwealth of Australia, Parliamentary Debates, Senate, Wednesday, 21 November 1973, No. 47, 2016–2017, 2018–2019 (Neville Bonner).

94. Hiatt et al., *Inquiry into the role*, 33, 36.

95. Weaver, 'Australian Aboriginal Policy', 8–9.

96. Read, *Charles Perkins,* 170–71; Robbins, 'Self-Determination or Welfare Colonialism', 149.

97. C. Perkins, *A Bastard Like Me* (Sydney, NSW: Ure Smith, 1975), 171, 196.

98. H. C. Coombs, P. H. Bailey, E. Campbell, J. E. Isaac and P. R. Munro, *Royal Commission on Australian Government Administration*, Commonwealth of Australia Report (Canberra, ACT: Australian Government Publishing Service, 1976), 336.

99. Read, *Charles Perkins*, 232.

100. Rowse, *Obliged to be Difficult*, 124.

101. Perkins, *A Bastard*, 172.

102. Rowse, *Obliged to be Difficult*, 116–17, 120–22, 125.

103. Read, *Charles Perkins*, 209–10.

104. Commonwealth of Australia, Parliamentary Debates, Senate, Tuesday, 17 February 1976, No. 8, 11.

105. Hiatt et al., *Inquiry into the role*, 27, 32, 45 57, 63.

106. Hiatt et al., *Inquiry into the role*, 69–83.

107. Commonwealth of Australia, Parliamentary Debates, House of Representatives, Monday, 30 May 1977, No. 22, 2104-13.

108. P. Hanks, 'Aborigines and Government: the developing framework', in *Aborigines and the Law*, Peter Hanks and Bryan Keon-Cohen, eds. (North Sydney, NSW: George Allen & Unwin Australia, 1984), 42.

109. Q. Beresford, *Rob Riley: An Aboriginal leader's quest for justice* (Canberra, ACT: Aboriginal Studies Press, 2006), 124–37; Robbins, *Self-Determination or Welfare Colonialism*, 211–14.

110. R. Pitty, 'The political aspects of creating a treaty', in *What Good Conditions? Reflections on an Australian Aboriginal Treaty 1986–2006*, Peter Read, Gary Meyers and Bob Reece, eds. (Canberra, ACT: ANU E Press, 2006), 51.

111. J. Wright, *We call for a Treaty* (Sydney, NSW: Fontana, 1985), 14–17, 31.

112. Commonwealth of Australia, Parliamentary Debates, Senate, Thursday, 19 September 1974, No. 38, 1267-73 (Neville Bonner).

113. S. Harris, 'Treaty of Commitment. Replacing charity to Aborigines with real responsibility', *The Canberra Times*, Wednesday, 8 September 1976, 2.

114. S. Harris, *'It's Comin Yet . . .' An Aboriginal Treaty Within Australia Between Australians* (Adelaide, SA: Griffin Press, 1979), 2–4; Rowse, *Obliged to be Difficult*, 174–77; Wright, *We call for a Treaty*, 95–106.

115. P. Read, 'Doubts about treaty: some reflections on the Aboriginal Treaty Committee', in *What Good Conditions? Reflections on an Australian Aboriginal Treaty*

1986–2006, Peter Read, Gary Meyers and Bob Reece, eds. (Canberra, ACT: ANU E Press, 2006), 32–33.

116. 'We Call for A Treaty Within Australia, Between Australians', *The National Times*, Week Ending 25 August 1979, 13.

117. *Two Hundred Years Later*, Report by the Senate Standing Committee on Constitutional and Legal Affairs on the feasibility of a compact or 'Makarrata' between the Commonwealth and Aboriginal people (Canberra, ACT: Commonwealth of Australia, Australian Government Publishing Service, 1983), 14–15.

118. 'Aborigines stake claim on Capitol Hill', *The Canberra Times*, Wednesday, 8 August 1979, 3; Wright, *We Call for a Treaty*, 122–23.

119. J. Hagan, *Makarrata Consultations*, 8 July 1980, National Aboriginal Conference Secretariat, Canberra.

120. *Makarrata Report*, National Aboriginal Conference Sub Committee on the Makarrata, Canberra (undated), https://aiatsis.gov.au/collections/collections-online/digitised-collections/treaty/national-aboriginal-conference; *Two Hundred Years Later*, 15–16.

121. Rowse, *Obliged to be Difficult*, 182; Wright, *We call for a Treaty*, 129, 155.

122. Wright, *We call for a Treaty*, 138–39.

123. *Two Hundred Years Later*, 17–18.

124. National Aboriginal Conference, *The Makarrata. Some Ways Forward*, Position Paper delivered to the World Council of Indigenous Peoples Canberra, 1981.

125. B. Keon-Cohen and B. Morse, 'Indigenous land rights in Australia and Canada', in *Aborigines and the Law*, Peter Hanks and Bryan Keon-Cohen, eds. (North Sydney, NSW: George Allen & Unwin, 1984), 87.

126. Robbins, 'Self-Determination or Welfare Colonialism', 221, 224–25; Rowse, *Obliged to be Difficult*, 183; Wright, *We call for a Treaty*, 152.

127. 'Call for draft Makarrata proposal', *The Canberra Times*, Friday, 28 August 1981, 8.

128. *Two Hundred Years Later*, 19, 177–78.

129. Rowse, *Obliged to be Difficult*, 184; Wright, *We call for a Treaty*, 163–65.

130. Wright, *We call for a Treaty*, 171.

131. *Two Hundred Years Later*, 121–25.

132. *Two Hundred Years Later*, 125–27, 155–56.

133. Commonwealth of Australia, Parliamentary Debates, House of Representatives, Thursday, 8 December 1983, No. 134, 3484–94, 3489–90, 3493.

134. P. Kelly, *The End of Certainty. Power, Politics and Business in Australia* (St Leonards, NSW: Allen & Unwin, 1994), 34–53, 46–47.

135. A. Markus, *Race: John Howard and the remaking of Australia* (Crows Nest, NSW, Allen & Unwin, 2001), 51, 53, 57–72.

136. Commonwealth of Australia, Parliamentary Debates, House of Representatives, Thursday, 16 May 1985, No. 142, 2635 (Roger Shipton).

137. Commonwealth of Australia, Parliamentary Debates, House of Representatives, Thursday, 16 May 1985, No. 142, 2639 (David Connolly).

138. Commonwealth of Australia, Parliamentary Debates, House of Representatives, Tuesday, 17 September 1985, No. 144, 1130-31 (Roger Shipton).

139. Commonwealth of Australia, Parliamentary Debates, House of Representatives, Wednesday, 16 October 1985, No. 144, 2228-29 (David Connolly).

140. S. Bennett, 'Federalism and Aboriginal Affairs', *Australian Aboriginal Studies* 1, (1988), 20, 21, 26.

141. The steering committee comprised NAC representatives and representatives from the Northern, Central, Kimberley, and North Queensland land councils plus Charles Perkins and the chairman of the Aboriginal Development Commission.

142. The lawyers panel included three appointed by NAC, two appointed by the National Federation of Aboriginal Land Councils, one from the Northern Land Council, one from the Department of Aboriginal Affairs, one representing the minister and one appointed by the minister to assist the panel.

143. R. T. Libby, *Hawke's Law, The Politics of Mining and Aboriginal Land Rights in Australia* (Nedlands, WA: University of Western Australia Press, 1989), 19–22, 26, 28, 34–35.

144. Commonwealth of Australia, *Cabinet Minute, National Aboriginal Land Rights Legislation*, Canberra, 12 August 1985, Decision No. 6505, Submission No. 3146.

145. The principles were: inalienable freehold title, protection of sacred sites, control in relation to mining, mining royalty equivalents, and compensation for lost land.

146. *Cabinet Minute, National Aboriginal Land Rights Legislation*, Canberra, 12 August 1985.

147. The Western Australia Land Inquiry chaired by Paul Seaman QC.

148. Libby, *Hawke's Law*, 35–37, 51–52.

149. Libby, *Hawke's* Law, 53–54, 139–46.

150. Libby, *Hawke's Law*, 61, 67, 76, 81, 85.

151. Libby, *Hawke's Law*, 107–14.

152. Commonwealth of Australia, Parliamentary Debates, House of Representatives, Tuesday, 18 March 1986, No. 147, 1437–80.

153. Editorial, 'A Shameful Back Down', *The Canberra Times*, Thursday, 6 March 1986, 2.

154. Commonwealth of Australia, Parliamentary Debates, House of Representatives, Thursday, 8 December 1983, No. 134, 3485-87 (Clyde Holding MP).

155. Commonwealth of Australia, Parliamentary Debates, House of Representatives, Thursday, 10 December 1987, No. 158, 3152-54.

156. Commonwealth of Australia, Parliamentary Debates, House of Representatives, Tuesday, 11 April 1989, No. 166, 1332.

157. 'Black power on the march', *The Sun*, Wednesday, 27 January 1988.

158. R. Tickner, *Taking a Stand*, Land Rights to Reconciliation (Crows Nest, NSW: Allen & Unwin, 2001), 33.

159. 'Celebrating Freedom', *The Canberra Times*, Tuesday, 26 January 1988, 2.

160. 'No reason to feel guilty, says Fraser', *The Canberra Times*, Saturday, 23 January 1988, 3.

161. J. F. Kerr, 'Today's whites not guilty; today's blacks not harmed', *The Canberra Times*, Tuesday, 26 January 1988, 2.

162. Markus, *Race: John Howard*, 69–71.

163. Tickner, *Taking a Stand*, 40–41; R. Broome, *Aboriginal Australians, A history since 1788,* Fourth Edition (Crows Nest, NSW: Allen & Unwin, 2010), 272.

164. 'Aboriginal treaty by "mid-1990"', *The Canberra Times*, Monday, 13 June 1988, 3.

165. K. Scott, 'Treaty absurd: Howard "A form of apartheid"' *The Canberra Times*, Tuesday, 14 June 1988, 1.

166. Tickner, *Taking a Stand*, 29.

167. Commonwealth of Australia, Parliamentary Debates, House of Representatives, Thursday, 30 May 1991, No. 178, 4498-504 (Robert Tickner).

168. A. Gunstone, *Unfinished Business: The Australian Formal Reconciliation Process* (Melbourne, VIC: Australian Scholarly Publishing, 2007), 47.

169. E. Johnson, *National Report, Overview and Recommendations*, Royal Commission into Aboriginal Deaths in Custody (Canberra, ACT: Commonwealth of Australia, Australian Government Printing Service, 1991), 7–11.

170. E. Johnston, *The Process of Reconciliation*, Royal Commission into Aboriginal Deaths in Custody, National Report, Vol. 5 (Canberra, ACT: Commonwealth of Australia, Australian Government Printing Service, 1991), chapter 38.

171. P. Dodson, M. Mowbray and W. Snowden, 'Promise, confrontation and compromise in Indigenous affairs', in *The Hawke Government, A critical Retrospective*, Susan Ryan and Troy Bramston, eds. (North Melbourne, Vic: Pluto Press Australia, 2003), 309–10.

FOUR

Recognition and the Limits of Tolerance

Although political will faltered in the 1980s, the High Court *Mabo* decision of 1992 provided a new impetus for Indigenous recognition because Australian governments and the Australian population now had to recognise that Indigenous people had rights to land; such rights preceded British colonisation of the continent. Indigenous leaders felt the *Mabo* judgment had laid the basis for a settlement, where the Australian state would develop a political relationship with Indigenous people. But the Commonwealth government did not accept this premise, choosing to interpret native title as a land management issue for the states. A hostile and racially charged response to the decision would dominate public debate, swaying the Commonwealth government to protect economic and private property interests by adopting an extinguishment approach to native title. When Indigenous leaders saw this approach gaining traction, they sought dialogue and formal negotiation with Prime Minister Paul Keating. Keating was open to dialogue and negotiation because he saw the *Mabo* decision as a moral challenge for Parliament and the nation.

Indigenous leaders representing various organisations, including the Aboriginal and Torres Strait Islander Commission (ATSIC), participated in direct negotiations over the native title legislation with Prime Minister Paul Keating, senior government ministers and ministerial staff. I was directly involved with the Indigenous organisations that participated in the processes. This chapter explains in detail how Indigenous leaders came to dialogue and negotiate with the prime minister of Australia to produce a legislative outcome that protected the basic core of native title. Getting direct access to the prime minister and operating within the inner workings of the Australian Parliament was a high point for Indigenous involvement in government policy and law-making processes. Indigenous people came close to a genuine intercultural dialogue with Prime Minister Paul Keating but ultimately were impeded by persisting colonial assumptions, as well as the striking power differential between Indigenous representatives, the government and industry groups. It is important to convey this story in detail because it shows there was hope, not only for Indigenous people but also for the Australian nation. But the progress made in Indigenous recognition and development in Australia since the 1970s would be undermined after the election of a conservative government in 1996. The dialogue and negotiation between the prime minister of Australia and Indigenous people has not been replicated since.

The last section of this chapter shows how a change of federal government can overturn years of positive development in Indigenous policy and wind back hard-fought Indigenous gains. The Howard Coalition government, which came to power in March 1996, pronounced that it would not be driven by a 'politically correct' agenda in regard to Indigenous affairs and instead would focus on health, education and job opportunities to deliver social justice to Indigenous Australians, so-called practical reconciliation. Howard believed that the standing approach to Indigenous policy was based on a paradigm of non-Indigenous shame and guilt and he rejected any responsibility for Indigenous dispossession or for past policies of assimilation. In regard to native title, especially the High Court *Wik* decision, Howard said the pendulum had swung too far towards Indigenous people and it was time to bring it back to balance. John Howard's discourse about Indigenous affairs and rights was similar to that of Pauline Hanson, an independent member elected to the seat of Oxley in Queensland in 1996. She claimed that Indigenous people were receiving special benefits from the government on the assumption that they were the most disadvantaged in Australia. She also rejected any responsibility for past policies of government in regard to Indigenous people.

This chapter provides insight into the political and public mindset regarding Indigenous rights in the 1990s and early 2000s. Importantly, it shows how political leadership can enhance Indigenous recognition or undermine it. Prime Minister Paul Keating created and led public and political dialogue to enhance Indigenous recognition, whereas Prime Minister John Howard used his power and public leadership to undermine Indigenous recognition. The impact of the Howard government and the upheaval of Indigenous affairs created a public and political environment that has undermined Indigenous rights and has restrained Indigenous voices and Indigenous political power. The Howard discourse on Indigenous recognition and rights still reverberates today.

THE ANTI-*MABO* DEBATE

Despite Prime Minister Paul Keating's moral and inclusive approach, which accorded recognition and respect, enabling Indigenous representatives to play an active role in negotiations, after *Mabo* Australian governments were more concerned with protecting the land titles of industry and private landholders. State and territory governments along with industry called for the extinguishment of native title; and in accordance with such calls the Commonwealth in its legislative approach sought to provide a mechanism to identify the existence of native title, define it and limit the extent of its impact. The representatives of Aboriginal land councils and other Indigenous organisations tried to present an alternative dialogic approach in the Aboriginal 'Peace Plan' as the basis for reconciliation and a just settlement. Indigenous leaders presented the Peace Plan to Prime Minister Paul Keating in April 1993. Recognition, respect, protection, negotiation, consent, coexistence and non-extinguishment were key principles of the plan. However, the government did not regard validation of existing land titles as a matter for negotiation with Indigenous people but as a decision to be made and imposed by the Commonwealth and state and territory governments. Native title was treated as though it were a property right that could be validated and/or extinguished by state governments as part of their land management responsibilities. By reducing native title to a land management issue – as opposed to recognising it as a pre-existing right that required a fundamental shift in the way Australians and governments perceived Indigenous ownership of land – Indigenous leaders were denied authority and political leverage.

There were two strands to the Commonwealth government response to the *Mabo* judgment: first, the recognition of Indigenous peoples' dispossession and the need for reconciliation to restore relationships; and second, the need to create certainty for industry and protect private property interests. These positions were diametrically opposed. The Australian political system always balances Indigenous rights and interests against the rights and interests of governments, industry, and the wider population, based on liberal principles of uniformity and equal treatment. However, as a minority in a country established by colonialism, Aboriginal people are consistently on the losing side of majority political decision-making because governments and politicians serve the interests of the majority. There is no legal obligation on Parliament or on elected representatives to consider the concerns, desires, aspirations or rights of Indigenous people. Further, because of their minority status, Indigenous people do not have the same sort of influence in government policy and law making.

These factors were apparent in the political process after the *Mabo* judgment, but receptive and sympathetic public and political representatives can open political and constitutional doors to recognise Indigenous rights and enable Indigenous people to play a role in government decision-making. Prime Minister Keating laid a moral foundation through which Indigenous people could play a role in the political and legislative process of his government. In launching the International Year of the World's Indigenous People for Australia at Redfern Park in Sydney on 10 December 1992, Keating said the starting point for justice was for Australians to recognise that the problem of dispossession and colonisation starts with white Australians. He said Australians had failed to make the most basic human response to Aboriginal people by asking, 'How would I feel if this were done to me?' According to Keating, the *Mabo* judgment was a 'practical building block' for change and was 'the basis of a new relation between Indigenous and non-Indigenous Australians'; there was nothing to fear or lose in the recognition of historical truths or the extension of social justice or indeed the inclusion of Indigenous people in Australian social democracy.[1]

Although initial public responses to *Mabo* were supportive, a full-scale attack on the High Court's decision, the High Court itself and Indigenous people ensued. The hostile public debate reflected 'deep seated and emotionally charged racial fear and fantasies about Aboriginal people'.[2] When Indigenous leaders pursued the realisation and protection of native title rights, it was apparent there was a body of public opinion that considered Indigenous people and their rights to be inferior. The public discussion about the *Mabo* judgment and native title showed the persistence of colonial assumptions and attitudes about Indigenous people and their rights in Australia.

Australian historian Geoffrey Blainey had difficulty accepting the existence of native title because he believed the *Mabo* judgment was based on a misunderstanding of history. He said the High Court had attempted to put eighteenth-century values on the importance of land to Aboriginal culture today and that the elected Parliament, and not an unelected High Court, should be the appropriate body to determine the contemporary values of Australian people. Blainey was one of many prominent individuals who made disparaging comments about the *Mabo* decision and Aboriginal people. The late Western Australian Aboriginal leader, Rob Riley, said, 'Aboriginal people are used to getting their guts kicked in by people who have money and power to influence public debate'. Riley was responding to negative comments of Geoffrey Blainey about Aboriginal use of land and land ownership.[3]

In an address to the Foreign Correspondent Association, chief minister of the Northern Territory, Marshall Perron, said Aboriginal people were centuries behind in their cultural attitudes and aspirations. He said that they lacked hygiene, slept with dogs and did not want to live in houses.[4] Perron said he was merely responding to questions in relation to expenditure of money on Aboriginal health and his comments were not racist because he was stating the 'facts'.[5] Marshall Perron could have been mouthing the words of W. H. Willshire in 1891. Willshire, a South Australian police officer in charge of interior police patrols in Central Australia said, from his experience, he could not speak much in favour of the 'blacks' describing Aboriginal people as 'ungrateful, deceitful, wily and treacherous' and 'indolent in the extreme, squalid and filthy in their surroundings, as well as disgustingly impure among themselves'.[6]

Tim Fischer, leader of the National Party at the time, asserted on radio that he was not going to apologise for '200 years of white progress in this country' and he would fight the 'guilt industry'.[7] Fischer said Aboriginal dispossession was inevitable because developing cultures would always overtake stationary cultures. He said an Aboriginal sense of nationhood and infrastructure was not highly developed because 'at no stage did Aboriginal civilisation develop substantial buildings, roadways or even a wheeled cart'.[8] Fischer denied he was being judgmental or derogatory, nor was he a racist or a redneck.[9] Tim Fischer could have read an article titled 'Savages and Civilised Men' in *Science of Man* from March 1903 before he spoke on radio. This article discussed the progress white people had made in Australia as compared to blacks. The article said that 'the blacks during all centuries of their undisturbed wanderings over the wilderness have never even thought of constructing a road, highway, bridge or street through their camp, or attempted to make a farm, garden, house or manufacture of any kind; instead, it seems ridiculous to expect such savages as the blacks to make any improvements'.[10]

Geoffrey Blainey argued that Aboriginal people changed and harmed the environment, extinguished species, and were being overcompensated with more valuable land for the land they lost since 1788. He said the 'Aboriginal way of life was bound to be overthrown eventually because it supported so few people on so much land'.[11] Blainey further wrote that land is not a right but a matter of negotiation and the land rights movement has by and large gone far enough to the extent of weakening the economy and the sovereignty of Australia. He said Aboriginal people can no longer be regarded as 'landless in their own land' because the average Aboriginal person has about twelve times as much land as the average non-Aboriginal.[12] Perhaps Geoffrey Blainey is a student of English philosopher John Locke who wrote in the seventeenth century that while God gave the world to men in common, it cannot be understood that it should always remain common and uncultivated because 'he gave it to the industrious and the rational'.[13] European and international jurist Emerich de Vattel followed in the eighteenth century, arguing that those who did not cultivate the land but continued to hunt, fish, and gather 'occupy more land than they would have need of under a system of honest labour, and they may not complain if other more industrious Nations, too confined at home, should come and occupy part of their lands'.[14]

Hugh Morgan, managing director of Western Mining Corporation, criticised the *Mabo* decision for recognising 'Aboriginal law as if it were the law of a foreign country' and for leaving property law in a 'state of disarray'. He said Aboriginal people had no agriculture and did not graze animals, and their utensils, weapons and ornaments were crude. Further he said Aboriginal people had 'no written language, no sense of time or history, no common spoken language and no political institutions which went beyond the life and boundaries of their many clans'.[15] In a later speech at the annual conference of the Victorian RSL, Hugh Morgan said, 'guilt industry people have great difficulty in accepting, or recognising, that Aboriginal culture was so much less powerful than the culture of the Europeans, that there was never any possibility of its survival. The necessity of choice forces us, in the end, to accept that cultures are not equal, that some cultures will wither away, and some cultures will expand and grow'.[16] Hugh Morgan could have been reading 'The Age' of 11 January 1888, where in discussing the report of the Board of the Protection of Aborigines the editor wrote, 'It seems a law of nature that where two races whose stages of progression differ greatly are brought into contact, the inferior race is doomed to wither and disappear. . . . Human progress has all been achieved by the spread of the progressive races and the squeezing out of the inferior ones'.[17]

Why did these prominent Australians parrot erroneous assumptions and opinions about Aboriginal people from a bygone era? Did they believe that Aboriginal people were inferior or did they feel vulnerable after losing the powerful psychological weapon of terra nullius? These public figures had influence and resources to control public discussion. This is how they maintained political and psychological ascendency over Indigenous people. Industry bodies were similarly hostile to the recognition of Indigenous land rights. The mining industry was only prepared to recognise 'customary rights' that did not amount to title in land. They also warned that if native title gave veto rights to Indigenous stakeholders, investors would go offshore. The Australian Mining Industry Council (AMIC) along with the Western Australian Chamber of Mines and Energy and the Association of Mining and Exploration Companies (AMEC) conducted a major campaign calling for the validation of existing mining titles as well as identifying and limiting native title. They also called for amendments to the Commonwealth Racial Discrimination Act 1975 (RDA) to prevent retrospective or future infringement on mining rights by Aboriginal interests.[18] The RDA was enacted in 1975 and limited the Commonwealth's capacity to pass legislation discriminating against anyone based on race. The National Farmers Federation (NFF) called for government legislation to validate all pastoral and agricultural titles already issued. However, the Western Australian Farmers Federation and the Pastoralists and Graziers Association of Western Australia took a more hard-line approach by supporting Premier Richard Court's legislative response to the *Mabo* decision.[19]

The public discussion was about protecting vested interests and thus discrediting Aboriginal culture, Aboriginal people and undermining the legitimacy of their rights. The discourse warned that devastating consequences would follow from the *Mabo* decision, including territorial dismemberment of the Australian continent. It attacked the High Court judges as unelected judges who had made a fatally flawed, politically driven decision; argued that dispossession was always going to happen and that Aboriginal people should be grateful for British arrival; that Aboriginal people were privileged; and that Aboriginal culture was not strong enough to survive competition with powerful cultures.[20] According to Noel Pearson, the public pronouncements of politicians after the *Mabo* decision showed the wide influence of social Darwinism.[21] In the negative colonial discourses that continue to form the narratives and conventional truth of many Australians – industry transforms the land, represents progress and modernity whereas Aboriginal people represent the archaic and the past, something that Europeans had left behind.[22]

Arguments that native title and Aboriginal rights to land would undermine the Australian system of land law, threaten the interests of other Australians, and threaten the national interest, sovereignty and Anglo identity of Australia are familiar narratives to Indigenous people. Although there was no significant danger to commercial interests, the mining industry was threatened by the *Mabo* decision and thus waged a campaign against native title employing tactical strategies that 'predicted industry crisis, the threat of job losses and declining investment, with disastrous consequences for the nation'.[23]

FEDERAL RESPONSE TO *MABO*

In the aftermath of the *Mabo* judgment, the Commonwealth government adopted an extinguishment approach by focussing on the 'uncertainty' of mining titles. The government aimed to promote national economic interests through the validation of all land titles that had been issued after 1975, which might have otherwise been invalidated because of the Racial Discrimination Act. The proposed solution was for the states and territories to extinguish native title and for the federal government to compensate native titleholders. The government also outlined a tribunal system to identify the existence of native title and a land fund for those Indigenous people who did not benefit from *Mabo*.[24] The Commonwealth government initiated a consultative process that was directed by a Mabo Ministerial Committee comprising the prime minister and other key ministers. The government consulted with state governments, the mining and pastoral industries, the Aboriginal and Torres Strait Islander Commission (ATSIC), the Council for Aboriginal Reconciliation and some Aboriginal land councils.

The Council for Aboriginal Reconciliation received the *Mabo* decision as a challenge and an opportunity. The council felt that tensions between competing interests could be resolved through the definition, recognition and negotiation of rights.[25] Patrick Dodson, chair of the Reconciliation Council, said Indigenous people should be recognised as legitimate stakeholders with an opportunity to argue their case, comment on the options being put forth by the government and participate in meaningful negotiations.[26] ATSIC also called on the Commonwealth government to maintain the integrity of the *Mabo* decision, to prevent further extinguishment of native title and to establish appropriate processes and legislation to negotiate the settlement of native title claims.[27] On 22 March 1993, Lois O'Donoghue, ATSIC chairperson, wrote to the prime minister advising of the need for a social justice component to compensate or provide land for dispossessed people who would not benefit from native title. She was also concerned about state government action to validate land granted to non-Indigenous people after 1975 as well as possible amendments to the Racial Discrimination Act to validate mining and other interests over land.

Apprehensive about the vulnerability of native title to extinguishment, the Kimberley, Cape York, Central and Northern Land Councils likewise wrote to the prime minister on 16 October 1992, urging protection of existing native title rights but also seeking recognition of native title over national parks, reserves and vacant Crown land as well as appropriate resources to consult and represent native title holders. Aboriginal land councils raised these issues directly with government officials in Darwin on 17–18 December 1992. While the officials at the Darwin meeting listened to Indigenous concerns about protecting native title from state government action, they appeared more interested in determining where native title existed and how it should be defined, as well as validating existing land titles. It soon became clear that the 'consultation' by government officials in Darwin was really about the government selling its policy position to the land councils. In later meetings with Aboriginal organisations on 31 March to 2 April 1993, in Canberra, government officials felt national economic imperatives required the validation of all land titles that had been issued after 1975 and which might have otherwise been rendered invalid. The land councils and the Western Australian Aboriginal Legal Service wanted a proper consultation process with Indigenous people and a negotiation process between Indigenous people and the government. They did not think that validating existing titles was as urgent as the mining industry had made out.

THE PEACE PLAN

When government officials completed their report, Indigenous representatives were invited to attend a meeting of the Ministerial Committee in
Canberra.[28] Not having seen the report, the Indigenous leaders were concerned it would be published before they had the opportunity to comment on it, so the four land councils and the Western Australian Aboriginal Legal Service proposed a meeting in Alice Springs on 19–20 April
1993, to formulate a position to present to the Ministerial Committee.
Other organisations such as the New South Wales Land Council, Aboriginal Legal Rights Movement of South Australia and some prominent Aboriginal individuals were invited.

At the Alice Springs meeting a statement of principles called the 'Red
Centre Statement' was developed. It later grew into the 'Aboriginal Peace
Plan' and was presented by Indigenous leaders to the prime minister and
Mabo Ministerial Committee in Canberra on 27 April 1993.[29] The Peace
Plan outlined eight key principles that the government was urged to
adopt: recognition and protection of Indigenous rights; no extinguishment of Indigenous title but coexistence and revival; no extinguishment
or impairment without Indigenous consent; a declaration of Indigenous
title in reserves and other defined lands; a tribunal to recognise Indigenous land title; a long-term settlement process for Indigenous benefit;
security for sacred sites and heritage areas; and negotiation with Indigenous people for constitutional recognition. In exchange, Indigenous people would accept validation of titles between 1975 and 1992 that might
otherwise be rendered invalid because of the RDA. They would accept
post-1975 titles on the condition that the Commonwealth government
and resource developers negotiated agreements with native titleholders
and if no agreement could be reached, a tribunal would have jurisdiction
to determine the dispute.

Prime Minister Paul Keating met with Indigenous leaders on 27 April
1993. Senior Indigenous representatives at the meeting spoke of their law,
history, culture, language, their attachment to country, the brutal dispossession of Indigenous people and their hope that the government would
provide justice. Younger Indigenous representatives explained the principles of the Peace Plan, advising the prime minister of their concerns that
the mining and pastoral industries would influence the passage of quick-
fix legislation and cautioning him not to dismiss or exclude Aboriginal
people from the process. Patrick Dodson concluded that reconciliation
would be rendered sterile if there was no Aboriginal participation to
resolve some of the dilemmas facing the nation. Prime Minister Keating
said the government had no intention of selling out Indigenous people,
but it would be difficult to sell the deal because the Peace Plan was
asking the Commonwealth to operate a land title system, which is the
business of the states under the Constitution. Nonetheless he believed

there was a possibility of developing a regime that provided national consistency. But other government ministers seemed preoccupied with determining the existence of native title and paying compensation for its extinguishment.

The Aboriginal Peace Plan implied an equal and coexisting relationship as the basis for Indigenous claims for recognition and political power. The proposition was that Indigenous people had something that the Australian nation needed—the validation of uncertain land titles. Among other demands the Peace Plan sought a role for Indigenous groups in the Commonwealth legislative process. But the Commonwealth government would not entertain the political premise of the Peace Plan, thereby denying Indigenous people political recognition and leverage. The government regarded validation as not a matter for negotiation but a decision of the Commonwealth government and state and territory governments; on that basis native title was construed as nothing more than a property right that could be extinguished and compensated.[30]

Indigenous representatives hoped that the *Mabo* decision could form the basis of a postcolonial settlement regarding rights to land, rights to compensation and restitution and jurisdictional rights.[31] However, the government would not recognise that Indigenous Australians held authority stemming from prior occupation and the continuity of their nationhood and cultural identities. The government did not recognise that Indigenous Australians should have an equal and exceptional constitutional status in Australia. Colonial assumptions about Indigenous people not having any form of political authority played a clear role in the government's rejection of the political premise of the Aboriginal Peace Plan. Hence, the Aboriginal representatives were merely equated with other lobby groups like the mining, farming and pastoral industries, albeit far less powerful.

INDIGENOUS CONCERNS AND THE GOVERNMENT'S PRINCIPLES

A smaller delegation of Indigenous representatives met with Prime Minister Keating and the Ministerial Committee on 18 May 1993, due to ongoing concern about the extinguishment of native title and the issue of compensation. The delegation informed the prime minister that the Commonwealth had to take responsibility in relation to protecting, affirming and dealing with native title and to override the states in much the same way it had done in industrial relations, corporations' law, equal opportunities and human rights. They also argued that providing Indigenous landowners with a right of consent was not granting them a superior right because it was no different to the protection farmers in Western Australia or wine growers and churchgoers in Victoria enjoyed.

The lack of Indigenous representation from Tasmania, Victoria and parts of Queensland moved the Indigenous organisations to arrange a meeting in Adelaide in May 1993 to inform a wider group about recent developments and seek their involvement in the process. Delegates in Adelaide were concerned that the Commonwealth government was focussed on providing certainty to farmers, pastoralists and miners and that the Commonwealth could bypass the Indigenous organisations and work through ATSIC and the Council for Aboriginal Reconciliation, which were not widely regarded by Indigenous people as representative. They also worried that the prime minister might leave the protection of native title to the states. The Adelaide meeting reaffirmed that Commonwealth legislation should not only deal with land tenure, but form part of a broader human rights package enshrining other Indigenous rights.

Indigenous organisations began looking at drafting legislation, but they were increasingly pulled into tighter Commonwealth time frames. The work of their lawyers was eclipsed by the Commonwealth government's *Mabo* principles and its discussion paper for proposed legislation that became public in early May 1993.[32] These principles included identification of native title by a tribunal and protection of native title by coexistence and revival; recognition of native title by Commonwealth, state and territory laws; validation of existing grants with the Commonwealth and states paying compensation but maintaining the integrity of the RDA; ensuring future grants are validly issued and subject to negotiation for the consent of native title holders but only where it is enjoyed by other title holders; compensation to be paid to native titleholders when a grant is made over native title land; and a social justice package to recognise past dispossession and commitment to reconciliation. Indigenous leaders Noel Pearson and Mick Dodson were forthright in their public criticism of the document, implying that the Commonwealth government was continuing the colonial legacy of dispossessing Aboriginal people.[33]

The Commonwealth also supported Northern Territory government legislation to fast-track development of the McArthur River mine by validating the mining leases and bypassing negotiation with the native title holders, a troubling indication of its attitude to Indigenous title. On 28 May 1993, the Northern Land Council wrote to the prime minister expressing concern about extinguishment of native title by the Northern Territory legislation and querying Commonwealth support for that legislation. The Commonwealth later moved to legislate that the McArthur River mine grants did not extinguish native title.

Talks collapsed when Prime Minister Keating sought agreement from the states and territories at the Council of Australian Governments (COAG) meeting in Melbourne on several core propositions, including allowing states to validate grants with the Commonwealth paying full compensation. There was resistance from Western Australia, Victoria and Tasmania, which called for extinguishment of native title.[34] The prime minister was disappointed that the states were reluctant to uphold the principles of recognition implied by the *Mabo* decision; however, he said the Commonwealth would proceed to draft legislation dealing with native title.[35] He warned the states not to go it alone, stating they had to accept native title as reality and accept a national approach.[36]

When Indigenous representatives met in Darwin in June 1993 to consider the outcome of the COAG meeting, they heard Prime Minister Keating was looking for a statement of support that his government's principles met Indigenous needs. But Indigenous representatives criticised the government's handling of the McArthur River project, as they were concerned that the prime minister had ignored their position and had not negotiated with Indigenous people. In their view, the prime minister appeared to respond narrowly to the *Mabo* decision rather than address the broader rights issues as set out in the Peace Plan. Indigenous leaders were concerned that the government had appeared to back away from the issues of revival of native title, the right to consent, historical claims to land and protection of sacred sites.

Nevertheless, Indigenous leaders agreed that it was preferable to negotiate rather than litigate. To negotiate, however, they had to develop a national representative body that had the authority to speak for all Indigenous people. Although not entirely representative, for the sake of continuity it was agreed the representative structure of land councils and legal services already in place should continue until the planned national meeting in August. Representative spokespersons included Noel Pearson, Mick Dodson, Esther Williams, Rob Riley and Peter Yu. Despite their misgivings the Indigenous representatives wrote to Prime Minister Keating on 20 June 1993, acknowledging his principled stand in dealing with the state premiers and chief ministers, but voicing Indigenous concerns that communication, consultation and negotiation had diminished and that his instructions to the premiers and chief ministers appeared to accept a narrow view of *Mabo*.

A MINIMALIST APPROACH

By July 1993, Indigenous organisations began to see drafting instructions for a possible Commonwealth Bill that provided for the validation of past grants and acts, future grants and future dealings with native title and a national native title tribunal. Although Indigenous representatives did not have formal discussions with government officials about drafting the legislation, they were able to make representations to the government through Phillip Toyne, the government's special advisor on *Mabo*. Indigenous representatives criticised that native title was being treated as a bundle of rights that did not amount to ownership, and that regulation of native title could extinguish it. There was no provision for revival of lapsed native title or for the coexistence of native title with other titles. There was also concern that pastoral leases would extinguish native title. The cut-off date for validation of pastoral land grants that might have been invalid had been extended to 30 June 1993, the question of Indigenous consent was being ignored, and there was no provision for negotiation of regional or local agreements. Finally, there was no social justice or reconciliation measure.[37]

In an address to the Press Club in Canberra, Prime Minister Paul Keating said the *Mabo* judgment placed a great responsibility upon the nation and like the United States, New Zealand and Canada, which faced up to their responsibilities, some aspects of Australian life had to be set right. He said the Commonwealth would set the benchmarks and would not accept the lowest common denominator or fail to establish national standards and mechanisms for dealing with native title.[38] The Indigenous representatives were greatly encouraged by the prime minister's public position, but his words were not reflected in the draft legislation. In a letter to the prime minister on 26 July 1993, the Victorian Aboriginal Legal Service, the Central Land Council, the Kimberley Land Council and the Northern Land Council stated that the draft legislation 'assimilated' and 'castrated' native title and advanced the vested interests of miners and pastoralists while doing nothing to protect Indigenous interests beyond the bare minimum required by law. The Left faction of the Labor Party also recognised the possible flaws in the draft legislation and commented on the 'boy fixers' in government services who wanted to 'fix it up for industry'.[39]

In late July. the federal cabinet received a detailed briefing from government officials on the progress of the legislation and addressed several issues, primarily extinguishment, compensation, right of consent and the tribunal. The cabinet only agreed to a 'right to negotiate', where native titleholders have a right of consultation and negotiation in respect to native title land, not a veto over land use development.[40] The government was of the view that freehold tourist leases extinguished native title and pastoral leases, except where there were reservations in favour of Indigenous people but not by mining leases, licences and permits. The cabinet agreed the Commonwealth would allow states to operate their own tribunals provided the state satisfactorily validated titles between 1975 and 1993 and providing the state tribunal complied with Commonwealth standards. However, the Commonwealth government could override the decision of the tribunal in the national interest. The government would also proceed with social justice initiatives to advance the process of reconciliation.[41]

The Indigenous organisations felt that Indigenous people should not have to prove the existence or nature of their title, particularly in those situations where it would most likely exist, such as vacant crown land, crown land allocated for conservation reserves and national parks, land vested for the benefit of Indigenous people, offshore areas and rivers and pastoral lease land. They believed the role of the tribunal should be to determine the extent to which native title had been impaired by a grant or act of government.

THE EVA VALLEY STATEMENT

To develop a national Indigenous position, ATSIC and the Council for Aboriginal Reconciliation sponsored a three-day national meeting at Manyallaluk on Jawoyn country in the Northern Territory in August 1993. More than four hundred Indigenous people attended. While many people supported the Peace Plan principles, there were expressed concerns that many people had not heard of them. Many did not understand the *Mabo* decision and they had not been part of the process initiated by the government. Some argued that the government was using certain Indigenous organisations as though they were representative of Indigenous people. However, a position was finally agreed on after people methodically worked through the principles of what became known as the 'Eva Valley Statement'. The outcome of the meeting was total rejection of the draft Commonwealth legislation and formation of a new representative body called the Eva Valley Working Group to act as a negotiating team.[42]

The main thrust of the Eva Valley Statement was that the Commonwealth must honour its obligations under international human rights instruments and international law. The Commonwealth also had to agree to a negotiating process to set national standards and pass legislation with the full and free consent of Indigenous peoples to advance Indigenous rights to land and to make redress for the impact of dispossession. The statement put forward five principles for how the Commonwealth should respond to the *Mabo* decision: (1) recognition and protection of Indigenous rights; (2) acknowledgment that Indigenous title cannot be extinguished by grants of other interests; (3) ensuring that interests cannot be granted over Indigenous title without the informed consent of all title holders; (4) declaring Indigenous title in reserves and other lands; and (5) providing security for sacred sites and heritage areas.

At the press conference after the meeting Galarrwuy Yunupingu, chairman of the Northern Land Council, said the prime minister had undermined the reconciliation process. Mick Dodson, the Aboriginal and Torres Strait Islander Social Justice commissioner, said the government had not bothered to talk with Aboriginal people, had not negotiated and did not have Aboriginal consent.[43] Prime Minister Paul Keating claimed that these accusations were untrue as the government had consulted widely and with goodwill. He said if Aboriginal people seek justice and equity, they must provide leaders that accepted responsibility and leadership.[44] When Indigenous representatives provided the Eva Valley Statement to the prime minister on 25 August, he insisted the legislative scheme would realise a broader and deeper settlement, even though he could not guarantee the support of all state premiers. Mick Dodson warned the prime minister that the legislation would fail significantly if Indigenous people were not happy with it.

THE PROPOSED LEGISLATION

Indigenous representatives could see they were rapidly being overrun by the government's timetable so they turned their attention to having full-time coordination in Canberra.[45] On 2 September, Prime Minister Paul Keating released an outline of the proposed legislation and invited state and territory leaders to join the Commonwealth in a national approach. The Commonwealth Native Title Bill would recognise, protect and set standards for future dealings with native title. However, to resolve 'uncertainties', it would validate Commonwealth, state and territory laws, acts and grants from before 1 July 1993, going back to 1788. Validation meant extinguishment of native title by freehold and a wide category of leases. For future grants tribunals would be established to decide native title claims and assist in resolving conflicting interests in land.[46]

Indigenous organisations and ATSIC objected that the legislation gave states unfair power as native title tribunals would be loaded against Indigenous interests. They argued that not providing a right of consent and allowing for the extinguishment of native title was unacceptable. The government had also failed to provide social justice measures.[47] Mick Dodson wrote to Attorney General Michael Lavarch on 22 September 1993, reporting that the legislation failed to fulfil its own objectives, failed to appropriately recognise native title and failed to recognise the true character of the title and its connection with the spiritual and cultural fabric of Indigenous societies. In an address to the National Press Club, Patrick Dodson said the proposals did not come close to providing justice or equality or attempt to bring forward reconciliation. He said more cooperation and a greater willingness by the nation to find a generosity of spirit was required.[48]

Another national Indigenous meeting was held in Canberra in late September 1993 to formulate a response to the proposed legislation, develop principles for a social justice package and consider the formation of a national Indigenous coordinating structure. However, it was a tall order to have a diverse group of Indigenous people develop a detailed and unified position in such a short time when there were different understandings of the issues and different priorities. Many people were bitter about the historical treatment of Aboriginal people; some perceived the proposed legislation as just another insult from the government. Some

Indigenous groups, including the New South Wales Aboriginal Legal Service, rejected the legislation outright, arguing there should be no further negotiation with the government.[49]

The overwhelming response from the Canberra meeting was to reject the Commonwealth proposals on the legislation and walk away. This meant the Eva Valley Working Group could not negotiate any further with the government. However, Indigenous groups could negotiate with the government or assert their rights so long as they did not purport to represent the general interest of all Indigenous peoples.[50] Representatives of the main land councils, some legal services and other organisations felt that while the government's legislative proposal was unacceptable, they needed to continue their participation in the process to protect the interests of their constituents. A coalition named the Coalition of Aboriginal Organisations Working Party (Aboriginal Coalition) was established. The government needed an Indigenous interlocutor. The Aboriginal organisations were wary that if they did not organise to participate in the legislative process, the government would negotiate with ATSIC, a body created by the government, which did not represent the interests of Indigenous landowners and native title holders. Indigenous peoples across Australia have never accepted government-constituted bodies as their representatives, nor do they accept that selective Indigenous bodies can act on their general behalf.

VALIDATION OF TITLES

The outline of the Commonwealth legislation did not specifically say so, but validation of past grants and acts of government between 1975 and 1993 would be fulfilled by overriding or suspending the Racial Discrimination Act 1975 (RDA). The Commonwealth government considered these grants and acts to be innocently issued or carried out because previous governments were not aware of the existence of native title. However, because the RDA operated from October 1975 onwards, these titles were potentially invalid as the rights of native titleholders had been ignored, they had not been paid compensation and they were not provided with a right of procedural fairness. Suspending the RDA to validate grants would withdraw the protection of the RDA for Indigenous people.

To the Indigenous organisations this was particularly abhorrent because not only was the government proposing to take away the protection of the RDA just for Indigenous people, it was intending to carry out an act of racial discrimination in breach of Australia's international obligations under the Convention on the Elimination of All Forms of Racial Discrimination. In fact, the Indigenous organisations had provided a method for validation of grants post-1975 in the Peace Plan, based on a process of negotiation and coexistence of native title and other interests in land, without sacrificing one interest in land to another.[51] But governments and industry would not accept negotiation on validation because they believed it would be a lengthy process of case-by-case negotiation.

Support groups such as the Australian Council for Overseas Aid, representing more than ninety nongovernment aid organisations, urged the government to uphold the RDA.[52] ATSIC gained political support from the Australian Democrats and West Australian Greens, who released a joint statement to the media voicing concern that the legislation should not be weakened any further to accommodate the states, also affirming that ATSIC's proposals to strengthen the legislation should be accommodated, and the social justice package had to be made explicit before the legislation was presented to the senate.[53]

In early October 1993 representatives of the Aboriginal Coalition signalled their intention to Prime Minister Keating to develop a position on the proposed legislation. Membership of the Aboriginal Coalition comprised the Cape York Land Council, Central Land Council, Northern Land Council, Kimberley Land Council, New South Wales Land Council, Aboriginal Legal Service of WA, Aboriginal Legal Rights Movement of SA and the Tasmanian Aboriginal Centre. Their focus would be on the government's plan to override the RDA to validate titles. The Aboriginal Coalition wanted to maintain the integrity of the RDA and they sought an alternative method of validation. They preferred validation by negotiation where the titleholder, government and the native titleholder would negotiate reasonable terms and conditions for such validation, including payment of compensation. If an agreement could not be reached, then the tribunal would arbitrate settlement.

Due to a perception that ATSIC had conceded a limited suspension of the RDA, the Aboriginal Coalition met with ATSIC commissioners and officials. ATSIC agreed to amend its positions to accord with the view of the Aboriginal Coalition, particularly regarding opposing any suspension of the RDA. The Aboriginal Coalition and ATSIC agreed to seek the support of the minor parties as the Greens and Democrats had the potential to block the legislation in the Senate. Pressure could also be applied to the prime minister through the ALP Caucus Committee on Aboriginal Affairs and Social Justice.

When the Aboriginal Coalition and ATSIC representatives met with Prime Minister Keating on 5 October 1993, they argued strongly against suspending the RDA. But the government was determined. Frank Walker, the special minister of state, said titles could not be validated without suspending the RDA. Prime Minister Keating said he wanted the support of the states for the legislation and believed he would get all of them to agree, except Western Australia. If there was no 'certainty' he believed the states would pass their own legislation. After the meeting with ATSIC and the prime minister, some of the organisations in the Aboriginal Coalition dropped out. Alongside ATSIC the remaining organisations continued the round of meetings and negotiations. They met with the Labor Party Aboriginal Affairs and Social Justice Caucus Committee who were concerned with the government's position.[54]

SUPPORT FROM MINOR PARTIES

Both the Greens and the Australian Democrats were supportive of the ATSIC and Aboriginal Coalition approach, although the Greens offered reluctant support because they had instructions from Aboriginal people in Perth, Western Australia, who were rejecting the legislation entirely. The Greens wanted something better than a minimum position. They stated they would only support the proposed legislation if there were coexistence of titles, Commonwealth tribunals, a social justice package and no suspension of the Racial Discrimination Act. When the Aboriginal Coalition, ATSIC, Greens and Democrats met with Prime Minister Keating on 6 October 1993, he confirmed that the government had made some concessions to the states to get their support, which included widening the definition of grants that extinguished native title to include industrial, commercial, farming, utilities, telecommunications and recreational leases, extending the validation date to 30 June 1994, allowing state tribunals to decide native title claims and future land use; the states would then accept the right of negotiation in regard to future grants of title and acts of government. It also included a 'technical suspension' of the RDA, but rights of negotiation and compensation would be provided. In a later meeting that day the prime minister tried to appease ATSIC and the Aboriginal Coalition regarding their concerns about the legislation by going through the twenty-one points of their position indicating support for some and possible movement on others; however, the proposed suspension of the Racial Discrimination Act and the situation of the tribunal at either state or Commonwealth level remained problematic.

Phillip Toyne, the government's own special advisor, was also deeply troubled. In a letter sent on 5 October 1993 to Frank Walker, special minister of state, he wrote that the government's approach and process was deficient because it did not provide for direct Indigenous input to the ministerial committee and did not provide for a social justice package for those people who had been most dispossessed. He wrote that the concept of validation by extinguishment was not justified on the High Court ruling. Patrick Dodson threatened to quit his post as chairman of the Council for Aboriginal Reconciliation because the integrity of the reconciliation process was being damaged. In his view the lack of strong central government leadership was close to a betrayal of Aboriginal people, and the actions by state governments were the closest thing he had seen to sedition. He said unless the federal government showed more commitment to the reconciliation process it might as well windup reconciliation.[55]

Prime Minister Keating attempted to placate Aboriginal Coalition representatives in a breakfast meeting at the Lodge, the official residence of the prime minister in Canberra, to discuss a framework for validation put forward by the Commonwealth and funding for non-statutory land councils, including a statutory land fund.[56] Later, a lengthy meeting took place on 7 October 1993, between ATSIC, the Aboriginal Coalition and the prime minister and his advisers. However, the government still insisted on suspending the RDA to validate titles and provided no choice between state and Commonwealth tribunals. The cut-off date for validation would also remain June 1993 and the category of leases that would extinguish native title would be extended to include public utilities, roads and railway lines. However, social justice measures would provide land and economic benefits to Indigenous people who would not directly benefit from the *Mabo* decision or whose native title had been impaired and extinguished. A statutory body would be set up by legislation to buy and manage land.

BLACK FRIDAY AND VALIDATING TITLES

In a letter to Prime Minister Keating on 7 October 1993, ATSIC and the Aboriginal Coalition representatives indicated that they wanted to maintain dialogue and would provide a more detailed response. However, there were major differences on a majority of points and they regarded several issues as fundamentally unacceptable.[57] Soon afterwards, the prime minister announced publicly that the original outstanding issues between the government and Indigenous representatives had been narrowed to three or four; however, he was concerned that two or three of the outstanding matters were incompatible with the position emerging in discussion with the states, which angered the Indigenous representatives.[58]

In an emotional press conference on 'Black Friday', Lois O'Donoghue, Mick Dodson and Noel Pearson said the government was clearly indicating it was more interested in protecting state rights than Indigenous human rights. They informed the media that Prime Minister Keating's statement was wrong, that only three or four issues of disagreement remained. In response the prime minister said he was 'deeply disappointed' and that he was 'not sure whether Indigenous leaders can ever psychologically make the change to decide to come into a process, be part of it and take the burden of responsibility that goes with it'.[59] Despite this public insult the Indigenous representatives informed the prime minister in writing on 11 October that they were ready to continue talks with him.

There were not 'three or four' but nineteen outstanding issues on which agreement had not been reached. However, at this point, Indigenous lobbying efforts within the Labor Party began to pay off. Labor Party left and central-left faction members began to raise their concerns privately and publicly about the government's plans. A coalition of organisations including the Australian Council of Trade Unions (ACTU), Australian Council of Social Service (ACOSS) and Australian Conservation Foundation (ACF) called on the prime minister not to suspend the RDA. Several church groups, the Australian Council of Churches, the Uniting Church, the Religious Society of Friends and prominent Australians began to voice their concerns about the proposed legislation.[60] Daryl Melham, Labor Left member, sought a legal opinion indicating that the RDA did not have to be suspended to validate titles if the 'special measures' approach was used. Special measures are a form of affirmative action intended as temporary measures to relieve disadvantage.[61] Melham was able to get the advice to Prime Minister Keating.[62] The special measures approach was thereafter confirmed as legally valid by the attorney general Michael Lavarch and the minister of state Frank Walker as well as government lawyers. Over the next couple of days, the prime minister had a series of discussions with all major stakeholders.

When the Indigenous representatives met with Prime Minister Keating on 14 October, his attitude had changed. In a lengthy meeting the prime minster said he wanted Indigenous support for the legislation to secure the support of the Greens and Democrats. He conceded that it was possible under the RDA to construct a series of special measures to validate title and that the Commonwealth would pay compensation. The Indigenous representatives and the prime minister then went through the outstanding issues. There were some matters the prime minister was not prepared to move on because in his view the cabinet would not accept them.

The next day negotiations continued with broad agreement on most matters.[63] Indigenous representatives believed that with the resolution of a few key issues they could seek the support of Indigenous people for the bill and negotiate with the Democrats and Greens for their support in the Senate. The government would not agree on the coexistence of native title on pastoral leases because the National Farmers Federation (NFF) wanted extinguishment for the sake of 'certainty' and to subject the legislation to the RDA because they wanted to avoid High Court challenges to the legislation. Prime Minister Keating was confident he could get everything through the cabinet but needed the support of the pastoralists and farmers.

'Black Friday' was a watershed moment for the Indigenous people. Their representatives called on the government to account for its approach in the legislative process as well as asserted their right to be heard and taken seriously. The government was confronted with the choice of continuing in the same direction and risking Indigenous opposition to the legislation or negotiating with Indigenous representatives to get the legislation through parliament.[64] The Indigenous organisations highlighted the collusion between governments and the willingness of the states and the Commonwealth government to suspend the RDA to validate land titles and in the process extinguish native title. By interfering with Indigenous property rights in this way, the Indigenous representatives argued that the government's approach was an act of racial discrimination. This consequence seemed to have been lost on state and Commonwealth governments even though Australia abides by the International Covenant on the Elimination of all Forms of Racial Discrimination. Indigenous representatives called on the Australian population to ensure politicians did not sacrifice human rights protection for political imperatives.[65] This strategy had some impact.

THE CABINET DECISION

The federal cabinet met on the evening of 18 October to consider the final shape of the legislation. Land council and ATSIC representatives were provided a room in the inner sanctum in Parliament House. Prime Minister Paul Keating informed the representatives that the cabinet would not agree on the coexistence of native title with pastoral leases. The cabinet did agree that pastoral leases issued between 1975 and 1993 would extinguish native title but preserve reservations in favour of Aboriginal people. Also, where native title could be proved, Aboriginal-owned pastoral leases could be converted to native title. The issue of coexistence of all other pastoral leases would be left to the common law.[66] The prime minister put the proposal to Rick Farley of the NFF, who agreed after being assured of extinguishment. Farley had gone out on a limb and felt it was the best possible deal for the NFF. The NFF's support had given the government's legislation 'vital legitimacy'.[67]

In a press conference the next day, dubbed 'Ruby Tuesday', Lois O'Donoghue called the cabinet decision historic and said that a 'remarkable settlement and historic agreement' had been secured.[68] Prime Minister Keating boasted about the outcome, calling the legislation 'a new deal between Indigenous and non-Indigenous Australians' and also paid tribute to the Aboriginal leadership who were able to work out Aboriginal interests and offset them against the economic interests of the country.[69]

The Victorian government supported the cabinet's resolution, whereas the premiers of New South Wales, Queensland, South Australia, Tasmania and the chief minister of the Northern Territory gave cautious support. Premier Richard Court of Western Australia rejected the Commonwealth's final position, insisting Western Australia would proceed with its own legislation.[70] Opposition leader John Hewson rejected the draft bill stating that there was a huge cloud of uncertainty over pastoral leases plus other problems with the bill, including the right to negotiate, which would become a veto on development, the costs of compensation and the issue of legal assistance to claimants.[71]

Rick Farley of the NFF said farm organisations had given their support to the legislative package and he urged the Federal Opposition to ignore the stance of Richard Court and to negotiate with the federal government. He also urged state governments to take a constructive approach to the legislation.[72] The Queensland Mining Council complained that the federal government discriminated against miners because mining leases did not extinguish native title. The Western Australian Chamber of Mines and Energy said critical elements of the legislation were unworkable.[73]

Indigenous reaction to the cabinet decision was mixed. Michael Mansell commented that the outcome revealed that Aboriginal land interests would always be subordinate to white interests.[74] Patrick Dodson similarly expressed that the legislation subordinated native title to all other interests. He was also concerned that state definition and control of native title without an explicit recognition of its cultural base may see the death of native title rights. Rob Riley was concerned about extinguishment of native title on pastoral leases and did not think that it was a step forward for reconciliation because reconciliation had to be based on a proper recognition of Aboriginal rights.[75] Isabelle Coe said the legislation did nothing for people in New South Wales and people on the eastern seaboard, and the people meeting with the prime minister did not speak for Wiradjuri people.[76] Ray Robinson, president of the National Aboriginal and Islander Legal Service, said the Indigenous representatives had no mandate and were dealing away the future of Aboriginal people.[77] Paul Coe said no one had authority to negotiate and the apparent 'closed doors conspiracy' between the prime minister and the Indigenous representatives denied natural justice and self-determination to Aboriginal people.[78]

Within days of the cabinet decision there was a cooling of relations between the group of land councils who had been negotiating with the government and the other Indigenous organisations that had initially been part of the process. While the Indigenous representatives were accused of selling out Indigenous interests, they had felt they had a duty to their constituents to negotiate. Their assessment was that the overall general reaction from the Indigenous community was positive despite the criticism and disappointment expressed by some factions.

A MODICUM OF JUSTICE

The government moved quickly to draft the bill and the focus of the Indigenous representatives turned to informing Indigenous people and supporters of the outcome of the negotiations, clarifying certain issues with the government, providing an input into the drafting process and seeking support from the Western Australian Greens and Australian Democrats in the Senate. An issue of concern to Aboriginal organisations in Western Australia was that the Court government would try to issue as many grants as possible before the cut-off date for validation, and would also try to validate unlawful acts and grants. Rick Farley thought it still technically possible to test for native title on validly issued pastoral leases. He urged Indigenous representatives to state publicly there was little point in pursuing native title rights on validly issued pastoral leases. Indigenous representatives agreed.[79]

To facilitate the passage of the bill, the Indigenous representatives publicly agreed that the government had met their key demands and they also sought the support of the minor parties in the senate. While the Democrats felt the government arrived at a 'reasoned position' that provided for the interest of Indigenous people and ensured certainty over land titles,[80] the Greens reserved their support of the bill. Their support would depend on the content of the legislation and its impact on the ground. They wanted to ensure that Aboriginal people were better off under the proposals.[81] Some final matters were dealt with in a meeting with the prime minister in early November.

The introduction of the Land (Titles and Traditional Usage) Bill into the Western Australian (WA) Parliament in early November 1993 brought a sense of urgency to getting the proposed Commonwealth legislation through Parliament. The WA legislation extinguished native title and replaced it with a lesser right of 'traditional usage'. Early advice to the Indigenous representatives was that it would be found to be invalid, considering the ruling in *Mabo*. In a doorstop interview Prime Minister Keating said Premier Richard Court was 'contemplating the most unconscionable extinguishment of private land titles in this country's history' and the Commonwealth would assert its primacy 'without fear or favour'.[82]

The Commonwealth Native Title Bill was introduced into the House of Representatives on 16 November 1993. In his second reading speech Prime Minister Paul Keating said 'a modicum of justice' was being offered to Indigenous Australians. The nation was taking 'a major step towardss a new and better relationship between Aboriginal and non-Aboriginal Australians'. The prime minister said that the negotiation process in developing the bill had extended the frontier of mutual understanding through which a great deal was learnt about each other and about how to work together.[83]

THE SENATE PROCESS

The Aboriginal Alliance emerged to extract further amendments in the senate process. It comprised the New South Wales Land Council, the Aboriginal Provisional Government (APG), the Tasmanian Aboriginal Centre, the Victorian Aboriginal Legal Service and the Aboriginal Legal Service of Western Australia. They commended Prime Minister Keating on his strong personal stand but they felt the legislation had to be further altered to ensure that it did not discriminate against Aboriginal people; did not restrict the capacity of the common law to develop its recognition of Aboriginal rights over time; and did not allow the states to interfere with the existence or development of common law Aboriginal rights in a manner adverse to Aboriginal people. The Aboriginal Alliance believed the Indigenous representatives in the Aboriginal Coalition had become too close to the government. With the emergence of two different Indigenous groups seeking a better deal in the Senate, the Indigenous representatives who had negotiated an outcome with the government were dubbed the 'A Team' and the Aboriginal Alliance, the 'B Team'.

Indigenous representatives began considering amendments to the bill in the Senate through the Greens and Democrats. The Greens, however, were reluctant to support the bill in its present form and wanted the legislation examined by a senate select committee.[84] The Aboriginal Coalition thought the Greens' stance on the bill was misguided and a threat to Indigenous people. It was also inconsistent with the position of the Aboriginal Legal Service of Western Australia and the Kimberley Land Council, which supported the passing of the bill with amendments. However, because the Greens held the balance of power in the Senate, the government agreed to refer the Native Title Bill to the Standing Committee on Legal and Constitutional Affairs.

The government wanted the Native Title Bill through Parliament before the Christmas break, but the Opposition and the Greens were threatening to delay it. The Greens believed the bill reasserted terra nullius by validating past discriminatory acts and by extinguishing native title. The call by the Green senators from Western Australia for more time and more consultation would bring an enormous amount of pressure to bear on them, especially from Aboriginal people in Western Australia because the premier Richard Court had rushed through state legislation to extinguish native title and replace it with rights of traditional usage. The Opposition said the bill was 'rotten to its core', against national interests and would harm investment and threaten employment. They had resolved to oppose every amendment to the bill, even amendments that were supported by industry groups.[85]

The Aboriginal Alliance and the Aboriginal Provisional Government worked through the Greens to obtain amendments to the bill. The Aboriginal Coalition and the ATSIC also worked with the Democrats to obtain further amendments. However, to keep the Greens honest, the Aboriginal Coalition, with assistance from Community Aid Abroad and the Australian Council of Churches, brought six Western Australian Aboriginal representatives to Canberra.[86] The Kimberley Land Council also brought Kimberley Aboriginal representatives to Canberra. The strategy was to apply as much pressure as possible to the Greens to secure their vote for the bill.

In the Senate the Opposition dragged the debate out by filibuster, debating the bill clause by clause.[87] The government sought an amendment for renewal or extension of pastoral leases and to provide perpetual rights to renew mining leases without negotiation with native title holders, but it was voted down. Rick Farley of the NFF withdrew his support. He felt betrayed because the NFF had negotiated in good faith to develop a national approach to native title issues.[88] An alternative amendment by the Democrats allowed for renewal, regrant or extension of pastoral, agricultural or residential leases without negotiation with native title holders, but not for mining leases. The NFF, the government and the Greens accepted this. The government also moved a guillotine motion that was supported by the Greens and Democrats to end the Opposition's filibustering.

When the Greens announced they would support the bill, stating they had won concessions and had achieved the best possible outcome for Aboriginal people, the Senate debate was all but over.[89] After more than fifty hours of debate, the bill passed in the Senate on the night of 21 December 1993, by a vote of thirty-four to thirty. There was immediate applause and a standing ovation. The Opposition were motionless. When the bill was returned to the House of Representatives the next morning the amendments were taken into consideration and the bill was passed. The prime minister said it was appropriate that the last thing the Parliament did on the last sitting day of the International Year for the World's Indigenous People was to pass the Native Title Bill. Opposition leader John Hewson said it was a day of shame for Australia and they were proud on behalf of all Australians to dissociate themselves from the legislation.[90]

PARTICIPATION IN GOVERNMENT

Indigenous representatives involved in the native title legislative process were asserting recognition of a legal right, not a moral obligation, on the part of government.[91] They sought to defend the values, traditions and customs of Indigenous society based on human rights and justice. These principles are reflected in the Aboriginal Peace Plan that emphasised a long-term settlement process with Indigenous people, constitutional recognition of Indigenous rights and coexistence of native title and other land titles. An emphasis on human rights is also seen in the Eva Valley Statement that urged the Commonwealth government to set national standards in accordance with international human rights obligations and international law, including full and free consent of Indigenous people. But the government treated native title as a land management issue to be integrated into the land law of Australia. Therefore, the Native Title Act is only 'a technical scheme of real estate law rather than a programme for working towards new, postcolonial political arrangements with Indigenous peoples'.[92]

The overall outcome of the negotiation fell far short of what the Indigenous representatives wanted. Indigenous representatives were forced into a political struggle to protect native title given the enormous power of industry and the state and territory governments. Accordingly, the Native Title Act was a political compromise that responded to the political weight of the interested parties, and the outcome was more about advancement of commercial titles rather than protection of native title.[93] Indigenous representatives had to concede several points in negotiation. However, at the time, the passing of the Native Title Act was considered a victory for Indigenous people. Not only did the Commonwealth government assert its primacy in making laws for Indigenous Australians, Indigenous aspirations and leadership gained prominence in Australia as Indigenous leaders secured a place in parliamentary processes that afforded them a measure of recognition and respect enabling dialogue and negotiations with Prime Minister Paul Keating and his government.

Precedent was set for inclusion of Indigenous Australians in the parliamentary process, which has not been replicated at such a scale since then because the political space only existed due to the grace and goodwill of Prime Minister Paul Keating. There are still no laws, conventions or recognised practices in Australian government that acknowledge Indigenous people as having a constitutional stake in policymaking and power sharing. In chapter 5 we will see how in 2017 Indigenous Australians put forward proposals for a constitutionally enshrined Indigenous representative advisory voice to Parliament and the negotiation of a treaty with Indigenous people. The proposals for an Indigenous voice and negotiation of a treaty have been met with significant resistance from the government.

The reality of the Native Title Act was its confirmation of the dispossession of Indigenous people by legally validating all past grants and acts of government right back to 1788. Societal assumptions grounded in the notion of terra nullius and fears that native title would impair or dispossess other Australians of their rights in land are evident in the legislation. Christabel Chamarette, the Western Australian Greens senator involved in passing the bill, said that the objective and effect of native title legislation was to provide security to other existing stakeholders in land and even extend those tenures so that native title would not challenge those interests. Further, she argues that the position of the Liberal-National Coalition was fundamentally based on terra nullius.[94] The government assumed that to prevent any challenge from native title they could restrict or extinguish it and pay native titleholders' financial compensation for the damage caused. But native title emanates from Indigenous culture and heritage, therefore the assumption that Indigenous people would accept extinguishment of their culture and heritage, reflects the kind of thinking that informed terra nullius discourse in the first place. Today, the Crown is able to extinguish native title even though its own claim to sovereignty lies in terra nullius. The concept of terra nullius is a historically wrong colonial doctrine that subjugates Indigenous people. It should be repudiated.

The Aboriginal organisations that participated in the legislative and political process came together to represent the land interests of their Aboriginal constituents and to protect native title rights. ATSIC was not involved in their initial meetings. As the Commonwealth government began to impose its schedule and process, the group of organisations saw the need to widen their representative status, which involved developing a cooperative partnership with ATSIC. Eventually, a group of land councils from northern Australia and ATSIC became the interlocutors for the government. From the government's perspective ATSIC was the national Indigenous representative body, acting as an advisor to the government on Indigenous policy. According to Paul Coe this provided the appearance that the government had consulted and negotiated with Indigenous people and obtained their endorsement.[95] However, ATSIC was a government created entity that negotiated with the government and therefore was perceived to have been co-opted by it.

While various Indigenous representatives asserted their rightful negotiating status, they were also criticised for negotiating with the government because most Indigenous people were disenfranchised during the process. While Indigenous participation was pivotal for bringing the bill into fruition, the government dictated much of the consultative process and the model for legislation. There were numerous calls by the Indigenous organisations for the government to provide resources to enable Indigenous people to participate more fully, but the government saw no need to develop a wide consultative programme or commit resources to a *Mabo* information programme for Indigenous people or for the general population. It is a common tactic of the government to keep consultations as narrow as possible and to only consult with select 'Aboriginal leaders'.[96]

DIALOGUE AND RESPECT

Although there is now symbolic recognition of Aboriginal people as prior occupiers of the Australian continent, this recognition has its basis in moral atonement. The reality in Australia is that there is no formal relationship of mutual recognition and respect between Aboriginal people and the government. Prime Minister Keating's Redfern Park speech in December 1992 provided the cornerstone for Indigenous inclusion and for resolving colonial grievances. Keating's willingness to meet and negotiate directly with Indigenous representatives created the political space for dialogue and negotiation. However, his recognition of Indigenous people was not based on recognition of Indigenous nationhood or any constitutional right of Indigenous people, even though his moral and inclusive approach enabled the Indigenous representatives to play an active role in the negotiated outcome. Despite early problems in the relationship, Indigenous representatives grew to respect Prime Minister Keating for his strong stance. As we will see in the final section of this chapter, this is in direct contrast to how Prime Minister John Howard treated Indigenous representatives during the further amendments made to the Native Title Act in 1996–1997 after the *Wik* High Court judgment,[97] when they were excluded from the government and constitutional process.

During the negotiation of the original Native Title Act, the executive director of the NFF, Rick Farley was a positive force. Farley had 'gone out on a limb' and provided legitimacy to the government's legislation. Although criticised by sections of the NFF constituency, he was able to rise above the politics of the debate.[98] Farley was a member of the Council for Aboriginal Reconciliation and sought to balance the interests of his rural constituency with a commitment to reconciliation, thus enabling NFF to remain in the negotiating process.[99] There was respect from the Indigenous representatives for Rick Farley and the NFF for its constructive approach. But the NFF's stance would change after the *Wik* High Court decision in 1996, which recognised that native title could coexist with pastoral leases.

The role of Phillip Toyne in linking the Indigenous voice into the government process was also constructive and his decent and respectful approach engendered respect from the Indigenous representatives. Left and central-left factions of the parliamentary Labor Party supported the Indigenous negotiating strategy building a relationship of respect. Although relations were often strained with the Greens, there was a relationship of respect between the Greens and the Aboriginal Coalition that also extended to the Democrats and the Aboriginal Alliance. However, the same could not be said of the government officials who drove an extinguishment agenda regarding native title. The officials set the government agenda and had direct access to Prime Minister Keating.

What troubled the Indigenous representatives was the conflict between the prime minister's public statement about *Mabo* being an opportunity and a basis for reconciliation and his bureaucratic advisors' interest in achieving 'certainty' for industry, state and territory governments. Taken to its logical conclusion, 'certainty' to industry, state and territory governments meant extinguishment of native title.

While there was dialogue and negotiation involving elements of recognition and respect between the prime minister and the Indigenous representatives, the process relied on the goodwill of Prime Minister Paul Keating. It was neither a postcolonial dialogue of mutual recognition nor was it a dialogue of reflection in which government would examine its underlying assumptions about Indigenous people and respond with a different political approach. The government's approach was driven by its assumption that economic and other land interests had to be protected from the impact of native title.

THE LIMITATIONS

The politics surrounding the recognition of native title meant that this significant development in the aftermath of the *Mabo* decision was unable to transform the colonial relationship in Australia. In 1992, the response of settler Australians to the *Mabo* judgment was to treat native title and Indigenous rights as a threat. In his Redfern Park speech, Prime Minister Keating attempted to focus Australians on the impact of dispossession on Indigenous people and their failure to make the 'most basic human response' to Indigenous people. In his leadership role he tried to create an environment in which Australians would confront these issues and examine their attitudes and opinions. However, the racially charged debate ultimately trumped the prime minister's goodwill. Settler colonialism continues, which is demonstrated in the attitudes, assumptions and practices of Australian governmental institutions. What continues to drive these negative assumptions and attitudes is the failure to acknowledge historical as well as contemporary truths about wrongdoing and injustice. This failure is reflected in the denial of injustice against Indigenous people, the projection of fears that culminate in assertions of Indigenous greed, privilege and illegality, as well as perceptions that Indigenous people are the enemy of the nation.[100]

Today, settler colonialism is a powerful, dominating force in Australia. Its operation is not dependent on the presence or absence of formal state intuitions[101] because it can manifest itself through 'private-public partnerships' where the state colludes with global capitalism to structure and manage contemporary social and economic life, particularly by securing land and resources while strategically managing Indigenous people to ensure that they do not threaten resource development projects.[102]

The validation provision of the Native Title Act and the absence of a veto right for Indigenous people over future development reflects the inequality of power held by Indigenous people in comparison to the mining industry.[103] It also reflects private/public collusion given the influence of the mining industries' propaganda campaign on the government and its successful outcome in forcing the government to take a validation and extinguishment approach in respect to native title.

Winning a High Court case can gain important recognition of rights for Indigenous people; however, the value of the decision depends on how others respond to Indigenous claims. Parliament, politicians and government officials respond according to the assumptions and attitudes of industry and the broader Australian population. If industry views Indigenous rights as a threat and the Australian population are in denial, apathetic or perceive Indigenous people as privileged, the government will act accordingly. This is clear in how the government responded to the *Mabo* judgment. While Indigenous people forced open a space for dialogue and negotiation, that space did not endure because of the absence of constitutional practices and conventions in Australia where Indigenous people can assert their claims and have them recognised. The rights and interests of Indigenous people in settler states are viewed as stakeholder interests in a constitutional system that balances Indigenous rights and interests against the those of Australian commercial and private interests. The Australian government is not inclined to accommodate political pluralism by valuing or respecting Indigenous voices and recognising Indigenous authority.

While the *Mabo* judgment developed new insights regarding inherent Indigenous rights and political leadership enabled a negotiated outcome, limitations are inherent because politicians serve institutions and traditions within Australian constitutional government that have, throughout history, resisted and discredited Indigenous claims for recognition. They are also inclined to find policy and legal solutions within a liberal nationalist approach that accords with what is acceptable to the dominant Australian population. In that regard, the politics of recognition does not significantly modify colonial relationships.[104] Real change in the situation of Indigenous people requires a fundamental shift in the structure of power that will allow Indigenous peoples to regain control over their lives.[105] There is a positive correlation between Indigenous people resuming responsibility for their societies and the well-being of their members.[106] The ongoing challenge is to find ways of going beyond the exclusion or assimilation of Indigenous difference, which includes consideration of Indigenous self-determination.[107]

After the *Mabo* decision Australian society had to accept that Indigenous Australians had pre-existing land rights, however there had been an ongoing resistance to Indigenous rights with the emergence of the New Right in the 1980s. With the election of the Howard Liberal-Coalition government in 1996, conservative political opposition to Indigenous rights would resurface.

A DECADE OF DESPONDENCY

When elected in March 1996, the Federal Liberal-Coalition government led by Prime Minister John Howard promoted the narrative that Indigenous self-determination, institutions, programmes and services had failed over the previous two decades, therefore assimilationist and coercive intervention was required.[108] The first move of the Howard government was to appoint a minister for Indigenous affairs who had no knowledge or experience of the portfolio and who focussed on the financial accountability of Aboriginal organisations, particularly the accountability of the Aboriginal and Torres Strait Islander Commission (ATSIC).[109] ATSIC was a statutory authority established by the Hawke Labor government in 1989. It had a representative, advisory, advocacy and programme delivery role. Following accusations of corruption, Minister John Herron ordered a special audit for Aboriginal organisations to monitor and approve all ATSIC funds disbursed to those organisations – 95 percent of the Aboriginal organisations audited had their funding approved and the remaining had only minor technical irregularities.[110]

John Howard also changed the focus of the reconciliation process when he came to power. In an aggressive and hectoring speech at the Australian Reconciliation Convention in May 1997, Howard distinguished between practical matters such as health care, housing, education, employment and so-called symbolic issues, such as Indigenous rights, the stolen generations and so on, which he believed premised reconciliation on national guilt and shame.[111] This dichotomy became the focus of the Howard government's agenda: abolishing the policy of Indigenous self-determination, which had existed since 1972, and redefining reconciliation on 'practical' terms, which merely reduced the concept of reconciliation to enable Indigenous people fair access to general citizenship rights. However, 'practical' reconciliation failed to address the delivery of equitable support to Indigenous people, and so failed to deliver better socioeconomic outcomes for Indigenous people.[112] The approach sought to ensure that blame or guilt was not apportioned to settler-colonials for past wrongs. It rejected key recommendations of the National Inquiry into the Separation of Aboriginal and Torres Strait Islander Children from their Families and refused to formally apologise to the stolen generations as well as reducing the Native Title Act of 1993 with a discriminatory package of amendments on the presumption that the pendulum had swung too far in favour of Indigenous rights.[113]

The Howard government would go on to dismantle national Indigenous representation, undermine Indigenous authority and political voices, and introduce an individual responsibility paradigm into policy and practice.[114] Contrary to the recommendations of its own review, the Howard government, with the support of the Labor Opposition, abolished ATSIC in 2004 and mainstreamed ATSIC funding and programmes to other Commonwealth departments and agencies.[115] The government appointed a National Indigenous Council of hand-picked people to replace the elected board of ATSIC. ATSIC was created to allow Indigenous people self-determination and a voice in government for Indigenous policymaking; by abolishing ATSIC the Howard government effectively abandoned the policy of self-determination.[116]

SUPPRESSING NATIVE TITLE

The case of the *Wik and Thayorre Peoples v the State of Queensland* (1996) is a judgment of the High Court of Australia on appeal from a decision of the Federal Court. In June 1993, the Wik and Thayorre peoples, whose traditional lands includes Cape York in Queensland, filed a claim for traditional ownership of land including rivers, tidal lands and seas. They sought a declaration of their Aboriginal and possessory title over traditional lands and claimed damages and other relief if it was found that these rights had been extinguished. The claim covered several titles granted over their traditional lands including mining leases, pastoral leases, Aboriginal reserve special leases, deed of grant in trust and national park and Crown land. The Wik people claimed land in which future rights to mine bauxite had been granted to the mining company Comalco; however, their claim was mostly to land that had once been part of the Holroyd pastoral lease. The Thayorre people claimed land that had been part of the Michellton pastoral lease. The issues that were appealed to the High Court related to two questions: Did the pastoral leases give a right of exclusive possession to the pastoralists, and if so, did the grant of a pastoral lease extinguish any native title in the land covered by the pastoral lease? Wik and Thayorre argued that native title coexisted with the pastoral lease.

On 23 December 1996, four judges comprising the majority of the High Court decided that pastoral leases did not confer exclusive possession to the pastoralist; in particular it did not give possession that excluded the rights and interests of the Indigenous inhabitants. A grant of a pastoral lease under the Queensland Land Act is not necessarily inconsistent with native title and does not necessarily extinguish native title. If there is any inconsistency between native title rights and the rights of the pastoralists, the pastoralist's rights would prevail. Three judges including Chief Justice Brennan, who had written the majority judgement in the *Mabo* case, dissented by deciding that the pastoral lease extinguished native title. The Wik people lost their challenge to the grant of special bauxite mining leases to the mining company and their challenge to agreements between the mining company and the Queensland government made under special legislation. The Court decided that the leases were valid and that the agreement negotiated by the government took on the force of the legislation.

The mining industry led by the Minerals Council of Australia accepted the existence of native title but called for validation of all mining leases granted over pastoral properties between 1994 and 1996 and for amendments to the Native Title Act, especially limitations on the right of native title claimants to negotiate in respect to mining projects on pastoral leases.[117] The pastoral and farming industry through the NFF provided the most outspoken extreme response to the *Wik* decision, calling for immediate federal legislation to provide for the exclusive possession by pastoralists of their leases, extinguishment of native title on pastoral leases and procedural amendments to the Native Title Act.[118] The National Party, the coalition partner of the Liberal government through its leader Deputy Prime Minister Tim Fischer, called for extinguishment of native title on pastoral leases and compensation for such extinguishment.[119] State governments, particularly the Northern Territory, Queensland and Western Australia called for the extinguishment of native title on pastoral leases, replacing native title with statutory access rights for Aboriginal people to pastoral leases.[120] Against such powerful opponents the National Indigenous Working Group—a coalition of Indigenous organisations and the ATSIC—called on the Commonwealth government to adopt a non-discriminatory policy in dealing with the property rights of all Australians, which included non-extinguishment or impairment of native title; no amendments to the Native Title Act that eroded existing Indigenous rights; and for the Commonwealth to negotiate with Indigenous people over proposed amendments to the Native Title Act.

The Howard government ignored the Indigenous position because it was working on amendments to the Native Title Act in the form of a '10 Point Plan'. By May 1997, the government had endorsed this plan, which among another things validated all acts and grants between 1994 and 1996: it confirmed extinguishment of native title on exclusive tenures including provision of governments services on land, future government and commercial development, and management of water and airspace; pastoral and agricultural leases would extinguish native title to the extent of any inconsistency; and continued statutory access by Aboriginal people to pastoral leases. The plan also endorsed a higher registration test for native title claimants seeking the right to negotiate on mining projects and a higher registration test for new and existing native title claims.[121] Deputy Prime Minister Tim Fischer described the plan as having 'bucketfuls of extinguishment'.[122] The cumulative effect of the ten-point plan was de facto extinguishment by marginalising and suppressing native title, plus significantly reducing the Indigenous right to negotiate.

The government ignored the National Indigenous Working Group and did not negotiate with them on amendments to the Native Title Act. In that regard the strategy of the Indigenous leaders was to improve the bill in the Senate by working with the Opposition Labor Party and the minor Greens and Democrat parties, as well as the independent senator Brian Harradine, to bring them closer to the Working Group amendments. The Native Title Amendment Bill of 1997 was introduced into parliament in September, starting a long and arduous process with many months of divisive debate. The government twice rejected the amendments proposed by the Senate before the bill eventually passed in July 1998 with the support of Senator Harradine, who held the balance of power. According to the Aboriginal and Torres Strait Islander Social Justice commissioner, William Jonas, the amendments to the Native Title Act enabled non-Indigenous interests to prevail over Indigenous interests and significantly eroded the gains made from the *Mabo (No. 2)* decision, the original Native Title Act, and the *Wik* decision.[123]

HOWARD'S DISCOURSE

John Howard had bad form in Indigenous affairs before he became prime minister. As leader of the Opposition in the 1980s, he promoted race politics thereby destroying political bipartisanship on Aboriginal affairs, immigration and multiculturalism.[124] In the 1990s, while still in Opposition, Howard's emphasis on Australian nationalism lead him to attack what he called the 'guilt industry' and 'political correctness' in respect to Indigenous affairs.[125] When Howard came to power he sought to change Australian political culture through a discourse that criticised political correctness.[126] Political correctness is a term formerly used by the liberal left of politics to critique dogmatic tendencies within their own movements, but it was co-opted and rebranded by the conservative political right in the 1990s as a weapon to disparage the social and cultural politics of the Left.[127] As a political tactic of the conservative right, use of a discourse to oppose 'political correctness' conjures in the public imagination an enemy or an insidious force that is trying to advance an ulterior agenda, or which is trying to silence ordinary people or trying to deny them their share of goods and benefits in society. It was a rallying call for those with links to the neoliberal political agenda and the political discourse of the New Right, disillusioned by the threat of economic insecurity and resentful of social and cultural change in society.

John Howard railed against political correctness to rally Australians against what he regarded as 'industries' benefiting from the Keating Labor government at the expense of mainstream Australians. He condemned political correctness as a form of social censorship whereby mainstream Australians were being constrained in freely expressing their views and beliefs about certain issues—namely immigration, multicultu-ralism and Aboriginal rights—because they were branded as racists and bigots. His attacks were directed at what he regarded as special interest groups who he believed had the ear of the Keating Labor government and were in receipt of government largesse. Indigenous rights, multicul-turalism, immigration, public broadcasting and others were part of this so-called politically correct industry. The coded message was that ordi-nary Australians were powerless to compete against these so-called spe-cial interest groups because they were influencing the Keating govern-ment and receiving government privileges.[128]

Howard also believed that political correctness was denigrating Aus-tralian history, national character, and Australian values. In 1985, Profes-sor Geoffrey Blainey argued that the Labor Party, who was in power at the time, was the captive of the 'multi-cultural industry' and were disre-spectfully promoting a dark side of Australian history.[129] Blainey coined the term 'black armband history' and this stereotype appealed to Howard because he, along with Blainey, was opposed to the critical stance that emerged in the early 1970s when Australian historians were writing colo-nial history from an Aboriginal viewpoint. In Howard's view this was an attempt to denigrate British-Australian history to coerce the nation into collective guilt about the past. He termed it 'black armband history' that promoted a 'guilt industry' and that was obsessed with 'political correct-ness'.[130] What became known as the 'history wars' was in fact a concerted intellectual and political campaign by Howard and intellectuals on the right of politics who sought to suppress the critical history that was ap-pearing in various contexts such as the stolen generations and Australian frontier conflict, and which influenced the teaching of history in schools.[131]

Howard believed that Australian history was overwhelmingly posi-tive but it had been hijacked and rewritten by revisionist historians for their own political agenda, setting ordinary Australians against each oth-er, thus causing divisions in Australian society.[132] Howard's assault on black armband history and political correctness was in fact an assault on the legacy of the Labor government, which had been in power for some thirteen years. As Labor Prime Minister Paul Keating attempted to recast the stridently nationalist Australian identity and acknowledge that present-day Australians should accept responsibility in atoning for the wrongs committed against Aboriginal people in the past. The representa-tion of Australian history was at the core of the Howard government's position on Australian national identity and self-image.[133] But Howard's version of Australian history had little room or sympathy for the Indige-nous experience of colonialism. While he said the injustices committed against Indigenous people were a 'significant blemish' in Australia's his-tory, he insisted settler Australians should not be held accountable or regarded as guilty.[134]

Howard's denouncement of political correctness was aimed at those whom he regarded as being intolerant of ideas and values in which he believed. His attack on the 'guilt industry' and 'political correctness' was directed at building resentment in the broader population thus facilitating a major public backlash against Aboriginal rights. The backlash included a disparaging and sneering public discourse about Aboriginal people and their culture. It enabled a rollback of Indigenous political and legal recognition and was instrumental in denying the need for an honest account of Australian colonialism and its impact on Indigenous people.

In regard to Aboriginal people, Howard's 'One Australia' rejected any ownership or responsibility for past government policies and practices; a refusal to accept that Aboriginal people had been dispossessed of their land, and a rejection of a treaty with Aboriginal people.[135] It also encompassed social and national unity based on identical treatment and uniform political processes that defined recognition of the special status of Indigenous people as destructive symbolism.[136] To Howard, Indigenous self-determination was a form of separatism and Indigenous people were just another ethnic group in society to be tolerated.[137] The fact that Aboriginal people were dispossessed was irrelevant to John Howard. His belief in equality, social unity and desire to treat people equally resulted in an unwillingness to recognise that past injustices required different treatment for some groups in society. Howard had a narrow frame of reference regarding Indigenous disadvantage – in his view it was a matter of denied opportunity that could be remedied by removing the obstacles that prevented Aboriginal people joining mainstream Australia. Hence, his concentration was on providing health care, education and other services – practical reconciliation – an approach that had little room for questions of land rights, identity, and self-determination.[138]

John Howard's views were like those of Pauline Hanson, a populist politician who was elected as an independent member in 1996. Like Howard, Pauline Hanson had a vision of 'One Nation', and she rejected any responsibility for the past policies of government regarding Indigenous people on the basis that white Australians should not feel guilty about the past. She called for the abolishment of multiculturalism and a halt to immigration. However, unlike Howard who supported assistance to Indigenous people, Hanson called for the abolishment of benefits to Aboriginal people. In her maiden speech to Parliament, Hanson attacked those who promoted political correctness and controlled taxpayer funded 'industries' that serviced Aboriginals, multiculturalists and other minority groups. She said governments were encouraging separatism by providing 'opportunities, land, money and facilities' only for Aboriginals. She said she was fed up with the inequalities being promoted by governments and paid for by taxpayers on the assumptions that Aboriginals are the most disadvantaged in Australia. She called for the abolition of ATSIC. She believed the country was in danger of being swamped by

Asians, stating that they have their own culture and religion, form ghettos and do not assimilate. She wanted immigration policy radically reviewed and multiculturalism abolished.[139] Hanson triggered a nationwide debate on race.

John Howard believed that Indigenous policy was based on a paradigm of non-Indigenous shame and guilt, on a rejection of the Australia that he grew up in, on a rights agenda that led to welfare dependency, and on a philosophy of separateness rather than shared destiny.[140] Viewed from an Indigenous perspective, Howard's thinking is wrongheaded. Recognising Indigenous rights, uncovering the truth of history and resolving outstanding issues by way of treaty was never about making settler Australians feel guilty. It is about justice as well as acknowledging and respecting Indigenous people and their human rights. Indigenous people want the nation to reflect, to look at itself and accept the legal and moral reality of the past, learn lessons and use that reality and those lessons to genuinely resolve contemporary and future issues. This requires the acknowledgement of historical and contemporary truths, an understanding of the unique situation of Indigenous people within the nation, a capacity to empathise and a genuine desire to improve relationships between governments and Indigenous peoples. But John Howard knew exactly what he was doing. In many respects he was following historical precedence where Australian governments and politicians have either ignored, dismissed, reinterpreted or crushed Indigenous claims for recognition.

Howard was able to popularise his attitudes, assumptions and personal beliefs about Indigenous people in his attacks on political correctness and the so-called guilt industry. He lacked genuine respect for Aboriginal people, and he failed to see the social and economic progress that was being made on the ground in communities and at the political level. Instead, he turned Indigenous affairs upside down through a neoliberal ideology of assimilation that was imposed top-down and which sought to disempower Indigenous people. The upheaval of Indigenous affairs during the Howard decade still reverberates today because his government returned Indigenous policy to a time in the past when policies of assimilation thwarted Indigenous peoples' prospects of determining their own future.[141] Indigenous policy has regressed in many ways since the decade of the Howard government. There is now political and social disinterest and resistance to Indigenous recognition. Indigenous people and their claims for recognition are no longer taken seriously, and it is much more difficult to engender a level of understanding and goodwill in Australian society about the need for a renewed relationship with Indigenous people.

SETTLER AUTHORITY

The Commonwealth government's intervention into Northern Territory Aboriginal communities in June 2007 is a clear example of how Australian government and society have always approached dealing with Indigenous people. The intervention was a low point in contemporary Indigenous affairs policy. The Federal Howard Coalition government carried out punitive action against Aboriginal people in the Northern Territory under the pretext of 'stabilising and protecting' Aboriginal communities to protect Aboriginal children from abuse and violence as detailed in the *Little Children Are Sacred* report of the Northern Territory government.[142] That report found child sexual abuse was serious and widespread in Aboriginal communities. The report also found that much of the violence in communities was a result of past, current, and continuing social problems (such as poor health care, alcohol and drug abuse, unemployment, gambling, pornography, poor education and housing, loss of identity and control), and it also found that government service provision to communities needs to be improved to break the cycle of poverty and violence. The report stated that Aboriginal people were committed to solving the problem, and that government should consult with and work with them to design initiatives that help communities prevent and tackle child sexual abuse.

However, on June 21, 2007, Prime Minister John Howard and Minister for Indigenous Affairs Mal Brough announced a 'national emergency', which became known as the 'Northern Territory Emergency Response' (NTER) or 'NT intervention'. The government announced a series of measures applying to all people living in seventy-three remote Northern Territory Aboriginal communities. The police and army were mobilised to help facilitate the implementation of these measures.[143] On 7 August 2007, the government introduced five bills containing the Northern Territory national emergency response legislation into the House of Representatives. After a brief one-day hearing in parliament, the legislation passed through the house with the support of the Australian Labor Party. The Legal and Constitutional Committee conducted a one-day public hearing tabling its report on the Emergency Response Legislation on 13 August. On 17 August, the bills passed through the Senate, received Royal Assent and were enacted as legislation on the same day.[144] The speed of the parliamentary process was breathtaking and unprecedented. The legislation enabled the government to control the way Aboriginal people lived in prescribed townships and how they spent welfare payments. It controlled goods and services into communities—particularly alcohol, pornographic material, gambling and tobacco; conferred new powers on the police to enter private property without a warrant; controlled the use of government-funded computers; excluded customary and cultural practices in bail and sentencing; controlled community organisations through funding agreements; supervised and controlled community government councils as well as community stores; and modified the permit system to allow greater access to Aboriginal land and enable compulsory acquisition of townships from Traditional Owners.[145]

While there was agreement that child abuse and family violence in Aboriginal communities should be treated as a national priority, Aboriginal leaders expressed concern at the possible harmful consequences of such a quick response, made without consulting with the communities involved. Combined Aboriginal organisations in the Northern Territory developed a proposal in response to the governments' intervention; however, the government was unwilling to enter any dialogue or negotiations with Aboriginal communities.[146] The federal government's approach raised questions in relation to Australia's international obligation to respect and promote Indigenous human rights. Several NTER measures discriminated against Aboriginal people.[147] However, the government exempted its action from the prohibition on racial discrimination under the Racial Discrimination Act (RDA) based on the emergency legislation and its purported benefit as special measures. The operation of the RDA was suspended so there could be no challenge to what government or government officials did under the legislation. The intervention legislation also suspended the operation of the Northern Territory Anti-Discrimination Act.[148] The government measures were overtly discriminatory, infringed Aboriginal rights of self-determination and further stigmatised Aboriginal communities.[149]

The United Nations Special Rapporteur on the situation of human rights and fundamental freedoms of Indigenous people stated that the NTER measures involved racial discrimination because firstly, they distinguished on the basis of race as they were intended to apply specifically to Aboriginal individuals and communities in the Northern Territory; and secondly, the differential treatment of Aboriginal people involved the impairment of the enjoyment of various human rights, which are recognised in the International Covenant on Civil and Political Rights and the United Nations Declaration on the Rights of Indigenous Peoples. The United Nations Special Rapporteur said the discriminatory aspects of the NTER did not qualify as 'special measures', adding that it would be 'quite extraordinary' to find measures that limit or infringe the rights of a disadvantaged group in order to assist the group or certain of its members to be consistent with the objectives of the Convention on the Elimination of Racial Discrimination.[150] The Australian Indigenous Doctors Association stated that while the NTER addressed physical and social and environmental determinants to improve child health-care outcomes, they forecast that any improvements in physical health would be outweighed by negative impacts on psychological health, spirituality and cultural integrity of the Aboriginal population in the prescribed communities. They said the NTER had overlooked the centrality of human dignity to health. However, these negative impacts could be mitigated if the NT and the Australian governments would commit to and invest in respectful partnerships with Aboriginal leaders and organisations.[151]

The politics around the intervention had much to do with its main protagonists, John Howard and Mal Brough, as well the chief minister of the Northern Territory, Clare Martin and her government. John Howard had a history of going hard on Aboriginal people and Aboriginal issues, and the NTER was no exception. For Howard, the intervention was not about saving Aboriginal people in the Northern Territory but about saving himself. It was a grand venture to politically reinvent himself, an attempt to transform his reputation as an uncaring, distant leader. To Mal Brough the intervention was a means to implement his political agenda in Indigenous communities in the Northern Territory, particularly in respect to Aboriginal town camps in Alice Springs, ninety-nine-year leases for townships on Aboriginal land, remote area housing and the permit system for Aboriginal land. Chief Minister Clare Martin also held the Indigenous affairs portfolio; however, she was averse to addressing the apathy and neglect in respect to health, housing, education, alcohol and violence in Aboriginal communities; this was a situation of neglect her government had inherited from the former Country Liberal Party government. Her lack of immediate action in responding to the *Little Children are Sacred* report, which her government had commissioned, provided the necessary authorisation for Howard and Brough to carry out the intervention.[152]

The intervention into Northern Territory Aboriginal communities illustrates how fear, prejudice and negative discourses of Aboriginal people, which have their basis in erroneous colonial assumptions, became part of the political and societal narrative to justify the intervention. The government and supporters of the intervention constructed Aboriginal identity and culture to conflate Aboriginality with abuse of children, who in turn needed rescuing from a defective Aboriginal culture. Aboriginality was again characterised as primitive, savage, violent and threatening and therefore in need of state-imposed control, discipline and forcible assimilation. Aboriginal communities were referred to as disorderly, independent cultural and political zones, which required authority to be extended over them to assimilate them into the moral order of the nation and reinforce the legitimacy and sovereignty of the settler state.[153] The discourse around the intervention problematised and pathologised Aboriginal people and their communities; it concurred with the historical treatment of Aboriginal people. The intervention hoped to remedy the 'problem of Aboriginality' through coercion and assimilation.

John Howard won four consecutive terms in government between 1996 and 2007. Over that period he successfully diminished or overturned nearly all of the significant advances Indigenous people had made in regard to self-determination, reconciliation, addressing the past, native title and the 'stolen generations'. This tells us much about Australian society, which repeatedly voted him into government. During his time in government, he dismantled the Indigenous rights agenda and smashed Indigenous authority. Did he lack compassion for Indigenous people? Why did most of Australian society let him do what he did? While there have been exceptions throughout history, it is clear that those who make policy and political decisions about Indigenous Australians are generally lacking in compassion and understanding. However, most crucially they have never looked at themselves or reflected on why they hold the assumptions, views and opinions they have about Indigenous people. It is incumbent upon politicians, public decision makers and Australian society to look at themselves and to question their own assumptions and attitudes about Indigenous people.

NOTES

1. P. Keating, Australian Launch of the International Year for the World's Indigenous People (Speech, Redfern, NSW, 10 December 1992).

2. G. Cowlishaw, 'Did the Earth Move For You? The anti-Mabo Debate', in *Mabo and Australia, On Recognising Native Title After Two Hundred Years*, Gillian Cowlishaw and Vivienne Kondos, eds. (Sydney, NSW: The Australian Journal of Anthropology, August 1995), 60–62.

3. J. Hammond and J. Walker, *The Australian*, 13 May 1993, 1–2.

4. T. Hewett and M. Magazanik, 'Blacks culturally backward: Perron', *The Age*, 7 July 1993.

5. N. Bita and D. Nason, 'Perron slated for hygiene remark', *The Australian*, 8 July 1993, 5.

6. W. H. Willshire, *The Aborigines of Central Australia* (Adelaide, SA: Government Printer, North Terrace, 1891), 28. https://digital.library.adelaide.edu.au/dspace/bitstream/2440/18481/1/Willshire1.pdf.

7. R. Peake, 'Fischer inciting fear: PM', *The Canberra Times*, Wednesday, 13 January 1993, 3.

8. J. Walker, N. Bita and M. Irving, 'Fischer opens split on Mabo', *The Australian*, 21 June 1993, 1–2.

9. J. Walker and A. M. Moodie, 'Downer attacks Fischer outburst', *The Australian*, 22 June 1993, 1.

10. 'Savages and Civilised Men', *Science of Man, Journal of the Royal Anthropological Society of Australasia* 6, no. 2, 21 March (1903), 34. http://nla.gov.au/nla.obj-525829330.pdf.

11. G. Blainey, 'Mabo: what Aboriginals lost', *The Age*, 31 July 1993.

12. G. Blainey, 'Land rights for all', *The Age*, 10 November 1993, 15.

13. J. Locke, *The Second Treatise of Civil Government*, chapter 5, no. 34, first published 1690, e-book with text derived from sixth edition 1764, University of Adelaide Library, South Australia, last updated 17 December 2014. https://ebooks.adelaide.edu.au/l/locke/john/l81s/complete.html [Accessed 10 September 2019].

14. E. de Vattel, 'The Status of Aboriginal People, The Law of Nations', book I, chapter 8, in *A Source Book of Australian Legal History*, John Michael Bennett and Alex Cuthbert Castles, eds. (Sydney, NSW: The Law Book Company, 1979) 250–52.

15. H. M. Morgan, 'Mabo Reconsidered' (The Joe and Enid Lyons Memorial Lecture, Australian National University, 12 October 1992), 4–6.

16. P. Chamberlin, 'Mining Chief lashes Mabo', *The Sydney Morning Herald*, 1 July 1993.

17. Observations of the Editor, *The Age*, Melbourne, 11 January 1888, 4 (column 6–7). https://trove.nla.gov.au/newspaper/page/18437362.

18. P. Gill, 'Miners put Mabo plan to Government', *The Australian Financial Review*, 16 September 1993; G. W. Ewing, 'The Australian Mining Industry Council and its Role in the Mabo Debate' (AUSIMM Student Conference, Pathway to Industry, Brisbane, 28–29 April 1994), 18.

19. D. Humphries and M. Irving, 'Court's Bill on Mabo sets scene for federal fight', *The Australian*, 29 October 1993, 1–2.

20. A. Markus, 'Between Mabo and a hard place: race and the contradictions of conservatism', in *In the age of Mabo: History, Aborigines and Australia*, Bain Attwood, ed. (St Leonards, NSW: Allen & Unwin, 1996), 88–92, 99.

21. N. Pearson, '204 Years Of Invisible Title', in *Mabo: A Judicial Revolution*, M. A. Stephenson and Suri Ratnapala, eds. (St Lucia, QLD: University of QLD Press, 1993), 77–78.

22. B. Attwood, 'Mabo, Australia and the end of history', in *In the Age of Mabo: History, Aborigines and Australia*, Bain Attwood, ed. (St Leonards, NSW: Allen & Unwin, 1996), 102–3, 111.

23. D. Short, 'The Social Construction of Indigenous "Native Title" Land Rights in Australia', *Current Sociology* 55, no. 6, 866.

24. Commonwealth of Australia, 'The High Court Decision on Native Title' (Canberra, ACT, Prime Minister and Cabinet, October 1992).

25. Council for Aboriginal Reconciliation, 'Making things rights: Reconciliation after the High Court's decision on native title' (Canberra, ACT, Council for Aboriginal Reconciliation, Australia, January 1993), 9–11.

26. Council for Aboriginal Reconciliation, 'Walking together: The first steps', Report to Federal Parliament 1991–1994 (Canberra, ACT, Council for Aboriginal Reconciliation, Australia, 1994), 52.

27. Aboriginal and Torres Strait Islander Commission, 'Response to the consultation process concerning the Mabo Decision' (Canberra, ACT, ATSIC, 1993).

28. The Kimberley, Cape York, Central and Northern Land Councils, the New South Wales Aboriginal Land Council, the Western Australian Aboriginal Legal Service, ATSIC, Patrick Dodson and Mick Dodson, the newly appointed Aboriginal and Torres Strait Islander social justice commissioner.

29. Indigenous representatives were: Mick Dodson—Aboriginal & Torres Strait Islander Social Justice Commissioner; Lois O'Donoghue, George Mye, Gerhardt Pearson—ATSIC; Jean George, Noel Pearson—Cape York Land Council; Kunmanara Breaden, David Ross—Central Land Council; Patrick Dodson, Wenten Rubuntja—Council for Aboriginal Reconciliation; John Watson, Peter Yu—Kimberley Land Council; Manual Ritchie, Danny Chapman—NSW Aboriginal Land Council; Galarrwuy Yunupingu, John Ah Kit—Northern Land Council; Tauto Sansbury, Esther Williams—SA Aboriginal Legal Rights Movement; Getano Lui—Torres Strait Island Coordinating Council; Ted Wilkes, Robert Riley—WA Aboriginal Legal Service. Government representatives were: Paul Keating, Robert Tickner, Frank Walker, John Dawkins, Simon Crean, Ralph Willis, Duncan Kerr, Warren Snowden, Michael Lee, Sandy Hollway, Simon Balderstone.

30. T. Rowse, *Obliged to be Difficult, Nugget Coombs' Legacy in Indigenous Affairs* (Cambridge, UK: Cambridge University Press), 197.

31. Pearson, '204 Years of Invisible Title', 89.

32. Commonwealth of Australia, 'The Mabo High Court Decision on Native Title', Discussion Paper (Canberra, ACT: Australian Government Publishing Service, 1993).

33. J. Brough, 'Govt backs off after black leaders' blast', *The Canberra Times*, 4 June 1993, 1, 4; P. Chamberlin, 'Mabo Paper "A Slimy Document"', *Sydney Morning Herald*, 4 June 1993.

34. R. Peake, 'State revolt over Mabo', *The Canberra Times*, 9 June 1993, 1, 2; R. Peake, 'States defiant on land titles', *The Canberra Times*, 10 June 1993, 1, 2.

35. P. Keating, 'Statement by the Prime Minister, the Hon. P. J. Keating MP', Council of Australian Governments Meeting, Melbourne, 9 June 1993.

36. P. Keating, 'Statement by the Prime Minister, the Hon. P. J. Keating MP', Canberra ACT, 18 June 1993.

37. The Indigenous organisation position was taken from several internal discussion and position papers produced by the Indigenous organisations.

38. P. Keating, 'Address by the Prime Minister, the Hon. P. J. Keating MP', National Press Club, Canberra, ACT, 22 July 1993.

39. 'Labor left warns PM of flaws in Mabo law', *The Australian*, 26 July 1993, 2.

40. P. Keating, Transcript of the Prime Minister, the Hon. P. J. Keating MP, interview with Paul Murphy, Dateline SBS, 28 July 1993.

41. R. Tickner, 'The importance of Negotiation and Certainty', Media Release, the Hon. Robert Tickner MP, Minister for Aboriginal and Torres Strait Islander Affairs, Canberra, ACT, 28 July 1993.

42. The members of this working group were: Peter Yu, Michael Mansell, Darryl Pearce, David Ross, Noel Pearson, Marcia Langton, Rob Riley, Sandra Saunders, Geoff Clark, Archie Barton, Danny Chapman, Manuel Ritchie, Phil Cooper, Billy Craigie, Terry O'Shane, Kaye Mundine, Barbara Flick, Isobelle Coe.

43. K. Scott, 'Blacks bounce Govt on Mabo', *The Canberra Times*, 6 August 1993, 1, 2.

44. P. Keating, 'Mabo—The truth about consultation', Statement by the Prime Minister, the Hon. P. J. Keating MP, Sydney, NSW, 6 August 1993.

45. The author began work as full-time coordinator in Canberra in September 1993 having taken over from the Central Land Council employee who had been coordinating the representative group.

46. Commonwealth of Australia, 'Mabo: Outline of Proposed legislation on Native Title', Canberra, ACT: Commonwealth of Australia, September 1993.

47. J. Sexton, D. Nason and F. Kennedy, 'It fails on three fronts, says ATSIC', *The Australian*, 3 September 1993, 2.

48. P, Gill, 'WA delays legislation clash over Mabo titles', *The Australian Financial Review*, 16 September 1993.

49. P. Coe, 'Position Paper on the Commonwealth Outline of the Proposed Legislation on Native Title and NSW Draft Native Title Bill 1993', NSW Aboriginal legal Service, Unpublished, Sydney, 24 September 1993.

50. 'Anger as Government sells out over Mabo', *Land Rights News*, October 1993, 3, 13.

51. Aboriginal and Torres Strait Islander Social Justice Commissioner, *First Report* Human Rights and Equal Opportunity Commission (Canberra, ACT: Australian Government Publishing Service, 1993), 19–26.

52. Australian Council for Overseas Aid, 'Australian Council for Overseas Aid Denounces Racist Legislation', Media Release, 27 September 1993.

53. ATSIC, Australian Democrats, Greens (WA), 'Mabo Statement', Joint Media Release, Canberra, ACT, 30 September 1993.

54. M. Henzell, 'Media Release', Marjorie Henzell MP, Federal Member for Capricornia, Canberra, ACT, 6 October 1993.

55. C. Forbes, 'Aboriginal leader threatens to quit over discord', *The Australia*, 6 October 1993, 3.

56. David Ross, Noel Pearson and Darryl Pearce attended this meeting.

57. These included any suspension or impairment of the RDA; any restriction on native title holders/claimants to choose and Commonwealth or State Tribunal; any cut-off date later than June 1993; and any failure to provide a genuine opportunity to negotiate a fair outcome through arbitration after negotiations fail.

58. P. Keating, 'Mabo Negotiations", Statement by the Prime Minister, the Hon. P. J. Keating MP, Canberra, ACT, 7 October 1993.

59. P. Chamberlin, 'Black fury over Mabo deal', *The Sydney Morning Herald*, 9 October 1993, 1; K. Scott, 'Aborigines "sold out' by Keating"', *The Canberra Times*, 9 October

1993, 1 and 2; L. Tingle, 'PM failed us on Mabo: Aborigines', *The Weekend Australian*, 9–10 October 1993.

60. R. Tickner, *Taking a Stand. Land Rights to Reconciliation* (Crows Nest, NSW: Allen & Unwin, 2001), 194.

61. In his book *Taking a Stand* (2001), Robert Tickner, Aboriginal and Torres Strait Islander Affairs minister at the time states that the special measures approach was originally put forward by AMIC to the government in early 1993 but reportedly raised again by two Sydney barristers who were consulted by Daryl Melham.

62. A. Ramsey, 'Sicking on the dogs at 30,000 feet', *The Sydney Morning Herald*, 16 October 1993, 33.

63. There was agreement on the government's position in relation to the following: Crown ownership of minerals, extension of negotiation time limits, negotiation rights for nonregistered claimants, Commonwealth tribunal, coexistence and mining leases, no sunset clause, funding Indigenous organisations and Social Justice Package. There was no shift on principles but reluctant acceptance of the government's position on the override of tribunal decision and validation cut-off date. Agreement was close on: negotiation rights for all grants, negotiation rights for compulsory acquisitions, no grants over native title unless over freehold and special attachment and compensation. A few major issues were outstanding on: no suspension of RDA, no extinguishment by validation, compensation for all past extinguishment, choice of Commonwealth/State tribunals, hunting, harvesting and fishing rights.

64. Tickner, *Taking a Stand*, 190.

65. N. Pearson, 'A troubling inheritance', *Race & Class* 35, no. 4 (1994), 5.

66. T. Burton, 'How the Mabo pact was struck', *The Financial Review*, 20 October 1993, 1 and 10; P. Cole-Adams, 'Backroom Mabo wrangling ends in coup for Keating', *The Canberra Times*, 20 October 1993, 13; L. Tingle, '11th hour offer clinched Farley', *The Australian*, 20 October 1993; Tickner, *Taking a Stand*, 197–98.

67. N. Brown and S. Boden, *A way through: the life of Rick Farley* (Sydney, NSW: New South Publishing, University of NSW, 2012), 223–24.

68. Aboriginal and Torres Strait Islander Commission, 'Mabo Agreement Reached', *The ATSIC Reporter* 2, no. 9, October 1993, 14.

69. P. Keating, 'Press Conference', Transcript of the Prime Minister, the Hon. P. J. Keating MP, Canberra, ACT, Parliament House, 19 October 1993.

70. 'Cautious support in all but the west', *The Canberra Times*, 20 October 1993, 14.

71. K. Scott, 'Hope of native-title law passing by end of year', *The Canberra Times*, 20 October 1993, 1–2.

72. 'Rural groups urging new negotiations', *The Canberra Times*, 20 October 1993, 14.

73. 'Decision 'the basis of discrimination'', *The Canberra Times*, 20 October 1993, 14.

74. M. Mansell, 'Mabo—Good and Bad for Aborigines', Press Release of Michael Mansell, National Secretary, Aboriginal Provisional Government, 19 October 1993.

75. R. Dixon and S. Freeman-Greene, 'The Mabo Dreaming', Opinion Analysis, *The Age*, 20 October 1993, 19.

76. Dixon and Freeman-Greene, 'The Mabo Dreaming', 19.

77. I. Willox and M. Magazanik, 'Greens say they won't be hurried on Mabo', *The Age*, 21 October 1993, 3.

78. L. Taylor and D. Nason, 'Black negotiators "negotiated away' basic rights"', *The Australian*, 12 November 1993, 6.

79. L. Tingle and R. Jinman, 'We won't fund challenges to valid leases, black groups say', *The Weekend Australian*, 30–31 October 1993, 4.

80. C. Kernot, 'Democrats Welcome Mabo Outcome', Media Release, Senator Cheryl Kernot, Australian Democrats, Canberra, ACT, 19 October 1993.

81. Willox and Magazanik, 'Greens say they won't be hurried on Mabo', 3.

82. P. Keating, 'Transcript of the Prime Minister, the Hon. P. J. Keating MP, Doorstop', Parliament House, Canberra, ACT, 7 November 1993.

83. Commonwealth of Australia, Parliamentary Debates, House of Representatives, 16 November 1993, No. 190, 2877–83.

84. C. Chamarette, 'Greens move to put Mabo legislation on Hold', Media Release, Christabel Chamarette, Senator for the Greens (WA), Canberra, ACT, 24 November 1993.

85. L. Taylor, 'Coalition delay on Mabo Bill', *The Australian*, 15 December 1993, 2; K. Scott, 'Hewson gives backing to WA solo on Mabo', *The Canberra Times*, 28 October 1993, 13; I. Willox, 'Mabo a national disaster: Hewson', *The Age*, 11 December 1993, 6.

86. Those who came to Canberra were: Frank Woods, Wheatbelt Aboriginal Corporation—Northam; Dean Collard—Perth; Mike Hill—Busselton; Wayne Warner—Geraldton; Brian Samson—Western Desert; Mary Attwood—Port Hedland. Those from the Kimberley region were: Ivan McPhee, Kimberley Land Council; Peter Yu, Kimberley Land council; Robert Watson—Derby; Eileen Torres—Broome; Sam Butters—Warmun; Pearl Gordon—Billiluna.

87. L. Taylor and M. King, 'Keating defies Opposition on Mabo Bill', *The Australian*, 21 December 1993.

88. K. Scott, 'Farm lobby attacks Libs', *The Canberra Times*, 20 December 1993, 1.

89. K. Scott, 'Mabo win a turning point: PM', *The Canberra Times*, 22 December 1993, 1.

90. Commonwealth of Australia, Parliamentary Debates, House of Representatives, 22 December 1993, No. 191, 4541–46.

91. Pearson, 'A troubling inheritance', 8.

92. P. H. Russell, *Recognising Aboriginal Title. The Mabo Case and Indigenous Resistance to English-Settler Colonialism* (Sydney, NSW: University of NSW Press Ltd, 2005), 310.

93. D. Short, 'The Social Construction of Indigenous "Native Title" Land Rights in Australia', *Current Sociology* 55, no. 6 (2007), 868–70.

94. C. Chamarette, 'Terra Nullius Then and Now: Mabo, Native Title, and Reconciliation in 2000', *Australian Psychologist* 35, no. 2 (2000), 169.

95. P. Coe, 'ATSIC: self-determination or otherwise', *Race & Class* 35, no. 4 (1994), 38–39.

96. Short, 'The Social Construction of Indigenous Native Title', 868.

97. Wik and Thayorre Peoples v State of Queensland (1996) 187 CLR 1.

98. Brown and Boden, *A way through*, 223–25.

99. Tickner, *Taking a Stand*, 91, 196.

100. Chamarette, 'Terra Nullius Then and Now', 170–71.

101. P. Wolfe, 'Settler Colonialism and the elimination of the native', *Journal of Genocide Research* 8, no. 4 (2006), 393.

102. J. Preston, 'Neoliberal settler colonialism, Canada and the tar sands', *Race & Class* 55, no. 2 (2013), 44, 49.

103. Short, 'The Social Construction of Indigenous Native Title', 868–69.

104. G. Coulthard, 'Subjects of Empire: Indigenous Peoples and the "Politics of Recognition" in Canada', *Contemporary Political Theory* 6, no. 4, (2007).

105. M. Dodson, 'Towardss the exercise of Indigenous rights: Policy, power and self-determination', *Race & Class* 35, no. 4, 68.

106. Russell, *Recognising Aboriginal Title*, 337.

107. P. Patton, 'Mabo and Australian Society: Towardss a Postmodern Republic', *The Australian Journal of Anthropology* 6, no. 1 and 2 (1995), 92.

108. P. Dodson, 'Whatever Happened to Reconciliation', in *Coercive Reconciliation: Stabilise, Normalise, Exit Aboriginal Australia*, Jon Altman and Melinda Hinkson, eds. (North Carlton, VIC: Arena Publications, 2007), 21–29; V. Watson, 'From the "quiet revolution" to "crisis" in Australian Indigenous affairs', *Cultural Studies Review* 15, no. 1 (2009), 91–92.

109. L. O'Donoghue, 'Past wrongs, future rights', *Indigenous Law Bulletin* 4, Issue 1 (1997), 19.

110. J. Cunningham and J. I. Baeza, 'An 'experiment' in Indigenous social policy: the rise and fall of Australia's Aboriginal and Torres Strait Islander Commission (ATSIC)', *Policy & Politics* 33, no. 3 (2005), 463–64.

111. A. Pratt, *Practising Reconciliation? The Politics of Reconciliation in the Australian Parliament 1991-2000* (Parliament of Australia, Department of Parliamentary Services, 2005), 105–7, 137–40.

112. J. Altman, 'Practical Reconciliation and the New Mainstreaming: Will it make a difference to Indigenous Australians?', *Dialogue* 23, no. 2 (2004), Academy of Social Sciences in Australia, 35–45.

113. A. Gunstone, 'These Blokes are Re-inventing the 19th Century: The Howard Government's Record on Indigenous Affairs 1996–2006', *Journal of Indigenous Policy*, Issue 7 (2007), 41–52; A. Gunstone, 'The Howard Government and Indigenous Affairs', in *Over a Decade of Despair: The Howard Government and Indigenous Affairs*, Andrew Gunstone, ed. (North Melbourne, Vic; Australian Scholarly Publishing, 2010), 3–4.

114. L. MacDonald and P. Muldoon, 'Globalisation, Neo-liberalism and the Struggle for Indigenous Citizenship', *Australian Journal of Political Science* 41, no. 2 (2006), 216–20.

115. A. Pratt and S. Bennett, *The end of ATSIC and the future administration of Indigenous affairs* (Parliamentary Library, Information and Research Services, 2004), 10–16.

116. Cunningham and Baeza, 'An 'experiment' in Indigenous social policy', 471.

117. L. Taylor, 'Miners want all leases validated', *The Australian Financial Review*, 4 February 1997, 2.

118. National Farmers Federation, 'NFF calls on Prime Minister to act on Wik', News Release, 31 January 1997.

119. 'Fischer pushes For Mabo change', *The West Australian*, 8 February 1997, 36.

120. L. Taylor, 'States' Wik action plan', *The Australian Financial Review*, 6 February 1997, 1.

121. For an explanation of the impact of the 1997 Amendment bill on Indigenous peoples see M. Dodson, *Submission to the Parliamentary Joint Committee on Native Title and the Aboriginal and Torres Strait Islander Land Fund, The Native Title Amendment Bill 1997* (Sydney, NSW: Aboriginal and Torres Strait Islander Social Justice Commissioner, 3 October 1997). https://www.humanrights.gov.au/sites/default/files/content/pdf/social_justice/submission_land_fund_october1997.pdf [Accessed 11 September 2019].

122. Tim Fischer on ABC Radio PM Program, 16 May 1997, quoted in ATSIC, *The Ten Point Plan on Wik and Native Title: Issues for Indigenous Peoples* (Canberra, ACT: Aboriginal and Torres Strait Islander Commission, 1997), 5.

123. Aboriginal and Torres Strait Islander Social Justice Commissioner, *Native Title Report 1999* (Sydney, NSW: Human Rights and Equal Opportunity Commission, 1999), 3.

124. A. Markus, *Race: John Howard and the remaking of Australia* (Crows Nest, NSW: Allen & Unwin, 2001), 85–90.

125. Markus, *Race: John Howard*, 90–100.

126. M. Kalantzis and B. Cope, 'An opportunity to change the culture', in *The Retreat from Tolerance*, Phillip Adams, ed. (Sydney, NSW: ABC Books, 1997), 57–85.

127. M. Weigel, 'Political correctness: how the right invented a phantom enemy', *The Guardian*, Wednesday, 30 November 2016. https://www.theguardian.com/us-news/2016/nov/30/political-correctness-how-the-right-invented-phantom-enemy-donald-trump; T. Lynch and R. Reavell, 'Through the Looking Glass: Hanson, Howard and the Politics of 'Political Correctness', in *Pauline Hanson, One Nation and Australian Politics*, Bligh Grant, ed. (Armidale, NSW: University of New England Press, 1997), 30–34.

128. Markus, *Race: John Howard*, 94–99; Kalantzis and Cope, *An opportunity to change the culture*, 59–62.

129. M. McKenna, 'Different Perspectives on Black Armband History', *Department of Parliamentary Library*, Information and Research Service, Research Paper No. 5 (1997), 5–6.

130. S. Breen, 'Howard's History War, 1996-2007', in *Over a Decade of Despair: The Howard Government and Indigenous Affairs*, Andrew Gunstone, ed. (North Melbourne, Vic; Australian Scholarly Publishing, 2010), 106–8.

131. Breen, 'Howard's History War, 1996–2007', 108–13.

132. T. Birch, 'Black Armbands and White Veils': John Howard's Moral Amnesia', *Melbourne Historical Journal* 25 (1997), 8–16; Markus, *Race: John Howard*, 70, 92–93.

133. McKenna, 'Different Perspectives on Black Armband History', 7–12.

134. Pratt, *Practising Reconciliation?*, 114.

135. Markus, *Race: John Howard*, 86.

136. J. Robbins, 'The Howard Government and Indigenous Rights: An Imposed national Unity?', *Australian Journal of Political Science* 42, no. 2 (2007), 316.

137. W. Errington and P. V. Onselen, *John Winston Howard* (Carlton, Vic: Melbourne University Press, 2007), 261, 264.

138. Errington and Onselen, *John Winston Howard*, 19, 260–61.

139. Commonwealth of Australia. Parliamentary Debates, House of Representatives, Tuesday, 10 December 1996, No. 8, 3860-3863 (Pauline Hanson).

140. J. Howard, 'A New Reconciliation', *Sydney Papers* 19, no. 4 (Spring 2007), 107.

141. Gunstone, 'These Blokes are Re-inventing the 19th Century', 49.

142. P. Anderson and R. Wild, *Ampe Akelyernemane Meke Mekarle: 'Little Children are Sacred'*, Report of the Northern Territory Board of Inquiry into the Protection of Aboriginal Children from Sexual Abuse (Darwin, NT: Northern Territory Government, 2007).

143. M. Hinkson, 'Introduction: In the name of the child', in *Coercive reconciliation: Stablisie, normalise, exit Aboriginal Australia*, Jon Altman & Melinda Hinkson, eds. (North Carlton, VIC: Arena Publications, 2007), 1–2.

144. Aboriginal and Torres Strait Islander Social Justice Commissioner, *Social Justice Report* (Sydney, NSW: Human Rights and Equal Opportunity Commission, 2007), 209–11.

145. Hinkson, *Introduction: In the name of the child*, 3–5; Australian Human Rights Commission, *The suspension and reinstatement of the RDA and special measures in the NTER*, 2 November 2011 (Sydney, NSW: Australian Human Rights Commission, 2011), 5–6. https://www.humanrights.gov.au/our-work/race-discrmination/publications/suspension-and-reinstatement-rda-and-speacial-measures-nter [Accessed 29 March 2017].

146. Aboriginal and Torres Strait Islander Social Justice Commissioner, *Social Justice Report*, 2007, 221–24, 226–32.

147. The measures included compulsory lease acquisition of Aboriginal land without consultation or consent and without compensation; taking control of Aboriginal town camps that are held under leases in perpetuity by Aboriginal associations; suspending the 'future act' provisions of the Native Title Act over areas held under leases acquired by the Commonwealth; intervening into the operations of Aboriginal community councils and associations including service delivery and management of funds; compulsory income management of social security benefits; termination of the Community Development Employment project to subject unemployment payments to income management; limiting the consideration of customary law or cultural practices in criminal proceeding for all alleged offences; according special powers to the Australian Crimes Commission to collect information on crimes affecting Indigenous communities (Anaya 2010, 28–29).

148. Aboriginal and Torres Strait Islander Social Justice Commissioner, *Social Justice Report*, 2007, 218–19.

149. S. J. Anaya, *Report by the Special Rapporteur on the situation of human rights and fundamental freedoms of indigenous peoples, Appendix B: Observations on the Northern Territory Emergency Response in Australia* (Human Rights Council Fifteenth Session, United Nations General Assembly A/HRC/15/37/Add.4, 1 June 2010), 3. https://documents-dds-ny.un.org/doc/UNDOC/GEN/G10/138/87/PDF/G1023887.PDF?OpenElement [Accessed 29 March 2017].

150. Anaya, *Report by the Special Rapporteur on the situation of human rights and fundamental freedoms of indigenous peoples*, 29–30, 31.

151. Australian Indigenous Doctor's Association and Centre for Health Equity Training, Research and Evaluation, UNSW, *Health Impact Assessment of the Northern Territory Emergency Response* (Canberra: Australian Indigenous Doctors' Association, 2010), 55.

152. P. Toohey, 'Last Drinks: The Impact of the Northern Territory Intervention', *Quarterly Essay*, no. 3 (2008), 16–17, 30–35, 22–27, 48–49.

153. A. Macoun, 'Aboriginality and the Northern Territory Intervention', *Australian Journal of Political Science* 46, no. 3 (2011), 520–21, 522–23, 524–25, 528–29.

FIVE

Dialogue and Indigenous Recognition

Indigenous people are not recognised as a polity within the Australian constitutional structure of government. Therefore, in matters of law and policy Indigenous people are treated as another stakeholder group along with all the other stakeholders and political lobby groups. As a minority group Indigenous Australians have to rely on the goodwill of political parties and the compassion of white politicians for protection of their rights or respect for human rights. Unfortunately, goodwill and compassion are most often lacking, as is illustrated on numerous occasions. In 2011, the Western Australian state government closed the Aboriginal community of Oombulgarri in the East Kimberley region of Western Australia and evicted the residents on the basis that the community was unviable. In 2014, the government bulldozed the community infrastructure effectively forcing the people from their traditional lands to be assimilated into nearby white townships. Residents of Oombulgarri spoke of a lack of consultation, a rushed government process and a lack of consent on their behalf.[1] The government also threatened to shut down services to another hundred and fifty small and remote Aboriginal townships because the Commonwealth government had devolved responsibility for municipal and essential services for these communities to the State government. The Western Australian government said these communities are unviable and dangerous because of suicide, poor health and abuse and neglect of children.[2] There was Aboriginal anger and offense when the premier of Western Australia linked the possible closure of the communities to child sexual abuse.[3] This anger and offence was compounded when Prime Minister Tony Abbott said the government could not 'endlessly subsidise lifestyle choices'.[4]

The Western Australian government had not sought consultation with Aboriginal communities or representative organisations in relation to their community closure policy and only promised formal consultation after nationwide protests and condemnation from the United Nations.[5] The Western Australian government's actions exemplify a relationship of deep historical disrespect towards Aboriginal people, where Australian law and government policy are used in authoritarian ways to subordinate Aboriginal people. As a result, Aboriginal people are excluded from the very process of policymaking and problem solving by government. Politicians, public sector bureaucrats, other experts and even judicial decision makers largely drive Indigenous policy and determine solutions primarily through the values, interests and ideology of government and the dominant society. There is a clash of ideas and values between Indigenous people and governments, which is implicit in structures, processes and institutional arrangements that give rise to power, authority and procedural rules. There is also a notable lack of respectful dialogue in the relationship because there is no national framework of partnership between Indigenous people and the Australian nation-state.[6]

The recent focus on constitutional recognition of Indigenous people in Australia has been far from satisfactory because the Australian state does not have a framework for dialogue and negotiation to make law and policy and to advance the nation to a renewed relationship with Indigenous people. Australian government derives from a system of law that did not recognise Indigenous Australians as having any land ownership, civil society or form of sovereignty. Indigenous polity was not recognised by the British. Indigenous people were excluded from recognition in colonial constitutions; and other than discriminatory provisions, the 1901 Constitution of the Commonwealth of Australia likewise did not recognise Indigenous people. Further, as discussed in chapter 2, the common law largely denied recognition to Indigenous people. The ongoing relationship between governments and Aboriginal people is grounded in paternalism, dominance and even racism. Consequently, Indigenous people have no stake in politics and power and Australian governments have not been able to remedy this situation.

This chapter examines Indigenous recognition politics in Australia, its limitations and the lack of political framework for relationship-building between governments and Indigenous peoples. The need for new foundations, created through a process of intercultural dialogue to develop new norms, language and practice in Australian social and political culture, is imperative if governments are to build a renewed relationship with Indigenous people. The Canadian Royal Commission on Aboriginal Peoples is one example of how Aboriginal people in Canada attempted a transformative dialogue with the state as the means to create a vision for a new relationship. Although there was no ringing endorsement for change by the Canadian government, the Royal Commission is an example of how a formal dialogical process can examine issues and generate a way forward in creating a renewed relationship. The Canadian Truth and

Reconciliation Commission is another example of a public dialogue process advocating for political change. It is further discussed in chapter 6 as an example of truth telling. Drawing on the Canadian experience, this chapter discusses how a vision for a new relationship can be created through intercultural dialogue.

RECOGNITION POLITICS IN AUSTRALIA

Australia's form of government originates from the Constitution of the Commonwealth and the Constitutions of the States, which were the former self-governing colonies established by the British in Australia. These constitutions derive from the British Crown and the Imperial Parliament. However, Australian constitutional government does not adequately represent the interests of Indigenous people. Its laws, institutions and ensuring legal and political power serve the interests of the majority settler Australian population. The constitutional institutions, rules and principles in Australia were created on the basis of Indigenous exclusion in colonial State constitutions and other than discriminatory provisions the 1901 Constitution of the Commonwealth of Australia also did not recognise Indigenous people. Further, the common law has largely denied recognition to Indigenous people. There were no treaties with Indigenous people in Australia, therefore Indigenous people are not recognised as a distinct source of political authority and have no recognised political or constitutional status. Consequently, there is no constitutionally recognised framework for cross-cultural political engagement between governments and Indigenous peoples. Hence, there is no obligation on governments to recognise or engage in respectful ways with Indigenous people. This is the established political and legal framework in which Indigenous policy and claims for recognition of rights are mediated. In this situation Indigenous rights and interests are either ignored, denied, demeaned, excluded, suppressed or there is reluctant recognition and minimal concessions.

Since the 1970s, Australian governments have attempted to accommodate Indigenous claims by way of a politics of recognition. Recognition is a political approach used by settler states to accommodate and reconcile Indigenous-identity claims and Indigenous assertions of nationhood within settler state sovereignty.[7] The recognition of land rights and native title are examples. The recognition of Indigenous people in the Australian Constitution is a contemporary public policy issue. It is also an example of how erroneous perceptions and assumptions about Indigenous people are part of the political processes that are driven and controlled by government. The formal process for constitutional recognition commenced in November 2010 when the Australian government established an expert panel to determine the best option for an amendment to

the Australian Constitution to recognise Aboriginal and Torres Strait Islander peoples. It recommended the repeal of potentially discriminatory
provisions of the Constitution (Sections 25 and 51 (xxxvi)) and the inser-
tion of new sections (Sections 51A and 116A) to enable the parliament to
make laws for Indigenous people and to prohibit discrimination based on
race.[8] The Australian Parliament passed the Aboriginal and Torres Strait
Islander Peoples Recognition Act 2013 to symbolically recognise Indigenous people as the first inhabitants and provided for a review of progress
on constitutional recognition. A Parliamentary Joint Select Committee on
Constitutional Recognition of Aboriginal and Torres Strait Islander Peoples was established soon after. The Joint Select Committee recommended in June 2015 that a referendum be held to recognise Indigenous
people in the Constitution. It also recommended repeal and recasting of
potentially discriminatory provisions in the Constitution (Sections 25 and
51xxvi) and set out three options to progress to a successful referendum.[9]

In 2012, the government established and funded 'Recognise', a public
relations campaign to lobby for a 'Yes' vote in a referendum even though
there was no referendum proposal. This raised the suspicions of Indigenous people.[10] Recognise was considered an advertising campaign for
the government's agenda.[11] By 2014, the focus and process of constitutional recognition began to stagnate, and the review panel established
under the Recognition Act 2013 noted this. Indigenous people were becoming frustrated by the delays and perceived lack of government commitment for constitutional recognition. There was a loss of public momentum and awareness of the issue of constitutional recognition and so
the review panel said Australians were not ready for a referendum. It
recommended a referendum council to finalise a proposal for constitutional amendment and that a referendum be held no later than the first
half of 2017.[12] The drift in the constitutional recognition debate, the lack
of a model for constitutional recognition, and the promotion of a 'softer
version of reform' by the Recognise campaign prompted Indigenous resistance.[13]

Throughout, the Australian government had been managing the process to achieve an outcome based on what would be acceptable to the
government. This became clear in July 2015 when the then Prime Minister Tony Abbott and then Opposition Leader Bill Shorten hosted forty
handpicked Indigenous leaders to discuss a way forward. Indigenous
leaders requested an Indigenous process to enable an Indigenous consensus on a model for recognition, but the prime minister rejected it[14] although he changed his mind some weeks later following meetings with
Indigenous leaders. The government had clearly predetermined a process for going forward as two ideas not discussed in the meeting were the
key outcome: broad community conferences with no mention of the need
for Indigenous conferences; and a referendum council, which most Indigenous leaders had not heard off.[15] The Australian government wants

minimal constitutional change. Issues such as recognition of Indigenous sovereignty, self-determination and treaty are deemed not acceptable for consideration in a referendum proposal since they are issues that Australians refuse to address. The expert panel made this clear in 2012, when it said the issue of Indigenous sovereignty would be 'highly contested' and any constitutional backing for a treaty would likely confuse Australians and therefore likely jeopardise public support for the panel's recommendations.[16]

As issues of Indigenous sovereignty and treaty were not addressed, 'recognition' in the Constitution became meaningless for many Indigenous people. This has resulted in some Aboriginal people questioning the need for and purpose of recognition. Prominent Aboriginal activist, Michael Mansell, has argued that Aboriginal people have never needed to be recognised to establish the fact of prior occupation, so why is there a need now for recognition by white Australians? He maintains that Indigenous recognition will not alter the institutional arrangements established by the Australian Constitution.[17] The contention is that recognition is something bestowed upon Indigenous people by white Australians to legitimise their colonial system, whereas 'treaties are legal mechanisms between two parties that recognise one another's sovereignty'.[18] This point is important because it explains why resistance to constitutional recognition by some Indigenous leaders is so strong.

However, aspirations for constitutional reform were overtaken by 'constitutional conservatives' who vowed to oppose any proposals that entrench rights in the Constitution.[19] Noel Pearson has attempted to find a middle ground between such a position and Indigenous aspirations for constitutional change. He proposed an alternative constitutional amendment to enable Indigenous people to have a say about laws and policies made about them. Parliament would create the Indigenous representative mechanism and symbolic statements of recognition would be achieved through a declaration outside of the Constitution.[20] But Michael Mansell says Pearson's proposal risks the 'constitutional entrenchment of subordination' and it cannot be described as a step towards self-determination.[21]

The Referendum Council, established in December 2015 to advise on steps to a successful referendum, conducted a national engagement and consultation programme with Indigenous peoples between December 2016 and May 2017. During these dialogues the proposal for an Indigenous voice in the Constitution along with the constitutional reforms proposed by the expert panel were discussed. In its recommendations of June 2017, the Referendum Council said a referendum should be held to provide for an Indigenous representative voice to the Commonwealth Parliament in the Australian Constitution and that all Australian parliaments enact legislation to articulate a symbolic statement of recognition. Importantly, although the issue of treaty was not part of the original expert panel reforms, proposals for a treaty or agreement making mechanism were strongly endorsed by the Indigenous dialogues.[22]

The Indigenous dialogues advanced a different view to that of the expert panel. Indigenous people were not persuaded by the benefits of a statement of acknowledgment in the Constitution nor were they supportive of removing potentially discriminatory clauses from the Constitution as they would confer no substantive benefit and the issues were considered low priority in many dialogues or rejected by other dialogues. There was ambivalence regarding a prohibition against adverse discrimination, however the dialogues supported a constitutionally entrenched voice to Parliament and an agreement making mechanism such as a treaty. The need for truth telling about Australia's history of colonisation was also stressed. An Indigenous or First Nation voice enshrined in the Constitution and a Makarrata Commission to supervise truth telling and agreement making between governments and Indigenous people were proposals later endorsed by a National Indigenous Constitutional Convention at Uluru in May 2017.[23] The Uluru Statement from the Heart arose from the national constitutional convention. It reflects the ideas and aspirations of Indigenous people.

When the Australian government considered the recommendations of the Referendum Council in October 2017, it flatly rejected the idea of a national Indigenous representative voice to parliament. Prime Minister Malcom Turnbull said it was a 'radical change' to the Constitution and was not 'desirable or capable of winning acceptance in a referendum', yet offered no evidence in that regard. He also said the proposal was inconsistent with a fundamental principle of Australian democracy: namely, that Australian citizens have equal civic rights to vote for, stand for and serve in the national Parliament.[24] Indigenous representatives were enraged that the prime minister could be so disrespectful by dictating what form Indigenous recognition should take. The purpose of the representative voice or advisory body was not to limit the power of Parliament but to ensure that Aboriginal and Torres Strait Islander voices were heard in the Commonwealth Parliament. Further, the representative voice is only an advisory body and its structure and establishment would be enacted in legislation by Parliament. The only difference with past Indigenous advisory bodies to government is that the Indigenous Voice would be enshrined in the Constitution. Despite this the government believed the Indigenous representative Voice proposal stood little chance of success. Their opposition appears to be driven by colonial views about the place of Indigenous people in the Australian nation, displaying the persistent influence of terra nullius in Australia.

The prime minister and the government said they remained committed to finding a constitutional amendment that would succeed and to an effective way to develop stronger local Aboriginal and Torres Strait Islander voices and local empowerment.[25] In March 2018, the Commonwealth Parliament established a Joint Select Committee on Constitutional Recognition relating to Aboriginal and Torres Strait Islander Peoples. The Select Committee was cochaired by Senator Patrick Dodson (Labor) and Julian Leeser MP (Liberal). It looked at matters raised in the Uluru Statement from the Heart including the establishment of the First Nation Voice, the Makarrata Commission, Truth telling and other proposals for constitutional change. The Select Committee called for written submissions, received private briefings from Aboriginal and Torres Strait Islander leaders and other stakeholders, and conducted public hearings. The Select Committee produced an interim report in July 2018 setting out key areas of its inquiry and asking specific questions for consultation particularly in regards to the proposal for a First Nations Voice and this included setting out some broad principles for the design of such an institution.[26] In its final report of November 2018, the Select Committee made four recommendations to the Australian Government: to (1) initiate a process of codesign with Aboriginal and Torres Strait Islander peoples for the First Nations Voice; (2) consider legislative, executive and constitutional options to establish the Voice; (3) support the process of truth telling; and (4) consider the establishment of a National Resting Place to be a place of commemoration, healing and reflection.[27]

The Select Committee reiterated principles, which it had identified in its interim report, that could underpin the design of a First Nations Voice. These included: support for local and regional structures; membership of the Voice to be chosen by Indigenous people; the design of local voices to reflect local practices; equal gender representation; the Voice to provide oversight and advice and enable dialogue and negotiations with government; and consideration of the interplay between any Voice body and existing Indigenous organisations.[28] The Select Committee concluded that the First Nations Voice should be codesigned by Aboriginal and Torres Strait Islander peoples, the Australian government and Parliament.[29] As to implementing the First Nations Voice, the Select Committee identified two approaches: (1) a referendum to constitutionally enshrine a Voice prior to finalising details of its structure and function and enactment by Commonwealth legislation and (2) enacting the Voice in Commonwealth legislation followed by a referendum to constitutionally enshrine the Voice. The Select Committee made no recommendation on either approach but simply advocated that there be a process of codesign and thereafter the Australian government balance the likelihood of referendum success to determine whether to proceed with implementation of the Voice by legislation, executive action or referendum.[30]

The Select Committee looked at other proposals for constitutional change. These included removing potential discriminatory provisions from the Constitution by repealing Section 25 of the Australian Constitution and replacing or amending Section 51(xxvi) of the Constitution, and a legislative extra-constitutional declaration of recognition to be passed by all Australian Parliaments. The extra-constitutional declaration was supported and recommended by the Referendum Council in 2017, however the Referendum Council said removing Section 25 would confer no substantive benefit and replacing section 51(xxvi) was ranked low in priority by the Indigenous dialogues in 2016–2017. Although these changes do not have wide support among Indigenous people, the Select Committee believes there would be broad political support for repealing section 25 and rewording section 51(xxvi) to remove references to 'race'. In regard to the extra-constitutional declaration of recognition, the Select Committee noted that it would unlikely be supported by Indigenous people if there is an absence of constitutional recognition.[31]

While there was not a lot of discussion on the idea of a Makarrata Commission in the Select Committee report, the Select Committee did comment on the concept of 'Makarrata' as a concept stemming from Yolngu traditions in northeast Arnhem Land in the Northern Territory, stating that it can be perceived as too culturally specific to be used across Aboriginal and Torres Strait Islander nations. In respect to agreement making, the Select Committee canvassed native title agreement making and the recent initiation of treaty processes in Australia. Ultimately, it merely observed that agreement making is happening in Australia and that once local and regional voices are established, they could pursue agreements. In respect to truth telling, the Select Committee looked at its importance and some possible models, commenting that there is a desire by Australians for a fuller understanding of history, that truth telling would empower Indigenous people and promote healing, and that truth telling would provide an honest account of the contested nature of Australian history. The Select Committee recommended the Australian government support truth telling and suggested this could involve local projects between Indigenous people and descendants of settlers.[32]

Current Liberal prime minister, Scott Morrison, who won a Liberal Party leadership spill in August 2018 and who went on to win a general election in May 2019, does not support an Indigenous or First Nations Voice enshrined in the Constitution as he claims it will create a third chamber of Parliament.[33] However, it is reported that the prime minister would support a national body established by legislation.[34] The minister for Indigenous Australians in the Liberal/National Coalition government, Ken Wyatt, an Aboriginal man, has promised to develop a consensus option for constitutional recognition to be put to referendum during the current parliamentary term. He also states he will work on progressing truth telling approaches that allow all Australians to reflect on the place of First Nations people and our shared past. In respect to treaty, he said it is important for the state and territory jurisdictions to take the lead.[35]

Ken Wyatt has a difficult task because not only does the prime minister not support a constitutionally enshrined Indigenous Voice, many in his own party, including front and backbenchers, resist the Voice proposal.[36] Patrick Dodson, shadow assistant minister for Indigenous Affairs and Aboriginal and Torres Strait Islanders, has called for a bipartisan approach. He wants the government to address constitutional recognition because he is concerned that the attitudes of the front bench members will prevent the nation from moving forward.[37] Galarrwuy Yunupingu, Yolngu leader from Gove Peninsula in the Northern Territory, has expressed frustration at the slow pace of constitutional recognition. He has declared to Minister Ken Wyatt that if the Australian Constitution does not recognise Yolngu and other Indigenous people, then his people will not recognise the Constitution; they will throw it into the salt water (the sea).[38]

THE LIMITS TO RECOGNITION

Malcolm Turnbull's response to the 2017 Uluru statement reflects the inability of the Australian government to address Indigenous claims for recognition. Turnbull failed to see the profound historical importance of the Uluru Statement, failed to appreciate the historical experience of Indigenous people, and failed to see that his government's contemptuous response is another episode in the long history of indifference, discrimination and injustice in the treatment of Indigenous people.[39] Prime Minister Scott Morrison's response to the First Nations Voice proposal casts a similar shadow. The Commonwealth government and politicians seem unable to change their thinking to move beyond the colonial relationship with Indigenous Australians. In delivering the 19th Annual Vincent Lingiari Memorial Lecture at Charles Darwin University in August 2019, Ken Wyatt said the challenge for constitutional recognition is finding a set of words that can be put to a referendum and which a majority of Australians will vote for. He also made clear that the referendum question would not result in an enshrined voice to Parliament. In regard to an Indigenous Voice, Wyatt stated that the Indigenous voice is multilayered and multidimensional and therefore to give voice is through conversation and understanding, working with individuals and community leaders to develop practical solutions.[40] If a constitutionally enshrined Voice does not result from a referendum then what is the point of constitutional recognition? Ken Wyatt is talking about a legislated voice to Parliament rather than a constitutionally enshrined representative Voice.[41] It also appears Wyatt may be talking about an Indigenous service delivery and policy voice, which is significantly different to an Indigenous political Voice. As for constitutional recognition, Wyatt may be talking about a statement of acknowledgement in the Constitution.

As a minority in Australian democracy, Indigenous people do not have equal access to or influence over government policy and decision-making and are therefore consistently on the losing side of majority decision-making processes.[42] Indigenous claims for recognition are not only constrained but are also treated with contempt by the tradition, language, norms and practices of Australian government. In that regard the Indigenous constitutional recognition process is constrained by the Constitution and its norms and traditions of cultural and legal uniformity, and also norms and traditions of exclusion of Indigenous people. Australian constitutional government is unable to accommodate difference or cultural diversity and this is historically illustrated because most politicians are not inclined to publicly defend or advocate the recognition of Indigenous claims.

The greatest constraint to recognising Indigenous rights in Australia is the intellectual framework that is embedded in the institutions of Australian governments and which in turn is implanted in the attitudes and opinions of public decision makers and many ordinary Australians. This intellectual framework is reflected in the political and legal thinking of Australian government and in public intellectual thinking and perceptions about Indigenous people. It has been shaped by erroneous colonial assumptions and attitudes about Indigenous people. John Howard's history war has not only sharpened the nation's resistance to facing up to the truth of history, but it also reinforced triumphalist narratives about Australian history that are contemptuous of Indigenous experience and history. Malcolm Turnbull's response to the 2017 Uluru Statement and Scott Morrison's response to the Voice proposal is reflective of this type of thinking and attitude. It is old thinking that has its genesis in colonial times. It is terra nullius thinking.

This thinking is reflected in societal attitudes, opinions and practices of governments, politicians, public decision makers and the influential public. The Australian nation is caught in a colonial mind-set unable to transcend their ingrained assumptions and attitudes about Indigenous people.

DIALOGUE, NOT DEBATE

Historical and contemporary examples of Indigenous struggles in Australia exemplify how colonial or terra nullius approaches are still implicit in the way governments treat Indigenous people. But finding alternate collaborative strategies to solve problems in Indigenous affairs is not enough because there is first a need for substantial transformation of the relationship between Indigenous people and governments so that Indigenous people can engage equally, formally and cross-culturally with governments.

The need for dialogue as a decolonising approach to the relations between Indigenous peoples and settler states is crucial because there is a limited range of formats in Australia to discuss and resolve Indigenous claims and grievances. Although his focus is North America, James Tully sets out a conception of postcolonial dialogue between Aboriginal people and settler or nation-states that could have application in Australia. He argues that a constitutional dialogue can recognise and accommodate the cultural difference of Aboriginal peoples.[43] Such dialogue would involve an ongoing intercultural conversation between Aboriginal and non-Aboriginal people over time. It would not be a once and for all agreement nor frozen in a constitutional document:

> Dialogue is the form of human relationship in which mutual understanding and agreement can be reached and, hence, consent can replace coercion and confrontation. Between Aboriginal and non-Aboriginal people, it is an intercultural dialogue in which the partners aim to reach mutual understanding and uncoerced agreements by contextually appropriate forms of negotiation and reciprocal questioning on how they should cooperate and review their relations of cooperation over time. Specific types of relations are agreed to, written down as treaties, put into practice, reviewed and renewed.[44]

In Australia, existing methods for resolving problems in Indigenous policy and in the government-Indigenous relationships have failed to transform the way in which governments interact with and respond to Indigenous claims and grievances. For example, the formal reconciliation process initiated by government (1991–2000) failed to confront the issues important to Indigenous people and failed to advance a new form of engagement and relationship.[45] The Australian reconciliation process did not correspond to the desires of Indigenous people for a broader decolonising approach to justice.[46] This is because Australian constitutional government lacks norms, conventions or practices that recognise, respect, or include Indigenous voices, perspectives and authority in constitutional and political matters. This demonstrates a need to transform the existing relationship between Indigenous people and governments because the existing structure subordinates the role and position of Indigenous people within the Australian state. Indigenous people have a genuine stake in political and constitutional matters because the legitimacy of Australian sovereignty is contingent upon Indigenous consent. Australians have yet to complete the step of gaining the consent of Indigenous people to legitimise the sovereignty of the Australian Crown.[47]

But to move from a relationship that subordinates Indigenous people to a relationship where Indigenous authority is recognised and respected, it is necessary to change the cultural and political beliefs and values that Australians have inherited from their colonial past. It also involves creating new norms and practices in government regarding Indigenous policy. Dialogue can change the political and cultural background that influences systems and society. But in Australia this means having difficult conversations that examine deeply held opinions and assumptions; and by extension this requires an examination of Australian social identity, societal beliefs and values.

What then is dialogue? A good starting point is the definition by David Bohm, legendary physicist and philosopher who wrote that 'the object of dialogue is not to analyse things, or to win an argument, or to exchange opinions', but rather to suspend your opinions and listen to the opinions of others, then suspend everybody's opinions to see what they mean and to find commonality, even if we don't agree with each other. Therefore, to be engaged in dialogue one must be *open to listening* and to *questioning one's own thinking*. Dialogue is usually associated with discussion or debate, but there is a difference. Debate is about trying to make your points of view prevail over the views of others; it is about attempting to win an argument or defeat an opponent. Similarly, in discussion people bat ideas back and forth to win points.[48] Discussion seeks closure and completion as in decision-making; this is different to dialogue, which seeks to open new possibilities. While discussion is necessary because it produces valuable results, it is limited in solving intractable problems, especially where people bring different assumptions and diverse points of view and have a deep investment in getting what they want.[49] Discussion lacks all or any of the following three features that are components of dialogue: equality and the absence of coercive influences; listening and empathy; and bringing assumptions into the open and suspending judgment.[50]

Deliberation, which is a process of narrowing options by careful consideration and weighing of options to make tough decisions, is not the same as dialogue—a process of joint inquiry and respectful listening to diverse views.[51] Dialogue differs from negotiation and mediation because its intention is to reach new understanding and in doing so form a new basis on which to think and act.[52] Mediation or negotiation aims for concrete agreement. These agreements define and satisfy material interests whereas dialogue creates new human and political capacities to solve problems. Negotiation deals with goods or rights that are divided and shared in tangible ways, whereas dialogue creates new ground for mutual respect and collaboration.[53] Dialogue is neither an instrument of decision-making nor is it a negotiating device to seek agreement leading to action,[54] but it can serve as a prelude to or an aspect of negotiation or mediation.[55]

Dialogue also differs from consensus, where people look for a view that reflects what most people can live with, assuming that shared action will arise out of a shared position. While consensus creates a measure of agreement, it does not explore or alter the underlying patterns of thought and meaning—the patterns that led people to disagree at the outset. Dialogue brings to the surface these patterns of thought so that people can gain insight into why they arise.[56] While debate, political activism, negotiation and mediation have a role in a democratic society, dialogue is essential because it encourages diversity of thinking and opinion, focusses on mutual understanding and builds new relationships.[57] As a discipline of collective thinking and inquiry, dialogue transforms the quality of conversation by transforming thinking in response to mutual receptivity, which in turn opens up new possibilities for people to discover new insights instead of seeking closure or completion.[58]

A THEORY OF DIALOGUE

As a collective learning process, dialogue examines 'tacit thought', especially exploring the underlying processes that govern tacit thought. Tacit thought is the know-how or knowledge that people use to think; it governs how we formulate our views, deal with differences, pay attention, and make casual connections.[59] People essentially see and understand the world through the images and interpretations that live in their memory. These images or memory are experienced as 'literally true and obvious', therefore people defend them under conditions of threat and embarrassment.[60] To understand one's own assumptions and opinions and to gain new insights it is necessary to examine or experience tacit thought in real-time conversation rather than look back and reflect on conversation. Hence, it is a reflective process that happens in real time. When people confront tough issues, their views and opinions collide and the environment heats up causing their association with each other to become unstable and incoherent. Dialogue seeks to produce a cooler shared environment by refocusing the group's shared attention enabling people to engage in high energy interactions with reduced friction, yet still recognise differences.[61]

William Isaacs, a leading authority on dialogue, outlines four elements: (1) human beings must invent ways to reduce defensiveness that arises face-to-face so that they can inquire together and learn from one another; (2) they must invent ways of inquiring into the shared 'field' or background conditions out of which they speak to harness the possibility of collective intelligence; (3) there is a development sequence where a pattern of inquiry and action unfolds over time, producing tangible effects; and (4) dialogue employs certain methods to expand the capacity of a group to inquire into and alter the formative forces that govern their experience.[62] The challenge of dialogue is to first reduce face-to-face defensiveness between people that leads them to advocate their views and not inquire into the views of others. The intent is to increase levels of self-reflection, increase psychological safety and increase the quality of collective attention to better contain the conflict. Dialogue occurs in the 'field' of shared meaning and energy of a group of people, which comprises the collective attention, images and tacit thought of people. It is within the collective shared field that people directly experience the nature of tacit patterns of thought and action. Therefore, face-to-face interactions are concerned with the quality and nature of effective listening, the tone and texture of interactions, the pattern of shared reasoning and the way in which people tend to reproduce and represent the content of their conversation. [63]

People divide the world according to how they perceive it. They generally do not recognise that they see the world through memory because their interpretations of the world are 'mechanistic processes of thought' that repeat themselves. These representations, or images of memory known as 'idols', comes across as real. Therefore, human experience is dominated by idols that are taken as literally valid. Bohm argues that humans have lost self-perception at the level of our thought. In that regard, our ideas or feelings arrive 'from nowhere' or are triggered by the environment and so we lack the ability to connect our perceptions with the nature of our thoughts. Hence, we cannot assess the direction of our thoughts because consciousness appears as literal and real. [64]

In collective dialogue the notion of idols and patterns of thought are brought to the surface through a 'container' in which dialogue takes place. A container is a collection of assumptions, shared intentions and beliefs of a group and it is in this space that the participants observe and hear their interactions and inquire into their underlying images, norms and perceptions. To explore underlying thinking and use self-perception to construct and comprehend the nature of the container, the participants suspend their assumptions, and this potentially enables them to transform their underlying patterns of thought. The key aspects of the container are people listening, respecting one another, suspending their judgements and speaking their own voice. [65]

In dialogue, suspension of standing assumptions makes self-perception or self-awareness possible, enabling one to see the impulses that lie behind everyday thought. When assumptions are suspended, they are neither expressed nor suppressed but are held in abeyance. This involves 'loosening our grip' on the temptation to fix, correct or problem-solve, stepping back to observe one's own thoughts and feelings in order to understand one's consciousness, but also to become aware of the processes that generated those thoughts and feelings as the precondition to transforming thoughts and feelings. Hence, dialogue is a transformational vehicle because it helps people 'notice the connection between the thoughts going on in dialogue, the feelings in the body and the emotions'. [66] This process is not about trying to change anybody's opinion but helping them see what their own and other people's assumptions and reactions mean; this is considered dialogue—when people realise what is on each other's mind, and not come to any conclusions or judgments. [67]

Isaacs proposes that dialogue evolves through a series of phases where a pattern of inquiry and action unfold over time. In the first phase (instability of the container) there is an 'initiatory crisis' because participants are concerned with safety and trust in dialogue. Participants struggle with polarisation and conflict in the second phase (instability in the container) as a result of the fragmentation or clash of beliefs and assumptions. By the third phase (inquiry in the container), the participants are able to inquire into polarisation and foreign ideas without taking divisive action on the group's fragmented knowledge. This leads to the final phase (creativity in the container) where participants begin to think generatively, and new understandings based on collective perception emerge. The result is an approach for dialogue that expands the capacity of individuals and groups of people to inquire into and alter the thoughts that govern and shape their experience in order to transform thinking processes to ultimately create a different kind of face-to-face interaction.[68]

STRUCTURED DIALOGUE

The most common form of dialogue is facilitated group dialogue where a group of people come together to reach a common understanding, solve problems, resolve conflict or engage in deliberative processes. At the beginning of a dialogue people get to know each other, build trust and establish relationships of sharing and negotiate a common way to proceed.[69] Relationship-building is an important aspect of any dialogue process and it emerges through direct interaction. Essential to developing new relationships is empathy, trust, sensitivity and responsiveness to the concerns of others, which can only be developed through direct interaction.[70] The quality of human experience and interaction creates a space for shared consciousness and creative thinking, which also includes differences and disagreements because in the dialogic process they are not obstacles but places for further exploration.[71] In the dialogue relationship people treat each other as equals, refrain from exerting coercive influences over one another, listen and respond empathically to one another and bring their deep-rooted assumptions to the surface without challenging or reacting judgmentally and defensively.[72]

For dialogue to be effective it must be facilitated by a third party that nurtures a free and open discussion by increasing participants' understanding of the process and creating enthusiasm and commitment to sustain the dialogue.[73] In a group dialogue there is no obligation on participants to do anything or come to any conclusions. However, in situations of conflict the emphasis is on helping participants see each other's perspectives and understand each other's 'concerns, needs, fears, priorities and constraints', and encouraging them to deal with the conflict analytically rather than to exacerbate and perpetuate conflict.[74] The focus is on transforming relationships. To play an effective role in dialogue, it is necessary to build capacities such as listening (without resistance or imposition), respecting (seeing others and their position as legitimate), suspending (suspend assumptions, judgment and unilateral conviction) and voicing (speaking the truth of one's own authority).[75] One of the most critical elements of dialogue is not to react when your assumptions are challenged but to suspend your assumptions and listen.

Dialogue must not be an instrument for one group to accomplish its agenda or to have a superficial consultation with people. A genuine dialogue process is characterised by certain principles such as inclusiveness, joint ownership, learning, humanity and a long-term perspective. To be *inclusive,* dialogue must give a voice to those people who have been excluded historically because of gender, age, economic status, race, ethnicity or religion. However, having a place in the dialogue does not immediately put people on an equal footing because there will be power imbalances. Steps must be taken to mitigate these imbalances by 'levelling the playing field'.[76] Dialogic inquiry requires questioning privileges afforded by socioeconomic status, knowledge, ethnicity or gender.[77]

Dialogue provides an opportunity for *joint ownership* when it enables people to shape their own future, which requires having conversations about what truly matters. The *learning* aspect of dialogue happens through self-reflection as people hear and reflect on what others are saying, what they are saying and what new insights and perspectives they gain. To create a safe place in dialogue it is important for people to display *humanity*, by being open to diverse points of view and behaving respectfully and responsibly towards each other. This is the safe place of dialogue where empathy (ability to put oneself in another's shoes) and authenticity (speaking the truth on one's own authority) are required. Finally, finding a sustainable solution to complex problems requires a *long-term perspective.* There are no quick fixes in dialogue. It takes time for sustainable change to emerge from changes in individual patterns of thinking and behaviour, and then even longer to transfer the impact of dialogue to the socio-political level.[78]

As a longer process, dialogue requires commitment, resources and time, and its impact is not immediate or measurable. There is also a degree of vulnerability that not everyone is comfortable with because to develop trust one must make certain sensitive or personal disclosures. This can expose a person to certain risks including the possibility of suffering harm because of engaging in intercultural dialogue. The risks may involve being misunderstood or making oneself vulnerable when our deepest convictions and even doubts are revealed to other parties. There is also risk associated with internal differences on each side of the dialogue. Groups, communities, and other large social formations have many internal divisions, and so it is impossible to find a representative voice able to speak with authority on behalf of others. In that regard, there first needs to be internal group or community dialogue.[79]

LACK OF DIALOGUE IN AUSTRALIA

Societal or public discussions about Indigenous issues are not constructive in Australia because of the command-and-control nature of Indigenous policy and the culture of argument. Authority for making Indigenous policy is held by governments and primarily white politicians who direct government bureaucracy to implement such policy. Indigenous policy and claims for recognition are caught in a Western culture of competition where challenging or responding to people or ideas is predominantly done by argument. Therefore attack, criticism, opposition or demonization tends to characterise the public discourse around Indigenous issues. This often leads to polarisation in public opinion. Polarisation encourages demonization of the other side, prevents exploration of alternative views and can obscure solutions to problems.[80] At a societal level, some writers note that the breakdown of relationships and communication in Western society occurs because people listen to others through the screen of their own thoughts and prejudices, which results in people not being able to cooperate or work together.[81] This breakdown of relationships stems from a number of causes, including the adversarial nature of a society where people advocate and defend their interests, beliefs and ideas, and fail to listen to others. [82]

The culture of argument is a barrier to solving problems because an adversarial frame of mind assumes that there are only two sides to every issue.[83] Therefore, finding common understanding in these circumstances is difficult. Argument prevents understanding because parties attack each other for perceived weaknesses in logic, facts are denied, information is filtered and, in the extreme, there can be misrepresentation and even lies. Confrontation does not lead to the truth. Further, by emphasising the need for evidence and reasons to support claims, the argument model can devalue other forms of knowledge, experience or reasons as fallacious or anecdotal. While debate can be constructive it can also polarise views and opinions, creating winners and losers in public discourse and fails to consider that there are more than two sides to every question. In a binary competition of reason, one position will emerge as the more acceptable.[84]

The adversarial nature of Australian political democracy plays out in public debate about Indigenous issues. Public debate on Indigenous issues is also heavily influenced by the tacit knowledge about Indigenous people, this being the erroneous and negative assumptions that have accumulated over centuries. There is an ingrained societal practice in Australia of denigrating and racialising Indigenous people. In public debate Indigenous issues are often exploited and manipulated by governments and politicians who demonize Indigenous people and discredit the Indigenous rights agenda to galvanise public support for their politics.[85] Governments are not invested in dialogue with Indigenous people because Indigenous affairs are largely orientated towards command and control, where governments have their own agenda for Indigenous people. The general perception is that Indigenous communities and people are problems, hence public debate is often about what is thought to be best for Indigenous people.[86]

Differences in social memories cause major divergences between Indigenous and non-Indigenous perspectives about the past.[87] The Australian population has a limited understanding of Indigenous people and their history, which includes minimal recognition that colonisation involved the massive dispossession of Indigenous people.[88] Indeed, many Australians, including the young, think that Indigenous people have 'too many rights' and that the recognition of Indigenous rights will result in reverse discrimination against them.[89] In addition to mainstream Australian denial and ignorance, there is Indigenous anger grounded in experiences of being dominated, excluded and denied redress. This anger fuels claims for justice and restitution and in return causes the dominant majority to frame their own anger as a denial of Indigenous rights claims, including a denial of responsibility for the past.[90] A fear of loss of white privilege coupled with fragility in respect to colonisation and dispossession of Indigenous people causes an angry and defensive reaction within the general Australian population.[91] Blaming Indigenous people and their culture for continuing disadvantage is a common projective defence to resentment, fear and anxiety.[92]

DIALOGUE AND DELIBERATION

When governments make decisions about important public policy issues, the norms of democracy provide an opportunity for citizens to engage in discussions and consensus on political issues.[93] Deliberative democracy or public deliberation is meant to give people a voice, agency, power and opportunity to have a say in the political system.[94] In the process, participants can advocate their opinions and persuade others of the rightness of their position, as well as inquire into and explore the reasoning and opinion of others.[95] However, public deliberation is often equated with public debate, where the best considered argument triumphs.[96] Further, the emphasis on rational argument through providing and defending reasons silences or devalues other ways in which people communicate meaningfully, though noncompetitively.[97] As a result, public deliberation often suits the majority culture because the opinions, interests and preferences of minority groups—including Indigenous people—are not represented with equal agency in formal institutions of decision-making such as Parliament.[98]

As a dominated minority group, Indigenous people in Australia lack the power, privilege and authority to influence public discussion and deliberative processes. Furthermore, as we have seen, deliberative processes of government in regard to Indigenous issues are influenced by a lack of respect or negative feelings and attitudes towards Indigenous people. Therefore, such processes can ignore Indigenous participation and discredit their voices. However, conflict over Indigenous claims for recognition can be resolved through dialogue and deliberation with Indigenous people rather than by the decisions of policy makers or the courts.[99] Public deliberation processes can be enhanced through dialogue when an open conversation explores public reasons, free from the urgency of selling or defending positions as happens in deliberation and decision-making.[100] In that regard, dialogue brings the benefits of constructive communication and listening, and this includes the dispelling of stereotypes and enabling honesty in relaying ideas; whereas deliberation brings critical thinking and reasoned argument in making decisions on public policy.[101] However, in an open dialogic process, government and policy makers need to step back and resist the temptation to fix so called 'Indigenous problems' or resist the urge to deny or suppress Indigenous claims. Instead, dialogue requires governments and policy makers to inquire into their own thinking about Indigenous people to transform the foundations for their thinking. Any deliberative process that follows would then involve a different form of interaction where ongoing dialogue and negotiation with Indigenous people becomes the norm in Indigenous policy making.

STRUGGLES OVER RECOGNITION

Norms of mutual recognition—laws, rules, conventions and customs—are a feature of any rules-based system; not just in formal political systems but also other systems such as organisations, bureaucracy, corporations, human rights regimes and so on. Individuals or groups often challenge these norms of recognition through various forms such as negotiation, resistance, grievance and dispute resolution, constitutional negotiations, civil disobedience campaigns, courts and referenda, or armed struggle. For Indigenous people the challenge against the prevailing norms of recognition may relate to a colonial failure to recognise their original sovereignty and authority, or colonial attempts to assimilate them. Therefore, Indigenous claims for recognition of their cultural identity, ways and customs, ownership of land and its resources and of their cultural knowledge directly challenge the norms of government and settler society because they constitute claims made as distinct 'peoples' with rights of self-determination based on prior occupancy and sovereignty. These Indigenous claims for recognition have typically been dealt with by theorists, courts and policymakers within a liberal and nationalist approach, which attempts to reconcile the legitimacy of minority recognition with the freedom and equality of individuals and national uniformity.[102]

However, the liberal and nationalist approach increases rather than resolves conflict. Two of the most problematic issues with this approach are the imposition of solutions devised by courts, theorists and policymakers, and the assumption that there are 'definitive and final solutions' to struggles over recognition. James Tully argues that we need to transform the way we think about conflicts over recognition, which entails resolving conflict by inclusive dialogue among those who are subject to the contested norm of mutual recognition, not by monological solutions handed down from above. Such a dialogic approach would accord with the democratic practice of civic participation, allowing people to have a say over the formulation of the norms of mutual recognition through free and open exchange of reasons and deliberation.[103]

Therefore, the primary aim of dialogue should not be the search for definitive and final procedures and solutions, but to allow a 'dialogical civic freedom' to emerge through universal participation in the practices and institutions of society:

> to ensure that those subject to and affected by any system of governance are always free to call its prevailing norms of recognition and action and coordination into question, to present reasons for and against modifying it, to enter into dialogue with those who govern and who have a duty to listen and respond, to be able to challenge the prevailing procedures of negotiation in the course of discussions, to reach or fail to reach an imperfect agreement to amend (or overthrow) the norm in question, to implement the amendment; and then to ensure that the implementation is open to review and possible renegotiation in the future.[104]

Tully argues that 'dialogical civic freedom' involves not only a right or freedom to speak out against oppressive, exclusionary or assimilative norms of recognition, but a corresponding duty on the part of the powerful to listen and respond in an open dialogue. However, dialogue is not a solution to all problems because theorists, courts and policymakers still have a counterbalancing role to play. The deliberations of citizens cannot become the unquestioned source and standard of justice as they are fraught with imperfections, injustices and disagreements. Minorities have limited power over the decisions of the powerful groups; at the end of the dialogue, they need to be able to appeal to other decision-making institutions (such as courts, parliament, international human rights bodies, nonpartisan adjudicators or mediators and global networks), who can provide checks and balances on the powers of the dominant group to manipulate the dialogue and manufacture agreement.[105]

Although there are a few exceptions, overall, there is no demonstrated culture or practice of genuine dialogue in regard to Indigenous claims for land and recognition of cultural and political rights in Australia. The stories of injustice and struggle for recognition that are discussed in this book reveal that the Indigenous struggle for recognition over the course of history has been ignored, undermined, denied or reinterpreted to accord with the limits of national tolerance in Australia.

INTERCULTURAL DIALOGUE

Dialogue can address intercultural conflicts in liberal democratic societies or solve tensions across societies with different cultures.[106] It can be an instrument for public discussion and transformation in a society divided by social or cultural conflict. Intercultural dialogue is a process of interaction between cultural groups with distinct identities to recognise and accommodate difference, promote mutual understanding and address cultural conflict. It may involve the state because intercultural dialogue is a political process that requires a deconstruction and reconstruction of power and power relations.[107] For colonised and oppressed peoples, dialogue is often regarded as a tool to construct a decolonised relationship of reciprocity.[108] In Australia this involves reimagining and creating new nation-building models that move away from the nationalist framework of a majority culture and 'others', and which duly acknowledges the belonging of all Australians—Anglo settlers, Indigenous peoples and migrants.[109]

Intercultural dialogue should be transformative, creating a context in which individuals and groups develop relationships and engage in conversation that goes beyond their values and beliefs to develop understanding in order to transform society.[110] In transformative dialogue certain practices are required to create the context for common understanding between the parties. These practices include relational responsibility rather than blame, self-expression through personal stories, affirming and embracing others, coordinating voice and co-constituting action, self-reflexive conversation and giving voice to multiple positions and co-creating new realities.[111] In situations of conflict and tension, intercultural dialogue must be grounded in nonviolence and mutual respect and be underpinned by the ideas of pluralism and multiculturalism, enabling historical reflection and mutual forgiveness.[112]

Talking across difference requires dialogue to be fair, and participants must have an attitude of openness and trust, an ability to listen and understand the complexities of other people's worldview and knowledge.[113] Understanding the perspectives and realities of others contributes to improving tolerance and reducing prejudice and conflict.[114] Individuals and groups only begin to understand one another, and gain new perspectives and change their assumptions, when they are treated equally, listened to with empathy and their beliefs are considered with respect.[115] The aim is to create meaning and understanding across cultures to generate a common frame of reference, a shared view of the world.[116] Importantly however, intercultural dialogue can enable 'others' to speak authoritatively in their own voices rather than being spoken for or interpreted by the dominant culture.[117]

For Indigenous people living within the Australian state, a different approach to intercultural dialogue is required for resolving claims to land and recognition of cultural and political rights. It will also include the formation of agreed principles of recognition on which new relationships of reconciliation can be negotiated.

CONSTITUTIONAL DIALOGUE

In his book *Strange multiplicity: Constitutionalism in an age of diversity*, James Tully discusses the failure of modern constitutional nation-states to accord recognition to various groups, particularly Indigenous peoples, because their claims for freedom and autonomy have been denied or suppressed by the structure, practices, language and traditions of the nation state. Modern constitutionalism is associated with the rise and formation of the modern nation state, its institutions and mechanisms beginning in the sixteenth and seventeenth century through to the nineteenth century in Europe and which is distinctive to the political philosophy of Liberalism.[118] Constitutionalism imposes limits on government power by a constitutional framework but it also requires a tradition to uphold the Constitution and an adherence to the rule of law and protection of fundamental rights.[119] While modern constitutionalism is based on popular sovereignty, national identity, uniformity of political and legal authority including institutions of representative government, separation of powers, the rule of law and individual liberty, it rests on the stages theory of human social and economic development in that constitutional nation-states are considered the highest and most developed form of society in comparison to 'ancient' constitutions or 'savage' societies.[120]

According to James Tully, a constitution should be an expression of popular sovereignty, but for Aboriginal peoples it is an 'imperial yoke' around their necks, causing dissent and resistance and which requires constitutional amendment.[121] The language and terms of modern constitutionalism has served to justify European imperialism, including the dispossession of Aboriginal nations of their territory and sovereignty. Recognition of cultural diversity is problematic for modern constitutionalism because it demands cultural uniformity as well as uniformity in legal and political institutions. Therefore, Indigenous people who live within established nation-states are subject to the traditions of modern constitutionalism, and in Australia that tradition is liberalism. When Aboriginal people make claims for recognition as peoples and nations with sovereignty or rights of self-determination, their claims are constrained by the prevailing language of constitutionalism and are adjudicated and tested by criteria and traditions of interpretation set by modern constitutionalism.[122]

James Tully maintains that the language and traditions of modern constitutionalism are held in place by customary language, the normative activities of modern constitutional society and the legal and political structures of a constitutional state. In that respect the language, activities and structures of the nation-state have worked to keep Aboriginal claims of recognition out of public discussion by discrediting the claim or silencing the claimants. However, the customary uses and criteria of modern constitutionalism are not fixed and unquestioned norms, but rather are open to change; and indeed, they have been changing to recognise and accommodate cultural diversity. In that regard, constitutionalism has been shaped in various ways by intercultural encounters and it is through these cultural interactions and the recognition of cultural diversity that hidden rules and language of modern constitutionalism have emerged. Tully calls these hidden rules and language the 'hidden constitutions of contemporary societies'. They are forgotten, ignored or misinterpreted common intercultural conventions that facilitate cultural recognition and which can be reconstructed to change the vision of a constitution or resolve an impasse.[123]

Hidden constitutions are found in the writings and constitutional arrangements of the agents of justice who have sought to recognise minority groups or Indigenous cultures. They are also found in applications of constitutional law, in particular cases in the common law of Commonwealth countries and in international law. Three 'hidden conventions' of constitutionalism are identified by Tully, deriving from the interactions between the Aboriginal and European systems of law in North America and Canada as a result of constitutional negotiations. They are: mutual recognition (the recognition of Aboriginal nations as independent and self-governing nations in constitutional negotiations); continuity (the cultural identities of Aboriginal nations as equal and sovereign nations continue through all treaty arrangements over time); and consent (Aboriginal consent is required by the Crown through a process of negotiation to acquire land and establish European sovereignty). These conventions are an authoritative part of the intercultural common ground between Aboriginal peoples and non-Indigenous society in the course of constitutional practice in North America and Canada.[124]

But notions of dialogue with Indigenous people are much more complex because of the political, social and economic power imbalance that exists between Indigenous and non-Indigenous peoples. Recognition is realised through social dialogue where there is a genuine attempt at understanding and valuing the other on their own terms and also reflecting on one's own assumptions and understanding of the other in order to develop a language of understanding and a 'shared horizon'. However, recognition is also based on the relation of dominant-subordinate, hence recognition is distorted by the deployment of power thus entrenching a relationship of conflict and hostility.[125] In that regard the politics of recognition does not significantly transform colonial relations between Indigenous peoples and the state because, in its contemporary form, it reproduces the very configuration of colonial power that Indigenous peoples have historically sought to transcend.[126]

While recognition and accommodation of cultural distinctiveness is a marked improvement on past policies of exclusion, genocide and assimilation, Indigenous commentators in Canada and the United States suggest there is no significant transcendence of power in the colonial relationship because recognition is something that is granted or accorded to Indigenous people who are in a subordinate relationship with a settler state. Therefore, Indigenous peoples must find the source of liberation in their own transformative practice of self-recognition: not only in their struggle against colonialism, but also to teach the Western world about relationships that are profoundly non-imperialist.[127] This analysis and criticism echoes the situation in Australia, as the incremental recognition of Indigenous claims throughout history has not transformed the colonial relationship. Likewise, it is also necessary for Indigenous people in Australia to develop their own practices of authority and self-determination for empowerment and liberation.

The conventions of 'consent' and 'mutual recognition' are also criticised on the basis that they reproduce the unequal position of power of Indigenous people with regard to settler colonial states. While 'consent' and 'mutual recognition' are useful ethical concepts, to address prevailing power imbalances there must be some acknowledgement of power difference and an examination of historical truths as a component of dialogue in order to give greater moral traction to the claims of Indigenous peoples in settler societies. Therefore, dialogue for Indigenous people is about opening practical and political possibilities in regard to the unmet expectations of Indigenous people in the processes of transitional justice, such as apology, reparations and new kinds of actions by the dominant powers in the future. Hence, a much more realistic condition of Indigenous and non-Indigenous dialogue is the freedom for Indigenous people to be able to reassert a history of injustice and unfulfilled promises without any closure. This would render the dialogue ongoing and open-ended.[128] The examination of historical truths through dialogue, and the need for dialogue to open practical and political possibilities for Indigenous people, are essential for postcolonial relations in Australia. Consent and mutual recognition are also necessary in Australia, just as much as they have been an essential aspect of constitutional practice in North America.

In North America, Indigenous consent is reflected in treaties. According to Tully this demonstrates that the British Crown did not always accept the historical theories and philosophies that deemed Indigenous consent unnecessary in the colonisation process because Indigenous societies were not considered sufficiently developed to acquire rights in land or sovereignty. Tully also refutes historical arguments that Indigenous societies in North America would eventually consent to the superiority of European institutions and embrace Western modernity as a necessary condition for their own development. He argues that Indigenous people have demanded the right to govern themselves and their territories and, in that regard, have refused to acquiesce or assent to the modern nation-states imposed on them in either colonial or decolonised form.[129]

Tully recognises that modern practices of consent through negotiation do reproduce the colonisation of Indigenous people rather than initiate processes of decolonisation because in the negotiation process, Indigenous people are subordinated by the hegemony of Western institutions. Hegemony in the relationship between Indigenous peoples and Western governments is difficult to confront in practice because it is so deeply woven into the thoughts and action of non-Indigenous peoples in the form of Western attitudes of superiority; and it affects Indigenous peoples in the form of attitudes of inferiority and ambivalence, or in alienation of their own institutions or beliefs. Further, it is difficult for Indigenous people to confront hegemony in contemporary forms of negotiation and consultation because they are so focussed on the pressing needs of the 'here and now'.[130] In that respect negotiations are framed in terms of the norms and customs of the dominant partner, and negotiations do take place within and through the hegemony of legal, political and economic institutions that have been imposed on Indigenous people without their consent. Further, negotiations take place within a set of unquestioned theses on 'modernity' that affirms the idea of human social progress through imperial expansion and the global ascendency of Western institutions. By entering negotiations under these conditions, Indigenous people do appear to tacitly consent to their acquiescence in the imposed institutions; this is the problem of subordination of one partner under the hegemony of the other.[131]

In that context, Tully suggests a four-step approach to move dialogue and negotiation forward. Firstly, negotiations should not be rejected because of the unequal situation because all negotiations begin under conditions of hegemony and subordination. In fact, the aim of negotiations is to change the unequal circumstances. Secondly, negotiation is not just between two partners in an official process with a fixed structure of conditions. Negotiations take place within the broader field and practice of consent and dissent, where multiple actors contribute to shaping the course of the negotiations. Also, negotiations can be ongoing, open-ended relationships that are continually modified by consent, agreement, negotiation and renegotiation. Thirdly, the modernity thesis—that there is a set of necessary and inevitable causal processes of modernisation or globalisation that organise the interactions of individuals and groups—should be rejected. There are movements around the world demanding diverse forms of political organisation and legal pluralism that do not conform to these modernisation theses. Lastly, dialogue and negotiation should be grounded in the alternative world one wants to defend and advance through negotiation. The resilience, survival, demographic growth and renaissance of traditional customs and ways can provide the groundwork for an alternative vision of the world. Therefore, strength in Aboriginal processes of negotiation is grounded in the way of life that is being defended and also in creating new community networks and partnerships with non-Aboriginal people.[132]

DIALOGUE AND NEW RELATIONSHIPS

One example of an attempt at dialogue is the Canadian Royal Commission on Aboriginal Peoples (1991–1996), which set out a vision of a new relationship between Aboriginal and non-Aboriginal people in that country. James Tully worked as advisor to the Canadian Royal Commission on Aboriginal Peoples. The Royal Commission investigated the evolution of the relationship among Aboriginal peoples (Indian, Inuit and Métis), the Canadian government and Canadian society, and sought to comprehend the problems that plagued those relationships that confront Aboriginal peoples.[133] The report said that the policy of assimilation was a failure and that Canada had to look to its historical treaty relationships to restructure a new relationship between Aboriginal and non-Aboriginal people.

The Royal Commission was established in response to demands by Aboriginal peoples to dismantle the current colonial relationship administered through the Indian Act. They wanted to establish a new relationship that is not only just, but able to provide workable solutions to the chronic social and economic problems faced by Aboriginal people. The vision of a new relationship came from Aboriginal people, through a dialogic process of consultation and discussion. The Royal Commission met for five years, conducting over 178 days of public hearings, and visiting ninety-six Aboriginal communities. It commissioned more than 1,200 specialised studies and discussed problems and solutions with Canadians. The vision of a new relationship was tested and redrafted through lengthy discussions with non-Aboriginal Canadians, with participants having expertise in areas of law, government, management, health care, business, education, economics, forestry, fisheries and the environment. The final draft gained wide consensus from Aboriginal and non-Aboriginal discussants.[134]

René Dussault, one of the cochairs of the Royal Commission, said it became apparent that to achieve change in many communities or in the relationships between Aboriginal and non-Aboriginal people in Canada, it was not sufficient just to tinker with government regulations, programmes and policies or the laws. What was needed was a report that would be a source of inspiration and provide a road map for change: a guide to begin again on a new footing of mutual recognition, respect, sharing and mutual responsibility. The report had to integrate Aboriginal and non-Aboriginal perspectives and include 'honourable compromises' in achieving a vision for reconciliation. The commissioners had to develop a broader vision of the sources of law to include treaties and customary law, and a broader vision of the Constitution to enable Aboriginal people to exercise their autonomy. With regard to land, resources and the economy, the vision had to foster reciprocity and sharing; and in regards to sociocultural matters, the vision had to stress the interconnection of all things and foster the protection of Aboriginal identity, languages, cultures and ways of life.[135]

The Royal Commission concluded that the primary cause of social and economic crisis facing Aboriginal people was the colonial relationship imposed on them by the Canadian government through the Indian Act. The relationship is more than one hundred and fifty years old and since the mid-nineteenth century its aim was to displace Aboriginal people from their traditional lands and assimilate them into Canadian society. Its effect has been to marginalise Aboriginal people and create a system of welfare dependency, alienation and frustration. The commissioners argued that for Aboriginal people to free themselves from this destructive relationship, they must first replace the ruinous paternalism of the Canadian government with control over their own lives. Second, they need their own land, resources and governments to reconstruct their societies, economies and political orders. Finally, they need time, space and respect from non-Aboriginal Canadians to heal their spirits and revitalise their cultures.[136]

The Royal Commission focussed on striving for a renewed relationship based, firstly, on the recognition of Aboriginal people as 'peoples', 'nations' or 'First Nations' that are not subordinate to federal or provincial governments but coordinate with them. This outlines a unique (sui generis) postcolonial relationship because Aboriginal peoples are not some sort of multicultural group or minority within Canadian society. Secondly, Aboriginal people are acknowledged as self-governing in that they have the inherent right and capacity to govern themselves in accordance with their own laws and cultures. They also possess native title, a right to land and resources to render themselves economically self-reliant and to finance their development. Thirdly, the First Nations authorities coexist through interrelations with the provincial and federal governments. Even if they agree to share or leave many of their powers in the hands of provincial and federal governments, their inherent right to govern themselves persists. This principle of continuity or coexistence nullifies the doctrine of terra nullius (that they have no rights of self-government over their territories) and it also nullifies the doctrine of extinguishment (that their status as self-governing First Peoples could be extinguished by acts of the federal government).[137]

According to the Royal Commission the new relationship should be built upon the principles of mutual recognition, mutual respect, sharing and mutual responsibility. The Royal Commission saw *mutual recognition* as involving non-Aboriginal and Aboriginal Canadians affirming and accepting each other as being part of Canada: Aboriginal people being recognised as the original inhabitants and caretakers of the land with distinctive rights and responsibilities flowing from that status; and non-Aboriginal people recognised as being part of the land by birth and adoption, having strong ties of affection and loyalty.[138]

The Royal Commission recognised the importance of *respect* between cultures for harmonious relations, however public attitudes of respect require an examination of the makeup, practices and symbols of public institutions to ensure they embody the basic consideration and esteem that are owed to Aboriginal and non-Aboriginal languages and culture. *Sharing and reciprocity* are also important components and can be built into a renewed relationship by recognising each other's rights and respecting each other's cultures and institutions, recognising unacknowledged histories, ensuring the return of land to Aboriginal people, addressing poverty and dependence and enhancing people's capacity to contribute. Finally, *mutual responsibility* involves the transformation of the colonial relationship of guardian and ward into a genuine partnership where Aboriginal peoples and Canada also have responsibilities to the land they share.[139]

In Canada, treaties are the preeminent means of creating and acknowledging relationships and are a key illustration of the importance of dialogue in creating and maintaining relationships. The negotiation and renewal of treaties is important for re-establishing and adjusting relationships because relationships among peoples are not static as 'once and for all' transactions. They need to be adjusted regularly and explicitly reaffirmed from time to time. Aboriginal and non-Aboriginal people meet, exchange ideas and negotiate the dialogue on an intercultural common ground, which already exists as a result of historical interaction and cooperation. The intercultural institutions and practices resulting from this cooperation and interaction provide the starting point for a renewed dialogue.[140] In considering the potential for reconciliation, the Royal Commission stressed that reconciliation is a matter of trust and this required that 'partners from both sides leave their comfort zone, question long held views, put aside prejudices often inspired by ignorance and fear, and accept the other in his or her difference'. Further, reconciliation should not be seen as a threat to Canada in reorienting Canadian society towards respect for Aboriginal autonomy and greater participation into mainstream institutions. [141]

The Canadian Royal Commission on Aboriginal Peoples is an example of a formal dialogical process that could examine issues and generate a way forward for a renewed relationship between Indigenous people and governments in Australia. Although there were no ringing endorsements or calls from governments for fundamental change of the kind envisaged by the Canadian Royal Commission on Aboriginal Peoples, [142] the lessons and principles enunciated by the Royal Commission can inform an intercultural dialogue in Australia because Indigenous people in this region likewise have never consented to British-Australian sovereignty or the imposition of a colonial relationship. This demands the negotiation of a new relationship in Australia through constitutionally recognised agreements. The other lesson of the Royal Commission is that it attempted to find solutions to the many problems and issues that originate from the colonial relationship.

The Canadian Truth and Reconciliation Commission is another example of a public dialogue process in respect to Indigenous grievances and/ or claims for recognition. It was established in 2008 under the terms of the Indian Residential Schools Settlement Agreement. The agreement was the result of a large class action against the Canadian government and Christian churches by Survivors of Indian Residential Schools. [143] The Canadian Truth and Reconciliation Commission acknowledged the work of the earlier Royal Commission on Aboriginal Peoples (1991–1996) and its emphasis on developing a vision for reconciliation, and especially the 'heavy onus' that reconciliation places on the Canadian government to change its ways. [144] Indeed, the Royal Commission called for a full investigation into the residential schools by documenting their purpose and the extent of their impact on Aboriginal peoples.

Residential schools with a remit to 'civilise' and 'Christianise' Aboriginal children in Canada were proposed from the early seventeenth century, however, after the British conquest of New France in 1763, the idea lay dormant until the early nineteenth century when British missionaries established residential schools throughout the colonies. After confederation of the British North American colonies in 1867 to form the Canadian state, the federal government became involved in Indian residential schools, increasing its involvement from the 1880s to the mid-1990s. Residential schools became official Canadian policy and practice because they were part of government's assimilation policy through the Indian Act and they materialised the government's intent to eliminate its government-to-government relationships with First Nations. The federal government became involved in residential schools at a time it was colonising Aboriginal lands in Western Canada. In negotiating treaties with Aboriginal people, the government feared it would be called upon to provide relief to Aboriginal people during times of economic stress. To divest itself of these financial and legal obligations the government invested in residential schools, thereby providing skills to Aboriginal people to participate in the market economy; they would politically and socially assimilate young Aboriginal people; they would change Aboriginal culture and beliefs by substituting these with Christian ideals and beliefs; and by dispersing individuals from communities, the schools would provide security to the government against aggression from any particular Aboriginal tribe.[145]

The commission documented the 'complex truth about the history and ongoing legacy of church-run residential schools' by examining 'individual and collective harms perpetrated against Aboriginal peoples'. Further, the commission had to guide and inspire a process of truth and healing, leading towards reconciliation within Aboriginal families, and between Aboriginal peoples and non-Aboriginal communities, churches, governments and Canadians generally. The process of the commission was to 'work to renew relationships on a basis of inclusion, mutual understanding and respect'. Specifically, it was required to hold seven national events to gather documents and statements about residential schools and their legacy; to fund truth and reconciliation events in the community; to recommend commemorative initiatives for the federal government to fund; to set up a research centre to house the commission's records and documents; and to issue a report with recommendations.[146]

An Indian Residential School Survivors Committee advised the commission. It met regularly with all parties to the Settlement Agreement to discuss opportunities and challenges in fulfilling its role. During its six years of operation, the commission held events in all parts of the country, with the most visible being the seven national events held between June 2010 and March 2014. More than nine thousand residential school survivors registered to attend. The national events provided a forum for survivors and their families and raised awareness of the history and legacy of residential schools. The commission also held two further regional events and held two hundred and thirty-eight days of local hearing in seventy-seven communities. The seven sacred teachings of the Anishinaabe— Respect, Courage, Love, Truth, Humility, Honesty and Wisdom— served as themes for the seven national events. Sacred fires were lit at the beginning of each event and the day's proceedings began with ceremony. Cultural performances were key elements of each national event.[147]

The commission also sponsored two town hall events to draw a greater number of participants. The commission received more than 6,750 statements from residential school survivors, members of their families and other individuals about the residential school system and its legacy. The commission also gathered statements from former staff of residential schools, conducting ninety-six separate interviews with former staff and children of former staff. Students were involved in all national events, with local schools invited to take part in the day of learning. More than fifteen thousand students participated by attending presentations, cultural performances, observing and taking part in panel discussions and workshops and visiting displays in learning places. Activities were organised to help teachers prepare students for National Event Education Days. Furthermore, the commission was able to connect with Canadian and worldwide audiences by live streaming the national events on the internet and posting on its website and social media platforms.[148]

The impact and legacy of the residential schools is seen today. It not only affected the survivors whose lives are shaped by their experiences in these schools, but has affected their partners, children, grandchildren, extended families and communities. The commission examined a range of impacts relating to child welfare, education, language, culture, health care and justice, making various recommendations. The impacts of the schools — including the historical political and legal policies — are reflected in educational, income, health care and social disparities between Aboriginal people and other Canadians. It is reflected in the 'intense racism' harboured against Aboriginal people and in systemic and other forms of discrimination experienced by Aboriginal people. It is also reflected in the 'critically endangered status' of most Aboriginal languages, the current disproportionate number of Aboriginal children removed from their families by child welfare authorities and the overrepresentation of Aboriginal people in custody and detention. Further, the astonishing number of Aboriginal victims of crimes — particularly women and girls — can partly be explained by how Aboriginal children were treated in residential schools: 'They were denied an environment of positive parenting, worthy community leaders, and a positive sense of identity and self-worth'. The violence, damage and trauma inflicted on Aboriginal children is intergenerational.[149]

The commission examined Indian residential schools and their legacy in the context of colonisation, the Indian Act (an instrument of the assimilation policy) and the Crown's failure to keep its treaty promises, which have damaged the relationship between Aboriginal and non-Aboriginal peoples. The most significant damage was to the trust between the Crown and Aboriginal peoples. Repairing the trust required a new vision for Canada: one that embraced Aboriginal people's right to self-determination within, and in partnership with, Canadian sovereignty.[150] The commission urged reconciliation to resolve the long-standing conflict between the Crown and Aboriginal peoples and set out ten guiding principles of truth and reconciliation to assist Canadians to move forward.[151] It defined reconciliation as an 'ongoing process of establishing and maintaining mutually respectful relationships' between Aboriginal and non-Aboriginal peoples. For this to happen 'there has to be awareness of the past, acknowledgement of the harm that has been inflicted, atonement for

the causes, and action to change behaviour'. Establishing respectful relationships also required the revitalisation of Indigenous law and legal
traditions. [152]

The commission considered that the United Nations Declaration on
the Rights of Indigenous Peoples is the appropriate framework for reconciliation in twenty-first-century Canada. It states that Aboriginal peoples'
rights to self-determination must be integrated into Canada's constitutional and legal framework and into civic institutions consistent with the
declaration. Aboriginal peoples in Canada have Aboriginal and treaty
rights and therefore have the right to access and revitalise their own laws
and governance systems within their communities and in their dealings
with government; they also have a right to revitalise their cultures, languages and ways of life and have the right to reparations for historical
harms. [153]

The spiritual, legal and moral foundations of reconciliation can be
found in early treaties and covenants negotiated and pledged between
Aboriginal peoples and the Crown. In accordance with traditions of di-
plomacy plus treaty and covenant making, the commission called on the
Canadian government to jointly develop with Aboriginal peoples a Royal
Proclamation of Reconciliation to be issued by the Crown that would
repudiate the Doctrine of Discovery and terra nullius; adopt the United
Nations Declaration on the Rights of Indigenous Peoples as a reconciliation framework; renew treaty relationships; and reconcile Aboriginal and
Crown constitutional and legal orders. A royal proclamation is an important symbol that would be recognised by all citizens. It would 'reaffirm
the long-standing, but often disregarded, commitment between Canada
and Aboriginal peoples'. Based on the principles enunciated in the royal
proclamation, the commission called for all parties to the Indian Residential Schools Settlement Agreement to develop and sign an action-orientat-
ed Covenant of Reconciliation to advance peace and healing in Canada. [154]

In regard to the Doctrine of Discovery and terra nullius, the commission said these concepts were used to justify European sovereignty over
Indigenous lands and to extinguish Aboriginal land and resource rights
in treaty and land claim processes; they have no legitimate place in describing the foundations of the country or in contemporary policymaking, law, and legislation because such concepts are factually, legally and
morally wrong. [155]

WHERE TO FOR AUSTRALIA?

The Canadian Royal Commission on Aboriginal Peoples set out a vision
for reconciliation based on building a renewed relationship between Aboriginal and non-Aboriginal people. The Canadian Truth and Reconcilia-

tion Commission set out guiding principles for truth and reconciliation in Canada. This type of public discussion to get to the bottom of what is required for truth and reconciliation in order to establish a framework for moving forward is lacking in Australia. As we will see in chapter 6, there have been attempts at truth telling in Australia but the failure to date of the constitutional recognition process is a reminder that there are major barriers to overcome if the nation is to genuinely recognise the status of Indigenous Australians. Constitutional recognition is constrained by the Australian Constitution that dictates a referendum must be supported by a majority of Australians in a majority of states. Further, the norms, traditions and attitudes of government also constitute barriers to moving forward. While the structured process for constitutional recognition in Australia enabled Indigenous people to engage in discussion and deliberation, the process was highly managed by government and politicians who clearly want a different outcome to Indigenous people. The early focus on reforming the Australian Constitution has since 2017 changed to focus more on what Indigenous people want, and this is reflected in the Uluru Statement from the Heart. However, in their struggles for constitutional recognition, Indigenous Australians are being subjected to approaches that enforce uniformity and assimilation, rather than recognise Indigenous difference or Indigenous authority.

It is important for Indigenous Australians to continue to engage with governments through dialogue and negotiation. However, missing in Australia is a constitutional framework through which Indigenous people can engage with governments on an ongoing basis to transform the current colonial relationship. The Indigenous proposal for a First Nations Voice enshrined in the Australian Constitution could provide such a constitutional framework, but the federal government does not accept it, and in that regard will not be supported in a referendum. Alternatively, a First Nations Voice established by federal legislation is possible. However, to move to a renewed relationship there needs to be processes of genuine dialogue and negotiation. The Indigenous proposal for a Makarrata Commission for treaty-making and truth telling is a structure that can move the process forward by way of intercultural dialogue. This dialogue could happen through a truth telling process that can be established by the federal government through its executive and legislative powers.

NOTES

1. Amnesty International, *WA Government must stop Oombulgurri demolitions after forcibly evicting community members* (Sydney: Amnesty International, 23 September 2014); T. Solonec, 'The trauma of Oombulgurri's demolition will be repeated across Western Australia', *The Guardian*, Thursday, 27 November 2014. https://

www.theguardian.com/commentisfree/2014/nov/27/the-trauma-of-oombulgurris-demolition-will-be-repeated-across-western-australia [Accessed 3 December 2014].

2. H. Davidson, 'WA plan to close 100 remote and Indigenous communities "devastating"', *The Guardian*, Tuesday, 18 November 2014. http://www.theguardian.com/australia-news/2014/nov/18/wa-plan-to-close-100-remote-and-indigenous-communities-devastating [Accessed 19 July 2015].

3. 'Colin Barnett links closure of remote Aboriginal communities to child abuse', *The Guardian*, Friday, March 20, 2015. http://www.theguardian.com/australia-news/2015/mar/20/colin-barnett-links-closure-of-remote-aboriginal-communities-to-child-abuse [Accessed 19 July 2015].

4. S. Medhora, 'Remote communities are 'lifestyle choices', says Tony Abbott', *The Guardian*, Tuesday, 10 March 2015. http://www.theguardian.com/australia-news/2015/mar/10/remote-communities-are-lifestyle-choices-says-tony-abbott [Accessed 19 July 2015].

5. C. Wahlquist, 'Remote Aboriginal communities still in limbo despite release of 'major reforms',' *The Guardian*, Thursday, 7 May 2015. http://www.theguardian.com/australia-news/2015/may/07/remote-aboriginal-communities-still-in-limbo-despite-release-of-major-reforms [Accessed 19 July 2015].

6. P. Dodson, *Reconciliation: Two Centuries On, Is Dialogue Enough?*, La Trobe University Centre for Dialogue, Working Paper [Online] 2008/1. www.latrobe.edu.au/dialogue/publications/workingpppaper-series/past-issues [Accessed 19 January 2012].

7. G. Coulthard, *Red Skin White Masks: Rejecting the Colonial Politics of Recognition* (Minneapolis: University of Minnesota Press, 2014), 151.

8. Commonwealth of Australia, *Recognising Aboriginal and Torres Strait Islander Peoples in the Constitution: Report of the Expert Panel* (Canberra, ACT: Department of Families, Housing, Community Services and Indigenous Affairs, January 2012), 153, 173.

9. Commonwealth of Australia, *Joint Select Committee on Constitutional Recognition of Aboriginal and Torres Strait Islander Peoples, Final Report* (Canberra, ACT: Parliament House, 2015).

10. G. M. Anderson, 'The Government is Asking You to Blindly Vote for Changes in a Referendum, without Even Clarifying the Final Wording', 23 May 2014, Sovereign Union—First Nations Asserting Sovereignty. http://nationalunitygovernment.org/content/government-asking-you-blindly-vote-changes-referendum-without-even-clarifying-final-words [Accessed 26 April 2018].

11. C. Liddle, 'I Don't Want Your Recognise Campaign—It's Nothing but a Sham', *The Guardian*, Monday, 18 August 2014. https://www.theguardian.com/commentisfree/2014/aug/18/i-dont-want-your-recognise-campaign-its-nothing-but-a-sham   [Accessed 26 April 2018].

12. J. Anderson, T. Hosch and R. Eccles, *Final Report of the Aboriginal and Torres Strait Islander Act of Recognition Review Panel* (Canberra, ACT: Department of Prime Minister and Cabinet, Australian Government, September 2014).

13. M. Davis and M. Langton, 'Introduction', in *It's Our Country: Indigenous Arguments for Meaningful Constitutional Recognition and Reform*, Megan Davis and Marcia Langton, eds. (Carlton, VIC: Melbourne University Press, 2016), 5.

14. N. Pearson, 'Process of recognition: The constitutional recognition of indigenous Australians requires meaningful consultation', *The Monthly* (August 2015). https://www.themonthly.com.au/issue/2015/august/1438351200/noel-pearson/process-recognition [Accessed 26 April 2018].

15. Pearson, 'Process of recognition'.

16. Commonwealth of Australia, *Recognising Aboriginal and Torres Strait Islander peoples in the Constitution: Report of the Expert Panel* (Canberra, ACT: Department of Families, Housing, Community Services and Indigenous Affairs, January 2012), 201, 213.

17. M. Mansell, 'Is the Constitution a better tool than simple legislation to advance the cause of Aboriginal Peoples?', in *It's Our Country: Indigenous Arguments for Meaningful Constitutional Recognition and Reform*, Megan Davis and Marcia Langton, eds. (Carlton, VIC: Melbourne University Press, 2016), 145–54.

18. N. Gorrie, 'Fuck Your Constitutional Recognition, I Want a Treaty', *VICE* [online], 17 March 2016. https://www.vice.com/en_au/article/qb5zdp/fuck-your-recognition [Accessed 26 April 2018].

19. G. Craven, 'The Law, Substance and Morality of Recognition', in *The Forgotten People: Liberal and Conservative Approaches to Recognising Indigenous Peoples*, Damien Freeman and Shereen Morris, eds. (Carlton, Victoria: Melbourne University Press, 2016), 38.

20. N. Pearson, 'There's no such thing as minimal recognition—There is only recognition', in *It's Our Country: Indigenous Arguments for Meaningful Constitutional Recognition and Reform*, Megan Davis and Marcia Langton, eds. (Carlton, Victoria: Melbourne University Press, 2016), 174.

21. M. Mansell, *Treaty and Statehood: Aboriginal Self-Determination* (Leichhardt, NSW: The Federation Press, 2016), 53.

22. Commonwealth of Australia, *Final Report of the Referendum Council* (Canberra, ACT: Department of Prime Minister and Cabinet, 30 June 2017), 2, 14.

23. Commonwealth of Australia, *Final Report of the Referendum Council*, 10–28.

24. M. Turnbull, G. Brandis and N. Scullion, *Response to Referendum Council's Report on Constitutional Recognition* (Department of Prime Minister and Cabinet, Australian Government, 26 October 2017), https://ministers.pmc.gov.au/scullion/2017/response-referendum-councils-report-constitutional-recognition [Accessed 8 November 2019].

25. M. Turnbull, G. Brandis and N. Scullion, *Response to Referendum Council's Report on Constitutional Recognition*.

26. Commonwealth of Australia, *Interim Report: Joint Select Committee on Constitutional Recognition relating to Aboriginal and Torres Strait Islander Peoples* (Canberra, ACT, July 2018).

27. Commonwealth of Australia, *Final Report: Joint Select Committee on Constitutional Recognition Relating to Aboriginal and Torres Strait Islander Peoples* (Canberra, November 2018).

28. Commonwealth of Australia, *Final Report: Joint Select Committee on Constitutional Recognition*, 10.

29. Commonwealth of Australia, *Final Report: Joint Select Committee on Constitutional Recognition*, 74–78.

30. Commonwealth of Australia, *Final Report: Joint Select Committee on Constitutional Recognition*, 102, 118.

31. Commonwealth of Australia, *Final Report: Joint Select Committee on Constitutional Recognition*, 122, 124, 132, 136.

32. Commonwealth of Australia, *Final Report: Joint Select Committee on Constitutional Recognition*, 158, 184–85.

33. P. Karp, 'Scott Morrison claims Indigenous voice to parliament would be a third chamber', *The Guardian*, Wednesday, 26 September 2018. https://www.theguardian.com/australia-news/2018/sep/26/scott-morrison-claims-indigenous-voice-to-parliament-would-be-a-third-chamber [Accessed 6 August 2019].

34. G. Brown and P. Taylor, 'Morrison to veto "voice" as part of Constitution', *The Australian*, Friday, 12 July 2019. https://www.theaustralian.com.au/nation/politics/morrison-to-veto-voice-as-part-of-constitution/news-story/c9753bbe3595470032ac7fa95636931e [Accessed 6 August 2019].

35. K. Wyatt, *Walking in Partnership to Effect Change*, National Press Club Address, Department of Prime Minister and Cabinet, Australian Government. https://ministers.pmc.gov.au/wyatt/2019/national-press-club-address-walking-partnership-effect-change [Accessed 18 August 2019].

36. D. Crowe, 'On Indigenous recognition, the PM has already drawn a line that might be impossible to cross', *The Sydney Morning Herald*, Thursday, 11 July 2019. https://www.smh.com.au/politics/federal/on-indigenous-recognition-the-pm-has-already-drawn-a-line-that-might-be-impossible-to-cross-20190711-p526c8.html [Accessed 15 August 2019].

37. L. Allam, 'Pat Dodson urges Coalition to 'deal with' Indigenous voice to parliament and referendum', *The Guardian*, Wednesday, 5 June 2019. https://www.theguardian.com/australia-news/2019/jun/05/pat-dodson-urges-coalition-to-deal-with-indigenous-voice-to-parliament-and-referendum [Accessed 6 August 2019].

38. H. Davidson, 'Ken Wyatt warned Indigenous Australians will throw constitution into seas unless recognition resolved', *The Guardian*, Saturday, 3 August 2019. https://www.theguardian.com/australia-news/2019/aug/03/ken-wyatt-warned-indigenous-australians-will-throw-constitution-into-sea-unless-recognition-resolved [Accessed 6 August 2019].

39. M. McKenna, 'Moment of Truth: History and Australia's Future', *Quarterly Essay* 69 (March 2018), 13.

40. K. Wyatt, *Looking Forward, Looking Back*, 19th Annual Vincent Lingiari Memorial Lecture, Charles Darwin University, Thursday, 15 August 2019. https://ministers.pmc.gov.au/wyatt/2019/19th-annual-vincent-lingiari-memorial-lecture-charles-darwin-university [Accessed 26 August 2019].

41. K. Murphy, 'Ken Wyatt says he has Indigenous voice to parliament plan for Scott Morrison', *The Guardian*, Thursday, 17 October 2019. https://www.theguardian.com/australia-news/2019/oct/17/ken-wyatt-says-he-has-indigenous-voice-to-parliament-plan-for-scott-morrison [Accessed 18 October 2019].

42. D. Cronin, 'Justice and the political future for Indigenous Australians', in *Practical Justice: Principles, Practice and Social Change*, Peter Aggleton, Alex Broom and Jeremy Moss, eds. (Abingdon Oxon, UK: Routledge, 2019), 167.

43. J. Tully, *Strange Multiplicity. Constitutionalism in an age of diversity* (Cambridge, UK: Cambridge University Press, 1995).

44. J. Tully, *Public Philosophy in a New Key, Volume 1: Democracy and Civic Freedom* (Cambridge, UK: Cambridge University Press, 2008), 239.

45. A. Gunstone, *Unfinished Business: The Australian Formal Reconciliation Process* (Melbourne, VIC: Australian Scholarly Publishing, 2007), 132–66.

46. D. Short, *Reconciliation and Colonial Power: Indigenous Rights in Australia* (Hampshire, England: Ashgate Publishing Group, 2008), 178, 180.

47. J. Tully, 'A Fair and Just Relationship. The Vision of the Canadian Royal Commission on Aboriginal Peoples', *Meanjin* 57, no. 1 (1998), 157.

48. D. Bohm, *On Dialogue* (London & New York: Routledge, 1996), 7, 30; D. Yankelovich, *The Magic of Dialogue: Transforming Conflict into Cooperation* (New York: Simon & Schuster, 1999), 38.

49. W. Isaacs, *Dialogue and the art of thinking together. A pioneering approach to communicating in business and in life* (New York: Doubleday, 1999), 45–46.

50. Yankelovich, *The Magic of Dialogue*, 38–45.

51. B. Pruitt and P. Thomas, *Democratic Dialogue: A handbook for practitioners* (New York: The General Secretariat of the Organisation of American States, and the United Nations Development Program, 2007), 22–23.

52. Isaacs, *Dialogue and the art*, 19.

53. Pruitt and Thomas, *Democratic Dialogue*, 21–22.

54. Yankelovich, *The Magic of Dialogue*, 15.

55. M. Herzig and L. Chasin, *Fostering Dialogue Across Divides: A Nuts and Bolts Guide from the Public Conversations Project* (Watertown, MA: Public Conversations Project, 2006), 3; A. Dessel and M. Rogge, 'Evaluation of Intergroup Dialogue: A Review of the Empirical Literature', *Conflict of Resolution Quarterly* 26, no. 2 (2008), 211.

56. W. N. Isaacs, 'Taking Flight: Dialogue, Collective Thinking, and Organizational Learning', *Organizational Dynamics* 22, no. 2 (1993), 26.

57. Herzig and Chasin, *Fostering Dialogue Across Divides*, 3; Pruitt and Thomas, *Democratic Dialogue*, 19–21.

58. Isaacs, 'Taking Flight', 25; Isaacs, *Dialogue and the art*, 45–46.

59. W. N. Isaacs, 'Towards an Action Theory of Dialogue', *International Journal of Public Administration* 24, no. 7 (2001), 718, 722.

60. Isaacs, *Dialogue and the art*, 307; Isaacs, 'Taking Flight', 31.

61. Isaacs, 'Taking Flight', 31–32.

62. Isaacs, *Towardss an Action Theory*, 729–44.

63. Isaacs, *Towardss an Action Theory*, 730–32; Isaacs, *Dialogue and the art*, 242.

64. Bohm, *On Dialogue*, 10, 28, 56; Isaacs, *Dialogue and the art*, 61; Isaacs, *Towardss an Action Theory*, 732–75.

65. Isaacs, 'Taking Flight', 34; Isaacs, *Towardss an Action Theory*, 733–34; Isaacs, *Dialogue and the art*, 242–44.

66. Bohm, *On Dialogue*, 23.

67. Isaacs, *Dialogue and the art*, 134–44, 146–47.

68. Isaacs, *Dialogue and the art*, 257–85; Isaacs, *Towardss an Action Theory*, 729–44.

69. Bohm, *On Dialogue*, 17–22.

70. H. C. Kelman, 'Group Processes in the Resolution of International Conflicts', *American Psychologist* 53, no. 3 (1997), 219.

71. O. Escobar, 'The dialogic turn: dialogue for deliberation', *In-Spire Journal of Law, Politics and Societies* 4, no. 2 (2009), 53.

72. N. C. Roberts, 'Calls for Dialogue', in *The Transformative Power of Dialogue*, Nancy Charlotte Roberts, ed. (London: Elsevier Book Series, 2002), 6.

73. H. M. Zoller, 'A place you haven't visited before: Creating the conditions for community dialogue', *Southern Communication Journal* 65, no. 2 (2000), 198; Kelman, *Group Processes*, 214.

74. Kelman, 'Group Processes', 214.

75. Isaacs, *Dialogue and the art*, 419.

76. Pruitt and Thomas, *Democratic Dialogue*, 26–28.

77. O. Escobar, *Public Dialogue and Deliberation, A communication perspective for public engagement practitioners* (Edinburgh: The University of Edinburgh, 2011), 32–33.

78. Pruitt and Thomas, *Democratic Dialogue*, 28–32.

79. A. Appadurai, 'The Risks of Dialogue', in *New Stakes for Intercultural Dialogue, Acts of the International Seminar, Paris 6–7 June 2006*, Samantha Wauchope and Odette Petit, eds. (UNESCO 2008), 33–37.

80. D. Tannen, *The Argument Culture* (New York: Random House, 1998), 21.

81. B. Bohm, *On Dialogue*, 2–4; D. Tannen, *The Argument Culture*, 24–25; D. Yankelovich, *The Magic of Dialogue*, 19–31.

82. W. Isaacs, *Dialogue and the art*, 17–18.

83. Tannen, *The Argument Culture*, 3–4,7–8, 9–11.

84. B. Hyde and J. L. Bineham, 'From debate to dialogue: Towards a pedagogy of nonpolarized public discourse', *Southern Communication Journal* 65, no. 2 (2000), 209–11.

85. Dodson, *Reconciliation: Two Centuries On, Is Dialogue Enough?*, 4.

86. L. Behrendt, 'Reconciliation: Forty Years On', *Australian Quarterly* 79, no. 3 (2007), 48.

87. D. Mellor and D. Bretherton, 'Reconciliation between Black and White Australia: the Role of Social Memory', in *The Role of Memory in Ethnic Conflict*, Cairns and Mícheál D. Roe, eds. (New York: Palgrave MacMillan, 2003), 51–53.

88. D. Mellor and D. Bretherton, 'Reconciliation between Black and White Australia', 49–50.

89. Commonwealth of Australia, *National Human Rights Consultation Report* (Barton, ACT: Attorney General's Department, September 2009), 209–10.

90. C. Lane West-Newman, 'Anger in Legacies of Empire, Indigenous Peoples and Settler States', *European Journal of Social Theory* 7, no. 2 (2004), 190–91.

91. G. Hage, 'Multiculturalism and White Paranoia in Australia', *Journal of International Migration and Integration* 3, nos. 3–4 (2002), 418–22.

92. R. Williams, 'Why Should I Feel Guilty?: Reflections on the Workings of Guilt in White-Aboriginal Relations', *Australian Psychologist* 35, no. 2 (2000), 136–42.

93. S. Wheatley, 'Deliberative Democracy and Minorities', *European Journal of International Law* 14, no. 3 (2003), 508–10.

94. M. L. McCoy and P. L. Scully, 'Deliberative Dialogue to Expand Civic Engagement: What Kind of Talk Does Democracy Need?', *National Civic Review* 91, no. 2 (2002), 118.

95. Escobar, *Public Dialogue and Deliberation*, 34–35.

96. Escobar, *Public Dialogue and deliberation*, 38.

97. V. L. Bonham, T. Citrin, S. M. Modell, T. H. Franklin, E. W. Bleicher and L. M. Fleck, 'Community-Based Dialogue: Engaging Communities of Colour in the United States' Genetics Policy Conversation', *Journal of Health Politics, Policy and Law* 34, no. 3 (2009), 332.

98. S. Wheatley, 'Deliberative Democracy and Minorities', 514.

99. J. Tully, 'Recognition and Dialogue: The Emergence of a New Field', *Critical Review of International Social and Political Philosophy* 7, no. 3 (2004), 93–94.

100. Escobar, *Public Dialogue and Deliberation*, 42–43.

101. McCoy and Scully, *Deliberative Dialogue to Expand Civic Engagement*, 117.

102. Tully, 'Recognition and Dialogue', 86–89, 90, 94.

103. Tully, 'Recognition and Dialogue', 91–93.

104. Tully, 'Recognition and Dialogue', 99.

105. Tully, 'Recognition and Dialogue', 99, 101.

106. M. R. James, 'Critical Intercultural Dialogue', *Polity* 31, no. 4 (1999), 587–607; Kelman, 'Group processes', 212–20; J. M. Ramirez, 'Peace Through Dialogue', *International Journal on World Peace* 14, no. 1 (2007), 65–81.

107. A. Karsten and B. Kűntzel, *Forum on Intercultural Dialogue: Discussion paper based on the Forum on Intercultural Dialogue, 22–26 November 2006* (Strasbourg, France: Council of Europe, 2006), 1–21. http://doku.cac.at/intercultural_dilaogue_discussion_paper.pdf [Accessed 9 September 2011].

108. P. Restrepo, 'Some Epistemic and Methodological Challenges within an Intercultural Experience', *Journal of Historical Sociology* 24, no. 1 (2011), 45–61.

109. K. Anderson, 'Thinking "Postnationally": Dialogue across Multicultural, Indigenous, and Settler Spaces', *Association of American Geographers* 90, no. 2 (2000), 381–91.

110. P. M. Jenlink, 'The Power of Dialogue on Social Systems', in *Dialogue as a Collective Means of Design Conversation*, Patrick M. Jenlink and Bela H. Banathy, eds. (New York: Springer, 2008), 51–52.

111. K. J. Gergen, S. McNamee and F. J. Barrett, 'Towards Transformative Dialogue', *International Journal of Public Administration* 24, no. 7 (2001), 679–707.

112. Ramirez, 'Peace Through Dialogue', 65–81.

113. L. Flower, 'Talking across Difference: Intercultural Rhetoric and the Search for Situated Knowledge', *College Composition and Communication* 55, no. 1 (2003), 38–68; M. R. James, 'Critical Intercultural Dialogue', *Polity* 31, no. 4 (1999), 587–607.

114. G. Sammut and G. Gaskell, 'Points of View, Social Positioning and Intercultural Relations', *Journal for the Theory of Social Behaviour* 40, no. 1 (2009), 47–64.

115. Roberts, 'Call for Dialogue', 6–7; Isaacs, 'Taking Flight', 25; Yankelovich, *The Magic of Dialogue*, 41–45.

116. B. H. Banathy, 'Searching Together, Approaches, Methods and Tools', in *Dialogue as a Collective Means of Design Conversation*, Patrick M. Jenlink and Bela H. Banathy, eds. (New York: Springer, 2008), 78.

117. Restrepo, 'Some Epistemic and methodological Challenges', 58.

118. D. T. Butle Ritchie, 'Critiquing Modern Constitutionalism', *Appalachian Journal of Law* 3, no. 37 (2004), 37–49.

119. G. Maddox, *Australian Democracy in Theory and Practice*, 5th Edition (Frenchs Forest, NSW: Pearson Education Australia, 2005), 62–64; M. Rosenfeld, 'Modern Constitutionalism As Interplay Between Identity And Diversity: An Introduction', *Cardozo Law Review* 14 (1993), 497.

120. J. Tully, *Strange Multiplicity: Constitutionalism in an age of diversity* (Cambridge, UK, Cambridge University Press, 1995), 62–70.

121. Tully, *Strange Multiplicity*, 5.

122. Tully, *Strange Multiplicity*, 39.

123. Tully, *Strange Multiplicity*, 40–41, 57, 99.

124. Tully, *Strange Multiplicity*, 100, 116, 119–24.

125. A. Schaap, 'Political Reconciliation Through A Struggle for Recognition', *Social & Legal Studies* 13, no. 4 (2004), 527–33.

126. G. Coulthard, 'Subjects of Empire: Indigenous Peoples and the "Politics of Recognition" in Canada', *Contemporary Political Theory* 6, no. 4 (2007), 438–39.

127. Coulthard, 'Subjects of Empire', 442–43, 456.

128. L. Lange, 'Dialogue, History, and Power: The Role of Truth', in *Philosophy and Aboriginal Rights: Critical Dialogues*, Sandra Tomsons and Lorraine Mayer, eds. (Oxford: Oxford University Press, 2013), 364–69.

129. J. Tully, 'Consent, Hegemony, and Dissent in Treaty Negotiations', in *Between Consenting Peoples: Political Community and the Meaning of Consent*, Jeremy Webber and Colin M. Macleod, eds. (Vancouver, British Columbia: The University of British Columbia Press, 2010), 237–40.

130. Tully, 'Consent, Hegemony, and Dissent', 242–45.

131. Tully, 'Consent, Hegemony, and Dissent', 241–42.

132. Tully, 'Consent, Hegemony, and Dissent', 246–51.

133. Canada, (R. Dussault, G. Erasmus, P. L. A. H. Chartrand, J. P. Meekison, V Robinson, M Sillett, and M. Wilson). *Royal Commission on Aboriginal Peoples, Looking Forward Looking Back*, Volume 1 (Ottawa: The Commission, 1996), 11–14.

134. Tully, 'A Fair and Just Relationship', 146–47.

135. R. Dussault, 'The Vision of the Royal Commission on Aboriginal Peoples', *Saskatchewan Law Review* 70, (2007), 93–94.

136. Tully, 'A Fair and Just Relationship', 147–48.

137. Tully, 'A Fair and Just Relationship', 148–50.

138. Canada, *Royal Commission on Aboriginal Peoples*, 645–48.

139. Canada, *Royal Commission on Aboriginal Peoples*, 649–51, 651–57.

140. Canada, *Royal Commission on Aboriginal Peoples*, 657–60.

141. Canada, *Royal Commission on Aboriginal Peoples*, 95–96.

142. P. L. A. H. Chartrand, 'Towardss Justice and Reconciliation: Treaty Recommendations of Canada's Royal Commission on Aboriginal Peoples', in *Honour Among Nations? Treaties and Agreements with Indigenous People*, Marcia Langton, Lisa Palmer, Maureen Tehan and Kathryn Shain, eds. (Carlton, Victoria Melbourne University Press, 2004), 132.

143. Truth and Reconciliation Commission of Canada, *Honouring the Truth, Reconciling for the Future, Summary of the Final Report of the Truth and Reconciliation Commission of Canada* (Winnipeg: Truth and Reconciliation Commission Canada, 2015), 23.

144. TRC Canada, *Honouring the Truth, Summary of the Final Report*, 186.

145. TRC Canada, *Honouring the Truth, Summary of the Final Report*, 50–58.

146. TRC Canada, *Honouring the Truth, Summary of the Final Report*, 23.

147. TRC Canada, *Honouring the Truth, Summary of the Final Report*, 23, 25, 30.

148. TRC Canada, *Honouring the Truth, Summary of the Final Report*, 25–26, 30–33.

149. TRC Canada, *Honouring the Truth, Summary of the Final Report*, 135–39.

150. Truth and Reconciliation Commission of Canada, *Canada's Residential Schools: Reconciliation, The Final Report of the Truth and Reconciliation Commission of Canada*, Volume 6 (Montreal, Quebec: McGill-Queen's University Press, 2015), 20.

151. TRC Canada, *Canada's Residential Schools, Final Report*, 16.

152. TRC Canada, *Canada's Residential Schools, Final Report*, 3, 11–12.

153. TRC Canada, *Canada's Residential Schools, Final Report*, 25–28.

154. TRC Canada, *Canada's Residential Schools, Final Report*, 29–38.

155. TRC Canada, *Canada's Residential Schools, Final Report*, 43.

SIX

The Pathway Ahead

A fundamental issue for the Australian nation is to transform the current colonial Indigenous-State relationship. To do so Australian governments must engage in genuine dialogue and negotiation with Aboriginal and Torres Strait Islander peoples. The former reconciliation process in Australia failed to transform the relationship because its goal of reconciliation differed from Indigenous aspirations of self-determination. Reconciliation is still outstanding. For genuine reconciliation to take root four key issues must be addressed: justice, historic truth, historical responsibility and restructuring the social and political relationship and consequently restructuring the state's constitutional structure to reflect such change.[1]

A genuine reconciliation in Australia should begin with an honest and frank dialogue to address historic truths and historical responsibility for injustices. This will involve examining and repudiating the erroneous assumptions and negative discourses about Indigenous people that originate from terra nullius discourse. The colonial mindset is still strong in Australia. Settler Australians have inherited erroneous assumptions and negative discourses about Indigenous people and they continue to reinforce them. This colonial mindset is a stumbling block to transforming the existing relationship with Indigenous peoples. Genuine reconciliation requires decolonising that mindset. While some of these assumptions have shifted, especially around public acceptance and understanding of Indigenous rights to land, it will require a sincere effort on the part of the Australian nation to examine how these assumptions, which deemed Indigenous people to have deficiencies in respect to European society, have played a significant role in the legal, moral, societal and constitutional formation of the Australian nation.

There is a master narrative at play in Australia about Indigenous people. Such master narrative is based on colonial thinking and terra nullius discourses, which legitimise dispossession of Indigenous peoples through colonialism, normalizes British sovereignty and privileges the position and status of settler Australians. This narrative has reassured settler Australians that the British appropriated the country legally and peacefully, that Australian history was overwhelmingly positive, and that they are not responsible for any injustices that were committed in the colonial project. But it is a flawed narrative because it originates from the fiction of terra nullius, a concept used to extinguish Aboriginal humanity, Aboriginal rights to land and Aboriginal resource rights. Terra nullius requires Aboriginal people to prove they are not 'savages', that they occupied and owned land and that they had sovereignty over those lands. The Truth and Reconciliation Commission in Canada says the doctrine of discovery and related concept of terra nullius is a 'manifestation of historical wrongs' and 'does not conform to international law or contribute to reconciliation' and should be formally repudiated by the Canadian government.[2]

Injustices were committed under the pretence of the Australian continent being characterised as terra nullius. This chapter examines how the Australia nation might transcend terra nullius discourses that constitute the master narrative and move to a relationship of recognition and respect with Aboriginal and Torres Strait Islander peoples.

TRANSCENDING TERRA NULLIUS THINKING

The 2017 Uluru Statement from the Heart and the report of the Referendum Council affirm that truth telling about Australian history is important for the relationship between Indigenous people and the Australian nation. Truth telling about history is a critical first step to addressing past injustices and creating new political and social foundations for the future. In that regard truth telling is not just about understanding Australian history from an Indigenous perspective, but also about understanding the thinking and beliefs that underlay historical and contemporary public policy in regard to Indigenous people. Understanding the basis of this thinking involves confronting the underlying assumptions and attitudes about Indigenous people and acknowledging that these have played an influential role in social policy, decision-making and public discussion about Indigenous people. Changing the beliefs behind such thinking is a prerequisite to recognising and resolving Indigenous claims. These claims for example range from having an Indigenous voice in government Indigenous policy making, partnership agreements with government in regard to delivering services to Indigenous communities, recognising the role of Indigenous organisations in providing services and further it includes the bigger issues such as constitutional recognition and treaty.

Many Australians perceive and understand Indigenous people through the colonial thinking and terra nullius discourse that has accumulated over the centuries. It has been instrumental in contributing to negative attitudes towards Indigenous people. Such thinking reinforces disrespect for Indigenous people, undermines Indigenous claims for recognition and constrains the ability of the Australian nation to have a positive and mutually beneficial relationship with Indigenous people. Individually and collectively, Australians need to understand why they think the way they do about Indigenous people, because to understand and be open to the views and opinions of others it is necessary to understand oneself, to be aware of one's own thoughts. In that regard it is necessary to understand the genesis of thinking about Indigenous people and what influences that thinking. To understand these patterns of thought, the Australian population must step back, suspend their preconceived assumptions about Indigenous people, resist the urge to defend those assumptions and self-reflect. This is the starting point to creating the foundations for tacking the big questions about the past and creating a future relationship between Indigenous people and the Australian nation. These big questions are most often hard and confronting questions to which there are no immediate answers. Asking the big questions means having difficult conversations that examine deeply held attitudes and assumptions and repudiating the underlying negative attitudes and erroneous assumptions about Indigenous people. Unfortunately, these sorts of conversations elicit anger, defensiveness and guilt in the Australian population. But to ask Australians to confront underlying assumptions and acknowledge the impact of colonialism is not to moralise about guilt. It is about liberating all Australians from the yoke of colonial thinking and creating new narratives for a future relationship. The Australian nation needs to find a way to liberate itself from corrosive colonial ideologies and discourses about Indigenous people, without feeling anger or guilt. Indigenous people do not want non-Indigenous Australians to feel guilt. They just want them to understand and accept the truth of history and then take action to resolve outstanding issues.

To move to a relationship where Indigenous people are recognised, respected and have authority it is necessary for the Australian nation to: (1) confront and repudiate cultural and political beliefs about Indigenous people that are inherited from the colonial past; (2) build a shared understanding about Australian history through an honest and frank process of truth telling; and (3) engage in genuine intercultural dialogue about addressing past injustices and creating new foundations for how Indigenous and other Australians should associate in the future.

ATTEMPTS AT TRUTH TELLING

Indigenous Australians have always understood that the master narrative about them is incorrect, unjust, forgetful and unkind, and that the truth about Indigenous dispossession and mistreatment is something the Australian population would prefer not dwell on. But there are Australians who want to promote truth, mutual understanding and reconciliation. There have also been instances where attempts have been made to understand Indigenous people and to publicly acknowledge or rectify injustice. The Royal Commission into Aboriginal Deaths in Custody (1987–1991), the National Inquiry into the Separation of Aboriginal and Torres Strait Islander Children from Their Families (1995–1997), the public statement of Prime Minister Paul Keating in his Redfern Speech (1992) and the apology to the Stolen Generation by Prime Minister Kevin Rudd (2008) are examples.

Commissioner Elliott Johnston in his overview report for the Royal Commission into Aboriginal Deaths in Custody (RCIADIC) said that all Australians need to understand the country's past and the treatment of Aboriginal people, especially understanding that dispossession and deliberate policies and practices of disempowerment of Aboriginal people were based on the assumption of superiority and associated racist attitudes.[3] Commissioner Johnston saw the 'extraordinary domination' of Indigenous people by non-Indigenous people as the underlying cause of disadvantage and that ending domination plus empowering Indigenous self-determination would eliminate disadvantage.[4] In his Redfern Park speech on 10 December 1992, to launch Australia's celebration of the 1993 International Year of the World's Indigenous People, Prime Minister Paul Keating attempted to focus the nation on historical truths and social justice. He said the starting point for justice was for Australians to recognise historical truths relating to dispossession and colonisation. Australians had failed to make the most basic human response to Aboriginal people, to ask, 'How would I feel if this were done to me?'[5]

In his formal apology to the stolen generations in the national Parliament on 13 February 2008, Prime Minister Kevin Rudd asked a similar question of the Australian people and of Australian parliamentarians. He asked, 'Imagine that this had happened to you': how would they feel if they were forcibly removed from their mothers, their families and their community, as the stolen generations were. According to Rudd the apology was necessary because human decency demanded that the nation right the historical wrong and that responsibility for the hurt, pain and suffering of the stolen generations had to be accepted by parliaments and governments because it was their decisions that made the laws that created the stolen generations.[6]

Former Prime Minister Paul Keating said he wanted to 'deal in truths, historical truths', making it clear that it was non-Aboriginal Australians who did the dispossessing, taking the lands and brutalising the tradition-al way of life. Keating said injustice could not be swept aside and that the 'callous disregard' of the Aboriginal and Torres Strait Islander people and the truth of their loss and their circumstances had degraded all Aus-tralians.[7] Former Prime Minister Kevin Rudd said that the stories of the stolen generations had cried out to be heard and for an apology, but instead were met with a 'stony and stubborn and deafening silence' from the Australian Parliament for more than a decade. Rudd said that there will always be a 'shadow hanging over us and our future' if the truth was not fully confronted in respect to the stolen generations.[8]

Both Paul Keating's speech and Kevin Rudd's apology acknowledged historical injustice, although Rudd did not address frontier history. Nor did Keating or Rudd use their acknowledgement of historical injustice to address political disempowerment, the disappearance or nonrecognition of what the Uluru Statement from the Heart refers to as Australia's 'an-cient sovereignty' that has never been ceded or extinguished. Facing up to the way in which the country was conquered and how a new relation-ship with Indigenous people might be renegotiated remains outstanding. There is a real fear to facing up to the truth of history. Australian history has largely been interpreted from the perspectives of the colonisers. Tri-umphalist stories of colonisation in Australia, which portray Indigenous people as inferior, along with nationalist narratives that erased or mini-mised the colonisation of Indigenous peoples and even portrayed Indige-nous people as invaders and settlers as defenders of their land, are still very influential in Australia. Since the late 1960s, historians began to critically write histories with an Indigenous focus, and from the 1980s these new histories became influential; however, such histories have met with resistance in the Australian consciousness, as became clear with the rise of Pauline Hanson and the election of the Howard government in 1996.[9]

TRUTH AND RECONCILIATION

Recognising that the dispossession of Indigenous people underwrote the material success of Australian society is a challenge for the nation, mak-ing government uncomfortable and causing many Australians to avert their eyes.[10] According to Aboriginal leader Mick Dodson, the fear of facing up to historical truths around the violence of colonisation and the dispossession of Indigenous people is embedded in the 'Australian psyche'.[11] Dodson is referring to an inherent resistance in the minds and hearts of the Australian people to address the wrongs of the past. Many Australians have difficulty accepting the stark reality of colonialism and its impact on Indigenous people, as well as accepting any responsibility for these wrongs that were perpetrated by governments and individuals.

For Australian governments this inherent resistance manifests in many ways, some of which are outlined in previous chapters. This resistance is a significant barrier to resolving the wrongs of the past and moving to a new and different future.

In its opening chapter, the *Report of the National Inquiry into the Separation of Aboriginal and Torres Strait Islander Children from Their Families* states that the devastation of the past 'cannot be addressed unless the whole community listens with an open heart and mind to the stories of what has happened in the past and, having listened and understood, commits itself to reconciliation'.[12] Stolen generation peoples had the opportunity to tell the truth about the past and how the harm and suffering continues to affect them and their families. The former Howard government refused to formally apologise for the harm caused by past state policies, shifting responsibility from government to the Australian people by arguing that current generations of Australians should not accept responsibility for the actions and policies of earlier generations, and in any case the actions of governments at the time were sanctioned by laws and considered to be in the best interest of Indigenous people. The Howard government was also keen to avoid any perceived legal liability that may flow from a formal apology and acknowledgement.[13] Although the Howard government accepted the need to understand the shared history in Australia and to acknowledge mistreatment of Indigenous people, it could only bring itself to express 'deep and sincere regret' for past injustices and the hurt and trauma.[14] Clearly, Howard and his government lacked sincerity. While the Rudd Labor government publicly acknowledged stolen generations' history and suffering, and accepted responsibility for policies, practices and consequences when Rudd formally apologised in Parliament, there was no offer of compensation made. The *Bringing Them Home* report explicitly recommended that reparation, including financial compensation, be made to individual people who were forcibly removed, their families, communities and descendants.

The lesson for truth telling in regard to the stolen generations is that public recognition and government acceptance of responsibility are necessary, but truth telling can be rendered meaningless if the government is resistant and denies responsibility for past policies and practices and if truth telling is not followed by some form of reparation. The need for truth telling about Australia's history is a long-standing issue. It received prominence during the 2017 Indigenous dialogues and the Uluru Convention of First Peoples in regards to recognising Indigenous people in Australia's Constitution, which emphasised that the true history of colonisation must be told and that a truth commission should be established prior to constitutional reform or as part of a treaty negotiation.[15] The Uluru Statement from the Heart, which was endorsed at the Uluru's First Peoples Convention, recommended a truth and justice commission.

TRUTH AND JUSTICE

Truth telling is an important aspect of transitional justice and the most popular transitional justice method is truth commissions. Truth commissions are official processes initiated to break with the past by uncovering 'the truth' about past injustices and wrongdoing that have been deliberately 'silenced'. Truth commissions can bring closure, healing and reconciliation, and generally assist society to move forward. They give voice or enable victims to tell their story, enabling public understanding of the form of reparation required as a restorative form of justice.[16] Public acknowledgement of the truth of injustice—to restore the victim's dignity and rebuild the integrity of those who have perpetrated harm—is the central premise of a truth commission.[17]

While truth commissions investigate history, they do not have prosecutorial powers; nor are they judicial bodies to investigate individual crimes. However, they can render a moral judgment about what was wrong and unjustifiable and in that way frame new national narratives of acknowledgement, accountability and civic values. Their purpose is to provide an authoritative account of a contested past, determine the major causes of violence or injustice and make recommendations about measures to avoid repetition in the future. A key role of the truth-finding exercise is documenting and acknowledging a legacy of conflict and human rights violations as a step towards healing wounds.[18]

Truth telling is considered an essential step towards reconciliation in Australia because it will enable a shared understanding of the history of colonisation in Australia and its continuing impact. According to Reconciliation Australia and the Healing Foundation, truth telling can bring collective healing enabling future generations of Australians to break the cycle of repetition and not repeat the wrongs of the past. Healing may occur when people tell their stories and when others bear witness to these stories, enabling all Australians to accept and own the past.[19]

Truthfulness in history and realigning the power relationship between Indigenous people and governments are essential elements for reconciliation in Australia. Efforts have been made in the past to educate and inform Australians about the truth of their country's history in order to commit to reconciliation. The Council for Aboriginal Reconciliation (1991–2000) was established for that purpose, but its focus on 'hearts and minds' reconciliation meant that reconciliation was left to individuals in a people's movement. Further, because the formal reconciliation process focussed on addressing socioeconomic disadvantage rather than encompassing a broader notion of justice, it avoided the impact of colonialism on Indigenous people. Ultimately, it did not advance a new form of political relationship between Indigenous people and other Australians.

The Joint Select Committee on Constitutional Recognition relating to Aboriginal and Torres Strait Islander Peoples (2018) examined the call for truth telling in the Uluru Statement from the Heart. It recognised the importance of truth telling in acknowledging the negative impacts and injustices of colonisation, both past and ongoing, affecting Indigenous people; but also saw truth telling as an opportunity for Indigenous people to share their culture, language, heritage and history. The Select Committee looked at current truth-telling practices, many of these being community initiatives. Evidence presented to the Select Committee pointed to the need for truth telling at the local and regional level, led by Indigenous peoples but engaging and involving the broader community. Oral history is a significant part of truth telling. Truth telling should also lead to change in the way Australian history is taught in schools. In that regard the Select Committee recommended that truth telling should involve local organisations and communities, libraries, historical societies and Indigenous associations.[20]

The contested nature of Australian history and the need for public acknowledgment of past and ongoing injustices against Indigenous peoples require the Australian government as representative of the Australian people to establish a legal and constitutional framework to ensure an authoritative account of Australian history. Australians need to own this history, which includes acknowledging that the Crown perpetrated serious injustices against Indigenous peoples when it failed to observe Aboriginal land ownership and sovereignty. Australia does not need another 'hearts and minds' reconciliation process reliant on individual goodwill, but a public political process that examines how the assumptions, policies and practices of the Crown impacted and affected Indigenous people and how those impacts and effects continue today. It must be a process that examines and encourages governments to take responsibility for its actions and to repair the harm done in the past and the continuing legacy of harm. But to encourage government to take responsibility for their actions, Australian society must own up and bear witness to past wrongs, acts of injustice and also violence.

INTERNATIONAL TRUTH TELLING

Often cited by commentators in Australia as an example of truth telling, the Truth and Reconciliation Commission in South Africa (South African TRC) emerged out of a negotiated settlement for power sharing in South Africa after the end of apartheid in 1994. It investigated gross violations of human rights committed between 1960 and 1994, the period of apartheid. In a court-like setting it used the narratives of both victims and perpetrators to conduct a public conversation about killings, torture, abduction and severe ill treatment during the apartheid regime. But in focussing on gross human rights violations, the South African TRC excluded other apartheid violations such as structural oppression; and having a limited time frame, it excluded historical violations that preceded the emergence of apartheid. Further, in using the narratives of victims and perpetrators, apartheid violence was reduced to individual acts of violence. Its use of a quasi-judicial process to hear the stories of victims and perpetrators enabled blame for illegal activities to be placed on a minority of individuals, thereby allowing the apartheid state apparatus to escape responsibility for structural violence.[21]

The influence of Archbishop Desmond Tutu as chairperson of the South African TRC shaped a spiritual reconciliation process within the Christian moral framework of sin, guilt, confession and redemption. The apartheid era was seen as a stain upon the nation that had to be cleansed through redemption and forgiveness. This 'confessional model' of truth allowed questions of personal culpability and guilt to override collective responsibility for the violence and injustice of apartheid. Hence the perpetrating community were able to abrogate collective responsibility.[22] The South African TRC is hardly an applicable model for truth telling in Australia because it focussed on truth and reconciliation between individual perpetrators and their victims, thereby excluding a broader sense of justice. The Truth and Reconciliation Commission in Canada (the commission) is more appropriate to Australia because it examined individual and collective harms perpetrated against Aboriginal families, communities, and nations and also examined the preconditions that permitted such violence and oppression to occur.[23]

As we saw in chapter 5, the commission examined Indian residential schools and their legacy in the context of European colonisation.[24] Christianity provided moral justification for colonisation, in that Christian nations believed they had a God-given right to colonise lands they had 'discovered' as long as they converted and 'civilised' the Aboriginal inhabitants. Christian missionaries were used to convert so called 'heathens' and although they often attempted to soften the impact of imperialism, they worked to undermine Aboriginal relationship to land, traditional economic pursuits and Aboriginal culture, practices and beliefs in accordance with European beliefs of self-superiority.[25]

According to the commission, the Crown in Canada pursued a policy of cultural genocide in dealing with Aboriginal peoples, intending to eliminate them as distinct peoples and assimilate them into Canadian society. This included the Crown divesting itself of its legal and financial obligations to Aboriginal people and gaining control over Aboriginal lands and resources. Residential schools became a central element in the Crowns Aboriginal policy. The commission defined cultural genocide as 'the destruction of those structures and practices that allow a group to continue as a group'. States that engage in cultural genocide destroy political and social institutions of the targeted group, seize their lands, forcibly transfer the group and restrict their movement, ban languages, persecute spiritual leaders, forbid spiritual practices, destroy or confiscate objects of spiritual value, and most significantly, disrupt families to prevent the transmission of cultural values and identity from one generation to the next.[26]

The Crown's Aboriginal policy and its historical legacies has damaged the relationship and broken the trust between Aboriginal and non-Aboriginal people in Canada through policies and practices of cultural genocide and assimilation. Further, the Crown's failure to keep its treaty promises with Aboriginal people, the Canadian government's reliance on the Doctrine of Discovery and terra nullius in establishing the validity of Crown sovereignty, plus the government's continuing unilateral and divisive actions in regards to Aboriginal title and rights have undermined the original relationship of mutual support, respect and assistance that was confirmed by the Royal Proclamation of 1763 and the various treaties negotiated with the Crown in good faith.[27]

The Commission said, 'without truth, justice and healing, there can be no genuine reconciliation', and that 'reconciliation cannot occur without listening, contemplation, meditation and deeper internal deliberation'.[28] To establish a legal, political and constitutional basis for reconciliation in Canada, the commission called for the government of Canada to develop with Aboriginal peoples a Royal Proclamation of Reconciliation to be issued by the Crown. In conjunction with the Royal Proclamation, the commission also called on all parties to the Indian Residential Schools Settlement Agreement to develop and sign a Covenant of Reconciliation to advance reconciliation in Canadian society. Among other things, and under the banner of reconciliation, the commission called for action in regards to the following:

- Adoption of the United Nations Declaration of the Rights of Indigenous Peoples as the framework for reconciliation in Canada.
- Recognising the Aboriginal people's right to self-determination and integrating it into Canada' constitutional, legal, and institutional framework.
- The renewal of treaty relationships by reaffirming the nation-to-nation relationship between Aboriginal peoples and the Crown on principles of mutual recognition, mutual respect, and shared responsibility.
- Repudiation of concepts such as the Doctrine of Discovery and terra nullius that were used to justify European sovereignty over Aboriginal nations and Aboriginal people.
- Reconciling Aboriginal and Crown constitutional legal orders to ensure Aboriginal people are partners in the Canadian federation and this includes recognising and integrating Aboriginal laws and legal traditions.

THE LIMITS OF AUSTRALIAN RECONCILIATION

Reconciliation emerged after the Hawke Labor government abandoned its national land rights policy and its 1988 promise to negotiate a treaty with Indigenous Australians. The premise for reconciliation is contained in the Council for Aboriginal Reconciliation Act 1991, which put in place the formal reconciliation process in Australia (1991–2001). The Commonwealth Parliament established the Council for Aboriginal Reconciliation (CAR). Its purpose was to promote reconciliation between Aboriginal and Torres Strait Islanders and the wider Australian community based on appreciation of Aboriginal and Torres Strait Islander cultures, achievements and their unique position as Indigenous peoples in Australia, which includes fostering an ongoing national commitment to address Indigenous disadvantage.[29] Reconciliation would be promoted through education and awareness, addressing Indigenous disadvantage and aspirations, and consulting widely with the public about a formal document of reconciliation.

CAR was given ten years to do its work. During that time, several significant events took place that had a marked impact on the reconciliation process. These events included the High Court *Mabo* decision (1992), the High Court *Wik* decision (1996), the election of a conservative Liberal Coalition government (1996), massive funding cuts to the Aboriginal and Torres Strait Islander Commission (1996), the Commonwealth government's ten-point plan amendment to the Native Title Act (1997) and the handing down of the 'Bringing them Home'—stolen generations report (1997). The conservative Liberal Coalition government under John Howard substantially changed the direction and focus of Indigenous affairs. Howard was opposed to the establishment of the Aboriginal and Torres Strait Islander Commission, a national Indigenous representative and funding authority, and the negotiation of a treaty with Aboriginal people. He considered both to be divisive, believing that genuine reconciliation with Indigenous people was about addressing basic needs.

In an aggressive speech at the Australian Reconciliation Convention in Melbourne in May 1997, where many of the audience turned their backs on him, Howard appeared hostile to the rights-based approach to reconciliation. Howard avoided raising the difficult conversation about past wrongdoings, thereby jettisoning any state or collective Australian responsibility for rectifying past wrongs. He failed to reframe and rebuild a different relationship with Indigenous people and even failed to create the psychological change necessary to building future relationships.[30] This hostility and failure was revealing in the government's response to the final report of the Council for Aboriginal Reconciliation. When the Council for Aboriginal Reconciliation presented two documents—Australian Declaration Towards Reconciliation and the Roadmap for Reconciliation—to the Howard government in May 2000 and its final report in

December 2000, the government did not respond to the documents until September 2002. According to Bill Jonas, the Aboriginal and Torres Strait Islander Social Justice commissioner at the time, the government had 'deliberately sought to shut down debate' by stating that they are committed to practical reconciliation.[31] Indeed the report disappeared from public view.

The declaration of commitment towards reconciliation was primarily an inspirational set of words and the roadmap for reconciliation contained four strategies to make reconciliation a reality. Neither contained substantive recognition of Indigenous political rights such as sovereignty, although the roadmap for reconciliation did refer to self-determination and constitutional reform. The final report to the Commonwealth government in December 2000 recommended that the Council of Australian Governments implement a national framework to overcome Indigenous disadvantage and that all parliaments and local governments pass motions to support the Australian Declaration Towards Reconciliation and the Roadmap for Reconciliation. The council also recommended the Commonwealth Parliament prepare legislation for a referendum to recognise Aboriginal and Torres Strait Islander peoples in the preamble of the Australian Constitution and remove discriminatory sections. The council also encouraged each government and parliament to advance reconciliation by negotiating treaties with Indigenous peoples. To give effect to its two documents, the council provided a draft reconciliation bill. The draft bill set out a process to identify unresolved issues for discussion and a mechanism for negotiation of unresolved issues.[32]

The recommendation of treaty went against the view of members of CAR who considered it divisive and highly emotive, however its inclusion was largely because of the efforts of Geoff Clarke, the chairperson of the Aboriginal and Torres Strait Islander Commission.[33] Responding to the CAR documents and final report, the Howard government accepted references and recommendations relating to equality of opportunity and access to health care, housing, education, employment and economic independence for Indigenous people. However, it did not accept recommendations relating to Indigenous rights. The government disagreed with the reference to recognising customary law because in their view all Australians are subject equally to a common set of laws. They refused to endorse the term 'self-determination' because in their view it implied the possibility of a separate Indigenous state, thereby challenging national sovereignty as well as implying that the Commonwealth must relinquish responsibility for and control over Indigenous well-being. Nor did they support a formal apology to Indigenous people for injustices of the past because such apology could imply that present generations are responsible and accountable for actions of earlier generations, actions that were sanctioned by laws of the time. The government did not support the concept of treaty because in their view a treaty is only made between sovereign states, therefore to pursue a treaty would be divisive, under-mining the idea of a single Australian nation and creating uncertainty and disputation. In the government's view, true reconciliation would be achieved when Indigenous Australians enjoyed the same opportunities and standards of treatment as other Australians. [34] This is the language of the former archaic assimilation policy.

The CAR's focus of promoting reconciliation meant that its role cen-tered on communication and public awareness, supporting a people's movement for reconciliation and consulting on the desirability of a docu-ment of reconciliation. [35] It was more a 'hearts and mind' campaign. No real definition or meaning of reconciliation was reached. While it was broadly about improving relationships between Indigenous and other Australians, the term reconciliation was 'broad and vague' thus enabling different players to attach different and even contradictory meanings to the term. [36] Hence, reconciliation meant different things to different peo-ple. For the CAR, reconciliation meant a united Australia that respects the land, values Aboriginal and Torres Strait Islander heritage, and pro-vides justice and equity for all. Clearly, this definition was in keeping with the CAR's function and its lack of power.

The CAR did not operate within existing formal or legal constitutional structures and its functions were limited to consulting and advising, hav-ing no power to implement its recommendations. Reconciliation was con-ceived as a process between Indigenous people and the wider commu-nity rather than between Indigenous people and the state. [37] The reconcil-iation process became dominated by nationalist discourse and interfer-ence by government. [38] It was susceptible to the influence of politicians and political intervention as John Howard did when he came to power. While there was Indigenous support for the reconciliation process, partic-ularly from the ATSIC, Indigenous people were not involved in the estab-lishment of the CAR, it was instigated by the Commonwealth govern-ment. Therefore, reconciliation was conducted on 'white' terms. It em-phasised private individual relationships rather than advising how the Australian state should relate to Indigenous people. This enabled the state to have an invisible role of facilitating reconciliation, allowing it to deny perpetration of harm and historical wrongs while at the same time bolstering its legitimacy and authenticity. [39]

Many Indigenous Australians had problems with the formal reconcili-ation process because it failed to address important issues and was con-fined to improving Indigenous socioeconomic disadvantage as well as educating Australians about Indigenous issues. Certainly, health care, education, housing and employment are important to Indigenous people but they are citizenship rights that most Australians take for granted. The Howard government focussed reconciliation on 'practical reconciliation' that addressed socioeconomic disadvantage particularly in health care, housing, education and employment. While governments do need to address Indigenous socioeconomic disadvantage, passing off access to basic citizenship rights and entitlements as some form of reconciliation with Indigenous people is not reconciliation because most Australians expect their governments to provide these societal goods and services to them as citizens of Australia.

The formal reconciliation process is a stark reminder that reconciliation has no meaning for Indigenous people if the nation is not prepared to deal with historical injustices or if reconciliation does not acknowledge and legitimise Indigenous claims for recognition of rights. Formal reconciliation did not educate the wider community about reconciliation and the historical causes of Indigenous disadvantage; this in turn removed national self-examination and reflection from the process.[40] Patrick Dodson, former chairman of the CAR, said reconciliation provided a doorway for a political settlement where the Australian state could recognise the status of Indigenous people and unravel the colonial legacy that continues to determine relationships between Indigenous communities and Australian governments.[41] While there was initial scepticism regarding reconciliation expressed by Indigenous people, there were good intentions from the Hawke Labor government who initiated the formal reconciliation process. However, the Howard Liberal-Coalition government deliberately derailed reconciliation and it tried to pass off access to basic citizenship rights and entitlements as reconciliation with Indigenous people. As a result, Indigenous scepticism towards reconciliation turned to distrust and disillusionment. Patrick Dodson would eventually resign from the Council for Aboriginal Reconciliation.

Genuine reconciliation should address substantive issues concerning Indigenous political rights and the transformation of existing power relationships. The formal reconciliation process avoided a broader notion of justice that included issues such as treaty, sovereignty, self-determination, land rights and challenging the existing power relations.[42] Thus, it was not established to address matters of historical truths, historical responsibility or to recognise Indigenous rights or restructure social and political relationships. For reconciliation to have any meaning the nation must face up to history, officially recognise past wrongs and recognise Indigenous people and their rights by way of constitutional recognition or formal treaty.[43] The Referendum Council's 2017 national Indigenous consultation process about constitutional recognition raised treaty or negotiated settlement and truth telling as important for the relationship between Indigenous peoples and the Australian nation and insisted that there should be a process to facilitate agreement making and truth telling.[44] The barriers or constraints to reconciliation in Australia are not just the nation's collective guilt over the legitimacy of the settler state.[45] Barriers are also found in political and legal frameworks of Australian constitutional government that subordinates Indigenous rights.[46] They are found in government methods and techniques for managing and governing Indigenous communities, referred to as 'internal colonisation,'[47] and in the false assumption that reconciliation is a unilateral exercise controlled by the state; an exercise that does not accept contesting ideas and beliefs nor recognising the fundamental difference of Indigenous peoples.[48]

Reconciliation is regarded as a process where a nation or peoples create a shared future by addressing the past and negotiating a collective way forward to decolonise existing relationships. However, reconciliation is superficial in Australia. Indeed, the differences in regard to what reconciliation means in Canada and Australia are stark. The Royal Commission on Aboriginal Peoples in Canada set out a vision for reconciliation premised on building a renewed relationship between Aboriginal and non-Aboriginal peoples. The fundamental elements to this renewed relationship include: (1) the rejection of principles that are remnants of the colonial era such as assimilation, control, intrusion and coercion. Outmoded doctrines such as terra nullius and discovery must likewise be abandoned because they reflect attitudes of racial and cultural superiority; (2) acknowledgement that Aboriginal people are nations, and understanding the nationhood dimensions of Aboriginal social and political organisations must be recognised and strengthened; (3) affirmation that Aboriginal nations were historically sovereign, self-governing peoples and that room must be made within the Canadian legal and political framework for Aboriginal nations to reassume their historical self-governing status. Respecting Aboriginal autonomy is not considered a threat to Canadians, nor it is a denial of the rights of other Canadians and it does not challenge the sovereignty of the Canadian state; and (4) the need for Canadians to better understand the place of Aboriginal peoples in Canadian society and for Canadian institutions to reflect that understanding. Aboriginal people are the original inhabitants of the land and they have historical rights; they are not another racial or cultural minority group in Canadian society.[49]

According to the Canadian Royal Commission on Aboriginal Peoples the responsibility for reconciliation rests on the Government of Canada because the state must resolve the fundamental contradiction in Canada: that it is a modern liberal democracy built upon the suppression of Aboriginal nations and at the expense of their cultural identity.[50] The Royal Commission recognised that colonisation is institutionalised in Canada because laws, governmental structures and institutions are founded upon assumptions of superiority that continues to form the basis of relationships between Aboriginal people and Canadian society. History privileges certain perspectives and it is the culture and values of mainstream Canadian society that are recognised and which shape governmental structures and institutions that control the lives of Aboriginal people.

The Crown as represented by government must solve the fundamental contradiction in Australia because colonisation is institutionalised in

Australia as well. In comparison with the discussion and recommendations on reconciliation of the Canadian Royal Commission on Aboriginal
Peoples, the outcome of the formal reconciliation process in Australia
seemed somewhat amateurish. The Council for Aboriginal Reconciliation
presented two documents—the Australian Declaration Towards Reconciliation and the Roadmap for Reconciliation—to the prime minister and
the Australian people at Corroboree 2000, a national reconciliation event
at the Sydney Opera House in May 2000. The declaration is simply a set
of nice words. However, it does mention the lack of treaty or consent in
Australia, owning the truth and healing the wounds of the past and
stopping injustice. The roadmap comprised three strategies to sustain the
reconciliation process, recognise Indigenous rights and overcome disadvantage. In its final report to Parliament titled *Reconciliation, Australia's
Challenge,* the Council for Aboriginal Reconciliation recommended that:

- the Council for Australian Governments work to overcome Indigenous disadvantage by agreeing on and implementing a national
  framework;
- all parliaments and local governments formally support the Australian Declaration and the Roadmap for Reconciliation;
- the Commonwealth prepare legislation to recognise Indigenous
  people in the preamble of the Australian Constitution and to remove discriminatory clauses from the Constitution;
- all levels of government, nongovernment, business, peak bodies,
  communities and individuals commit to reconciliation and support
  Reconciliation Australia;
- each government and parliament recognise that reconciliation
  would be advanced by treaties or agreements negotiated with Indigenous peoples; and
- the Commonwealth Parliament enact legislation to put in place a
  process for an agreement or treaty.

While the Council for Aboriginal Reconciliation said all the right words,
this was hardly visionary because it was based on the premise of over-
coming Indigenous disadvantage and improving understanding and relationships with Indigenous people within the Australian community. By
the time the Council for Aboriginal Reconciliation had handed down its
final report, the notion of reconciliation had lost its significance for most
Indigenous people. The focus on a 'feel good' or 'hearts and minds' form
of reconciliation is reflected today in the mode of justice that is promoted
by Reconciliation Australia. Reconciliation Australia, a nongovernment
body set up to carry on the work of reconciliation after the formal process
ceased in 2001, considers reconciliation to be primarily about strengthening relationships between Aboriginal and Torres Strait Islander peoples
and non-Indigenous peoples. From this perspective there are five integral
and interrelated dimensions to measure reconciliation: historical accep-

tance of past wrongs and amending those wrongs; race relations based on a relationship of trust and respect; equality and equity where Indigenous people are recognised and participate in life opportunities; institutional integrity supporting reconciliation; and unity where Australian society values and recognises Indigenous culture and heritage.[51] These social dimensions of reconciliation tiptoe around the difficult political issues that have their genesis in colonisation and that need to be resolved if reconciliation is to become reality in Australia. The type of reconciliation promoted by Reconciliation Australia assumes that when Indigenous people are recognised and are unified within the single polity of the nation state, reconciliation will ensure. The former reconciliation process promoted this type of reconciliation. It failed.

FINDING TRUTH IN AUSTRALIA

Indigenous Australians have put forward a proposal for an Indigenous representative Voice to Parliament, the negotiation of a treaty, and the need for truth telling about Australia's history of colonisation. These proposals are enshrined in the Uluru Statement from the Heart. Much of the focus of the Indigenous proposal has been on seeking change to the Australian Constitution to recognise an Indigenous Voice to Federal Parliament. In the Indigenous proposal, the need for truth telling is linked to agreement-making or treaty. But truth telling about Australia's history is fundamental for societal change, which needs to happen in Australia if constitutional recognition and treaty making become reality. Most of the Australian population has little understanding or awareness of colonisation and its impact on Indigenous people. Therefore, if Australians are to vote in a referendum for an Indigenous constitutional Voice to Parliament or if the Australian government is to accept that a treaty or treaties is integral to reconciliation then attitudinal and societal change is required. There is a need to move beyond the colonial relationship and a truth-telling mechanism can dismantle these colonial barriers to justice.

In that regard, truth telling in Australia should explore how the nation can move to a postcolonial relationship with Indigenous peoples. In examining how the nation needs to change its relationship with Indigenous people, the truth commission must examine Australian colonial and contemporary history and practice. Specifically, the truth commission must first uncover Australian history from an Indigenous perspective, exposing the myths and assumptions of colonisation and rejecting colonial principles that reflect racial and cultural superiority. Further, the truth commission must examine human rights violations that took place over the course of colonial and contemporary history, particularly abuses relating to extermination, assimilation, exploitation, neglect, oppression and mistreatment that occurred with the support of governments or under the pretext of government policies. The purpose is not to promote guilt or lay blame but to examine and explain why these abusive and harmful practices are morally wrong and why it is no longer justifiable for a liberal democratic state to maintain the current colonial relationship with Indigenous peoples. The exercise of truth telling should then challenge colonial assumptions, narratives and histories that continue to operate in the social and political landscape of the nation. These need to be understood in the context of contemporary government policymaking, to realise how they are barriers to achieving justice for Indigenous Australians and barriers to moving to a postcolonial relationship with Indigenous people. These assumptions, narratives and histories have been imposed on Indigenous people because they impose a view of the world that is an outcome of colonial power.[52] Finally, a truth commission must examine how the damage and harm to Indigenous people can be repaired through restorative measures including reparation and reconciliation.

The truth commission must build new national narratives of acknowledgement, accountability and civic values in regards to how the state and its citizens relate with Indigenous people. There is a current discourse in Australia around reconciliation that is based on the idea that telling the truth will progress reconciliation between Indigenous and other Australians because it will break from the past, heal the wounds of the past as well as unify the nation. But the logic of putting the past behind us in order to create a unified nation is problematic because it glosses over deeper issues of injustice and compensation for past harms and continuing injustice. Therefore, breaking or moving from the past generally follows the script of 'forgiving and forgetting' and 'unifying the country' while brushing aside any deeper discussions of restitution and justice; hence, 'reconciliation becomes a way for the dominant culture to re-inscribe the status quo rather than to make amends for previous injustices'.[53]

The truth commission must confront historical truths or untruths, and this involves examining the colonial foundations of the nation and the treatment of Indigenous people in that regard. It must not only confront historical colonialism but also continuing colonialism. This will be uncomfortable for Australians and therefore such an examination may not be politically acceptable to settler Australians who wield significant political power. But new possibilities for the future of the Australian nation will only emerge when settler Australians confront truths about the colonisation of Australia and are moved out of their comfort zone in order to change attitudes.[54]

TRUTH TELLING AS DIALOGUE

There has never been a practice or culture of dialogue on the part of government in regard to Indigenous rights in Australia. Throughout history Indigenous people have challenged and engaged the Australian state to create dialogic space in which to resolve their grievances against government policies and practices and resolve their claims for recognition. However, these forms of engagement cannot properly be described as dialogue because Indigenous claims for recognition are made within a constitutional system that ignores, excludes, discredits or redefines Indigenous claims. The structure and language of Australian government have historically excluded or demeaned Indigenous people and their cultural or political rights. Therefore, Indigenous efforts at engaging with governments have been constrained and deliberately excluded by a framework that subordinates their humanity and their rights. The traditions and conventions of parliaments, the courts, bureaucracy and systems of authority have reinforced this framework and have not been able to respond in ways that remove injustice and positively recognise Indigenous difference.

Indigenous people have not only contested laws and policies of governments that have denied their rights but have also struggled against the beliefs, assumptions and norms of settler Australian society that have sought to destroy or assimilate Indigenous culture and exclude Indigenous rights. The engagement by Indigenous people with governments has always been unequal. This unequal standing means that Indigenous people are excluded from having a political voice in government. There is no formal political or constitutional relationship between governments and Indigenous people. Any dialogue between Indigenous people and the Australian state is limited by the mentality and practice of settler colonialism because it is characterised by the eradication of Indigenous social, political and cultural practices, therefore negotiations of sovereignty only happen within the polity of the settler state, resulting in the formal erasure of Indigenous sovereignty.[55]

While Australian governments have accorded limited recognition to Indigenous rights over the last two centuries, the recognition of Indigenous aspirations for political and cultural rights is constrained by the traditions, language and practices of Australian constitutionalism. Australian constitutional government is based on principles that enforce uniformity in identity of citizens and treating them equally. Therefore, the Australian state is unable to understand or recognise Indigenous difference or engage with Indigenous people other than through the traditions and practices of uniformity and formal equality. Furthermore, however, colonisation has created persistent and deep-seated erroneous assumptions about Indigenous people and their culture and it is through this screen that Australians perceive the difference of Indigenous people. Settler colonialism does not have an alternative imagination, nor is it able to offer a narrative in regard to reconciliation and the decolonisation of the settler state because the basis for settler-Indigenous relations is a paradigm of Indigenous displacement, dispossession or erasure.[56]

The history of Indigenous-State relations in Australia is littered with examples of limitations placed on Indigenous aspirations and claims for recognition, because of the ingrained negative attitudes and erroneous assumptions about Indigenous people. They are barriers to truth and reconciliation. To break down the barriers and create a space where Indigenous people and governments can freely talk about Indigenous aspirations and claims without governments falling back to their default position, it is necessary to initiate an intercultural dialogue to get to the bottom of why there is such resistance to Indigenous recognition claims. A truth and treaty commission would serve as a constitutional mechanism to examine and uncover truths and untruths to create a public conversation about the constitutional and political status of Indigenous people in the Australian nation. A truth and treaty commission would provide a pathway for the future and for decolonising the existing colonial relationships.

The theory and practice of dialogue are applicable to a truth-telling process because the emphasis is on mutual understanding for all parties involved in the process to build common understanding. Mutual understanding is achieved when participants become more conscious of their own thinking and begin to understand the thinking of others. Therefore, participants in the truth-telling process must examine their underlying patterns of thoughts and open themselves to the views and opinions of others. The idea is to listen to what others have to say and to observe your own thoughts and feelings in a reflective process as the basis for transforming thinking. While dialogue is useful for creating discussion between conflicting parties to build common understanding, it is not necessarily useful or meaningful for Indigenous Australians who are claiming recognition of rights in a colonial state. The Australian state has been reluctant to recognise Indigenous claims for rights and refuses to recognise that Indigenous people have political authority that derives from Indigenous sovereignty.

To be meaningful, a truth-telling process must create an intercultural political dialogue that addresses the political and cultural rights of Indigenous people and examine how they can be accommodated within the constitutional structure of the nation by way of dialogue and negotiation. Indigenous claims for justice are political because they challenge the beliefs, practices, and narratives of the nation-state that emphasise cultural and political uniformity and where the norms and language of state institutions adjudicate and interpret Indigenous claims, which are usually considered subordinate to the interests of the state. The relationship between Indigenous people and governments must be transformed through a political process to deconstruct the existing colonial relationship and to create a vision and framework for mutual recognition and political association into the future. To that end a truth-telling process in Australia should focus on creating mutual understanding between Indigenous people and government to encourage recognition of and respect for Indigenous people. This means thinking positively about Indigenous cultural and political difference, appreciating that difference and creating new ways of understanding and incorporating it within the political institutions of the nation.

An intercultural dialogue is an important mechanism to shape public recognition of Indigenous people. Genuine recognition requires understanding Indigenous Australians on their own terms and examining how policies and practices of colonialism have impacted Indigenous people. This requires non-Indigenous Australians to reflect upon and understand their assumptions and attitudes about Indigenous people and for governments to reflect upon how they can recognise and value Indigenous difference within Australian society and reflect that recognition in the institutions of Australian government. However, mutual understanding through dialogue is not simply about transforming the thinking of individuals or groups in Australian society to change dominant assumptions about Indigenous people. Mutual understanding also extends to resolving the historical grievances and claims of Indigenous people for cultural and political recognition within the traditions, practices and laws of the Australian state.

INTERCULTURAL DIALOGUE

The purpose of intercultural dialogue is to engage across cultural differences to build mutual recognition and respect with the aim of reaching understanding and agreement through appropriate discussion and negotiation. While there have been instances of dialogue between Indigenous people and government in Australia, it has hardly been genuine or structurally guaranteed. The structural conditions for genuine dialogue have been lacking in the historical encounters, as outlined in this and other chapters. Indeed, the historical context, assumptions and attitudes that prevailed about Indigenous people at those particular times in history explain why these historical encounters cannot be understood as dialogue. Negative assumptions and attitudes about Aboriginal people have accumulated over the years and have constrained or blocked efforts at dialogue, although as we saw in chapter 4, the negotiations in 1993 over the Native Title Act contained several elements of a genuine dialogue.

A genuine intercultural dialogue in Australia requires a set of principles to underpin a reconciled relationship between Indigenous and settler Australians. But these elements are lacking in Australia, so it is useful to look to Canada for examples. The Truth and Reconciliation Commission in Canada said the United Nations Declaration on the Rights of Indigenous peoples provides the necessary principles, norms and standards for reconciliation in twenty-first-century Canada. The commission also set out guiding principles for truth and reconciliation to assist Canadians to not only talk about reconciliation but to also practice it.[57] Not all principles are applicable in Australia where there were no historical treaties negotiated, however, as general principles, they are relevant. The principles are as follows:

1. The United Nations Declaration on the Rights of Indigenous Peoples is the framework for reconciliation in Canada.
2. First Nations, Inuit and Métis peoples have treaty, constitutional and human rights that must be recognised and respected.
3. Reconciliation is a process of healing relationships through public truth sharing, apology and commemoration to acknowledge and redress past harms.
4. Reconciliation must constructively address the ongoing legacies of colonialism that have had destructive impacts on Aboriginal peoples.
5. Reconciliation must close the gaps in social, health care and economic outcomes that exist between Aboriginal and non-Aboriginal Canadians.
6. All Canadians share responsibility for establishing and maintaining mutually respectful relationships.
7. The perspectives and understandings of Aboriginal Elders and Traditional Knowledge Keepers are vital to long-term reconciliation.
8. It is essential to support Aboriginal peoples' cultural revitalisation and to integrate Indigenous knowledge systems, oral histories, laws, protocols and connections to the land into the reconciliation process.
9. Political will, joint leadership, trust-building, accountability and transparency, as well as a substantial investment of resources are important requirements for reconciliation.
10. There must be sustained public education and dialogue for reconciliation about the history and legacy of residential schools, treaties, Aboriginal rights and Aboriginal contribution to Canadian society.

In chapter 5, the principles identified by James Tully in his book *Strange Multiplicity: Constitutionalism in an Age of Diversity*—mutual recognition, continuity, and consent—are suggested as relevant guidance for the Australian settler state on recognising and accommodating Indigenous aspirations in a new relationship of reconciliation. Although he specifically refers to the situation in Canada, James Tully argues that Aboriginal people should be recognised as equal, coexisting and self-governing nations, that should be accommodated by the renewal of treaty relationships. Accordingly, a just relationship consists of the following principles: mutual recognition, intercultural negotiation, mutual respect, sharing and mutual responsibility.[58] These principles have been endorsed by the Truth and Reconciliation Commission in Canada, which referred to the principles for a new relationship put forward by the Royal Commission on Aboriginal Peoples and called for the establishment of a new treaty relationship in Canada between Aboriginal and non-Aboriginal people based on mutual recognition, mutual respect and shared responsibility.[59]

In negotiating a postcolonial relationship, Aboriginal and non-Aboriginal peoples must engage in *intercultural dialogue* of negotiation to work out how they will address past injustices and associate in the future. In this middle ground, or cultural interface, the partners listen and speak with each other in their 'own language and customary ways' and on equal footing in order to reach fair agreement. Non-Aboriginal people do not speak for Aboriginal people either in the 'imperial monologue of command and obedience' or by only permitting Aboriginal people to speak in the 'languages, traditions and institutions of the dominant society'. A fundamental convention of intercultural dialogue is *mutual recognition* where Aboriginal and non-Aboriginal people recognise and accept each other as equal peoples (equality) who govern themselves and their lands according to their own laws and cultures (self-government) and their governments and culture coexist and continue through all their relations and interdependencies over time (coexistence). In a coexisting relationship people live side by side governing their own affairs. It is not separation or isolation. Mutual recognition must be affirmed publicly in the institutions and symbols of the nation-state.[60]

Once Aboriginal and non-Aboriginal peoples recognise each other as equals they must show respect for each other, share legal and political power and act responsibly towards each other. To create a positive and supportive climate for harmonious relations a public attitude of *mutual cultural respect* is required. It includes showing respect to each other in their languages, cultures, laws and government and in their dialogue with each other. In a renewed relationship future prosperity and well-being rests on equitable *sharing* in the future. It includes sharing legal and political power, which involves supporting Aboriginal self-government and returning land and resources unjustly taken for Aboriginal economic self-sufficiency. This also includes recognising and publicly acknowledging the sharing extended by Aboriginal people that have been unacknowledged and unreciprocated throughout history. Finally, the partners must act *responsibly* towards each other and to the environment they share. The notion of responsibility in Aboriginal society involves responsibility to others and to the environment. In non-Aboriginal society a high value is placed on individual responsibility and individual freedom. However, there is now a growing awareness that cultural and ecological diversity is a prime responsibility of humans. [61]

There are no recognised principles or conventions in Australian constitutional government to guide reconciliation or relationship building. The principles enunciated by the Truth and Reconciliation Commission in Canada to guide truth and reconciliation can be adapted to the Australian situation. Further the principles of mutual recognition, intercultural dialogue, mutual respect, sharing and mutual responsibility put forward by the Canadian Royal Commission on Aboriginal Peoples and by James Tully, and which are supported by the Canadian Truth and Reconciliation Commission, have application in Australia to guide the transformation of the colonial relationship between Indigenous and other Australians.

These principles can guide genuine intercultural dialogue in Australia through a Truth and Justice Commission, a proposal put forward in the Uluru Statement from the Heart. This body must be empowered by legislation or executive order and it would conduct a dialogic inquiry at different levels. At the national level, a Truth and Justice Commission could conduct an inquiry, similar to the Royal Commission on Aboriginal Peoples and the Truth and Reconciliation Commission in Canada. At a local and regional level, the commission could facilitate local group dialogue projects around history, truth telling and historical relationships between Indigenous and other Australians. The facilitated dialogue groups would act as a microcosm of the larger Australian society and be a vehicle for change at the societal level. Insights, ideas, evidence and outcomes from the local or regional dialogue could be fed into the national inquiry as well as the discussion and decision-making of national policy and political culture.

The role of the Truth and Justice Commission in Australia will be to examine the historical and continuing relationship including the lack of relationship between Aboriginal and Torres Strait Islander peoples and the Crown in England and thereafter Australia, and in doing so set the record straight about problematic and unjust aspects of Australian history. In its investigations it should examine the history and impact of past and continuing colonisation on Indigenous peoples, which includes uncovering historical conventions or practices where Indigenous people and governments have engaged cross-culturally as well as examine shared history where Indigenous and settler Australians have developed respectful relationships. It should propose specific solutions, actions, or principles in regard to how truth telling should continue into the future so it becomes accepted knowledge in understanding the history of Australia. Further, and most importantly, the commission should propose solutions, actions, or principles in respect to how Indigenous peoples, the

Crown, and other Australians might associate in the future in a relationship of mutual recognition, mutual respect and shared responsibility. This should also include making recommendations about expressions of regret and forgiveness. It may also include making recommendations regarding compensation or reparation for damage and loss suffered as a result of injustices committed on Indigenous communities. Examining history will be a huge undertaking; therefore, it will be necessary for the truth and justice commission to identify particular events, incidences or themes to inquire into. This can be done by way of written submission or hearing oral submissions on what it should inquire into. Truth telling should accept both oral evidence and stories as well as documented or research supported evidence.

As part of its investigative function the proposed Truth and Justice Commission should create a dialogic conversation that engages with the nation. To do so it should establish certain conditions on how it would undertake a genuine dialogue. Therefore, a truth-telling dialogue in Australia should:

- examine historical truths and reflect on those truths in order to address past injustices;
- recognise and respect that Aboriginal and Torres Strait Islander peoples are the original peoples and are self-determining peoples;
- recognise and respect the continuity of Aboriginal and Torres Strait Islander cultures and identities;
- embrace and recognise different values and beliefs and accommodate cultural diversity;
- acknowledge power differences and address them through appropriate checks and balances;
- recognise that a truth-telling dialogue entails a right and freedom to speak out against injustice and oppression;
- allow participants to speak in their own voice and in their own way;
- encourage participants to listen without resistance and remain open to the perspectives and realities of others;
- urge participants to suspend, not defend, their assumptions about others and self-reflect in order to understand one's own thinking;
- examine and interrogate attitudes and deeply held assumptions about Indigenous people;
- ensure that participants behave and act responsibly towards each other to build trust;
- guard against coercion, blame, violence, or enforcement of authority, which have no place in the dialogue;
- allow participants to put forward solutions rather than accept the imposition of solutions by politicians, courts, theorists or bureaucratic advisors; and

- encourage political and social leadership to build relationships across existing cultural and political divides.

The Joint Select Committee on Constitutional Recognition recommended in November 2018 that the Australian government support a process of truth telling through local projects where Indigenous peoples and descendants of local settlers with the support of local organisations, libraries and historical societies develop a fuller understanding of history of the area. While it is important to examine local histories, Indigenous Australians should be vigilant about the type of truth telling they want because the Joint Select Committee may well have given the Australian government a mechanism to avoid accepting responsibility for truth telling and to avoid having an honest and frank intercultural dialogue. The Australian government could easily fund a series of local history projects thereby reducing truth telling to an exercise between individual citizens; a 'feel good' or 'hearts and minds' project rather than a constitutional process between Indigenous peoples and Australian governments. A constitutional truth-telling process is not a story-telling project or a history seminar but must be regarded as a process of public inquiry that examines issues of political recognition including treaty, Indigenous sovereignty, Indigenous governance and constitutional recognition, such as a constitutionally recognised Indigenous Voice or constitutional recognition of Indigenous rights.

A genuine truth-telling dialogue in Australia could establish the political and social space for ongoing discussions and negotiations to agree on guiding principles to create the framework for a new relationship. In order to recognise and respect Indigenous cultures and identities, a truth-telling dialogue may consider possibilities for a distinct constitutional status for Indigenous people as is the case in other British settled countries. It may also address issues of Indigenous social and economic development examining models that embrace plurality and diversity and consider Indigenous knowledge and perspectives of development. Importantly, an intercultural truth-telling dialogue would establish principles and a framework for negotiation and agreement with Indigenous people, although outcomes would be open to review and revision. In that regard dialogue is ongoing and requires a long-term perspective.

NOTES

1. N. Rouhana, 'Reconciling History and Equal Citizenship in Israel: Democracy and the Politics of Historical Denial', in *The Politics of Reconciliation in Multicultural Societies*, Will Kymlicka and Bashir Bashir, eds. (Oxford: Oxford University Press, 2008), 76.

2. Truth and Reconciliation Commission of Canada, *Canada's Residential Schools: Reconciliation, The Final Report of the Truth and Reconciliation Commission of Canada*, Volume 6 (Montreal, Quebec: McGill-Queen's University Press, 2015), 32–33.

3. E. Johnson, *National Report, Overview and Recommendations*, Royal Commission into Aboriginal Deaths in Custody (Canberra, ACT: Australian Government Publishing Service, 1991), 7–11.

4. Johnson, *National Report, Overview and Recommendations*, 15–20.

5. 'Paul Keating Redfern Park Speech', 10 December 1992, *Indigenous Law Bulletin* 5, Issue 11 (2001), 9.

6. Commonwealth of Australia, Parliamentary Debates, House of Representatives, Wednesday, 13 February 2008, No. 1, 168–70 (Kevin Rudd).

7. P. Keating, *Redfern Reprise: 23rd Anniversary of Redfern Speech*, Address by the Hon. Paul Keating, Australian Museum, Sydney, 9 December 2015. www.keating.org.au/shop/item/redfern-reprise-23rd-anniversary-of-redfern-speech [Accessed 17 April 2019].

8. Commonwealth of Australia, Parliamentary Debates, House of Representatives, Wednesday, 13 February 2008, No. 1, 169–70 (Kevin Rudd).

9. A. Curthoys, 'Disputing National Histories: Some Recent Australian Debates', *Transforming Cultures eJournal* 1, no. 1 (March 2006), 7–9. https://epress.lib.uts.edu.au/journals/index.php/Tfc/article/view/187 [Accessed 22 March 2019].

10. M. McKenna, 'Moment of Truth: History and Australia's Future', *Quarterly Essay* 69, (March 2018), 15–16.

11. K. Middleton, 'Mick Dodson on fixing the constitution', *The Saturday Paper*, Edition No. 177, 7–13 October 2017. https://www.thesaturdaypaper.com.au/news/politics/2017/10/07/mick-dodson-fixing-the-constitution/15072948005319 [Accessed 22 April 2019].

12. Human Rights and Equal Opportunity Commission, *Bringing Them Home: National Inquiry into the Separation of Aboriginal and Torres Strait Islander Children from Their Families* (Sydney, NSW: Commonwealth of Australia, 1997), 3.

13. Senate Legal and Constitutional References Committee, *Healing: A Legacy of Generations*, The Report of the Inquiry into the Federal Government's Implementation of the Recommendations Made by the Human Rights and Equal Opportunity Commission in *Bringing Them Home* (Canberra, ACT: Commonwealth of Australia, November 2000), 112–13.

14. Senate Legal and Constitutional References Committee, *Healing: A Legacy of Generations*, 116.

15. Commonwealth of Australia, *Final Report of the Referendum Council* (Canberra, ACT: Department of Prime Minister and Cabinet, 30 June 2017), 25–26, 32.

16. P. Lundy and M. McGovern, 'Whose Justice? Rethinking Transitional Justice from the Bottom Up', *Journal of Law and Society* 35, no. 2 (2008), 270.

17. A. Chapman and P. Ball, 'The Truth of Truth Commissions: Comparative Lessons from Haiti, South Africa, and Guatemala', *Human Rights Quarterly* 23, no. 1 (February 2001), 12.

18. Chapman and Ball, 'The Truth of Truth Commissions', 2–3.

19. Reconciliation Australia & Healing Foundation, *Truth Telling Symposium Report*, 5–6 October 2018, 18–19.

20. Commonwealth of Australia, *Final Report: Joint Select Committee on Constitutional Recognition*, 160–62, 164, 171–72, 175, 179, 185.

21. C. Van der Walt, V. Franchi and G. Stevens, 'The South African Truth and Reconciliation Commission: 'Race', historical compromise and transitional democracy', *International Journal of Intercultural Relations* 27 (2003), 256–57.

22. P. Muldoon, 'Reconciliation and Political Legitimacy: The Old Australia and the New South Africa', *Australian Journal of Politics and History* 49, no. 2 (2003), 191–93.

23. Truth and Reconciliation Commission of Canada, *Canada's Residential Schools: Reconciliation, The Final Report of the Truth and Reconciliation Commission of Canada*, Volume 6 (Montreal, Quebec: McGill-Queen's University Press, 2015), 162.

24. Truth and Reconciliation Commission of Canada, *Honouring the Truth, Reconciling for the Future, Summary of the Final Report of the Truth and Reconciliation Commission*

of Canada (Canada, Winnipeg: Truth and Reconciliation Commission of Canada, 2015), 49–50.

25. Truth and Reconciliation Commission of Canada, *Honouring the Truth, Reconciling for the Future*, 43, 46, 48, 49.

26. Truth and Reconciliation Commission of Canada, *Honouring the Truth, Reconciling for the Future*, 1.

27. Truth and Reconciliation Commission, *Canada's Residential Schools: Reconciliation, The Final Report* (Volume 6), 19, 20, 24, 32–33, 53–54.

28. Truth and Reconciliation Commission of Canada, *Canada's Residential Schools: Reconciliation, The Final Report*, 7, 13.

29. See also Robert Tickner, Minister for Aboriginal Affairs and Minister Assisting the Prime Minister for Aboriginal Reconciliation, Second Reading, Council for Aboriginal Reconciliation Bill 1991, Parliamentary Debates, House of Representatives Official Hansard, no. 178, Thursday, 30 May 1991, Commonwealth of Australia, 4498–504.

30. S. Maddison, *Beyond White Guilt: The real challenge for black-white relations in Australia* (Crows Nest, NSW: Allen & Unwin, 2011), 133.

31. Aboriginal and Torres Strait Islander Social Justice Commissioner, *Social Justice Report* (Sydney, NSW: Human Rights & Equal Opportunity Commission, 2001), 198.

32. Council for Aboriginal Reconciliation, *Reconciliation: Australia's Challenge, Final Report of the Council for Aboriginal Reconciliation to the Prime Minister and the Commonwealth Parliament* (Canberra, ACT: Council for Aboriginal Reconciliation, Australia, 2000), 105–8.

33. A. Gunstone, 'Indigenous rights and the 1991–2000 Australian Reconciliation Process', *Cosmopolitan Civil Societies: An Interdisciplinary Journal* 1, no. 3 (2009), 44, 46. https://epress.lib.uts.edu.au/journals/index.php/mcs/article/view/1141 [Accessed 14 August 2019].

34. Commonwealth of Australia, *Commonwealth Government Response to the Council for Aboriginal Reconciliation Final Report, Reconciliation—Australia's Challenge* (Canberra, ACT: Dept. of Immigration and Multicultural and Indigenous Affairs, 2002).

35. S. Brennan, 'Reconciliation in Australia: The Relationship between Indigenous Peoples and the Wider Community', *The Brown Journal of World Affairs* 11, no. 1 (2004), 152–53.

36. A. Pratt, *Practising Reconciliation? The Politics of Reconciliation in the Australian Parliament 1991–2000* (Parliamentary Library: Parliament of Australia, Department of Parliamentary Services, 2003), 151–53.

37. E. Moran, 'Is reconciliation in Australia a dead end?', *Australian Journal of Human Rights* 12, no. 1 (2006), 115–17.

38. A. Gunstone, *Unfinished Business: The Australian Formal Reconciliation Process* (Melbourne, VIC: Australian Scholarly Publishing, 2007), 48–93.

39. M. McMillan and S. Rigney, 'Race, reconciliation, and justice in Australia: from denial to acknowledgment', *Ethnic and Racial Studies* 41, no. 4 (2018), 769.

40. Gunstone, *Unfinished Business*, 132–66.

41. P. Dodson, 'Whatever Happened to Reconciliation', in *Coercive Reconciliation: Stabilise, Normalise, Exit Aboriginal Australia*, Jon Altman and Melinda Hinkson, eds. (North Carlton: Arena Publications Association, 2007), 21.

42. Gunstone, *Unfinished Business*, 301–3

43. Maddison, *Beyond White Guilt*, 135.

44. Commonwealth of Australia, *Final Report of the Referendum Council*, 25, 27, 31, 32.

45. Maddison, *Beyond White Guilt*, 86–88.

46. Moran, 'Is reconciliation in Australia a dead end?', 132–33.

47. Maddison, *Beyond White Guilt*, 89–90.

48. R. De Costa, 'Reconciliation or Identity in Australia', *National Identities* 2, no. 2 (2000), 280, 287.

49. Canada (R. Dussault, G. Erasmus, P. L. A. H. Chartrand, J. P. Meekison, V. Robinson, M. Sillett, M. Wilson), *Royal Commission on Aboriginal Peoples, Looking Forward Looking Back*, Volume 1, (Ottawa: The Commission, 1996), 582–86.

50. Canada, *Royal Commission on Aboriginal Peoples, Looking Forward Looking Back*, Volume 1, 582.

51. Reconciliation Australia, *Grounded in Truth, Walk Together with Courage*, National Reconciliation Week 2019. https://www.reconciliation.org.au/wp-content/uploads/2019/05/ra-nrw-2019-guide_v8.pdf [Accessed 7 June 2019].

52. J. Corntassell, Chaw-win-is and T'lakwadzi, 'Indigenous Storytelling, Truth-telling, and Community Approaches to Reconciliation', *English Studies in Canada* 35, Issue 1 (March 2009), 139.

53. Corntassell, Chaw-win-is and T'lakwadzi, 'Indigenous Storytelling, Truth-telling', 144.

54. Leigh, 'Leadership and Aboriginal Reconciliation', *The Australian Journal of Social Issues* 37, no. 2 (2002), 140–42.

55. L. Veracini, *Settler Colonialism: A Theoretical Overview* (Basingstoke, UK: Palgrave Macmillan, 2010), 105, 108–9, 114–15.

56. Veracini, *Settler Colonialism, A Theoretical Overview*, 99, 101, 108–9, 112–13, 115.

57. Truth and Reconciliation Commission, *Canada's Residential Schools, The Final Report*, 16.

58. J. Tully, *Public Philosophy in a New Key, Volume 1: Democracy and Civic Freedom* (Cambridge: Cambridge University Press, 2008), 229.

59. Truth and Reconciliation Commission of Canada, *Canada's Residential Schools, Final Report*, 23.

60. Tully, *Public Philosophy in a New Key*, 229–32, 239–41.

61. Tully, *Public Philosophy in a New Key*, 242–44, 244–49, 250–52.

Epilogue

There are many Australians who want a transformed relationship with Indigenous people but there is no broad public support for Indigenous aspirations in Australian society. There is reluctance in Australia to move forward or take the next step because it involves having difficult and uncomfortable conversations about history and injustices committed against Indigenous peoples. A common public and political refrain often heard in Australia when Indigenous people talk about or make claims of injustices is: Why don't Indigenous people shut up, get over the past and move on? Telling Indigenous Australians to get over their past is an avoidance mechanism to deflect or dismiss claims of injustice. There is a deep fear of acknowledging and owning the injustices that have been committed against Indigenous peoples. There is also a fear that any challenge to the master narrative about Australia will not only expose the fiction upon which it is based but also expose the untruths, racial biases and prejudicial attitudes that have underpinned thinking about Indigenous people in Australia. The question is, how we can have a conversation in Australia that does not create guilt, fear, anxiety, anger, disrespect or hatred? Unfortunately, conversations about race, particularly the clash of racial realities, are difficult and uncomfortable.

After more than two hundred and thirty-three years of colonialism in Australia there is a clear need for transformation and redress without having to revert to terra nullius thinking. The Crown, as represented by government in Australia, is responsible for building a just relationship with Indigenous Australians. However, to achieve a just relationship it is necessary to dismantle the barriers to recognising and respecting Indigenous people. To move forward requires confronting the truth and questioning the erroneous assumptions and negative discourses about Indigenous people that have been inherited from the colonial past. There must be a commitment by the Crown to acknowledge and rectify past injustice through a genuine truth and reconciliation process that has restorative and transformative dimensions. It will involve restructuring social and political relationships between the State, Australian society and Indigenous peoples. Fundamentally, it will require a new relationship based on the recognition of Indigenous political authority within the Australian constitutional and governmental structure. To move forward towards a just relationship, it is first necessary to identify the principles upon which an Indigenous-State relationship should be based and to recognise these

principles as important conventions and obligations of Australian constitutional government. There is need for a genuine road map to guide
change and build the foundations for a renewed relationship.

Settler states like Australia can accommodate Indigenous difference
by recognising Indigenous social and political institutions within constitutional and governmental structures. This requires the Crown, as represented by government, to engage in dialogue and negotiation with Indigenous peoples in a process of political reconciliation. But history shows
that governments in Australia are rigid; refusing or reluctant to recognise
Indigenous rights. The rigidity, however, appears to be more in the
minds of politicians and those who represent the interests of the Crown
because in the past, government has been able to recognise and accommodate Indigenous rights to land – rights to land that preceded British
colonisation. Political reconciliation requires the creation of political
space in which Indigenous peoples and governments can discuss the
terms of their political association. While Australian governments have
created limited political space from time to time to discuss important
public policy issues with Indigenous people, the conversations are rarely
dialogic and they focus on assimilationist and/or nationalist outcomes,
thereby avoiding the political questions of Indigenous sovereignty and
treaty.

The need for an ongoing dialogical space for a genuine conversation
about the constitutional and political status of Indigenous people in the
Australian nation is vital. However, the national discussion has to move
to a broader notion of justice for Indigenous people beyond the perception that justice is about closing the socioeconomic gap between Indigenous and other Australians or educating white Australians to appreciate
Indigenous culture. Australian political leaders have the power to create
this political and social space. A truth-telling dialogue commissioned by
the federal government is the starting point. A truth-telling dialogue can
lay the moral and intellectual framework and the principles for reconciliation. A constitutionally recognised First Nations Voice to Parliament
and a treaty process with Indigenous Australians are pivotal steps towards genuine reconciliation. But they are not definitive and final because they are mechanisms by which Indigenous people participate in
the institutions of Australian constitutional government and through
which frameworks are created for an ongoing consensual political association.

Meaningful dialogue requires a predisposition to understanding and
helping others through an approach built on openness, absence of resistance and building trusting relationships. The Australian population can
assist Indigenous people by thinking positively about cultural difference
and appreciating the value of such difference within the nation as well as
adopting an openness and willingness to tackle issues important to Indigenous people. This also includes facing up to historical and contemporary

truths about colonialism and confronting underlying erroneous assumptions and discourses about Indigenous people. While these are sensitive matters for non-Indigenous Australians and may evoke guilt or anger, the purpose is not to moralise about guilt but to assist Australians to understand historical truths as well as repudiate assumptions and attitudes about Indigenous people based on racial superiority or deficit discourses. Indigenous people can also support Australians to emancipate themselves from deeply held erroneous assumptions and attitudes, free from feelings of guilt, fear or anger.

Although Indigenous people lack the necessary political power to affect outcomes in policy and law-making processes, they must still confront the hegemony and inertia of Australian legal, political and economic institutions that assert significant power and influence in opposing their rights or claims for recognition. In this context, Indigenous people need to rebuild their political and cultural values and practices to challenge and undercut the hegemony and inertia of colonialism. Importantly, Indigenous political leaders must articulate new models of Indigenous-State constitutional relationships based on Indigenous values and practices. An openness and willingness to change prevailing attitudes and opinions is necessary to transform the colonial relationships between Indigenous and non-Indigenous Australians and to create renewed relationships that will provide the foundation for achieving real and enduring justice for Indigenous people.

Bibliography

Aboriginal and Torres Strait Islander Social Justice Commissioner. *Social Justice Report.* Sydney, NSW: Human Rights and Equal Opportunity Commission, 2007.
———. *Social Justice Report.* Sydney, NSW: Human Rights and Equal Opportunity Commission, 2001.
———. *Native Title Report 1999.* Sydney, NSW: Human Rights and Equal Opportunity Commission, 1999.
———. *Native Title Report.* Canberra, ACT: Human Rights and Equal Opportunity Commission, January–June 1994.
———. *First Report 1993.* Human Rights and Equal Opportunity Commission. Canberra, ACT: Australian Government Publishing Service, 1993.
Aboriginal and Torres Strait Islander Commission. *The Ten Point Plan on Wik and Native Title: Issues for Indigenous Peoples.* Canberra, ACT: Aboriginal and Torres Strait Islander Commission, 1997.
———. 'Mabo Agreement Reached'. *The ATSIC Reporter* 2, no. 9 (October 1993).
Aboriginal and Torres Strait Islander Commission, Australian Democrats, Greens (WA). 'Mabo Statement'. Joint Media Release. Canberra, ACT, 30 September 1993.
Aboriginal and Torres Strait Islander Commission. 'Response to the consultation process concerning the Mabo Decision'. Canberra, ACT: ATSIC, 1993.
Aborigines Welfare Board. *Report for the Year Ending 30th June 1940.* Parliament of New South Wales, Sydney: Government Printer, 1941.
Altman, J. 'Practical Reconciliation and the New Mainstreaming: Will it make a difference to Indigenous Australians?' *Dialogue* 23, no. 2 (2004): 35–45.
Amnesty International. *WA Government must stop Oombulgurri demolitions after forcibly evicting community members.* Sydney: Amnesty International, 23 September 2014.
Anderson, J., T. Hosch, and R. Eccles. *Final Report of the Aboriginal and Torres Strait Islander Act of Recognition Review Panel.* Canberra, ACT: Department of Prime Minister and Cabinet, Australian Government, September 2014.
Anderson, G. M. 'The Government is asking you to blindly vote for changes in a Referendum, without even clarifying the final wording'. 23 May 2014, Sovereign Union—First Nations Asserting Sovereignty. Accessed 26 April 2018. http://nationalunitygovernment.org/content/government-asking-you-blindly-vote-changes-referendum-without-even-clarifying-final-words.
Anderson, P. and R. Wild. *Ampe Akelyernemane Meke Mekarle: 'Little Children are Sacred'.* Report of the Northern Territory Board of Inquiry into the Protection of Aboriginal Children from Sexual Abuse. Darwin, NT: Northern Territory Government, 2007.
Anderson, K. 'Thinking "Postnationally": Dialogue across Multicultural, Indigenous, and Settler Spaces'. *Association of American Geographers* 90, no. 2 (2000): 381–91.
Anaya, S. J. *Report by the Special Rapporteur on the situation of human rights and fundamental freedoms of indigenous peoples, Appendix B: Observations on the Northern Territory Emergency Response in Australia.* Human Rights Council Fifteenth Session, United Nations General Assembly A/HRC/15/37/Add.4, 1 June 2010. Accessed 29 March 2017. https://documents-ddsny.un.org/doc/UNDOC/GEN/G10/138/87/PDF/G1023887.PDF?OpenElement.
Appadurai, A. 'The Risks of Dialogue'. In *New Stakes for Intercultural Dialogue, Acts of the International Seminar, Paris 6–7 June 2006,* edited by Samantha Wauchope and Odette Petit. UNESCO 2008, 33–37.

Attwood, B. 'Mabo, Australia and the end of history'. In *In the Age of Mabo: History, Aborigines and Australia*, edited by Bain Attwood. St Leonards, NSW: Allen & Unwin, 1996.

———. *Rights for Aborigines*. Crows Nest, NSW: Allen & Unwin, 2003.

Attwood, B. and A. Markus. *The 1967 Referendum. Race Power and the Australian Constitution*. Canberra, ACT: Australian Institute of Aboriginal and Torres Strait Islander Studies, 2007.

———. *Thinking Black. William Cooper and the Australian Aborigines' League*. Canberra, ACT: Aboriginal Studies Press, Australian Institute of Aboriginal and Torres Strait Islander Studies, 2004.

———. *The Struggle for Aboriginal Rights. A Documentary History*. Sydney, NSW: Allen & Unwin, 1999.

Australian Human Rights Commission. *The suspension and reinstatement of the RDA and special measures in the NTER*. 2 November 2011. Sydney, NSW: Australian Human Rights Commission. Accessed 29 March 2017. https://www.humanrights.gov.au/our-work/race-discrmination/publications/suspension-and-reinstatement-rda-and-speacial-measures-nter.

Australian Indigenous Doctor's Association and Centre for Health Equity Training, Research and Evaluation, UNSW. *Health Impact Assessment of the Northern Territory Emergency Response*. Canberra: Australian Indigenous Doctors' Association, 2010.

Australian Council for Overseas Aid. 'Australian Council for Overseas Aid Denounces Racist Legislation'. Media Release, 27 September 1993.

Banathy, B. H. 'Searching Together, Approaches, Methods and Tools'. In *Dialogue as a Collective Means of Design Conversation*, edited by Patrick M. Jenlink and Bela H. Banathy. New York: Springer, 2008.

Banner, S. *Possessing the Pacific. Land, Settlers, and Indigenous People from Australia to Alaska*. Cambridge, MA: Harvard University Press, 2007.

———. 'Why terra nullius? Anthropology and property law in early Australia'. *Law and History Review* 23, no. 1 (2005): 95–131.

Barta, T. 'Sorry, and not sorry, in Australia: How the apology to the stolen generation buried a history of genocide'. *Journal of Genocide Research* 10, no. 2 (2008): 201–14.

Bartlett, R. H. 'The Land (Titles and Traditional Usage) Act Western Australia, A Racist and Invalid Enactment'. In *Mabo: The Native Title Legislation*, edited by M. A. Stephenson. St Lucia, Queensland: University of Queensland Press, 1995.

Barwick, D. *Rebellion at Coranderrk*. Canberra, ACT: National Capital Printing, 1998.

Beaglehole, J. C. *The Journals of Captain James Cook on his Voyages of Discovery. The Voyage of the Endeavour 1768–1771*. Part Two. Millwood, NY: Hakluyt Society, 1988.

Behrendt, L. 'Reconciliation: Forty Years On'. *Australian Quarterly* 79, no. 3 (2007): 48–53.

———. *Achieving Social Justice: Indigenous rights and Australia's future*. Leichhardt, NSW: Federation Press, 2003.

Bennett, S. 'Federalism and Aboriginal Affairs'. *Australian Aboriginal Studies* 1 (1988): 18–27.

Beresford, Q. *Rob Riley. An Aboriginal leader's quest for justice*. Canberra, ACT: Aboriginal Studies Press, 2006.

Berndt, R. M. 'The Gove dispute: The question of Australian Aboriginal land and the preservation of sacred sites'. *Anthropological Forum: A Journal of Social Anthropology and Comparative Sociology* 1, no. 2 (1964): 258–95.

Birch, T. '"Black Armbands and White Veils": John Howard's Moral Amnesia'. *Melbourne Historical Journal* 25 (1997): 8–16.

Blackstone, W., and T. M. Cooley. *Commentaries on the Laws of England*. Chicago: Callaghan and Cockcroft, 1871.

Bonham, V. L., T. Citrin, S. M. Modell, T. H. Franklin, E. W. B. Bleicher and L. M. Fleck. 'Community-Based Dialogue: Engaging Communities of Colour in the United States' Genetics Policy Conversation'. *Journal of Health Politics, Policy and Law* 34, no. 3 (2009): 325–59.

Bohm, D. *On Dialogue*. London and New York: Routledge, 1996.

Borch, M. 'Rethinking the Origins of Terra Nullius'. *Australian Historical Studies* 32, no. 117 (2001): 222–39.

Breen, S. 'Howard's History War, 1996–2007'. In *Over a Decade of Despair: The Howard Government and Indigenous Affairs*, edited by Andrew Gunstone. North Melbourne, Vic; Australian Scholarly Publishing, 2010.

Brennan, S. 'Reconciliation in Australia: The Relationship between Indigenous Peoples and the Wider Community'. *The Brown Journal of World Affairs* 11, no. 1 (2004): 149–61.

Briscoe, G. 'The origins of Aboriginal political consciousness and the Aboriginal Embassy 1907-1972'. In *The Aboriginal Tent Embassy. Sovereignty, Black Power, Land Rights and the State*, edited by Gary Foley, Andrew Schaap and Edwina Howell. Abingdon, Oxon: Routledge Taylor & Francis, 2014.

Broome, R. *Aboriginal Australians, A history since 1788*. Fourth Edition. Crows Nest, NSW: Allen & Unwin, 2010.

———. *Aboriginal Victorians, A History Since 1800*. Crows Nest, NSW: Allen & Unwin, 2005.

———. *Aboriginal Australians: Black Response to White Dominance 1788–1980*. North Sydney: Allen & Unwin, 1982.

Brown, N. and S. Bowden. *A way through: The life of Rick Farley*. Sydney, NSW: New South Publishing, University of NSW, 2012.

Brunton, P. *The Endeavour Journal of Joseph Banks*. Angus and Robertson and the State Library of New South Wales, 1998.

Bryant, G. M. 'Government Policy Towards Aborigines'. *Australian Government Digest* 1, no. 3 (1973): 899–904.

———. 'Press Statement 6 April 1973'. *Australian Government Digest* 1, no. 2 (1973): 502.

———. *Report on Yirrkala, Northern Territory, and Bauxite Deposit Leases*. The Federal Council for Aboriginal Advancement, 1963. National Museum of Australia. http://indigenousrights.net.au/document.asp?iID=684.

Buchan, B. 'The empire of political thought: Civilization, savagery and perceptions of Indigenous government'. *History of Human Sciences* 18, no. 2 (2005): 1–22.

———. 'Traffick of Empire: Trade, Treaty and Terra Nullius in Australia and North America, 1750-1800'. *History Compass* 5, no. 2 (2007): 386–405.

Buchan, B., and M. Heath. 'Savagery and civilization: From terra nullius to the "tide of history"'. *Ethnicities* 6, no. 1 (2006): 5–26.

Butle Ritchie, D. T. 'Critiquing Modern Constitutionalism'. *Appalachian Journal of Law* 3, no. 37 (2004): 37–49.

Canada, (R. Dussault, G. Erasmus, P. L. A. H. Chartrand, J. P. Meekison, V. Robinson, M. Sillett and M. Wilson). *Royal Commission on Aboriginal Peoples, Looking Forward Looking Back*. Volume 1. Ottawa: The Commission, 1996.

Cane, S. *First footprints: The epic story of the First Australians*. Crows Nest, NSW: Allen & Unwin, 2013.

Castles, A. *An Australian Legal History*. Sydney: The Law Book Company, 1982.

Chamarette, C. 'Terra Nullius Then and Now: Mabo, Native Title, and Reconciliation in 2000'. *Australian Psychologist* 35, no. 2 (2000): 167–72.

———. 'Greens move to put Mabo legislation on Hold'. Media Release. Christabel Chamarette, Senator for the Greens (WA). Canberra, ACT, 24 November 1993.

Chapman, A. and P. Ball. 'The Truth of Truth Commissions: Comparative Lessons from Haiti, South Africa, and Guatemala'. *Human Rights Quarterly* 23, no. 1 (February 2001): 1–43.

Chartrand, P. L. A. H. 'Towards Justice and Reconciliation: Treaty Recommendations of Canada's Royal Commission on Aboriginal Peoples'. In *Honour Among Nations? Treaties and Agreements with Indigenous People*, edited by Marcia Langton, Lisa Palmer, Maureen Tehan and Kathryn Shain. Carlton, Vic: Melbourne University Press, 2004.

Chesterman, J., and B. Galligan. *Indigenous people and Citizenship. Individual, Community, Nation: the 50th Anniversary of Australian Citizenship Conference.* University of Melbourne, 1999. Accessed 28 August 2013. web.archive.org/web/20100706073856/ http://www.law.unimelb.edu.au/events/citizen/chesterman.pdf.

———. *Citizens Without Rights, Aborigines and Australian Citizenship.* Cambridge, UK: Cambridge University Press, 1997.

Christie, M. F. *Aborigines in Colonial Victoria 1835–1886.* Sydney, NSW: Sydney University Press, 1979.

Coe, P. 'ATSIC: self-determination or otherwise'. *Race & Class* 35, no. 4 (1994): 35–39.

———. 'Position Paper on the Commonwealth Outline of the Proposed Legislation on Native Title and NSW Draft Native Title Bill 1993'. New South Wales Aboriginal Legal Service. Unpublished, Sydney, 24 September 1993.

Corntassell, J., Chaw-win-is and T'lakwadzi, 'Indigenous Storytelling, Truth-telling, and Community Approaches to Reconciliation'. *English Studies in Canada* 35, Issue 1 (March 2009): 137–59.

Craven, G. 'The Law, Substance and Morality of Recognition'. In *The Forgotten People: Liberal and Conservative Approaches to Recognising Indigenous Peoples*, edited by Damien Freeman and Shereen Morris. Carlton, Vic: Melbourne University Press, 2016.

Cronin, D. 'Justice and the political future for Indigenous Australians'. In *Practical Justice: Principles, Practice and Social Change*, edited by Peter Aggleton, Alex Broom and Jeremy Moss. Abingdon Oxon, UK: Routledge, 2019.

———. 'Trapped by history: Democracy, human rights and justice for Indigenous people in Australia'. *Australian Journal of Human Rights* 23, no. 2 (2017): 220–41.

Clark, J. *Aborigines and Activism. Race, Aborigines and the Coming of the Sixties to Australia.* Crawley, WA: University of Western Australia Press, 2008.

Commonwealth of Australia. *Final Report: Joint Select Committee on Constitutional Recognition relating to Aboriginal and Torres Strait Islander Peoples.* Canberra, ACT November 2018.

———. *Interim Report: Joint Select Committee on Constitutional Recognition relating to Aboriginal and Torres Strait Islander Peoples.* Canberra, ACT, July 2018.

———. *Final Report of the Referendum Council.* Canberra, ACT: Department of Prime Minister and Cabinet, 30 June 2017.

———. *Joint Select Committee on Constitutional Recognition of Aboriginal and Torres Strait Islander Peoples, Final Report.* Canberra, ACT: Parliament House, 2015.

———. *Recognising Aboriginal and Torres Strait Islander Peoples in the Constitution: Report of the Expert Panel.* Canberra, ACT: Department of Families, Housing, Community Services and Indigenous Affairs, January 2012.

———. *National Human Rights Consultation Report.* Barton, ACT: Attorney General's Department, September 2009.

———. *Commonwealth Government Response to the Council for Aboriginal Reconciliation Final Report, Reconciliation—Australia's Challenge.* Canberra, ACT: Department of Immigration and Multicultural and Indigenous Affairs, 2002.

———. *Mabo: Outline of Proposed legislation on Native Title.* Canberra, ACT: Commonwealth of Australia, September 1993.

———. *The Mabo High Court Decision on Native Title.* Discussion Paper. Canberra, ACT: Australian Government Publishing Service, 1993.

———. *The High Court Decision on Native Title.* Canberra, ACT, Prime Minister and Cabinet, October 1992.

———. *Cabinet Minute, National Aboriginal Land Rights Legislation.* Canberra, 12 August 1985, Decision No. 6505, Submission No. 3146.

———. *Cabinet Minute, Committee on Aboriginal Affairs.* Sydney, 6 December 1971, Decision No. 613 (AA), Submission No. 457.

———. *Cabinet Minute, Committee on Aboriginal Affairs.* Canberra, 13 and 14 October 1971, Decision No. 480 (AA) and 486 (AA).

———. *Cabinet Minute, Committee on Aboriginal Affairs.* Sydney, 3 August 1971, Decision No. 341 (AA) with attached submission No. 245.

————. *Cabinet Minute, Committee on Aboriginal Affairs*. 3 August 1971, Decision No. 341 (AA) with attached Submission No. 285.

————. *Report from the Select Committee on Grievances of Yirrkala Aborigines, Arnhem Land Reserve. Part 1—Report and Minutes of Proceedings, House of Representatives*. Canberra, ACT: Commonwealth Government Printer, 1963.

————. *Native Welfare, Meeting of Commonwealth and State Ministers held at Canberra, 3rd and 4th September 1951*. Canberra, ACT: Commonwealth Government Printer, 1951.

————. *Aboriginal Welfare: Initial Conference of Commonwealth and State Aboriginal Authorities*. Canberra, ACT: Commonwealth Government Printers, 1937.

Coombs, H. C. *Trail Balance*. South Melbourne: The MacMillan Company, 1981.

————. *Kulinma. Listening to Aboriginal Australians*. Canberra, ACT: Australian National University Press, 1978.

Coombs, H. C., P. H. Bailey, E. Campbell, J. E. Isaac and P. R. Munro. *Royal Commission on Australian Government Administration*. Commonwealth of Australia Report. Canberra, ACT: Australian Government Publishing Service, 1976.

Council for Aboriginal Reconciliation. *Reconciliation: Australia's Challenge, Final Report of the Council for Aboriginal Reconciliation to the Prime Minister and the Commonwealth Parliament*. Canberra: Council for Aboriginal Reconciliation, December 2000.

————. *Walking together: The first steps*. Report to Federal Parliament 1991–1994. Canberra, ACT, Council for Aboriginal Reconciliation, Australia, 1994.

————. *Making things rights: Reconciliation after the High Court's decision on native title*. Canberra, ACT, Council for Aboriginal Reconciliation, Australia, January 1993.

Coulthard, G. *Red Skin White Masks: Rejecting the Colonial Politics of Recognition*. Minneapolis: University of Minnesota Press, 2014.

————. 'Subjects of Empire: Indigenous Peoples and the "Politics of Recognition" in Canada'. *Contemporary Political Theory* 6, no. 4 (2007): 437–60.

Cowlishaw, G. 'Did the Earth Move for You? The anti-Mabo Debate'. In *Mabo and Australia: On Recognising Native Title After Two Hundred Years*, edited by Gillian Cowlishaw and Vivienne Kondos. Sydney, NSW: The Australian Journal of Anthropology, August 1995.

Cunningham, J., and J. I. Baeza. 'An "experiment" in Indigenous social policy: The rise and fall of Australia's Aboriginal and Torres Strait Islander Commission (ATSIC)'. *Policy & Politics* 33, no. 3 (2005): 461–73.

Curthoys, A. 'Disputing National Histories: Some Recent Australian Debates'. *Transforming Cultures eJournal* 1, no. 1 (March 2006), 6–18. Accessed 22 March 2019, https://epress.lib.uts.edu.au/journals/index.php/Tfc/article/view/187.

Darwin, C. *On the Origins of Species by Means of Natural Selection or the Preservation of Favoured Races in the Struggle for Life*. (London: John Murray, 1859).

Davis, M., and M. Langton. 'Introduction'. In *It's Our Country: Indigenous Arguments for Meaningful Constitutional Recognition and Reform*, edited by Megan Davis and Marcia Langton. Carlton, Vic: Melbourne University Press, 2016.

De Costa, R. 'Reconciliation or Identity in Australia'. *National Identities* 2, no. 2 (2000): 277–91.

Dessel, A., and M. Rogge. 'Evaluation of Intergroup Dialogue: A Review of the Empirical Literature'. *Conflict of Resolution Quarterly* 26, no. 2 (2008): 199–237.

de Vattel, E. 'The Status of Aboriginal People, The Law of Nations'. Book I, chapter 8. In *A Source Book of Australian Legal History*, edited by John Michael Bennett and Alex Cuthbert Castles. Sydney, NSW: The Law Book Company, 1979.

————. 'The Law of Nations; or, Principles of the Law of Nature, applied to the Conduct and Affairs of Nations and Sovereigns'. In *The Law of Nations*, edited by J. Chitty. Philadelphia: T & J W Johnson & Co., 1863.

Dodson, M. 'Towards the exercise of Indigenous rights: policy, power and self-determination'. *Race & Class* 35, no. 4 (1994): 65–76.

Dodson, M. *Submission to the Parliamentary Joint Committee on Native Title and the Aboriginal and Torres Strait Islander Land Fund, The Native Title Amendment Bill 1997*. Sydney, NSW: Aboriginal and Torres Strait Islander Social Justice Commissioner, 3

October 1997. https://www.humanrights.gov.au/sites/default/files/content/pdf/social_justice/submission_land_fund_october1997.pdf.

Dodson, M., and L. Strelein. 'Australia's Nation-Building: Renegotiating the Relationship between Indigenous Peoples and the State'. *University of New South Wales Law Journal* 24, no. 3 (2001): 826–39.

Dodson, P. *Dialogue and Nation Building in Contemporary Australia. So What?* Lecture. University of New South Wales, Sydney, 20 August 2009.

———. *Reconciliation: Two Centuries On, Is Dialogue Enough?* La Trobe University Centre for Dialogue Working Paper (2008). Accessed 19 January 2012. www.latrobe.edu.au/dialogue/publications/workingpppaper-series/past-issues.

———. 'Whatever Happened to Reconciliation'. In *Coercive Reconciliation: Stabilise, Normalise, Exit Aboriginal Australia*, edited by Jon Altman and Melinda Hinkson. North Carlton: Arena Publications Association, 2007.

Dodson, P., M. Mowbray and W. Snowden. 'Promise, confrontation and compromise in Indigenous affairs'. In *The Hawke Government: A critical Retrospective*, edited by Susan Ryan and Troy Bramston. North Melbourne, Vic: Pluto Press Australia, 2003.

Dodson, P. L. *Regional report of inquiry into underlying issues in Western Australia*. Royal Commission into Aboriginal Deaths in Custody. Canberra, Australian Government Publishing Service, 1991.

Douglas, H., and M. Finnane. *Indigenous Crime and Settler Law: White Sovereignty after Empire*. United Kingdom: Palgrave MacMillan, 2012.

Dussault, R. 'The Vision of the Royal Commission on Aboriginal Peoples', *Saskatchewan Law Review* 70 (2007): 93–98.

Eatock, P. 'Black Demo'. In *The Aboriginal Tent Embassy. Sovereignty, Black Power, Land Rights and the State*, edited by Gary Foley, Andrew Schaap and Edwina Howell. Abingdon, Oxon: Routledge Taylor & Francis, 2014.

Edmonds, P., and J. Carey. 'Australian Settler Colonialism over the long Nineteenth Century'. In *The Routledge Handbook of the History of Settler Colonialism*, edited by Edward Cavanagh and Lorenzo Veracini. Abingdon, Oxon, UK: Routledge, 2017.

Egan, R. *Neither Amity nor Kindness: Government policy towards Aboriginal people of NSW 1788 to 1969*. Paddington, NSW: Richard Egan, 2012.

Elkin, A. P. *The Australian Aborigines. How to Understand Them*. Sydney, NSW: Angus & Robertson, 1964.

———. *Citizenship for Aborigines: A National Aboriginal Policy*. Sydney, NSW: Australasian Publishing Co. Pty Ltd, 1944.

———. 'Anthropology and the Future of the Australian Aborigines'. *Oceania* 5, no. 1 (1934): 1–18.

———. *Understanding the Australian Aborigine*. The Morpeth Booklets, No. 2, 1933). Accessed 24 October 2013.. http://handle.slv.vic.gov.au/10381/121093.

Ellinghaus, K. 'Absorbing the "Aboriginal problem": controlling interracial marriage in Australia in the late 19th and early 20th centuries'. *Aboriginal History* 27 (2003): 183–207.

Errington, W., and P. V. Onselen. *John Winston Howard*. Carlton, Vic: Melbourne University Press, 2007.

Escobar, O. *Public Dialogue and Deliberation, A communication perspective for public engagement practitioners*. Edinburgh: The University of Edinburgh, 2011.

———. 'The dialogic turn: dialogue for deliberation'. *In-Spire Journal of Law, Politics and Societies* 4, no. 2 (2009): 42–70.

Ewing, G. W. 'The Australian Mining Industry Council and its Role in the Mabo Debate'. AUSIMM Student Conference, Pathway to Industry. Brisbane, 28–29 April 1994.

Fitzmaurice, A. 'Discovery, Conquest, and Occupation of Territory'. In *The History of International Law*, edited by Bardo Fassbender and Anne Peters. Oxford, United Kingdom: Oxford University Press, 2012.

———. 'The Genealogy of Terra Nullius'. *Australian Historical Studies* 38, no. 129 (2007): 1–15.

Flower, L. 'Talking across Difference: Intercultural Rhetoric and the Search for Situated Knowledge'. *College Composition and Communication* 55, no. 1 (2003): 38–68.

Foley, G. 'An Autobiographical Narrative of the Black Power Movement and the 1972 Aboriginal Embassy'. PhD Dissertation: University of Melbourne, 2012.

Foley, G. and T. Anderson. 'Land Rights and Aboriginal Voices'. *Australian Journal of Human Rights* 12, no. 1 (2006): 83–108.

Ford, L. *Settler Sovereignty: Jurisdiction and Indigenous People in America and Australia 1788–1836*. Cambridge, MA: Harvard University Press, 2010.

Frost, A. 'New South Wales as terra nullius: The British denial of Aboriginal land rights'. *Historical Studies* 19, no. 77 (1981): 513–23.

Gergen, K. J., S. McNamee and F. J. Barrett. 'Towards Transformative Dialogue'. *International Journal of Public Administration* 24, no. 7 (2001): 679–707.

Gilbert, K. *Because A White Man'll Never Do It*. Sydney: Angus & Robertson, 1973.

Goodall, H. *Invasion to Embassy: Land in Aboriginal Politics in New South Wales 1770–1972*. St Leonards, NSW Allen & Unwin with Black Books, 1996.

Gorrie, N. *Fuck Your Constitutional Recognition, I Want a Treaty*, VICE [online] 17 March 2016. Accessed 4 April 2018. https://www.vice.com/en_au/article/qb5zdp/fuck-your-recognition.

Gorton, J. *Address by the Prime Minister, Right Hon. John Gorton at the Conference of Commonwealth and State Ministers responsible for Aboriginal Affairs at Parliament House*. Department of Prime Minister and Cabinet, Melbourne, 12 July 1968.

Grammond, S. 'Treaties as Constitutional Agreements'. In *The Oxford Handbook of the Canadian Constitution*, edited by Peter Oliver, Patrick Macklem and Nathalie Des Rosiers. New York: Oxford University Press, 2017.

Greene, J. 'Colonial History and National History: Reflections on a Continuing Problem'. *William and Mary Quarterly* 6, no. 2 (2007): 235–50.

Gunstone, A. 'The Howard Government and Indigenous Affairs'. In *Over a Decade of Despair: The Howard Government and Indigenous Affairs*, edited by Andrew Gunstone. North Melbourne, Vic; Australian Scholarly Publishing, 2010.

———. 'Indigenous rights and the 1991-2000 Australian Reconciliation Process'. *Cosmopolitan Civil Societies: An Interdisciplinary Journal* 1, no. 3 (2009): 35–51. Accessed 14 August 2019. https://epress.lib.uts.edu.au/journals/index.php/mcs/article/view/1141.

———. 'These Blokes are Re-inventing the 19th Century: The Howard Government's Record on Indigenous Affairs 1996–2006'. *Journal of Indigenous Policy*, Issue 7 (2007): 41–52.

———. *Unfinished Business: The Australian Formal Reconciliation Process*. Melbourne, Vic: Australian Scholarly Publishing, 2007.

———. *Reconciliation, Nationalism and the History Wars*. Refereed paper presented to the Australasian Political Studies Association Conference, University of Adelaide, 29 September–1 October 2004. Accessed 12 February 2016. http://pandora.nla.gov.au/pan/39515/200607190000/www.adelaide.edu.au/apsa/docs_papers/Aust%20Pol/Gunstone.pdf.

Hagan, J. *Makarrata Consultations*. National Aboriginal Conference Secretariat, Canberra. 8 July 1980.

Hage, G. 'Multiculturalism and White Paranoia in Australia'. *Journal of International Migration and Integration* 3, nos. 3–4 (2002): 417–37.

Hanks, P. 'Aborigines and Government: the developing framework'. In *Aborigines and the Law*, edited by Peter Hanks and Bryan Keon-Cohen. North Sydney, NSW: George Allen & Unwin Australia, 1984.

Harris, S. '*It's Comin Yet . . . ' An Aboriginal Treaty Within Australia Between Australians*. Adelaide, SA: Griffin Press, 1979.

———. *This Our Land*. Canberra, ACT, Australian National University Press, 1972.

Henzell, M. 'Media Release'. Marjorie Henzell, MP. Federal Member for Capricornia. Canberra, ACT, 6 October 1993.

Herzig, M., and L. Chasin. *Fostering Dialogue Across Divides: A Nuts and Bolts Guide from the Public Conversations Project*. Watertown, MA: Public Conversations Project, 2006.

Hiatt, L. R., L. O'Donoghue and J. H. Stanley. *Inquiry into the role of the National Aboriginal Consultative Committee*. Report of the Committee of Inquiry. Canberra, ACT: Commonwealth of Australia, 1976.

Hinkson, M. 'Introduction: In the name of the child'. In *Coercive reconciliation: Stablisie, normalise, exit Aboriginal Australia*, edited by Jon Altman and Melinda Hinkson. North Carlton, Vic: Arena Publications, 2007.

Horner, J. *Bill Ferguson, Fighter for Aboriginal Freedom*. Canberra, ACT: Published by Jack Horner, 1994.

Horner, J., and M. Langton. 'The Day of Mourning'. In *Australians 1938*, edited by Bill Gammage and Peter Spearritt. Sydney, NSW Fairfax: Syme & Weldon Associates, 1987.

Howard, J. 'A New Reconciliation'. *Sydney Papers* 19, no. 4 (Spring 2007): 104–10.

———. *Opening Address to the Australian Reconciliation Convention, Melbourne*. Transcript of the Prime Minister, the Hon. John Howard MP, 26 May 1997.

Howell, E. 'Black Power—by any means necessary'. In *The Aboriginal Tent Embassy. Sovereignty, Black Power, land Rights and the State*, edited by Gary Foley, Andrew Schaap and Edwina Howell. Abingdon, Oxon: Routledge, Taylor & Francis, 2013.

Howson, P. *The Howson Diaries: The Life of Politics*. Ringwood, Vic: Penguin Books, 1984.

Howson, P., and R. Hunt. *Press Statement issued by the Minister for the Interior, Hon. Ralph Hunt, and the Minister for the Environment, Aborigines and Arts, Hon. Peter Howson*. Canberra ACT, 29 July 1972.

Hyde, B., and J. L. Bineham. 'From debate to dialogue: Toward a pedagogy of nonpolarized public discourse'. *Southern Communication Journal* 65, no. 2 (2000): 208–23.

Human Rights and Equal Opportunity Commission. *Bringing Them Home: National Inquiry into the Separation of Aboriginal and Torres Strait Islander Children from Their Families*. Sydney, NSW: Commonwealth of Australia, 1997.

Isaacs, W. *Dialogue and the art of thinking together. A pioneering approach to communicating in business and in life*. New York: Doubleday, 1999.

Isaacs, W. N. 'Towards an Action Theory of Dialogue'. *International Journal of Public Administration* 24, no. 7 (2001): 709–48.

———. 'Taking Flight: Dialogue, Collective Thinking, and Organizational Learning'. *Organizational Dynamics* 22, no. 2 (1993): 24–39.

James, M. R. 'Critical Intercultural Dialogue'. *Polity* 31, no. 4 (1999): 587–607.

Jenlink, P. M. 'The Power of Dialogue on Social Systems'. In *Dialogue as a Collective Means of Design Conversation*, edited by Patrick M. Jenlink and Bela H. Banathy. New York: Springer, 2008.

Johnson, E. *National Report, Overview and Recommendations*. Royal Commission into Aboriginal Deaths in Custody. Canberra, ACT: Commonwealth of Australia, Australian Government Printing Service, 1991.

———. *The Process of Reconciliation*, chapter 38. Royal Commission into Aboriginal Deaths in Custody. National Report, Volume 5. Canberra, ACT: Commonwealth of Australia, Australian Government Printing Service, 1991.

Kalantzis, M., and B. Cope. 'An opportunity to change the culture'. In *The Retreat From Tolerance*, edited by Phillip Adams. Sydney, NSW: ABC Books, 1997.

Karsten A., and B. Küntzel. *Forum on Intercultural Dialogue: Discussion paper based on the Forum on Intercultural Dialogue, 22–26 November 2006*. Strasbourg, France: Council of Europe, 2006: 1–21. Accessed 9 September 2011. http://doku.cac.at/intercultural_dialogue_discussion_paper.pdf.

Keal, P. *European Conquest and the Rights of Indigenous Peoples*. United Kingdom: Cambridge University Press, 2003.

Keating, P. *Redfern Reprise: 23rd Anniversary of Redfern Speech*. Address by Hon. Paul Keating, Australian Museum. Sydney, 9 December 2015. Accessed 17 April 2019.

www.keating.org.au/shop/item/redfern-reprise-23rd-anniversary-of-redfern-speech.

———. 'Transcript of the Prime Minister'. The Hon. P. J. Keating MP, Doorstop. Parliament House, Canberra, ACT, 7 November 1993.

———. 'Press Conference'. Transcript of the Prime Minister. The Hon. P. J. Keating MP. Parliament House, Canberra, ACT, 19 October 1993.

———. 'Mabo Negotiations'. Statement by the Prime Minister. The Hon. P. J. Keating MP, Canberra, ACT, 7 October 1993.

———. 'Mabo—The truth about consultation'. Statement by the Prime Minister. The Hon. P. J. Keating MP, Sydney, NSW, 6 August 1993.

———. Transcript of the Prime Minister. The Hon. P. J. Keating MP. Interview with Paul Murphy, Dateline SBS, 28 July 1993.

———. 'Address by the Prime Minister'. The Hon. P. J. Keating MP. National Press Club, Canberra, ACT, 22 July 1993.

———. 'Statement by the Prime Minister'. The Hon. P. J. Keating MP. Canberra ACT, 18 June 181993.

———. 'Statement by the Prime Minister'. The Hon. P. J. Keating MP. Council of Australian Governments Meeting, Melbourne, 9 June 1993.

———. 'Australian Launch of the International Year for the World's Indigenous People'. Speech. Redfern, NSW, 19 December 1992.

Kelly, P. *The End of Certainty. Power, Politics and Business in Australia.* St Leonards, NSW: Allen & Unwin, 1994.

Kelman, H. C. 'Group Processes in the Resolution of International Conflicts'. *American Psychologist* 53, no. 3 (1997): 212–20.

Keon-Cohen, B., and B. Morse. 'Indigenous land rights in Australia and Canada'. In *Aborigines and the Law,* edited by Peter Hanks and Bryan Keon-Cohen. North Sydney, NSW: George Allen & Unwin, 1984.

Kernot, C. 'Democrats Welcome Mabo Outcome'. Media Release. Senator Cheryl Kernot, Australian Democrats, Canberra, ACT, 19 October 1993.

Kimberley Land Council. 'Transcript of Richard Court's meeting with the Kimberley Land Council Executive and Representatives of the Council of Kimberley Aboriginal Organisations'. Purnululu National Park, Friday, 30 July 1993.

Lane West-Newman, C. 'Anger in Legacies of Empire, Indigenous Peoples and Settler States'. *European Journal of Social Theory* 7, no. 2 (2004): 189–208.

Lange, L. 'Dialogue, History, and Power: The Role of Truth'. In *Philosophy and Aboriginal Rights: Critical Dialogues,* edited by Sandra Tomsons and Lorraine Mayer. Oxford: Oxford University Press, 2013.

Leigh, A. 'Leadership and Aboriginal Reconciliation'. *The Australian Journal of Social Issues* 37, no. 2, (2002): 131–52.

Libby, R. T. *Hawke's Law, The Politics of Mining and Aboriginal Land Rights in Australia.* Nedlands, WA: University of Western Australia Press, 1989.

Lindley, M. F. *The Acquisition of Government of backward Territory in International Law.* London: Longmans, Green and Co., 1926.

Locke, J. *Two Treatise of Government.* New York: Hafner Publishing, 1947.

———. *The Second Treatise of Civil Government,* chapter 5, # 34. First Published 1690. E-book with text derived from sixth edition, 1764. University of Adelaide Library, South Australia. Last updated 17 December 2014. Accessed 10 September 2019. https://ebooks.adelaide.edu.au/l/locke/john/l81s/complete.html.

Lovell, M. 'Settler Colonialism, Multiculturalism and the Politics of Postcolonial Identity'. Australasian Political Studies Association Conference, Melbourne. 23–26 September 2007. Accessed 1 May 2013. https://digitalcollections.anu.edu.au/bitstream/1885/9387/3/Lovell_Settler2007.pdf.

Lundy, P., and M. McGovern. 'Whose Justice? Rethinking Transitional Justice from the Bottom Up'. *Journal of Law and Society* 35, no. 2 (2008): 265–92.

Lynch, T., and R. Reavell. 'Through the Looking Glass: Hanson, Howard and the Politics of "Political Correctness"'. In *Pauline Hanson, One Nation and Australian*

Politics, edited by Bligh Grant. Armidale, NSW: University of New England Press, 1997.

MacDonald, L., and P. Muldoon. 'Globalisation, Neo-liberalism and the Struggle for Indigenous Citizenship'. *Australian Journal of Political Science* 41, no. 2 (2006): 209–23.

Macoun, A. 'Aboriginality and the Northern Territory Intervention'. *Australian Journal of Political Science* 46, no. 3 (2011): 516–31.

Maddison, S. 'Settler Australia in the Twentieth Century'. In *The Routledge Handbook of the History of Settler Colonialism*, edited by Edward Cavanagh and Lorenzo Veracini. Abingdon, Oxon, UK: Routledge, 2017.

———. *Beyond White Guilt: The real challenge for black-white relations in Australia*. Crows Nest, NSW: Allen & Unwin, 2011.

Maddox, G. *Australian Democracy in Theory and Practice*. Fifth Edition. Frenchs Forest, NSW: Pearson Education Australia, 2005.

Maguire, A. 'Law Protecting Rights: Restoring the law of self-determination in the neo-colonial world'. *Law Text, Culture* 12 (2008): 12–39.

Makarrata Report. National Aboriginal Conference Sub Committee on the Makarrata. Canberra (undated). Accessed 6 June 2014. https://aiatsis.gov.au/collections/collections-online/digitised-collections/treaty/national-aboriginal-conference.

Manne, R. 'Comment, The History Wars'. *The Monthly* (November 2009): 15–17.

———. 'In Denial: The Stolen Generations and the Right'. *Quarterly Essay*, no. 1 (2001): 1–113.

Mansell, M. *Treaty and Statehood: Aboriginal Self-Determination*. Leichhardt, NSW: The Federation Press, 2016.

———. 'Is the Constitution a better tool than simple legislation to advance the cause of Aboriginal Peoples?' In *It's Our Country: Indigenous Arguments for Meaningful Constitutional Recognition and Reform*, edited by Megan Davis and Marcia Langton. Carlton, Vic: Melbourne University Press, 2016.

———. 'Mabo—Good and Bad for Aborigines'. Press Release of Michael Mansell. National Secretary, Aboriginal Provisional Government, 19 October 1993.

Markus, A. *Race: John Howard and the remaking of Australia*. Crows Nest, NSW: Allen & Unwin, 2001.

———. 'Between Mabo and a hard place: race and the contradictions of conservatism'. In *In the age of Mabo: History, Aborigines and Australia*, edited by Bain Attwood. St Leonards, NSW: Allen & Unwin, 1996.

Massola, A. *Coranderrk. A History of the Aboriginal Station*. Kilmore, Vic: Lowden Publishing Co., 1975.

McCoy, M. L. and P. L. Scully. 'Deliberative Dialogue to Expand Civic Engagement: What Kind of Talk Does Democracy Need?' *National Civic Review* 91, no. 2 (2002): 117–35.

McEwen, J. *The Northern Territory of Australia: Commonwealth Government's Policy with respect to Aboriginals*. Canberra, ACT: Department of the Interior, February 1939. Accessed 30 October 2013. http://nla.gov.au/nla.aus-vn4690481.

McGregor, R. 'Another Nation: Aboriginal Activism in the late 1960s and Early 1970'. *Australian Historical Studies* 40, no. 3 (2009): 343–60.

———. *Imagined Destinies, Aboriginal Australians and the Doomed Race Theory, 1880–1939*. Carlton South, Vic: Melbourne University Press, 1997.

McKenna, M. 'Moment of Truth: History and Australia's Future'. *Quarterly Essay* 69 (March 2018): 1–86.

———. 'Different Perspectives on Black Armband History'. *Department of Parliamentary Library*. Information and Research Service, Research Paper No. 5 (1997).

McMahon, W. *Australian Aborigines, Commonwealth Policy and Achievements*. Statement by the Prime Minister. The Rt. Hon. William McMahon, 26 January 1972.

———. *Statement by the Prime Minister the Rt. Hon. William McMahon to the Conference of Commonwealth and State Ministers Responsible for Aboriginal Affairs*. Cairns, 23 April 1971.

McMillan, M. and S. Rigney. 'Race, reconciliation, and justice in Australia: from denial to acknowledgment'. *Ethnic and Racial Studies* 41, no. 4 (2018): 759–77.

McNeil, K. *Common Law Aboriginal Title*. Oxford: Clarendon Press, 1989.

McPherson, B. H. *The Reception of English Law Abroad*. Brisbane: The Supreme Court of Queensland Library, 2007.

Mellor, D., and D. Bretherton. 'Reconciliation between Black and White Australia: the Role of Social Memory'. In *The Role of Memory in Ethnic Conflict*, edited by Ed Cairns and Mícheál D. Roe. New York: Palgrave MacMillan, 2003.

Miller, R. J., J. Ruru, L. Behrendt and T. Lindberg. *Discovering Indigenous Lands. The Doctrine of Discovery in the English Colonies*. Oxford: Oxford University Press, 2010.

Moran, E. 'Is reconciliation in Australia a dead end?'. *Australian Journal of Human Rights* 12, no. 1 (2006): 109–40.

Morgan, H. M. 'Mabo Reconsidered'. The Joe and Enid Lyons Memorial Lecture. Australian National University, 12 October 1992.

Morphy, H. 'Title to their land'. *Quadrant* 22, no. 9 (1978): 36–39.

Moses, A. Dirk. 'An antipodean genocide? The origins of the genocidal moment in the colonization of Australia'. *Journal of Genocide Research* 2, no. 1 (2000): 89–106.

Muldoon, P. 'Reconciliation and Political Legitimacy: The Old Australia and the New South Africa'. *Australian Journal of Politics and History* 49, no. 2 (2003): 182–96.

Muldoon, P., and A. Schaap. 'The constitutional politics of the Aboriginal Embassy'. In *The Aboriginal Tent Embassy. Sovereignty, Black Power, land Rights and the State*, edited by Gary Foley, Andrew Schaap and Edwina Howell. Abingdon, Oxon: Routledge, Taylor & Francis, 2013.

Nanni, G., and A. James. *Coranderrk. We Will Show the Country*. Canberra, ACT Aboriginal Studies Press, 2013.

National Aboriginal Conference. *The Makarrata. Some Ways Forward*. Position Paper delivered to the World Council of Indigenous Peoples Canberra, 1981.

National Farmers Federation. 'NFF calls on Prime Minister to act on Wik'. News Release, 31 January 1997.

Nettelbeck, A. '"A Halo of Protection": Colonial Protector and the Principle of Aboriginal Protection through Punishment'. *Australian Historical Studies* 43, no. 3 (2012): 396–411.

Nettheim, G. 'Western Australia v The Commonwealth: The Wororra Peoples and Anor v Western Australia; Teddy Biljabu and Ors v Western Australia', *Aboriginal Law Bulletin* 3, Issue 73 (1995): 4–7.

Newfong, J. 'The Aboriginal Embassy: Its purpose and aims'. *Aboriginal & Islander Identity* 1, no. 5, 4–6 July 1972. Aboriginal Publications Foundation: Perth.

O'Connell, J. F., and J. Allen. 'Dating the colonization of Sahul (Pleistocene Australia–New Guinea): A review of recent research'. *The Journal of Archaeological Science* 31 (2004): 835–53.

O'Donoghue, L. 'Past wrongs, future rights'. *Indigenous Law Bulletin* 4, Issue 1, (1997): 18–21.

O'Neill, N., S. Rice and R. Douglas, eds. *Retreat from Injustice: Human Rights in Australia*. Second Edition. Leichhardt, NSW: The Federation Press, 2004.

Patten, J. T. 'Our Historic Day of Mourning and Protest'. Aborigines Conference. Held at Australian Hall, Sydney, 26 January 1938. Report of Proceedings. *The Australian Abo Call*. April 1938, 2. Accessed 19 September 2013. http://www.aiatsis.gov.au/_files/archives/r000006632049n1p2.pdf.

Patten, J. T. 'Our Ten Points'. *The Australian Abo Call*. April 1938. Accessed 11 October 2013. http://www.aiatsis.gov.au/_files/archive/r000006632049n1p1.pdf.

Patten, J. T. and W. Ferguson. *Aborigines Claim Citizen Rights: A Statement of the Case for the Aborigines Progressive Association*. Sydney, NSW: The Publicist, 1938.

Patton, P. 'Mabo and Australian Society: Towards a Postmodern Republic'. *The Australian Journal of Anthropology* 6, nos. 1 and 2 (1995): 83–94.

'Paul Coe and Bobbi Sykes. Monday Conference Interview'. ABC Television, 20 March 1972. In *The Aboriginal Tent Embassy. Sovereignty, Black Power, Land Rights and the*

State, edited by Gary Foley, Andrew Schaap and Edwina Howell. Abingdon, Oxon: Routledge Taylor & Francis, 2014.

'Paul Keating Redfern Park Speech'. 10 December 1992, *Indigenous Law Bulletin* 5, Issue 11 (August/September 2001): 9–11.

Pearson, N. 'There's no such thing as minimal recognition—There is only recognition'. In *It's Our Country: Indigenous Arguments for Meaningful Constitutional Recognition and Reform,* edited by Megan Davis and Marcia Langton. Carlton, Vic: Melbourne University Press, 2016.

———. 'Process of recognition: The constitutional recognition of Indigenous Australians requires meaningful consultation'. *The Monthly.* (August 2015). Accessed 26 April 2018. https://www.themonthly.com.au/issue/2015/august/1438351200/noel-pearson/process-recognition.

———. 'A troubling inheritance'. *Race & Class* 35, no. 4 (1994): 1–9.

———. '204 Years of Invisible Title'. In *Mabo: A Judicial Revolution,* edited by M. A. Stephenson and Suri Ratnapala. St Lucia, QLD: University of QLD Press, 1993.

Perkins, C. *A Bastard Like Me.* Sydney, NSW: Ure Smith, 1975.

Pitty, R. 'The political aspects of creating a treaty'. In *What Good Conditions? Reflections on an Australian Aboriginal Treaty 1986–2006,* edited by Peter Read, Gary Meyers and Bob Reece. Canberra, ACT: ANU E Press, 2006.

Pratt, A. *Practising Reconciliation? The Politics of Reconciliation in the Australian Parliament 1991–2000.* Parliament of Australia, Department of Parliamentary Services, 2005.

Pratt, A., and S. Bennett. *The end of ATSIC and the future administration of Indigenous affairs.* Parliamentary Library, Information and Research Services, 2004.

Preston, J. 'Neoliberal settler colonialism, Canada and the tar sands'. *Race & Class* 55, no. 2 (2013): 42–59.

Price, A. G. *The Explorations of Captain James Cook in the Pacific as told by selections of his own Journals 1768 – 1779.* New York: Dover Publications Inc., 1971.

Pruitt, B., and P. Thomas. *Democratic Dialogue: A handbook for practitioners.* New York: The General Secretariat of the Organisation of American States, and the United Nations Development Program, 2007.

Ramirez, J. M. 'Peace Through Dialogue'. *International Journal on World Peace* 14, no.1 (2007): 65–81.

Read, P. 'Doubts about treaty: some reflections on the Aboriginal Treaty Committee'. In *What Good Conditions? Reflections on an Australian Aboriginal Treaty 1986-2006,* edited by Peter Read, Gary Meyers and Bob Reece. Canberra, ACT: ANU E Press, 2006.

———. *Charles Perkins . A Biography.* Ringwood, Vic: Penguin Books Australia, 1990.

Reconciliation Australia and Healing Foundation. *Truth Telling Symposium Report.* 5–6 October 2018.

Reconciliation Australia. *Grounded in Truth, Walk Together with Courage.* National Reconciliation Week 2019. Accessed 7 June 2019. https://www.reconciliation.org.au/wp-content/uploads/2019/05/ra-nrw-2019-guide_v8.pdf.

Reed, A. W. *Captain Cook in Australia: Extracts from the journals of Captain James Cook.* Wellington: New Zealand, A H & A W Reed, 1969.

Reed, L. '"Mrs Bon's Verandah Full of Aboriginals", Race, Class, Gender and Friendship'. *History Australia* 2, no. 2 (2005): 1–15.

Report from the Select Committee on Aborigines (British Settlements). Great Britain Parliament, House of Commons. Select Committee on Aboriginal Tribes. London, 1837.

Resolutions by National Conference of Aboriginal Councillors. Canberra, 10–11 August 1972. National Archives of Australia.

Restrepo, P. 'Some Epistemic and Methodological Challenges within an Intercultural Experience'. *Journal of Historical Sociology* 24, no. 1 (2011): 45–61.

Reynolds, H. 'Reviving Indigenous Sovereignty'. *Macquarie Law Journal* 6 (2006): 5–12.

————. *Aboriginal Sovereignty, Reflections on race, state and nation*. St Leonards: Allen & Unwin, 1996.

————. *Dispossession: Black Australians and White Invaders*. St Leonards: Allen & Unwin, 1989.

Ritter, D. 'The "Rejection of Terra Nullius" in Mabo: A Critical Analysis'. *Sydney Law Review* 5 (1996): 5–33.

Roberts, N. C. 'Calls for Dialogue'. In *The Transformative Power of Dialogue*, edited by Nancy Charlotte Roberts. London: Elsevier Book Series, 2002.

Roberts-Wray, K. *Commonwealth and Colonial Law*. London: Stevens & Sons Ltd, 1966.

Robbins, E. J. 'Self-Determination or Welfare Colonialism: Aborigines and Federal Policy Making'. PhD Dissertation, Flinders University, South Australia, 1994.

Robbins, J. 'The Howard Government and Indigenous Rights: An Imposed national Unity?' *Australian Journal of Political Science* 42, no. 2 (2007): 315–28.

Robinson, S. 'The Aboriginal Embassy: An Account of the protests of 1972'. *Aboriginal History* 118, no. 1 (1994): 49–63.

————. 'The Aboriginal Embassy'. Master of Arts, Australian National University, 1993.

Rosenfeld, M. 'Modern Constitutionalism as Interplay Between Identity And Diversity: An Introduction'. *Cardozo Law Review* 14 (1993): 497–531.

Rouhana, N. 'Reconciling History and Equal Citizenship in Israel: Democracy and the Politics of Historical Denial'. In *The Politics of Reconciliation in Multicultural Societies*, edited by Will Kymlicka and Bashir Bashir. Oxford: Oxford University Press, 2008.

Rowse, T. *Obliged to be Difficult. Nugget Coombs' Legacy in Indigenous Affairs*. Cambridge: Cambridge University Press, 2000.

Russell, P. H. *Recognising Aboriginal Title. The Mabo Case and Indigenous Resistance to English-Settler Colonialism*. Sydney, NSW: University of NSW Press Ltd, 2005.

Sammut, G., and G. Gaskell. 'Points of View, Social Positioning and Intercultural Relations'. *Journal for the Theory of Social Behaviour* 40, no. 1 (2009): 47–64.

Sanders, W. *Towards an Indigenous order of Australian Government: Rethinking self-determination as Indigenous affairs policy*. Canberra, ACT: Centre for Aboriginal Economic Policy Research, Australian National University, 2002.

'Savages and Civilised Men'. *Science of Man*. Dr A. Carroll, ed. *Journal of the Royal Anthropological Society of Australasia* 2, no. 6 and 21 (March 1903), 34. Accessed 1 November 2018. http://nla.gov.au/nla.obj-525829330.pdf.

Secher, U. 'The High Court and Recognition of Native Title: Distinguishing between the Doctrine of Terra Nullius and "Desert and Uncultivated"' *University Western Sydney Law Review* 11 (2007): 1–39.

Senate Legal and Constitutional References Committee. *Healing: A Legacy of Generations*. The Report of the Inquiry into the Federal Government's Implementation of the Recommendations Made by the Human Rights and Equal Opportunity Commission in *Bringing Them Home*. Canberra, ACT: Commonwealth of Australia, November 2000.

Schaap, A. 'Political Reconciliation Through A Struggle for Recognition'. *Social & Legal Studies* 13, no. 4 (2004): 523–40.

Schwarz, J. 'Beyond Familiar Territory: Decentering the Centre (An analysis of visual strategies in the art of Robert Smithson, Alfredo Jaar and the Bark Petitions of Yirrkala)'. PhD Dissertation, Australian National University, 1999.

Short, D. 'Australia: a continuing genocide?'. *Journal of Genocide Research* 12, nos. 1–2 (2010): 45–68.

————. *Reconciliation and Colonial Power: Indigenous Rights in Australia*. Hampshire, England: Ashgate Publishing Group, 2008.

————. 'The Social Construction of Indigenous "Native Title" Land Rights in Australia'. *Current Sociology* 55, no. 6 (2007): 857–76.

Simpson, G. 'Mabo, International Law, Terra Nullius and the Stories of Settlement: An Unresolved Jurisprudence'. *Melbourne University Law Review* 19 (1993–1994): 195–210.

Smith, L. Tuhiwai. *Decolonizing Methodologies: Research and Indigenous Peoples.* Second Edition. London, UK: Zed Books, 2012.

Souter, G. 'Skeleton at the Feast'. In *Australians 1938,* edited by Bill Gammage and Peter Spearritt. Sydney, NSW: Fairfax, Syme & Weldon Associates, 1987.

'Speeches at the Aboriginal Embassy 30 July 1972'. Recorded by Derek Freeman. In *The Aboriginal Tent Embassy: Sovereignty, Black Power, land Rights and the State,* edited by Gary Foley, Andrew Schaap and Edwina Howell. Abingdon, Oxon: Routledge, Taylor & Francis, 2013.

Strakosch, E., and A. Macoun. 'The Vanishing Endpoint of Settler Colonialism'. In *Stolen Lands, Broken Cultures: The Settler-Colonial Present,* edited by John Hinkson, Paul James and Lorenzo Veracini. North Carlton, Vic: Arena Publications, 2012.

Standfield, R. '"These unoffending people": myth, history and the idea of Aboriginal resistance in David Collins Account of the English Colony in New South Wales'. In *Myth, Memory and Indigenous Australia,* edited by Francis Peters-Little, Ann Curthoys and John Docker. Canberra: ANU E Press, 2010.

Tannen, D. *The Argument Culture.* New York: Random House, 1998.

Tickner, R. *Taking a Stand. Land Rights to Reconciliation.* Crows Nest, NSW: Allen & Unwin, 2001.

————. 'The importance of Negotiation and Certainty'. Media Release. The Hon. Robert Tickner MP. Minister for Aboriginal and Torres Strait Islander Affairs, Canberra, ACT, 28 July 1993.

'Tim Fischer on ABC Radio PM Program'. 16 May 1997. Quoted in ATSIC. *The Ten Point Plan on Wik and Native Title: Issues for Indigenous Peoples.* Canberra, ACT: Aboriginal and Torres Strait Islander Commission, 1997.

Toohey, P. 'Last Drinks: The Impact of the Northern Territory Intervention'. *Quarterly Essay,* no. 3 (2008): 1–97.

Truth and Reconciliation Commission of Canada. *Honouring the Truth, Reconciling for the Future, Summary of the Final Report of the Truth and Reconciliation Commission of Canada.* Winnipeg: Truth and Reconciliation Commission Canada, 2015.

————. *Canada's Residential Schools: Reconciliation, The Final Report of the Truth and Reconciliation Commission of Canada.* Volume 6. Montreal, Quebec: McGill-Queen's University Press, 2015.

Two Hundred Years Later . . . Report by the Senate Standing Committee on Constitutional and Legal Affairs on the feasibility of a compact or 'Makarrata' between the Commonwealth and Aboriginal people. Canberra, ACT: Commonwealth of Australia, Australian Government Publishing Service, 1983.

Tully, J. 'Consent, Hegemony, and Dissent in Treaty Negotiations'. In *Between Consenting Peoples. Political Community and the Meaning of Consent,* edited by Jeremy Webber and Colin M Macleod. Vancouver, British Columbia: The University of British Columbia Press, 2010.

————. *Public Philosophy in a New Key, Volume 1: Democracy and Civic Freedom.* Cambridge, UK: Cambridge University Press, 2008.

————. 'Recognition and Dialogue: The Emergence of a New Field'. *Critical Review of International Social and Political Philosophy* 7, no. 3 (2004): 84–106.

————. 'A Fair and Just Relationship. The Vision of the Canadian Royal Commission on Aboriginal Peoples'. *Meanjin* 57, no. 1, (1998): 146–66.

————. *Strange Multiplicity. Constitutionalism in an age of diversity.* Cambridge, UK: Cambridge University Press, 1995.

————. 'Aboriginal property and Western theory: Recovering a middle ground'. *Social Philosophy and Policy Foundation* 11, no. 2 (1994): 153–80.

Turnbull, M., G. Brandis and N. Scullion. *Response to Referendum Council's Report on Constitutional Recognition.* Department of Prime Minister and Cabinet, Australian Government, 26 October 2017. Accessed 8 November 2019. https://ministers.pmc.gov.au/scullion/2017/response-referendum-councils-report-constitutional-recognition.

Van der Walt, C. V. Franchi and G. Stevens. 'The South African Truth and Reconciliation Commission: "Race", historical compromise and transitional democracy'. *International Journal of Intercultural Relations* 27 (2003): 251–67.

Veracini, L. *Settler Colonialism: A Theoretical Overview*. Basingstoke, UK: Palgrave Macmillan, 2010.

———. Settler Colonialism and Decolonisation, Borderlands e-journal [Online] (2007). Accessed 1 May 2013. http://www.borderlands.net.au/vol6no2_2007/veracini_settler.htm.

Watson, I. 'Indigenous Peoples' Law-Ways: Survival Against the Colonial State'. *The Australian Feminist Law Journal* 8 (1997): 39–58.

Watson, V. 'From the "quiet revolution" to "crisis" in Australian Indigenous affairs'. *Cultural Studies Review* 15, no. 1 (2009): 88–109.

Weaver, S. M. 'Australian Aboriginal Policy: Aboriginal Pressure Groups or Government Advisory Bodies?'. *Oceania* 54, no. 1 (1983): 1–22.

Wells, E. *Reward and Punishment in Arnhem Land 1962 – 1963*. Canberra, ACT: Australian Institute of Aboriginal Studies, 1982.

Wheatley, S. 'Deliberative Democracy and Minorities'. *European Journal of International Law* 14, no. 3 (2003): 507–27.

Whitlam, G. *Aboriginal and Society*. Statement by the Prime Minister. The Hon. E. G. Whitlam. Conference of Commonwealth and State Ministers concerned with Aboriginal Affairs. Adelaide: Department of Prime Minister and Cabinet, Friday, 6 April 1973.

———. *The closure of the Aboriginal Embassy*. Statement by the Leader of the Opposition. Canberra ACT, 20 July 1972.

Williams, R. 'Why Should I Feel Guilty? Reflections on the Workings of Guilt in White-Aboriginal Relations'. *Australian Psychologist* 35, no. 2 (2000): 136–42.

Willshire, W. H. *The Aborigines of Central Australia*. Adelaide, SA: Government Printer, North Terrace, 1891. Accessed 1 November 2018. https://digital.library.adelaide.edu.au/dspace/bitstream/2440/18481/1/Willshire1.pdf.

Wolfe, P. 'Settler Colonialism and the elimination of the native'. *Journal of Genocide Research* 8, no. 4 (2006): 387–409.

Wright, J. *We call for a Treaty*. Sydney, NSW: Fontana, 1985.

Wright, S. *International Human Rights, Decolonisation and Globalisation*. London and New York: Routledge, 2001.

Wyatt, K. *Looking Forward, Looking Back*. 19th Annual Vincent Lingiari Memorial Lecture. Charles Darwin University, Thursday, 15 August 2019. Accessed 26 August 2019. https://ministers.pmc.gov.au/wyatt/2019/19th-annual-vincent-lingiari-memorial-lecture-charles-darwin-university.

———. *Walking in Partnership to Effect Change*. National Press Club Address. Department of Prime Minister and Cabinet, Australian Government, 10 July 2019. Accessed 18 August 2019. https://ministers.pmc.gov.au/wyatt/2019/national-press-club-address-walking-partnership-effect-change.

Yankelovich, D. *The Magic of Dialogue: Transforming Conflict into Cooperation*. New York: Simon & Schuster, 1999.

Zoller, H. M. 'A place you haven't visited before: Creating the conditions for community dialogue'. *Southern Communication Journal* 65, no. 2 (2000): 191–207.

Newspapers Articles

'150 Years After'. *The Sydney Morning Herald*, Tuesday 18 January 1938, 10.

'A price on our guilt'. *The Australian*, Wednesday 26 January 1972, 8.

'A Turning Point'. *The Canberra Times*, Friday 21 July 1972, 2.

'Aboriginal Art'. *The Sydney Morning Herald*, Saturday 22 January 1938, 10.

'Aboriginal Conference. Demand on land ownership'. *The Canberra Times*, Friday 11 August 1972, 1.

'Aboriginal Petition on Bark. Novel Plea by Tribal Group'. *The Canberra Times*, Thursday 15 August 1963, 3.

'Aboriginal treaty by 'mid-1990'. *The Canberra Times*, Monday 13 June 1988, 3.

'Aboriginal women gather for conference'. *The Canberra Times*, Friday 28 January 1972, 3.

'Aborigines' Protest'. *The Argus*, Melbourne, Monday 17 January 1938, 10.

'Aborigines stake claim on Capitol Hill'. *The Canberra Times*, Wednesday 8 August 1979.

'Aborigines to fly flag'. *The Canberra Times*, Wednesday 2 February 1972, 3;

'Aborigines' Day of Mourning. Emotional Protest Criticised, David Unaipon's Statement'. *The Sydney Morning Herald*, Thursday 13 January 1938, 8.

'Anger as Government sells out over Mabo'. *Land Rights News*, October 1993, 3, 13.

'Black power on the march'. *The Sun*, Wednesday 27 January 1988.

'Call for draft Makarrata proposal'. *The Canberra Times*, Friday 28 August 1981, 8.

'Cautious support in all but the west'. *The Canberra Times*, 20 October 1993, 14.

'Celebrating Freedom'. *The Canberra Times*, Tuesday 26 January 1988, 2.

'Colin Barnett links closure of remote Aboriginal communities to child abuse'. *The Guardian*, Friday 20 March 2015. Accessed 19 July 2015. http://www.theguardian.com/australia-news/2015/mar/20/colin-barnett-links-closure-of-remote-aboriginal-communities-to-child-abuse.

'Court ruling ends foolish adventure'. Editorial. *The West Australian*, Friday 17 March 1995, 14.

'Court: Act on Mabo'. *Northern Territory News*, 13 May 1993.

'Courts $4m Mabo Folly'. *The West Australian*, Friday 17 March 1995, 1.

'Criticism follows 'embassy' action'. *The Canberra Times*, Friday 21 July 1972, 3.

'Decision the basis of discrimination'. *The Canberra Times*, 20 October 1993, 14.

'Fischer pushes For Mabo change'. *The West Australian*, 8 February 1997, 36.

'House Hears Plea in Strange Tongue'. *The Age*, Thursday 15 August 1963.

'Howson hits black power sign'. *The Sydney Morning Herald*, 29 January 1972.

'Labor left warns PM of flaws in Mabo law'. *The Australian*, 26 July 1993, 2.

'Labor promises Aborigines land'. *The Canberra Times*, Wednesday 9 February 1972, 3.

'"New Deal" Policy, Education of Aborigines'. *The Argus*, Wednesday 14 December 1938, 13.

'No reason to feel guilty, says Fraser'. *The Canberra Times*, Saturday 23 January 1988, 3.

'Police to move Aboriginal embassy'. *The Canberra Times*, Tuesday, 18 July 1972, 1.

'Rehearsal at Farm Cove, Preparation for Pageant'. *The Sydney Morning Herald*, Saturday 15 January 1938, 11.

'Rural groups urging new negotiations'. *The Canberra Times*, 20 October 1993, 14.

'Victorious Day in the High Court'. *Kimberley Land Council News*, June 1995, no. 1, 5.

'We Call for A Treaty Within Australia, Between Australians'. *The National Times*, Week Ending 25 August 1979, 13.

Allam, L. 'Pat Dodson urges Coalition to "deal with" Indigenous voice to parliament and referendum'. *The Guardian*, Wednesday 5 June 2019. Accessed 6 August 2019. https://www.theguardian.com/australia-news/2019/jun/05/pat-dodson-urges-coalition-to-deal-with-indigenous-voice-to-parliament-and-referendum.

Bita, N. and Nason, D. 'Perron slated for hygiene remark'. *The Australian*, 8 July 1993, 5.

Blainey, G. 'Land rights for all'. *The Age*, 10 November 1993, 15.

———. 'Mabo: what Aboriginals lost'. *The Age*, 31 July 1993.

Brough, J. 'Govt backs off after black leaders' blast'. *The Canberra Times*, 4 June 1993, 1, 4.

Brown, G. and Taylor, P. 'Morrison to veto "voice" as part of Constitution'. *The Australian*, Friday, 12 July 2019. Accessed 6 August 2019. https://www.theaustralian.com.au/nation/politics/morrison-to-veto-voice-as-part-of-constitution/news-story/c9753bbe3595470032ac7fa95636931e.

Brown, K., and M. Duffield. 'Lawyers kept hopes high'. *The West Australian*, Friday 17 March 1995, 6.

Burton, T. 'How the Mabo pact was struck'. *The Financial Review*, 20 October 1993, 1 and 10.

Chamberlin, P. 'Black fury over Mabo deal'. *The Sydney Morning Herald*, 9 October 1993, 1.

———. 'Mabo Paper 'A Slimy Document'. *Sydney Morning Herald*, 4 June 1993.

———. 'Mining Chief Lashes Mabo'. *The Sydney Morning Herald*, 1 July 1993.

Cole-Adams, P. 'Backroom Mabo wrangling ends in coup for Keating'. *The Canberra Times*, 20 October 1993, 13.

Crowe, D. 'On Indigenous recognition, the PM has already drawn a line that might be impossible to cross'. *The Sydney Morning Herald*, Thursday 11 July 2019. Accessed 15 August 2019. https://www.smh.com.au/politics/federal/on-indigenous-recognition-the-pm-has-already-drawn-a-line-that-might-be-impossible-to-cross-20190711-p526c8.html.

Davidson, H. 'Ken Wyatt warned Indigenous Australians will throw constitution into seas unless recognition resolved'. *The Guardian*, Saturday 3 August 2019. Accessed 6 August 2019. https://www.theguardian.com/australia-news/2019/aug/03/ken-wyatt-warned-indigenous-australians-will-throw-constitution-into-sea-unless-recognition-resolved.

———. 'WA plan to close 100 remote and Indigenous communities 'devastating'. *The Guardian*, Tuesday, 18 November 2014. Accessed 19 July 2015. http://www.theguardian.com/australia-news/2014/nov/18/wa-plan-to-close-100-remote-and-indigenous-communities-devastating.

Dixon, R., and S. Freeman-Greene. 'The Mabo Dreaming'. Opinion Analysis. *The Age*, 20 October 1993, 19.

Dodson, P. 'Intervention turned our backs on reconciliation'. Opinion Piece. *The Sydney Morning Herald*, 20 August 2009, 17.

Editorial, 'A Shameful Back Down'. *The Canberra Times*, Thursday, 6 March 1986, 2.

Forbes, C. 'Aboriginal leader threatens to quit over discord'. *The Australia*, 6 October 1993, 3.

Gill, P. 'Miners put Mabo plan to Government'. *The Australian Financial Review*, 16 September 1993.

———. 'WA delays legislation clash over Mabo titles'. *The Australian Financial Review*, 16 September 1993.

Hammond, J., and J. Walker. *The Australian*, 13 May 1993, 1–2.

Harris, S. 'Treaty of Commitment. Replacing charity to Aborigines with real responsibility'. *The Canberra Times*, Wednesday 8 September 1976, 2.

Hewett, T., and M. Magazanik. 'Blacks culturally backward: Perron'. *The Age*, 7 July 1993.

Humphries, D., and M. Irving. 'Court's Bill on Mabo sets scene for federal fight'. *The Australian*, 29 October 1993, 1–2.

Karp, P. 'Scott Morrison claims Indigenous voice to parliament would be a third chamber'. *The Guardian*, Wednesday, 26 September 2018. Accessed 6 August 2019. https://www.theguardian.com/australia-news/2018/sep/26/scott-morrison-claims-indigenous-voice-to-parliament-would-be-a-third-chamber.

Kerr, J. F. 'Today's whites not guilty; today's blacks not harmed'. *The Canberra Times*, Tuesday 26 January 1988, 2.

Liddle, C. 'I Don't Want Your Recognise Campaign—It's Nothing but a Sham'. *The Guardian*, Monday, 18 August 2014. Accessed 26 April 2018. https://www.theguardian.com/commentisfree/2014/aug/18/i-dont-want-your-recognise-campaign-its-nothing-but-a-sham.

Medhora, S. 'Remote communities are 'lifestyle choices', says Tony Abbott'. *The Guardian*, Tuesday 10 March 2015. Accessed 19 July 2015. http://www.theguardian.com/australia-news/2015/mar/10/remote-communities-are-lifestyle-choices-says-tony-abbott.

Meertens, G. 'State acts over Mabo'. *The West Australian*, 17 May 1993, 5.

Middleton, K. 'Mick Dodson on fixing the constitution'. *The Saturday Paper*, Edition No. 177, 7–13 October 2017. Accessed 22 April 2019. https://www.thesaturdaypaper.com.au/news/politics/2017/10/07/mick-dodson-fixing-the-constitution/15072948005319.

Murphy, K. 'Ken Wyatt says he has Indigenous voice to parliament plan for Scott Morrison'. *The Guardian*, Thursday, 17 October 2019. Accessed 18 October 2019. https://www.theguardian.com/australia-news/2019/oct/17/ken-wyatt-says-he-has-indigenous-voice-to-parliament-plan-for-scott-morrison.

Observations of the Editor. *The Age*, Melbourne, 11 January 1888, 4 (column 6–7). Accessed 1 November 2018. https://trove.nla.gov.au/newspaper/page/18437362.

O'Leary, T. 'Advisory capacity to continue'. *The Canberra Times*, Wednesday 13 February 1974, 1, 3.

Peake, R. 'States defiant on land titles'. *The Canberra Times*, 10 June 1993, 1, 2.

———. 'State revolt over Mabo'. *The Canberra Times*, 9 June 1993, 1, 2.

———. 'Fischer inciting fear: PM'. *The Canberra Times*, Wednesday 13 January 1993, 3.

Pryer, W., and S. Manchee. 'Historic win in fight for land rights'. *The Western Australian*, 4 June 1992, 3.

Quekett, M. 'Court vows to fight decision'. *The West Australian*, Friday, 17 March 1995, 7.

Ramsey, A. 'Sicking on the dogs at 30,000 feet'. *The Sydney Morning Herald*, 16 October 1993, 33.

Reynolds, H. 'Western Australian justice won't come from within'. *The Sydney Morning Herald*, 22 November 1993.

Scott, K. 'Aborigines 'sold out' by Keating'. *The Canberra Times*, 9 October 1993, 1, 2.

———. 'Blacks bounce Govt on Mabo'. *The Canberra Times*, 6 August 1993, 1, 2.

———. 'Farm lobby attacks Libs'. *The Canberra Times*, 20 December 1993, 1.

———. 'Hewson gives backing to WA solo on Mabo'. *The Canberra Times*, 28 October 1993, 13.

———. 'Hope of native-title law passing by end of year'. *The Canberra Times*, 20 October 1993, 1, 2.

———. 'Mabo win a turning point: PM'. *The Canberra Times*, 22 December 1993, 1.

———. 'Treaty absurd: Howard "A form of apartheid"'. *The Canberra Times*, Tuesday 14 June 1988, 1.

Sexton, J., D. Nason and F. Kennedy. 'It fails on three fronts, says ATSIC'. *The Australian*, 3 September 1993, 2.

Solonec, T. 'The trauma of Oombulgurri's demolition will be repeated across Western Australia'. *The Guardian*, Thursday 27 November 2014. Accessed 3 December 2014. https://www.theguardian.com/commentisfree/2014/nov/27/the-trauma-of-oombulgurris-demolition-will-be-repeated-across-western-australia.

Stoney, K. 'Victory comes with mixed emotions'. *The West Australian*, Friday, 17 March 1995, 9.

Taylor, L. 'Coalition delay on Mabo Bill'. *The Australian*, 15 December 1993, 2.

———. 'Miners want all leases validated'. *The Australian Financial Review*, 4 February 1997, 2.

———. 'States' Wik action plan'. *The Australian Financial Review*, 6 February 1997, 1.

Taylor, L., and M. King. 'Keating defies Opposition on Mabo Bill'. *The Australian*, 21 December 1993.

Taylor, L. and Nason, D. 'Black negotiators 'negotiated away' basic rights'. *The Australian*, 12 November 1993, 6.

Tingle, L. '11th hour offer clinched Farley'. *The Australian*, 20 October 1993.

———. 'PM failed us on Mabo: Aborigines'. *The Weekend Australian*, 9–10 October 1993.

Tingle, L., and R. Jinman. 'We won't fund challenges to valid leases, black groups say'. *The Weekend Australian*, 30–31 October 1993, 4.

Wahlquist, C. 'Remote Aboriginal communities still in limbo despite release of "major reforms"'. *The Guardian*, Thursday 7 May 2015. Accessed 19 July 2015. http://www.theguardian.com/australia-news/2015/may/07/remote-aboriginal-communities-still-in-limbo-despite-release-of-major-reforms.

Walker, J., N. Bita and M. Irving. 'Fischer opens split on Mabo'. *The Australian*, 21 June 1993, 1–2.

Walker, J., and A. M. Moodie. 'Downer attacks Fischer outburst'. *The Australian*, 22 June 1993. 1.

Weigel, M. 'Political correctness: how the right invented a phantom enemy'. *The Guardian*, Wednesday 30 November 2016. Accessed 27 November 2018. https://www.theguardian.com/us-news/2016/nov/30/political-correctness-how-the-right-invented-phantom-enemy-donald-trump.

Willox, I. 'Mabo a national disaster: Hewson'. *The Age*, 11 December 1993, 6.

Willox, I., and M. Magazanik. 'Greens say they won't be hurried on Mabo'. *The Age*, 21 October 1993, 3.

Parliamentary Debates

Commonwealth of Australia. Parliamentary Debates. House of Representatives, Wednesday 13 February 2008, No. 1. (Hon. Kevin Rudd).

Commonwealth of Australia. Parliamentary Debates. House of Representatives, 22 December 1993, No. 191.

Commonwealth of Australia. Parliamentary Debates. House of Representatives, Tuesday 10 December 1996, No. 8. (Pauline Hanson).

Commonwealth of Australia. Parliamentary Debates. House of Representatives, 16 November 1993, No. 190.

Commonwealth of Australia. Parliamentary Debates. House of Representatives, Thursday 30 May 1991, No. 178. (Robert Tickner).

Commonwealth of Australia. Parliamentary Debates. House of Representatives, Tuesday 11 April 1989, No. 166.

Commonwealth of Australia. Parliamentary Debates. House of Representatives, Thursday 10 December 1987, No. 158.

Commonwealth of Australia. Parliamentary Debates. House of Representatives, Tuesday 18 March 1986, No. 147.

Commonwealth of Australia. Parliamentary Debates. House of Representatives, Wednesday 16 October 1985, No. 144. (David Connolly).

Commonwealth of Australia. Parliamentary Debates. House of Representatives, Tuesday 17 September 1985, No. 144. (Roger Shipton).

Commonwealth of Australia. Parliamentary Debates. House of Representatives, Thursday 16 May 1985, No. 142. (Roger Shipton).

Commonwealth of Australia. Parliamentary Debates. House of Representatives, Thursday 16 May 1985, No. 142. (David Connolly)

Commonwealth of Australia. Parliamentary Debates. House of Representatives, Thursday 8 December 1983, No. 134. (Clyde Holding).

Commonwealth of Australia. Parliamentary Debates. House of Representatives, Monday 30 May 1977, No. 22.

Commonwealth of Australia. Parliamentary Debates. Senate, Tuesday 17 February 1976, No. 8.

Commonwealth of Australia. Parliamentary Debates. Senate, Thursday 19 September 1974, No. 38. (Neville Bonner).

Commonwealth of Australia. Parliamentary Debates. Senate, Wednesday 21 November 1973, No. 47. (Neville Bonner).

Commonwealth of Australia. Parliamentary Debates. House of Representatives, Thursday 11 May 1972, No. 19.

Commonwealth of Australia. Parliamentary Debates. House of Representatives, Wednesday 23 February 1972, No. 8, 125–29. (Gough Whitlam).

Commonwealth of Australia. Parliamentary Debates. House of Representatives, Wednesday 23 February 1972, No. 8. (Peter Howson, Ralph Hunt).

Commonwealth of Australia. Parliamentary Debates. House of Representatives, Thursday 3 September 1970, No. 36. (Peter Nixon).

Commonwealth of Australia. Parliamentary Debates. House of Representatives, Thursday 7 September 1967, No. 36.

Commonwealth of Australia. Parliamentary Debates. House of Representatives, Tuesday 9 April 1963, No. 15. (Paul Hasluck).

Commonwealth of Australia. Parliamentary Debates. House of Representatives, Thursday 23 May 1963, No. 21. (Kim Beasley).

Commonwealth of Australia. Parliamentary Debates. House of Representatives, Thursday 23 May 1963, No. 21. (Gordon Bryant).

Commonwealth of Australia. Parliamentary Debates. House of Representatives, Thursday 23 May 1963, No. 21. (Peter Howson).

Commonwealth of Australia. Parliamentary Debates. House of Representatives, Wednesday 14 August 1963, No. 33. (Jock Nelson).

Commonwealth of Australia. Parliamentary Debates. House of Representatives, Tuesday 20 August 1963, No. 34. (Paul Hasluck).

Commonwealth of Australia. Parliamentary Debates. House of Representatives, Thursday 12 September 1963, No. 37. (Kim Beasley).

Commonwealth of Australia. Parliamentary Debates. House of Representatives, Thursday 12 September 1963, No. 37. (Paul Hasluck).

Commonwealth of Australia. Parliamentary Debates. House of Representatives, Thursday, 20 April 1961, No. 16. (Paul Hasluck).

Commonwealth of Australia. Parliamentary Debates. House of Representatives, Thursday 8 June 1950, No. 23. (Paul Hasluck).

Commonwealth of Australia. Parliamentary Debates. House of Representatives, Thursday 18 October 1951, No. 42. (Paul Hasluck).

Legal Cases

Coe v the Commonwealth [1978] 18 ALR 592.

Coe v Commonwealth of Australia and Another [1979] 24 ALR 118.

Coe v Commonwealth [1993] 118 ALR 193.

Cherokee Nation v State of Georgia [1831] 5 Pet 1.

Cooper v Stuart [1889] 14 App. Cas, 286.

Mabo and Others v The State of Queensland [No. 2] [1992] 175 CLR 1; 107 ALR 1; 66 ALJR 408.

Milirrpum and Others v Nabalco Pty Ltd and The Commonwealth of Australia [1970] 17 FLR, 141.

R v Jack Congo Murrell [1836] 1 Legge 72.

R v Murrell and Bummaree [1836] NSWSupC 35 (5 February 1836).

R v Wedge [1976] 1 NSWLR 581.

Walker v The State of New South Wales [1994] 182 CLR 45.

Western Sahara Advisory Opinion [1975] ICJ Reports, 12.

Wik and Thayorre Peoples v State of Queensland [1996] 187 CLR 1.

Index

Abbott, Tony, 157, 160
abolishing self-determination, 139
Aboriginal Alliance, 132, 136
Aboriginal Day of Mourning 1936, 8, 12, 16; anniversary of the First Fleet landing, 11; Aboriginal voice and perspective, 15; Cooper, William, 12, 16; Cumeroogunga protest, 14; dying relic of a dead past, 13; Ferguson, Bill, 8, 11, 12–13, 14, 16; Patten, Jack, 8, 11, 12–13, 14, 16; policy for Aborigines, 14; language of equal rights, 15; Nicholls, Doug, 12
Aborigines Protection Board (NSW), 7; assertiveness of Aboriginal people, 9; biological absorption and assimilation, 7; child removals, 9; concentrating Aboriginal people on reserves, 10
Aborigines' Progressive Association, 13
Aboriginal policy, Australia Day 1972, 74
Aboriginal tent embassy, 70, 75; Aboriginal place, 47, 79, 81; blatant contempt, 80; end the protest honourably, 80; greatest act of defacement, 82; inspired by Black Power movement, 82; police march in paramilitary style, 78; statement of demand, 76; turning point in Aboriginal policy, 83; violent encounter with police, 78; White Australians took up the challenge, 83
Aboriginal and Torres Strait Islander Commission (ATSIC), 98, 116, 119, 122, 124, 125, 126, 127, 132, 135, 139, 141, 144, 208

acquisition of foreign territory, 47, 48; Australian continent considered unclaimed territory, 47; Aboriginal sovereignty, 47–48; doctrine of discovery, 48; denial of sovereignty to Indigenous people, 50; implied recognition of Aboriginal jurisdiction, 52; modern doctrine of terra nullius, 50; terra nullius applied to Australia, 50; territories totally uninhabited, 49
AMIC and AMEC, 114
amendments Aboriginal Heritage Act (WA) 1972, x
assert claims for recognition, xv
Assimilation policy, 16–17, 19; assimilation and citizenship, 18; assumptions that Aboriginal society inferior, 69; exemption from Aboriginal legislation, 19; 'new deal' for Aborigines, 17; no legal or moral rights to land, 70
assumptions about inferiority, 8
assumption of protection policies, 9
Australian Aboriginal Progressive Association (AAPA), 10
Australian federalism, 94
Australian Reconciliation Convention 1997, 207

Banks, Joseph, xiv, 40, 42, 43, 49, 51–52
Barak, William, 4, 6
Barunga Statement, ix, xixn2, 99
Beazley, Kim, 23, 25
Blackstone, William, 49
black-arm band history, 143
black moratorium protest, 77
Blainey, Geoffrey, 93, 99, 112, 113, 143
Bohm, David, 168, 170
Bonner, Neville, 88

Bringing Them Home Report 1997,. *See*
    Report of the National Inquiry into
    the Separation of Aboriginal and
    Torres Strait Islander Children from
    Their Families 29; crime of
    genocide, 29–30; cultural genocide,
    30, 205; program of eugenics, 30;
    refusal to apologise, 30; stolen
    generations, 29, 202
Brough, Mal, 146, 148
Bryant, Gordon, 23
bucketfuls of extinguishment, 141
Burke, Brian, 95, 97

Cape York Land Council, 116
Cook, Captain James, xiv, 41, 42, 43, 49,
    51–52; blinded by his assumptions,
    42; Botany Bay and Gweagal
    people, 41; dismissal of Aboriginal
    polity, 44; erroneous assumptions,
    40; Guugu Yimithirr people, 42;
    musket fired at Aboriginal men, 41;
    not able to form any connection, 42;
    Possession Island, 43; twelve turtles,
    42
Central Land Council, ix, 116, 121
challenge to Land (Titles and
    Traditional Usage) Act 1993, xii
change beliefs and values, 167
Chamarette, Christabel, 134
Clarke, Geoff, 208
Coalition of Aboriginal Organisations
    Working Party (Aboriginal
    Coalition), 124, 125, 126, 127
Coe, Isabelle, 61, 130
Coe, Paul, 57, 80, 81, 130, 135
colonial attitudes within DAA, 86
colonial ideologies and practices, xiii
colonial mindset still strong, 197
colonial relationship, 2
colonial thinking and terra nullius
    discourse, 199
Common Law, 51; acquisition of New
    South Wales an act of State, 61;
    barbarian theory as law, 54;
    erroneous colonial assumptions in
    the common law, 52–54, 59; Coe v
    Commonwealth of Australia and
    Another 1979, 57–58; Coe v

Commonwealth 1993, 61; Cooper v
    Stuart 1889, 53; Mabo and Others v
    The State of Queensland [No. 2]
    1992, 59–60; Millirrupum v Nabalco
    1979, 55–56; New South Wales
    treated as practically unoccupied,
    51; rejection of Aboriginal
    sovereignty, 62–63; R v Jack Congo
    Murrell 1836,2.47-2.48; R v Wedge,
    56; Walker v The State of New
    South Wales, 61–62

confront hegemony and inertia of
    Australian state, 229
Constitutional dialogue, 178;
    Constitution, an imperial yoke, 178;
    consent and mutual recognition,
    180–181; four steps to dialogue and
    negotiation, 181; hidden
    constitutions or conventions, 179;
    modern constitutionalism, 178; no
    significant transcendence of power,
    180; power imbalance in dialogue,
    179; treaties and consent in North
    America, 181
Coombs, Herbert "Nugget", 71, 73, 75,
    79, 80, 84, 86, 88, 89
Coranderrk, 3; Aborigines Protection
    Act, 4, 5; Board for Protection of
    Aborigines, 4, 5, 7; challenge to
    protection policies, 6; policies of
    removal, 5

Council for Aboriginal Affairs (CAA),
    71, 73, 75, 79, 84, 87
Council for Aboriginal Reconciliation
    (CAR), 99, 116, 119, 122, 203, 207,
    209
Court, Richard, x, xii
culture of competition and argument,
    173

Davis, Jack, 88
de Vattel, Emmerich, 49, 113
deep and sincere regret, 202
deliberative democracy, 174
Department of Interior, 72, 73, 77, 84
denigrating and racializing Indigenous
    people, 173

dialogue as a decolonising approach, 166

dialogue conditions for Australia, 221–222

dialogical civic freedom, 176

dialogue elements, 169

dialogue, facilitated group, 171

dialogue, intercultural, 177, 216, 217, 220

dialogue phases, 170

dialogue, predisposition to understanding and helping others, 228

dialogue risks, 172

dialogue, what is, xiv, 168

differences in social memories, 174

discourse of terra nullius, 39–40

Dodson, Patrick, 31–32, 116, 117, 123, 126, 130, 164, 210

Dodson, Mick, 119, 120, 122, 123, 127, 201

doomed race theory, 5

Durack, Peter, 89

eliminate native title, xi

Elkin, A P, 16, 17

erroneous colonial assumptions and beliefs, xviii; accepted as fact, 51; continent regarded as uninhabited, 1; embedded in Australian institutions, 2

European assumptions of superiority, 44; Aboriginal people regarded as racially inferior, 44; Indigenous authority devalued, 47; savages and barbarians, 45–46; Social Darwinism, 46; stages theory of human development, 45, 46

exclusion of Aboriginal natives, 8

failure to accommodate Indigenous rights, 39

false assumptions and beliefs, xiii

Farley, Rick, 129, 130, 131, 133, 136

fear of historical truths, 201

Fischer, Tim, 113, 141

forcefully dispossessed, 1

Fraser Government, self management and self-sufficiency, 87

genuine dialogue, 172

genuine intercultural dialogue, 109

genuine reconciliation in Australia, 197, 210

genuine relationship with Aboriginal and Torres Strait Islander peoples, xiii

Giese, Harry, 25

greatest constraint to Indigenous recognition, 166

Gurindji people, 72

Hanson, Pauline, 110, 144, 201

Harris, Stewart, 88

Hawke Government, self-determination and national land rights, 92

Hasluck, Paul, 18, 19, 20, 22, 25

Hewson, John, 133

history wars, 30, 143

High Court Mabo judgement, x, 59–60

Holding, Clyde, 92, 94, 97, 98

Howard, John, 30, 98, 99, 110, 139, 142–144, 145, 146, 148, 207

Howard Government response to CAR documents, 208

Howard's One Australia, 144

Howson, Peter, 22–23, 72, 74, 75, 77, 80, 81

Hunt, Ralph, 77, 78

Indigenous claims for recognition, 175

Indigenous voices and perspectives, xvi

Indigenous recognition in Australia's Constitution, 159; constitutional conservatives, 161; expert panel, 159; Indigenous dialogues, 162; Indigenous sovereignty and treaty not addressed, 161; Joint Select Committee on Constitutional Recognition, 162–164, 203; minimal constitutional change, 160; 'Recognise' campaign, 160; Referendum Council, 161; rejection of Indigenous Voice to Parliament,

162
intercultural dialogue principles for
  Australia, 220
Isaacs, William, 169, 170

Jonas, Bill, 207
justice for Indigenous Australians is
  limited, 1
justice is more than closing the
  socioeconomic gap, 228
just relationship principles, 218–219

Keating, Paul, 109, 111, 117, 121, 122,
  123, 125, 127, 129, 131, 136, 143, 200
Kimberley Land Council, ix, 116, 121

Land (Titles and Traditional Usage)
  Act 1993, xi, 131
language and structure of government
  is exclusive, 215
Lavarch, Michael, 123, 128
lease of land, social and economic
  purposes, 73
Leopold Downs Station, x
liberating Australians from
  colonialism, 199
Locke, John, 46, 113

Manne, Robert, 30
manifesto, Aborigines claim
  citizenship rights, 13
Mansell, Michael, 130, 161
Martin, Claire, 148
master narrative, Australia, 197, 200
Maynard, Fred, 10
McMahon, William, 71–72
Melham, Daryl, 128
Minerals Council of Australia, 141
Morgan, Hugh, 93, 99, 114
Morrison, Scott, 164, 165
move to a new relationship, 199

National Aboriginal Consultative
  Committee (NACC), 83, 85, 87
National Aboriginal Conference
  (NAC), 87; aspirations for treaty
  stymied, 90; confidence trick by
  government, 91; criticism of NAC,
  91; treaty consultations, 89; two

phase negotiation for Makarrata, 91
Nationality and Citizenship Act 1948,
  18
National Conference of Aboriginal and
  Torres Strait Islander Councillors,
  79–80, 81–82
National Farmers Federation, 114, 141
National Federation of Land Councils,
  91
National Indigenous Council, 139
National Indigenous Working Group,
  141, 142
National land rights 92–93;
  abandonment of national land
  rights legislation, 97; Aboriginal
  land rights steering committee, 94;
  boycott by NAC and Federation of
  Land Councils, 96; mining industry
  campaign of fear, 96; preferred
  national land right model, 95;
  response to preferred land rights
  model, 95; removal of Aboriginal
  negotiating powers, exploration
  and mining, 95; Western Australian
  Labor Party opposition to land
  rights, 95, 97
Native Title Act, 134
native title, legislative recognition:
  Aboriginal land council urge
  protection of native title, 116;
  Aboriginal Peace Plan, 111, 117, 118,
  133; Australian Democrats, 126, 131,
  136; Australian Greens, 126, 131,
  132, 133, 136; basis of a post-colonial
  settlement, 118; Black Friday, 127,
  128; cautious support from states,
  129; Commonwealth urged to take
  responsibility, 118; Commonwealth
  government response to Mabo, 111,
  115; Commonwealth government
  Mabo principles, 119;
  Commonwealth Native Title Bill,
  123, 131; Council of Australian
  Governments (COAG), 119; Eva
  Valley Statement, 122, 133; Eva
  Valley Working Group, 122, 124;
  fast track of McArthur River mine,
  119; Federal Cabinet decision, 129;
  government insist on suspending

RDA, 127; hostile public discussion against Mabo, 112, 115; Indigenous leaders ask not to be dismissed or excluded, 117; Indigenous representatives feel ignored, 120; legislation assimilates and castrates native title, 121; legislation give states unfair power, 123; Mabo Ministerial Committee, 115, 117, 118; maintain integrity of Racial Discrimination Act, 125; protecting private and industry land titles, 111; RDA does not have to be suspended, 128; reject government proposals, no further negotiation, 123; Ruby Tuesday, 129; suspending the Racial Discrimination Act, 124–125

negative attitudes and erroneous assumptions are barriers, 216

New Right, 93; attack on land rights and government Aboriginal programs, 93; nationalism and raced based politics, 93

no broad public support for Indigenous aspirations, 227

no constitutional status, x

no national framework of partnership, 157

no constitutional framework for cross cultural engagement, 159

no guilt or responsibility for the past, 98

no legitimate status or political authority, 1

no power to influence deliberative processes, 174

no rights to traditional land, 71, 72

Northern Land Council, ix, 116, 121

not entitled to citizenship rights, 7

Northern Territory Emergency Response (NTER), 146, 155n147; fear, prejudice, and negative discourse, 148; prohibition on racial discrimination, 147; NTER involved racial discrimination, 147

non-discrimination and no extinguishment, 141

O'Donoghue, Lois, 116, 127

Oombulgarri, 157

opposition to native title, Court government, B03.7

on the losing side of majority decision making, 165

Parliamentary Select Committee, 25–26; deficiency of guardian-wardship relationship, 27; vindication of Yolngu grievance, 26; Yolngu evidence, 26

Pearson, Noel, 115, 119, 120, 127, 161

Perkins, Charles, 84, 86

Perron, Marshall, 112

petition to King George VI, 12

political correctness, 142

political dialogue, 216

political imbalance, 101; exclusion and barriers, 101; balancing rights and interests, 102; inability to engage equally with Indigenous people, 102; lack of political power and privilege, 102

politics of recognition, 159

potential for genuine dialogue, xvi

practical reconciliation, 139, 144, 209

public acknowledgement of injustice, 200

Racial Discrimination Act, xii, 83, 114, 115, 117, 119, 124, 125, 126, 128

reconciliation and historical injustices, 210

reconciliation, barriers in Australia, 210

reconciliation, call for action Canada, 206

reconciliation, deliberately derailed, 210

reconciliation, failed to address important issues, 209

recognition is constrained by constitutionalism, 215

reconciliation, premise in Australia, 207

reconciliation process, Australia 1991-2000, 167, 211–212

reconciliation, what is, 211
reconciliation with Indigenous people, 98
Redfern Park Speech 1992, 111, 136, 137, 200
refusal to apologise for harm caused, 202
relationship of paternalism, dominance, disrespect and racism, 157–158
Report from the House of Commons Select Committee on Aborigines (British Settlement) 1837, 3
Report of the National Inquiry into the Separation of Aboriginal and Torres Strait Islander Children from Their Families,. *See also* Bringing Them Home Report 202
repudiation of terra nullius, xiv, 188, 206, 211
responsibility of Crown to build just relationship, 227–228
responsibility for reconciliation, 211
restructure the relationship, xv
Reynolds, Henry, xi, 47, 54, 64
Richard Courts "foolhardy pursuit", xii
rights to land policy controversial, 74
Riley, Rob, 87, 112, 120, 130
Robinson, Ray, 130
Royal Commission into Aboriginal Deaths in Custody, 100, 200
Royal Commission on Aboriginal Peoples, Canada, 182; colonial relationship creates dependency and alienation, 183; dismantle the colonial relationship, 182; lessons and principles for Australia, 185; principles for a new relationship, 184; renewed relationship, 183; treaties create relationships, 184; vision and roadmap for change, 183
Rudd, Kevin, 200

self-determination, Whitlam Government, 83; self-management and self-reliance, 84; Department of Aboriginal Affairs (DAA), 84; self-determination is about empowering local communities, 84; growing assertiveness of Indigenous people, 85; Whitlam Government reforms, 83
Senate inquiry into feasibility of Makarrata 1981, 91–92
settler colonialism, 7, 29, 30–31, 137, 215
stolen generation apology, 200
stumbling block to justice, 2
subordination and domination of Indigenous people, x, 39, 167

tacit thought or knowledge, xiv, 169, 173
ten point plan, 141
terra nullius, B03.11 6.2
terra nullius discourse and thinking, xiii–xiv, 39–40
terra nullius, psychological, 39
Toyne, Phillip, 120, 126, 136
trapped by history, 31
transformation of colonial relationship, xv, 197
Treaty, 2; treaty with Aboriginal people, 88; Aboriginal Treaty Committee, 88; Makarrata treaty, 89; Senate Standing Committee inquiry, 91–92
treaty promise and retreat, 99
Truth and Reconciliation Commission, Canada, 185, 205–206; colonisation and the Crown's failure, 187; Covenant of Reconciliation, 188, 206; doctrine of discovery and terra nullius, 188; documenting truth and ongoing legacy, 186; framework for reconciliation, 188; impact and legacy of residential schools, 187; Indian Residential Schools Survivors Committee, 186; national and town hall forums, 186; reconciliation to resolve long-standing conflict, 187; residential schools for assimilation, 5.89; Royal Proclamation of Reconciliation, 188, 206
Truth and Reconciliation Commission, South Africa, 204–205

Truth Commissions, transitional justice, 203
Truth and Justice Commission in Australia, role of, 220
truth telling about history, 198
truth telling and dialogue, 216–217
truth telling and reconciliation, 203
truth and reconciliation principles, Canada, 217
truth telling, framework for in Australia, 204
truth telling in Australia, 213–214; build new national narratives, 214; challenge colonial assumptions and narratives, 213; confront historical truths or untruths, 214
truth telling is a constitutional process, 222
truth telling lessons regarding stolen generations, 202
Turnbull, Malcolm, 162, 165
Tully, James, 166, 176, 178, 179, 181, 218

Uluru Convention of First Peoples, 202
Uluru Statement from the Heart, 198, 202
unable to change thinking, 165
understand the genesis of thinking, 199
unequal engagement with government, 215
upheaval of Indigenous affairs, 145

value of court decision, 138
Victorian Aboriginal Legal Service, 121

Walker, Frank, 125, 128
Watson, Irene, 64
Wells, Edgar, 21, 23
Western Australian Aboriginal Legal Service, 116, 117
Western Australian Government "glorious victory", xii
where to for Australia, 188–189
Whitlam, Gough, 76, 83
Wik and Thayorre native title claim, 140
Williams, Esther, 120
Willshire, W H, 112
Wyatt, Ken, 164, 165

Yolngu bark petition, 24; political statement and claim to land, 27
Yolngu people, 20; assumptions of inferiority, 20; exclusion of Yolngu, 21; mining on Yolngu land, 20; status of a minor, 18; traditional values, 23–24, 27; wards of the state, 20
Yu, Peter, xii, 87, 120
Yunupingu, Galarrwuy, 122, 164

About the Author

Darryl Cronin is the Coordinator of the First Nations Programme with the Edmund Rice Centre for Justice and Community Education in Sydney, Australia. His research focusses on promoting human rights and justice for Indigenous Australians. Cronin has a doctor of philosophy degree from the University of New South Wales, a master of environmental law degree from Macquarie University and a bachelor of law degree from Adelaide University. He has worked in both academic and nongovernment organisation roles, having worked with Aboriginal organisations in northern Australia on land rights and socioeconomic development.

www.ingramcontent.com/pod-product-compliance
Lightning Source LLC
Chambersburg PA
CBHW030644270326
41929CB00007B/205